MORAL EDUCATION

Interdisciplinary Approaches

Edited by
C. M. BECK
B. S. CRITTENDEN
E. V. SULLIVAN

NEWMAN PRESS
New York, N.Y. Paramus, N.J.

ISBN 0-8091-1756-8

Published by Newman Press

Editorial Office: 1865 Broadway, N.Y., N.Y. 10023

Business Office: 400 Sette Drive, Paramus, N.J. 07652

Printed and Bound in the

United States of America

Preface

THIS BOOK is based on the proceedings of a conference on Moral Education held in June of 1968 in Toronto under the sponsorship of The Ontario Institute for Studies in Education. Specifically, the conference was jointly funded and organized by the Department of Applied Psychology and the Department History and Philosophy of Education within the Institute.

The publication is not simply a reproduction of the conference proceedings. As a result of the conference some of the papers were revised considerably, and the original discussion material underwent a major process of integration and reorganization. Professors Beck and Sullivan were responsible for editing the conference papers, and Professor Crittenden undertook the editing of the discussion section. We would like to thank the many research assistants and students from both departments who helped in the planning and execution of the conference and the preparation of this publication. In particular, we would like to express appreciation of the assistance given by Rowland Lorimer, Mary Stager, Nancy Taylor, and Ira Welch, in Applied Psychology, and by Erwin Biener, Theresa Haq, Michael Jackson, and Malcolm MacInnis, in History and Philosophy. We would like especially to thank Professor Abraham Edel whose wise and skilful chairing of the conference did so much to ensure its success. Finally, we would like to express our deep regret at the untimely death of Dr. Vivian Paskal, one of the conference participants, in January 1969.

Contents

Contributors

JUSTIN ARONFREED
Department of Psychology, University of Pennsylvania

DAVID P. AUSUBEL
Department of Educational Psychology, City University of New York

KURT BAIER
Department of Philosophy, University of Pittsburgh

MARY JO BANE
School of Education, Harvard University

CLIVE M. BECK
Department of History and Philosophy of Education,
Ontario Institute for Studies in Education and University of Toronto

BRIAN S. CRITTENDEN
Department of History and Philosophy of Education,
Ontario Institute for Studies in Education and
University of Toronto

ABRAHAM EDEL
Chairman of Conference, Philosophy Department,
City College of City University of New York

DAVID P. GAUTHIER
Department of Philosophy, University of Toronto

DAVID E. HUNT
Department of Applied Psychology, Ontario Institute for
Studies in Education and University of Toronto

LAWRENCE KOHLBERG
School of Education, Harvard University

JAN J. LOUBSER
Department of Sociology in Education
Ontario Institute for Studies in Education and University of Toronto

A. I. MELDEN
Department of Philosophy, University of California at Irvine

JAN NARVESON
Philosophy Department, University of Waterloo

DONALD OLIVER
School of Education, Harvard University

VIVIAN PASKAL
At time of her death, Department of Psychology,
University of Toronto

MICHAEL SCRIVEN
Department of Philosophy, University of California at Berkeley

EDMUND V. SULLIVAN
Department of Applied Psychology,
Ontario Institute for Studies in Education and University of Toronto

ELLIOT TURIEL
School of Education, Harvard University

PARTS ONE TO FOUR

Papers

edited by C. M. Beck and E. V. Sullivan

Introduction

C. M. BECK and E. V. SULLIVAN

THE CONTEMPORARY significance of a conference on moral education may be subject to question in some quarters, but it is nevertheless obvious that the general problem of moral education is being taken seriously by practical educators on this continent and in Europe. In England, the Farmington Trust Reasearch Unit is involved in a long-term study with the objectives of devising, improving, and clarifying programs in moral education for English schools (Wilson, Williams, and Sugarman 1967). Here in Canada, the recent report of the Committee on Religious Education has suggested making widespread changes in school curricula in Ontario and encouraging more extensive research and development in the area of value education in the school setting. This conference focuses on several themes which appear whenever discussion of morality centres on the role of the school in the development of virtue. Certainly, the questions and topics discussed in this conference are not new. Meno's question to Socrates concerning the nature of virtue is, in some ways, the basic underlying theme of the conference:

> Can you tell me, Socrates, whether virtue is acquired by teaching or by practice; or if neither by teaching nor practice, then whether it comes to man by nature, or in what other way?

This question provoked a rather extended discussion of the nature of morality and virtue which has continued on through the centuries to the present day. As can be seen in the papers and discussions of the conference, the topic of moral education still raises interesting questions which are as significant for contemporary education as they were in Socrates' time.

The importance of this subject may be underestimated, however, if morality is defined too narrowly, as has often been the case. To describe a conference as concerned with "moral education" is to run the risk of misleading some readers. Morality is frequently linked with the last vestiges of Puritanism in America, or with the moral prescriptions of pious Victorians on the topics of sex, alcohol, and gambling. Furthermore, linking the term "moral" with "education" in the school context incurs a further risk of being considered to have gone beyond the proper domain of school learning and to have encroached on areas of behaviour which are the concern of the family. The claim that the development of "intelligence" is the school's responsibility, whereas the proper place for "moral" training and "character" development is the home, is frequently heard when the domain of morals is thus narrowly interpreted.

It would be unfortunate, however, simply to accept such narrow interpretations, and to abandon traditions of usage of longer standing. Morality and ethics historically have had much wider scope and conceptual significance, going far beyond the delineation of a few choice behaviours or virtues. John Dewey was well aware of this earlier tradition when he argued for a more serious consideration of moral principles in the educational process:

> We have associated the term ethical with certain special acts which are labeled virtues and are set off from the mass of other acts, and are still more divorced from the habitual images and motives of the children performing them. Moral instruction is thus associated with teaching about these particular virtues, or with instilling certain sentiments in regard to them. The moral has been conceived in too goody-goody a way. Ultimate moral motives and forces are nothing more or less than social intelligence – the power of observing and comprehending social situations – and social power – trained capacities of control – at work in the service of social interest and aims. There is no fact which throws light upon the constitution of society, there is no power whose training adds to social resourcefulness that is not moral (Dewey 1959, pp. 42–43).

Dewey lamented the separation in the schools of intellectual and moral training, since it was indicative of a failure to conceive of and construct the school as a social institution having social life and value in itself. In *Democracy and Education* Dewey made note of a paradox that is often exhibited in discussions of morals. On the one hand, morality is identified with rationality, where reason is set up as the faculty for critical deliberation in moral choices. On the other hand, morality is thought of as an area in which ordinary knowledge and intellectual skills have no place. Dewey saw this separation as having a special significance for moral education in the schools, since, if valid, it would render such an enterprise hopeless by setting up the development of character as supreme, and, at the same time, treating the acquisition of knowledge and the development of understanding as something separate from character development. The ultimate outcome of this separation would be the reduction of moral education to some kind of catechetical instruction, or lessons about morals.

One becomes aware of a further paradox when one realizes that, in spite of Dewey's clear statements on the subject, the ultimate interpretation of his ideas in North American education led to educational environments and objectives that were contradictory to some of Dewey's educational tenets, especially in the area of character education. Dewey's interpretors, in stressing the 'needs" of the child, became extremely preoccupied with the child's "adjustment to life" as a means of counteracting the "formal discipline movement" (Hofstadter 1964). The 1940s and 1050s saw the goals of education phrased in terms of the child's social traits and values that led to "social adjustment" (Hofstadter, 1963; Kohlberg, 1966). The stress on "life adjustment" encouraged more entrenched conformity to socially acceptable values and a movement in American education which has been characterized by Richard Hofstadter as essentially "anti-intellectual." Dewey's desire for a curriculum which would graduate students who would be critically informed and intellectually and morally activated by their reason was not realized because of the excessive emphasis on "adjustment to life." In the schools the pendulum had swung away from "intellectual goals" that were advocated by "formal disciplinarians" towards a distorted emphasis on the "emotional life," which was detached from both intellectual and moral concerns.

The late 1950s and early 1960s saw a re-evaluation of the school's goals and commitments in contemporary society in the light of the rapid technological changes of the post-war era. Secondary education was severely criticized by Conant (1959) who suggested a major reorganization of the curriculum to one stressing mathematics, foreign languages, science, and social studies. Bruner's *The Process of Education* (1965) conveyed a similar message with respect to elementary school curricula by indicating that intellectual skills could be taught to very young children without producing accompanying emotional deficits, provided that the programs were geared to the child's cognitive level.

The major portion of emphasis in this "new" curriculum approach has, thus far, been strictly on scientific subjects, with social studies and humanities receiving less attention in both elementary and secondary schools. The stress on "technology" and "skills" has reduced the stature of the humanities and social studies to a degree where the functioning of the society as a democratic institution is affected, for the moral prerequisites of our expanding technological system have been neglected. The acquisition of technical knowledge and competence cannot supplant the need for a personal policy which informs and gives direction to changing technology (Niblett 1963). "A technical knowledge of, say, navigation, can be immensely interesting in itself. But the course the ship is to take is chosen for quite other reasons than the navigator's skill in plotting it. The educated man needs to discuss his direction of progress and the 'whys' of conduct as well as to build up knowledge and skills" (Niblett 1963, p. 27).

Contemporary education needs programs and curricula which are designed to be more "reflective" if students are going to be adequately prepared to live in a time in which all social institutions are being questioned. The school, as an institution, has, by and large, neglected those subjects (e.g., social studies, morality) that tend to deal with controversial topics. In general, such subjects as minority-group relations, nationalism, religion, morality, nuclear warfare, and other contemporary issues are bypassed by the school and left to the individual student's initiative outside of class hours. A focus on these topics in no way undermines the value of technological skills and methods and results of natural science, since in many instances solutions to socially important problems presuppose the use of scientific findings. Problems such as insanity, poverty, city planning, governmental operations, etc., demand many skills that natural science and technological advancement supply. However, in most cases the schools have focused on the skills and have ignored the social conditions to which they might be applied.

If education is to be something other than "indoctrination," it is necessary that the schools discuss controversial issues freely. Certainly a precondition of a democratic system of government is a citizenry which exercises its rights after an informed search for adequate solutions. Moral education may be broadly conceived of as the formulation and application of principles for action on complex societal issues. This type of education does not happen by accident and the school is one of the institutions which can encourage a more reflective understanding of these issues. Educational institutions in North America, in both Canada and the United States, have neglected controversial topics dealing with both private and public morality. Two examples in the areas of social studies and citizenship training will illustrate the neglect about which we are speaking.

In a recent survey of social studies and civics education in Canada, Hodgetts (1968) came to this rather pessimistic conclusion:

The study of government in our schools provides another good illustration of how the actual results of classroom instruction may be the very opposite of those desired by the teacher. According to provincial prescriptions, the civics part of Canadian studies is designed not only "to impart information concerning the form and functioning of our government" but also to give students "a deep and abiding appreciation of our heritage of free government." Every Canadian "should be thoroughly familiar with the working of our democratic institutions, his rights and duties under the rule of law and the responsibilities of those elected to public office." Again, the great majority of teachers that we interviewed accepted these objectives and felt that their students were developing "a constructive and positive attitude towards citizenship." Our evidence suggests that, far from even approximating these aims, the strongest, most widely held attitude of the students in our Survey was either complete indifference or deep cynicism toward politicians and political life (p. 78).

A similar conclusion is reached by Hess (1968) concerning political socialization of students in the United States:

Much of the political socialization that takes place at elementary and high-school levels is lacking in candor, is superficial with respect to basic issues, is cognitively fragmented, and produces little grasp of the implications of principles and their application to new situations ... political values and principles are often learned as slogans rather than as concepts to be applied to social issues. Students who have learned the Bill of Rights may still oppose the right of a speaker from an unpopular ideology, such as Communism, to speak in the town square; they may be able to recite the phrases about freedom of religion but be opposed to hiring an atheist as a teacher in the schools ... These responses suggest that teaching of the phrases has not sufficiently involved a comprehension of the underlying principles nor of the long-term consequences that will follow from ignoring basic rights (p. 532).

Existing social studies and citizenship training thus appears to be a subtle form of "indoctrination," where national or provincial myths are created. The schools appear to be superficial in their treatment of important social issues and, in general, to encourage the use of slogans and stereotypes instead of critical thinking (Hodgetts 1968, Hess 1968). R.S. Peters, in his *Ethics and Education,* points out that democratic systems of government need more than a set of slogans in order to function as vital institutions. People must have relevant experience to which they can refer abstract principles. The formulation and justification of principles is one thing, "but it is still another thing to apply moral principles intelligently to concrete circumstances" (Peters 1966, p. 203).

We have thus far argued that the domain of "moral education" is wider than the narrow definitions usually applied to it suggest. Moral education can encompass both private and public virtue, and our preliminary comments were designed to show that the topic deserves extensive exploration in contemporary North American education. The topic was explored along interdisciplinary lines in the conference with the participants representing the disciplines of philosophy, psychology, sociology, and social studies. Obviously, some important disciplines (e.g., history, theology, anthropology) were not represented. This limitation of participating disciplines was dictated only by considerations of available space and the format for discussion considered most appropriate. The conference participants were given a series of questions, thought to be pertinent for the discussion of "moral education" in contemporary North America, by the conference organizers. These questions centred around four general topic areas: (1) the general nature and scope of "moral education," (2) the problem of "ethical pluralism," (3) psychological considerations significant for a program of moral education, and (4) the social structure of the school as it relates to moral education. Each of these topics will now be considered in more detail in order to provide an overview of the conference papers.

THE GENERAL NATURE AND SCOPE OF MORAL EDUCATION

The conference papers express a variety of views about the nature and scope of moral education and about the proper use of the term "moral education." The variations are partly a reflection of differing opinions on relevant factual issues, but are also partly the result of different approaches to the general problem of definition.

There is fairly wide agreement in the papers that moral education, when it is successful, is concerned with something worthwhile or valuable. People do on occasion talk of "a bad moral education" or "a harmful moral-education program," but without some specific qualification to the contrary, one may assume that people who speak of themselves as developing a moral-education program are striving to achieve what they consider to be a worthwhile end. Both morality and moral education are seen as typically representing a set of important values.

How, then, do we distinguish moral education from other worthwhile activities? To begin with, moral education is distinctive in that it is moral *education,* rather than moral conditioning or moral training. Kohlberg and Baier strongly support this sort of distinction, maintaining that in moral education the reasoning of the student is fully engaged:

he reflects upon moral issues, invoking certain clearly defined principles of moral reasoning. Loubser, Melden, and Gauthier are somewhat more reserved in endorsing the distinction. Loubser sees moral education as taking place at least in part by means of a "socializing" process; and although he assumes that reasoning will be involved, he is primarily concerned with the functional nature of the actions which an ego performs with respect to an alter, rather than with the psychological processes that lead up to the actions. Melden speaks almost indifferently of training and education, allowing moral education to extend downwards to quite an early age, while perhaps thinking of the earlier stages as more typically training and the later stages as more typically education. He places a great deal of emphasis upon the role of understanding in truly moral behaviour, and for this reason does not conceive of there being such a thing as moral training which is radically different from moral education. Gauthier's reason for playing down the distinction runs in the opposite direction. He feels that the early moral "conditioning" which the child receives is so important in establishing basic patterns of moral behaviour that, even though it is "conditioning," it is to be described as the work of an "educator." Within moral education in this broad sense, however, he does distinguish between moral training (his first and second stages) and moral education (his third stage), the latter being concerned with the establishing of relevant general knowledge and awareness rather than with the development of basic dispositions and strategies.

Moral education is also a distinctive good in that it is *moral,* rather than, for example, mathematical or physical, education. On this point there is substantial agreement in the papers at a very general level, but considerable disagreement at more specific levels. Opinions differ concerning the nature of the moral and concerning the bearing of the nature of the moral on the definitional problem.

Aronfreed feels that there are both methodological and substantive reasons for loosening up the concept of the moral. He notes, for example, that the study of conscience has been greatly facilitated when psychologists have departed from the standard "pure" notion of conscience and acknowledged the presence of so-called nonmoral elements. Further, he maintains that various affective mechanisms commonly thought to have no moral significance play a much larger role in moral behaviour than moral theorists have normally allowed.

In certain respects, Baier keeps the concept of the moral relatively narrow: he emphasizes the necessity of moral reasoning, and furthermore concentrates upon a particular set of criteria for moral value to be used in moral reasoning, namely, the minimization of harm and suffering and the just distribution of burdens and benefits. Moral issues, for Baier, are a rather definite subset of value issues; and correspondingly, moral education is a narrower task than value education.

Kohlberg tends to support Baier and oppose Aronfreed in maintaining that distinctively moral features emerge only at a relatively late stage in development, when some minimum capacity for moral reflection has been established. Melden and Gauthier both opt for an earlier emergence of moral elements; however, once again, they do so for different reasons. Melden feels that at a quite early age children begin to recognize others as persons (in both senses of recognize), and, since such recognition is the essence of morality, there is equally the beginning of the development of a moral personality. Gauthier maintains, by contrast, that the young infant has no thought for the needs of others; but moral development is nevertheless already taking place, since important moral dispositions are being established.

In the discussion of the nature of morality in the papers, there is something of a conflict between what might be called the objective requirements and the subjective requirements. Kohlberg emphasizes the objective requirement that moral behaviour be in accordance with justice, and Baier the objective requirements that moral behaviour minimize harm and suffering and distribute goods justly. For both these writers, however, there are also subjective requirements. For Kohlberg, there is the requirement that one should reason one's way to a moral action, following certain appropriate canons of moral reasoning. It is not sufficient that one's action should be objectively beneficial. For Baier, similarly, there is the requirement that one's action be performed for a moral reason, and furthermore the requirement that one perform it *because* it is morally required. It is essential, then, that moral education concern itself with producing behaviour which involves acting for reasons, and acting for the right reasons. One might raise the question why, if a type of behaviour is beneficial to the parties concerned, we should withold from it the description "moral" and from its production the description "moral education," simply because reasoning is not centrally involved. To this question Kohlberg and Baier would probably give the answer that, if reasoning is not centrally involved, it is not *moral* behaviour and its production is not *education*. And this is a plausible position. However, the question that remains is how can we describe the kinds of dispositions Gauthier identifies and the kinds of behaviours Aronfreed discusses; these share many of the features of moral dispositions and behaviours and are objectively beneficial, but are not particularly rational.

THE PROBLEM OF ETHICAL PLURALISM

As we have seen, it is difficult to provide a very adequate account of the nature and scope of moral education without determining the nature of morality. All we have done in the previous section is note a few general distinctions and indicate some of the main problem areas. In the academic world at present, however, there is a considerable amount of controversy over the nature of morality and over the criteria for deciding moral issues. It is difficult to see, then, how academics can agree upon what form moral education should take.

Baier in his paper takes a fairly strong line on the problem. He defines ethical pluralism in societal terms rather than with reference to the differing views of philosophers. He rejects the suggestion that we might overcome the problem of ethical pluralism in society by accepting a procedural, formal, content-independent method of arriving at a common course of action in moral education, maintaining that such a method is arbitrary, that it constitutes an admission of the irrelevance of moral considerations and the impossibility of a rational solution, and that it is quite contrary to the moral approach to problems of the kind in question. However, Baier believes that we are not therefore left with no viable program of moral education. He feels that there are certain broad aims which can be adopted in moral education because they are generally accepted "in our society" and morevoer can be shown (in some significant sense) to be appropriate aims. The aims Baier mentions embrace producing in the child (*a*) an interest in and favourable attitude towards morality, (*b*) an understanding of the nature and purpose of public morality, (*c*) an understanding of the need for *some* public moral order, and (*d*) an understanding of (and, presumably, acceptance of) the criteria of acceptability which any public moral order must satisfy, namely, the minimization of the infliction of harm and suffering and the just distribution of burdens and benefits (that is, an equal distribution except where there are differences of desert). The general conception of morality which in Baier's view can legitimately be taught in the schools is at various points still controversial in the philosophical world, but Baier is undaunted by this. He maintains that, while we must avoid making pronouncements on clearly controversial public issues, we have sufficient public support and philosophical authority to teach this general conception of morality and so provide students with the basis for a "method" of tackling moral problems. Thus, he acknowledges that we must settle at least some very general substantive moral questions if we are to be able to develop a moral-education program, but considers that several questions of this kind may, for practical purposes, be taken as already settled.

By contrast, Kohlberg, Oliver, and Bane sometimes express the view that one *can* teach the form of moral reasoning without making pronouncements on content. (They do not seem to be altogether consistent advocates of this position). However, it is difficult to assess their claim since neither they nor any of the other writers provide an adequate account of a content-free method of tackling moral problems. It might be felt that Kohlberg's principle of justice provides us with a content-free criterion for judging moral matters. However, on the one hand, the advocacy of this criterion could not by itself be taken as a solution to the problem of ethical pluralism, for there is considerable disagreement among philosophers about what justice consists of and, indeed, whether justice is an independent criterion of moral value. Baier brings out some of the complexity inherent in the notion of justice when he distinguishes between equal distribution of goods and distribution according to desert. Baier himself is willing to provide a criterion of desert, in terms of one's contribution to lightening the total burden of a community and increasing the total benefit. But Kohlberg explicitly rejects such utilitarian approaches in moral reasoning, and does not tackle the problem of how we determine desert.

On the other hand, even if we could agree on the nature of the criterion of justice, it is difficult to see how it is a content-free criterion of moral goodness. It would seem that one is making a value judgment in claiming that justice, defined, for example, in terms of equality, is a good thing. One might well maintain that it is often a bad thing, or that it is only one consideration among many. And if one defines it in terms of equality or desert, or both, there is still the problem of determining desert. And it is no solution to say that from the point of view of morality justice is not a value but a given; for it is still a content that one has to teach, and the fact that it is not a moral content does not seem to solve anything. It may be that justice in some clearly defined sense is a valuable objective, and can be shown to be so; this is the line Baier takes. But to accept a criterion because it has been established as a sound one is different from accepting it on the ground that it is content-free and so in some sense does not need to be established.

It might be felt that even if a general criterion such as that of justice cannot be shown to be purely methodological or formal, there is one major methodological principle which did emerge from the papers, namely, that sound reasoning is essential to the moral life. However, it is difficult to see how far the bare acceptance of this principle will take us, without the affirmation of some definite principles of moral reasoning, which will have at least general substantive import. It might be suggested that at least it means that we must include in our moral-education program instruction in principles of logical and critical thought, principles common to reasoning in general. But is this really so? It means this for Baier, since he seems to embrace a kind of objectivist theory of value, maintaining that a group may hold something to be wrong without it, in fact, being wrong, that one can be mistaken about what is wrong, and so on. But does Kohlberg hold to such a theory? His rejection of utilitarianism and the deference he pays to R.M. Hare and other contemporary nonobjectivists would suggest not. Certainly he provides no objectivist defence of his own acceptance of the principle of justice. And do Oliver and Bane hold to such a theory? Towards the end of their paper they talk as if, in order to succeed in the moral domain, one must at certain points abandon the general principles of logical and critical thought.

But what of the proposition that reason of *some* sort is essential to moral behaviour? Surely this is a principle we can teach to children while we wait for the day when the principles of moral reasoning are discovered (assuming that they have not been already). But in fact, even on this matter, the conference papers exhibit some disagreement. There is the suggestion by Kohlberg that the exercise of reason is a necessary condition of morality, whereas Aronfreed and Gauthier tend to take the view that if certain ends can be achieved without the use of reason and are beneficial, then we should be prepared to call them good. Now, this may not be an unresolvable difference. Kohlberg may see reasoning as a necessary condition of moral value simply because, as a matter of fact, one cannot achieve the peculiar values of morality without the exercise of reason. It would then be an answerable empirical question whether or not reasoning is always necessary. Alternatively, Kohlberg may see moral behaviour as involving reasoning by definition: we simply would not call behaviour "moral" if it did not involve reasoning in a central way. It would then be a resolvable verbal dispute. But the fact remains that there is at present this difference of viewpoint, suggesting that even the proposition that reason of some sort is essential to moral behaviour is not content-free.

The question of whether a content-free methodology of morals can be found is, nevertheless, an extremely interesting one and must be explored further. It would seem, however, in the light of the conference papers, that there is also good reason to follow up Baier's suggestion that certain general substantive principles are already sufficiently well established to justify their being taught in the schools, despite the academic controversy which surrounds them. Of course, even this suggestion does not take us very far, because the principles Baier outlines are extremely general. But it might open the way for an important beginning.

We might note in closing this section that Kohlberg has an alternative suggestion concerning a possible solution to the problem of ethical pluralism. Like Baier, he in part turns away from the academic world and appeals to the wisdom of society, where, we find, people pass through certain identifiable stages of moral thought and behaviour as their age and experience increases. Kohlberg feels that the universal incidence of this sequence of development may be significant, reflecting man's increasingly accurate perception of how he must behave in society if he is to achieve his ideals. One might adopt the position, then, that certain broad moral principles have stood the "test" of generations of human experience and for this reason can be taught in the schools. Indeed, Kohlberg suggests, perhaps they are so natural and sensible that they do not really have to be taught: their emergence needs merely to be stimulated. This interesting possibility arising out of the conference papers is also deserving of close attention.

PSYCHOLOGICAL CONSIDERATIONS SIGNIFICANT FOR A PROGRAM IN MORAL EDUCATION

The relationship between the discipline of psychology and moral education stems from the obvious consideration that a program in moral education must take into account empirical findings and theoretical accounts of the development of the child and adolescent. Although historically psychologists have not been strictly interested in moral development, morality, broadly conceived, clearly involves such psychological dimensions as reasoning ability, intelligence, personality, and impulse control. At this conference, we were interested in several broad questions in moral education which centred on psychological theory and research. These questions were: What are the skills and dispositions that are required for moral action? What are some of the psychological constructs that may be related to morality (e.g., personality development, intelligence, character)? Can types of moral judgments be distinguished and graded according to their degrees of "rationality" or "sophistication"? How does the capacity of children for moral reasoning change with age? In what ways can the child's moral development be facilitated and enhanced? Are there some types of environments or training conditions that are especially important in promoting moral growth? These questions were broad enough to allow the conference participant considerable latitude in developing his own ideas on the topic of moral development.

Kohlberg's paper presents normative findings on the development of children's moral reasoning in childhood and adolescence. Kohlberg advances the notion, on the basis of his findings, that the ability to make moral judgments follows a stage developmental pattern. The stage developmental pattern moves from a premoral punishment orientation in the youngest children to an autonomous morality based on individual conscience and choice in the oldest children. Kohlberg, who places a heavy emphasis on moral judgment, is very critical of the psychological studies designed to assess virtue simply in terms of behavioural criteria. According to Kohlberg, his stages represent an increasing differentiation and disentangling of moral values and judgments from other types of values and judgment. He does not ignore behaviour in his presentation, but stresses the fact that consistent moral action is of necessity informed by mature and articulate moral judgments.

Kohlberg and his colleagues have also delineated a clear-cut position on the factors which facilitate growth in "moral reasoning" ability. Kohlberg regards growth in moral reasoning as a result of "cognitive conflict" at the stage in which the child is currently operating. Consequently, he proposes that programs in moral education must include conflict and controversy if more mature stages of moral judgment are to be reached. The amount of conflict considered optimal for growth is engendered when the child is exposed to arguments which are structurally one stage above his present level. Kohlberg uses evidence, both experimental and educational, to support this contention. The social-studies program described by Oliver and Bane was designed around controversial issues and dilemmas of either historical or contemporary significance, and was intended to provoke "conflict" which could be resolved by more analytic reasoning. Although their program involves many ideas that are similar to those of Kohlberg, they are more sceptical than he is concerning the long-term effects of a program that is based exclusively on fostering "moral reasoning." Oliver and Bane believe that moral reasoning is too restrictive for a general program in moral education, and that resolutions of moral conflicts are more complex and visceral than most curriculum planners suspect. Their alternative to "moral reasoning" programs will be discussed shortly.

Aronfreed's paper also indicates some disagreements, on several theoretical and practical grounds, with Kohlberg's position. Aronfreed feels that the ultimate criterion for assessing moral maturity should be, not judgment and reasoning, but a person's conduct or behaviour. Although he concedes that "moral judgment" may be a powerful determinant of some forms of conduct, he is not convinced that moral judgments enter extensively into the vast majority of social behaviour.

Instead of focusing on "reasoning," he addresses himself to the question, "How do the effects of social experience become represented in such a way that the child acquires internalized control over his behaviour?" He develops the thesis, in attempting to answer this question, that "moral judgment" is not the essential component for moral behaviour. He also points out that the discrepancy between conscience and conduct reveals the importance of *affective* components of cognitive structures. He outlines several experimental studies on children's reactions to punishment that support his emphasis on behaviour rather then Kohlberg's emphasis on judgment. Aronfreed also questions the validity of the idea of "stages" of moral reasoning and advances the interpretation that cognitive development of moral judgments is a continuous process.

Hunt, who generally accepts Kohlberg's criteria for moral maturity and uses Kohlberg's stages, addresses himself in more specific terms to the factors or conditions that facilitate or impede moral development. His paper attempts to derive a "metatheoretical" framework within which "matching" models can be considered. "Matching" involves the selection of an appropriate environment, which, when "matched" with the person's "personality" characteristics, produces more mature stages of development. Hunt outlines several specific examples of "matching models" and gives empirical evidence for their utility. A question that Hunt considers important is, "What environment is prescribed for a person in order to produce desired change?" In discussing this question, he suggests that "desired change" can be considered "genotypically," where "structural" or "stage" changes are emphasized, as in Kohlberg's system, or "phenotypically," where changes in specific behaviour are stressed, as in Aronfreed's system. In considering "matching models" for moral development, Hunt delineates four aspects of the model which require clarification: (1) desired change must be spelled out in clear and unambiguous criteria; (2) the person must be conceptualized on some relevant personality or stage dimensions; (3) the conception of the environment must be classified (e.g., "authoritarian versus laissez-faire); and (4) the interaction between the person and environment must be spelled out theoretically and empirically. Hunt analyzes Kohlberg's "cognitive conflict" matching model and several other matching models, and develops the thesis that those models that are for functional goals of immediate performance and satisfaction tend to prescribe an exact person-environment fit, whereas those models that aim for long-term developmental change tend to prescribe greater disparity in the match between person and environment. Kohlberg's use of the "conflict" engendered by arguments from one stage higher than the person's present level is an example of the latter type of model.

Ausubel stresses the importance of "moral reasoning" but frames the emphasis within the context of his ego-development theory. He summarizes literature on normative changes in value assimilation and discusses two main personality types – the satellizer and the nonsatellizer – who, because of their differing biosocial status, take different approaches to value assimilation. Satellizing and nonsatellizing are forms of identification which occur during early parent-child relationships. In a satellizing relationship, the subordinate party (child) renounces an independent, earned status of his own, and the superordinate party, in turn, accepts him as an intrinsically valuable entity. The satellizer thereby acquires a vicarious or derived biosocial status which is a function of the dependent relationship and independent of his own competence or performance ability. In contrast, a nonsatellizing relationship occurs when the parents do not "intrinsically" value the child, and give status on the basis of his competence or performance ability. If the act of identification occurs, it consists solely in the child's use of the parent as an emulatory model for learning the model's skills and methods of operation. The implications for the assimilation of moral values of these two types of "biosocial status" are then spelled out.

Ausubel's paper explicitly describes the roles of the family and of peers in the development of the child's moral orientation. Loubser takes a position similar to Ausubel's, delineating the role of peers and family in moral life. Ausubel develops the thesis that psychologists have undervalued the rational component in "moral obligation," ignoring the fact that, with increasing age, the child's increasing cognitive and role-taking skills enable him to take more rational approaches to moral obligation. Moral obligation is a core value of the moral system which organizes all other values together within an integrated and coherent system. Ausubel then proceeds to describe the age-developmental history of moral obligation. Ausubel also attempts in his paper to relate "moral beliefs" to behaviour or conduct, and he proposes an explanation of the discrepancy between one's beliefs and one's actions.

THE SOCIAL STRUCTURE OF THE SCHOOL AS IT RELATES TO MORAL EDUCATION

Psychology represents only one aspect of moral development. The topic of moral education also demands that we look at the school as a "social institution" since there are many implicit value assumptions and premises which can enhance or detract from a program in moral education. The school as a "social system contributes to the learning of certain norms such as independence, achievement, and universalism and specificity" (Dreeben 1967). Independence and achievement are self-explanatory, but the norms of universalism and specificity demand further explanation, especially since they are stressed in Loubser's paper on the development of moral sentiments. Dreeben clarifies the difference between universalism and specificity in the following way: "The relevant distinction here is whether individuals are treated as members of categories or as special cases. In one respect or another, an individual can always be viewed as a member of one or more categories; he is viewed particularistically if, notwithstanding his similarity to others in the same category or circumstances, he still receives special treatment ..." (1967, p. 228). The questions here concern the influence which the school has on the child's learning of these various values and the effect of this learning on the moral education of the child. More specifically, what is peculiar about the school as a "social institution" which makes it an important influence on the child's moral education?

Kohlberg maintains that the school is unwittingly a training ground for certain moral values, since the classroom situation requires enforcing rules by the teacher and this usually emerges as moralizing about the necessities of classroom management. He also compares the values transmitted in the Russian and American systems of education; the Russian system suffers from state indoctrination, whereas the American system is extremely effective in teaching the value of "competitive achievement." Oliver and Bane develop a similar thesis in their paper on the "achievement" ethic. For Kohlberg, the vehicle for a moral-education program in the schools is "social studies" and he sees Oliver's program as being obviously "moral" in terms of its value assumptions and goals. Kohlberg also proposes a "participatory program" in school management which would encourage fuller student participation and in which "justice" would become a living matter in the normal operations of school. Oliver and Bane advocate greater student participation in the school community and they give the schools a wider social radius than is apparent in Kohlberg's paper.

Loubser examines the structural characteristics of the school and compares them to those of the family. Although he contends that the school could be much more, he sees it, at present, as a weak extension of the family. He believes that the contemporary school is "in loco parentis," the major difference being that the school does not provide *care* as the parents do, that the school does not, in Ausubel's terms, "intrinsically value" the child. Loubser extensively discusses the development of the norms of universality and specificity (particularism) as they are learned in the schools, either explicitly in the curriculum or implicitly by the structure of the institution itself. He identifies the development of the "moral sentiment" with the development of "universalistic norms." The school's use of homogeneous age grouping and sex discrimination tends to discourage the developing of more universal moral values and sentiments. Age and sex differentiation tend to alienate children from potential human bonds which transcend the competitive (particularistic) aspects of both of these phenomena. Moreover, achievement and performance standards as discussed by Oliver and Bane and Kohlberg are held to discourage a more expansive and universalistic ethic which transcends the "particularism" engendered by competition. The provincial and local character of the school caused by such factors as language, religion, and race, also cuts down the possibility of having a more "universal" and humanistic ethic. Given some of these structural features of the school, Loubser does not find it surprising that individuals do not go beyond Kohlberg's "authority-maintaining" stage of moral development.

Oliver and Bane's paper makes similar criticism concerning the present school structure and its goals and calls for a radical new approach to moral education, involving a wider community which includes the family and the school. They suggest that an "experimental school," quite different in structure from the present school, will have more lasting effects on the child's moral values. Questions essential to the life of the community would be discussed in small groups of equals; this contrasts with the present school which is organized in large groups of students responsive to the authority constraints of the teacher. Moral development in the school context must be pursued outside an environment where conventional knowledge is taught. Oliver and Bane maintain that the school has historically operated within a limited range of human experience and they try to provide a rough outline of what a program with a wider social basis would look like. As Loubser does, they demand a freedom from traditional status distinctions as a prerequisite for a more serious program in moral education.

REFERENCES

Bruner, J.S. *The process of education* Cambridge, Mass.: Harvard University Press 1960

Conant, J.B. *The American high school today: A first report to interested citizens* New York: McGraw-Hill 1959

Dewey, J. *Moral principles in education* New York: Philosophical Library 1959

Dewey, J. *Democracy and education* New York: Free Press 1966

Dreeben, R. The contribution of schooling to the learning of norms *Harvard Educational Review* 1967 *37*(2) 211–37

Hess, R.D. Political socialization in the schools *Harvard Educational Review* 1968 *38*(3) 528–36

Hodgetts, A.B. *What culture? What heritage? A study of civic education in Canada* The Report of the National History Project, Ontario Institute for Studies in Education, curriculum series no. 5, 1968

Hofstadter, R. *Anti-intellectualism in American life* New York: Vintage Books 1963

Kohlberg, L. Moral education in the schools: A developmental view *The School Review* 1966 *74* 1–30

Niblett, W.R. (ed.) *Moral education in a changing society* London: Faber and Faber Ltd. 1963

Peters, R.S. *Ethics and education* New York: Keystones of Education Series, Scott, Foresman & Co. 1966

Report of the Committee on Religious Education in the Public Schools of the Province of Ontario, Ontario Department of Eduction 1969

Wilson, J., Williams, N., Sugarman, B. *Introduction to moral education* Middlesex: Penguin 1967

PART ONE

The search for common norms within a pluralistic society: some psychological and philosophical considerations

CHAPTER I

*Stages of moral development as a basis for moral education**

LAWRENCE KOHLBERG

INTRODUCTION

CONFERENCES on morality and moral education tend toward the equal-time view, one anthropologist, one psychologist, one theologian, one social commentator. The present conference is organized with the recognition that there are only two disciplines that have any basic scholarly generalizations to make about moral education; these are developmental social psychology and moral philosophy. Many other scholarly fields have an interest in moral education, but insofar as this interest leads to scholarly generalizations discussed on their intellectual merits, they are generalizations about either developmental social psychology or the nature of ideal morality. Let me cite two examples. A Catholic theologian and educator may have a great deal of interest in, and working knowledge of, the aims and processes of Catholic moral education. This knowledge will be of use to non-Catholic educators, however, only insofar as the Catholic educator has formulated a conception of morality that is defensible by reference to moral philosophy, rather than Catholic theology, and insofar as he has studied the development of such morality in terms of the general methods and concepts of developmental social psychology. Similarly, an anthropo-

*The research reported in this paper was supported by NICHD Grant H.D. 02469–01. Philosophic positions of the paper are in part drawn from the writer's conference paper "From Is to Ought" in T. Mischel (ed.) *Genetic Epistomology* New York: Academic Press 1971. Psychological findings are amplified in Kohlberg and Turiel (eds.) *Moralization Research, the Cognitive – Developmental Approach* New York: Holt Rhinehart and Winston 1971. An amplification of the practical implications of our approach for teachers is presented in Kohlberg and Turiel "Developmental Methods in Moral Education" in G. Lesser (ed.) *Psychological Approaches to Teaching* Chicago: Scott, Foresman 1971. The writer wishes to acknowledge the helpful editorial comments of Clive Beck and Edmund Sullivan.

logist's study of socialization in a tribe in New Guinea may provide a fresh perspective on moral education, but it will do so only by generating social psychological generalizations about development in terms of philosophically defensible goals of moral education.

But not only is it the case that there are just two basic "disciplines" or ways of thinking central to moral education. It seems to me that anything worthwhile any of us can say about moral education requires our being simultaneously a social psychologist and a philosopher. An approach to moral education based on putting together some consensus of current psychology and current philosophy is the typical camel, the commitee-constructed animal, whose only virtue is that it does not drink. In other places (e.g., Kohlberg 1969) I have argued that the social psychology of moral development has spent the last two generations in the wilderness because it thought it could carry on its studies without attention to the issues of moral philosophy. I suspect that Edel, Scriven, and Baier might say something similar about moral philosophy's neglect of psychology. Certainly there have been no classical or exciting treatments of moral education in the last two generations to compare with the work of Dewey (1909) and Durkheim (1925), in which a moral philosophy and a social psychology form a single unified whole.

While somewhat embarrassed at my own presumption, I have, in this and other papers, joined the list of aspirants to the grand tradition and claimed to have defined an approach to moral education which unites philosophic and psychological considerations and meets, as any "approach" must, the requirements A of being based on the psychological and sociological facts of moral development, B of involving educational methods of stimulating moral change, which have demonstrated long-range efficacy, C of being based on a philosophically defensible concept of morality, and D of being in accord with a constitutional system guaranteeing freedom of belief.

The chief focus of this paper (as distinct from my previous papers in the area) is the attempt to set forth explicitly the philosophic basis for my definition of moral maturity. However, I would like to propose to this conference that my conception of moral maturity be criticized and discussed with regard to its adequacy as a starting point for planned moral education in the public schools, not just in terms of its congruity with particular disciplinary perspectives. In order to lead the discussion in this direction, I have begun by considering two approaches to moral education alternative to mine, the ethically relative "hidden curriculum" approach dominant in the United States, and the "bag of virtues" approach which is favoured when the implicit moral education of a "hidden curriculum" is traded for explicit moral education. In criticizing these approaches, I have tried to bring out a set of standards for moral education which can then be used to test my own approach. For purposes of discussion, I have made the strongest possible claim, namely, that I can define a culturally and historically universal pattern of mature moral thought and action that meets philosophic criteria of rationality or optimality about as well as such criteria can be met. It is not necessary to accept such a strong claim in order to accept my general approach to moral education, but to the extent to which the claim can be accepted, it certainly provides a more adequate basis for the approach.

THE HIDDEN CURRICULUM

Most teachers are not fully aware that they must deal with issues of moral education, that they have no clear views on the subject, and that they have never had any training or education in it. Nevertheless, they are constantly acting as moral educators, because they are continually telling children what to do, continually making evaluations of their behaviour, continually monitoring their social relations in the classroom, and doing all of this as part of a larger social institution called the school, which is defined by a still larger institution called society. For example, my second-grade son one day told me that he did not want to be one of the bad boys in school, and when asked "who are the bad boys?" he replied "the ones who don't put their books back where they belong." His teacher would probably be surprised to know that her trivial classroom-management concerns defined for children what she and her school thought were basic moral values, and that as a result she was unconsciously miseducating them morally.

In recent years, these moralizing activities of the teacher have been called the "hidden curriculum," and some writers (Jackson 1968, Dreeben 1968) have argued that the unconscious shaping of teachers' activities by the demands of classroom management and of the school as a social system performs hidden services in adapting children to society.

Jackson (1968) summarizes three central characteristics of school life: the crowds, the praise, and the power. Learning to live in the classroom means, first, learning to live and to be treated as a member of a crowd of same-age, same-status others. Second, it means learning to live in a world in which there is impersonal authority, in which a relative stranger gives orders and wields power. Dreeben (1968) emphasizes similar characteristics, especially learning to live with authority. Both Jackson and Dreeben stress the fact that the hidden curriculum provides a way-station between the personal relations of the family and the impersonal achievement and authority-oriented roles of adult occupational and sociopolitical life. The perspectives of Jackson and Dreeben derive from a long and great tradition of educational sociology founded by Emile Durkheim in France at the end of the nineteenth century. According to Durkheim (1925),

There is ... a great distance between the moral state in which the child finds himself as he leaves the family and the one toward which he must strive. Intermediaries are necessary. The school environment is the most desirable. It is a more extensive association than the family or the little societies of friends. It results neither from blood relationships nor from free choice, but from a fortuitous and inevitable meeting among subjects brought together on the basis of similar age and social conditions. In that respect it resembles political society. On the other hand, it is limited enough so that personal relations can crystallize ... It is precisely groups of young persons, more or less like those constituting the social system of the school, which have enabled the formation of societies larger than the family ... [Even in simple societies without schools] the elders would assemble the young after they had reached a given age, to initiate them collectively into ... the intellectual and moral patrimony of the group (1925, pp. 230–2).

These views of the hidden curriculum depend upon the value-perspective of functional sociology, the perspective that the invisible hand of societal survival guides the shaping of human institutions and gives them a value or wisdom not apparent at first glance. Durkheim understood that functional sociology (which he founded) was not value-free but essentially represented a moral point of view. He articulately and explicitly argued that the sociologists's definition of the invisible hand of the social system was also the definition of the rational or scientific morality. Durkheim goes further than saying that acceptance of authority is one of the key elements of the child's moral development. He argues that the crowds, the praise, and the power which look so wasteful from the point of view of intellectual development are the necessary conditions for the moral development of the child. According to Durkheim

Although ... familial education is an excellent first preparation for the moral life, its usefulness is quite restricted – above all, with respect to the spirit of discipline. That which is essential to the spirit of discipline, that is to say, respect for the rule, can scarcely develop in the familial setting. The family ... is a very small group of persons ... their relationships are not subject to any general, impersonal, immutable regulation; they always have and normally should have an air of freedom ... But meanwhile the child must learn respect for the rule; he must learn to do his duty because it is his duty ... even though the task may not seem an easy one. Such an apprenticeship ... must devolve upon the school ... Too often, it is true, people conceive of school discipline so as to preclude endowing it with such an important moral function. Some see in it a simple way of guaranteeing superficial peace and order in the class. Under such conditions, one can quite reasonably come to view these imperative requirements as barbarous – as a tyranny of complicated rules ... In reality, however, the nature and function of discipline is something altogether different. It is not a simple device for securing superficial peace in the classroom ... It is the morality of the classroom (as a small society) (1925, pp. 146–8).

I shall not go into Durkheim's system of moral education in detail in this paper except to say it is the most philosophically and scientifically comprehensive, clear, and workable approach to moral education extant. Its workability has been demonstrated not in France, but in Soviet Russia where it has been elaborated from the point of view of Marxist rather then Durkheimian sociology. Like Durkheim, the Russians hold that altruistic concern or sacrifice, like the sense of duty, is always basically directed towards the group rather than towards another individual or towards an abstract principle. Durkheim reasons that altruism is always sacrificing the self for something greater than the self and another self can never be greater than the self except as it stands for the group or for society. Accordingly a central part of moral education is the sense of belonging to, and sacrificing for, a group.

One of the logical but to us rather horrifying innovations in the hidden curriculum that Durkheim and the Russians suggest on this basis is the use of collective responsibility, collective punishment and reward. Here is how a Russian moral education manual (quoted by Bronfenbrenner 1968) tells us these and other aspects of moral education are to be handled in a third-grade classroom:

Class 3-B is just an ordinary class; it's not especially well disciplined.

The teacher has led this class now for three years, and she has earned affection, respect, and acceptance as an authority from her pupils. Her word is law for them.

The bell has rung, but the teacher has not yet arrived. She has delayed deliberately in order to check how the class will conduct itself.

In the class all is quiet. After the noisy class break, it isn't so easy to mobilize yourself and to quell the restlessness within you! Two monitors at the desk silently observe the class. On their faces is reflected the full importance and seriousness of the job they are performing. But there is no need for them to make any reprimands: the youngsters with pleasure and pride maintain scrupulous discipline; they are proud of the fact that their class conducts itself in a manner that merits the confidence of the teacher. And when the teacher enters and quietly says be seated, all understand that she deliberately refrains from praising them for the quiet and order, since in their class it could not be otherwise.

During the lesson, the teacher gives an exceptional amount of attention to collective competition between "links." (The links are the smallest unit of the Communist youth organization at this age level.) Throughout the entire lesson the youngsters are constantly hearing which link has best prepared its lesson, which link has done the best at numbers, which is the most disciplined, which has turned in the best work.

The best link not only gets a verbal positive evaluation but receives the right to leave the classroom first during the break and to have its notebooks checked before the others. As a result the links receive the benefit of collective education, common responsibility, and mutual aid.

"What are you fooling around for? You're holding up the whole link," whispers Kolya to his neighbor during the preparation period for the lesson. And during the break he teaches her how better to organize her books and pads in her knapsack.

"Count more carefully," says Olya to her girl friend. "See, on account of you our link got behind today. You come to me and we'll count together at home."

I do not need to say any more to indicate that Durkheim and the Russians know how to make the hidden curriculum work. Furthermore, it is clear that Durkheim has simply taken to its logical conclusion a justification of the hidden curriculum which many teachers vaguely assume, the justification that the discipline of group life directly promotes moral character. We see, however, that when this line of thinking is carried to its logical conclusion, it leads to a definition of moral education as the promotion of collective national discipline which most of us feel is consistent neither with rational ethics nor with the American constitutional tradition. What I am arguing is that the trouble with Durkheim's approach to the hidden curriculum is not that he starts from a conception of moral development, but rather that he starts from an erroneous conception of moral development.

Oddly enough, permissive rejection of Durkheim's worship of collective authority can open the way for educational practices which, just as much as Durkheim's, are based upon a culturally relative notion of the moral. A.S. Neill says: "We set out to make a school in which we should allow children freedom to be themselves. To do this we had to renounce all discipline, all direction, all moral training. We have been called brave but it did not require courage, just a complete belief in the child as a good, not an evil, being. A child is innately wise and realistic. If left to himself without adult suggestion of any kind he will develop as far as he is capable of developing. I believe that it is moral instruction that makes the child bad, not good" (1960, p. 4).

A philosopher could while away a pleasant afternoon trying to find out just what ethical framework Neill is using when he says children are good but morality is bad. It is more instructive, however, to recognize that even at Summerhill moral problems arise, and to see how Neill handles them. Some years ago, Neill says,

we had two pupils arrive at the same time, a boy of seventeen and a girl of sixteen. They fell in love with each other and were always together. I met them late one night and stopped them, "I don't know what you two are doing," I said, "and morally I don't care for it isn't a moral question at all. But economically, I do care. If you, Kate, have a kid my school will be ruined. You have just come to Summerhill. To you it means freedom to do what you like. Naturally, you have no special feeling for the school. If you had been here from the age of seven, I'd never have had to mention the matter. You would have such a strong attachment to the school that you would think of the consequences to Summerhill" (1960, p. 57).

What the quotation makes clear, of course, is that the hidden moral curriculum of Summerhill is the "explicit" curriculum of Durkheim and the Russians. Unquestioned loyalty to the school, to the collectivity, seems to be the ultimate end of moral education at Summerhill. The radically child-centred approach, which denies morality, has a "hidden curriculum" which is the same "hidden curriculum" as that of the teacher who preached that moral virtue was putting your books away. For both the radical libertarian and the Philistine bureaucrat a point comes where the wish of the child conflicts with the convenience and welfare of the school (or its managers) and, for both, the latter is the ultimate good. If exposed to reflection, and made explicit as moral education, this implicit teaching of conformity to the school becomes Durkheim's use of loyalty to the school and its rules as a symbol of, and preparation for, loyalty to the national society.

The term "hidden curriculum," then, refers to the fact that teachers and schools are engaged in moral education without explicitly and philosophically discussing or formulating its goals and methods. On the face of it, engaging in moral education without thinking about its goals and methods seems as dubious as it would be in intellectual education. There is, however, a school of functional sociology which claims that unreflective moral education reflects the unconscious wisdom of society and its needs for "socializing" the child for his own welfare as well as that of society. When such "socialization" or rule enforcement is viewed as implying explicit positive educational goals, it generates a philosophy of moral education in which loyalty to the school and its rules is consciously cultivated as a matter of breeding loyalty to society and its rules.

RELATIVITY AND UNIVERSALS IN MORAL DEVELOPMENT

Although Durkheim's philosophical and psychological development of the hidden curriculum of everyday public-school practice seems repellent, we shall argue that it is the only logically consistent rationale for deliberate moral education under the central common assumption of most social scientists, the assumption of the cultural and historical relativity of moral values. Before we can consider other approaches to moral education, then, we must consider the issue of value-relativity.

Most contemporary psychologists and sociologists who write about moral values in child development and education start with the assumption that there are no universal, nonarbitrary moral principles and that each individual acquires his own values from the external culture. The following definition of moral values clearly reflects such a relativistic view: "moral values are evaluations of actions generally believed by the members of a given society to be either 'right' or 'wrong,'" (Berkowitz 1964, p. 44). While there are major theoretical differences among sociological role-theorists, psychoanalytic theorists, and learning theorists, and among different learning theorists themselves, they all do have a common characteristic: they view moral development and other forms of socialization as "the whole process by which an individual, born with behavioral potentialities of enormously wide range, is led to develop actual behavior which is confined within a much narrower range – the range of what is customary and acceptable for him according to the standards of his group" (Child 1954 n. 655). Thus, development is defined as the direct internalization of external cultural norms. The growing child is trained to behave in such a way that he conforms to societal rules and values.

The first educational position derived from the assumption of relativity is Durkheim's advocacy of moralization by collective discipline. According to this position, although all values are relative, the child must be taught to accept the dominant values of his society for his own adaptation and for the survival of his society, and the school plays a necessary role in this process.

A second position derived (in America) from the assumption of the relativity of values is that the public schools cannot teach the moral values of American society to children without infringing the rights of minority groups, and hence that value education should be conducted by having publicly supported schools which teach one or another system of values, leaving parents free to send their children to a Catholic parochial school, a school teaching Black nationalistic values, etc.

A third position (the Neill position) derived from the assumption is that moral values should not be taught or enforced in schools at all, since they are arbitrary and irrational.

In practice, most working educators who believe in ethical relativity shuttle from one of these three positions to the other depending upon the situation with which they are confronted. They have no assurance about the nature of any universal ethical principles to be transmitted to children, but they cannot be completely ethically neutral either. The customary result is to focus moral instruction on the trivial and immediate, rather than on the universal and important, because this approach gives rise to fewer headaches about philosophic or ethical justification.

An example of this shuttling between positions based on relativity comes from my observation of an enlightened and effective young fourth-grade teacher. The teacher was at the back of the room working with a project group, while the rest of the class were engaged with their work-books. In the front row, a boy said something to his neighbour who retaliated by quietly spitting in his face. The first boy equally quietly slugged the other without leaving his seat, by which time the teacher noted the disturbance. She said calmly, "Stop that and get back to your work-books." The boy who had done the slugging said, "Teacher I hit him because he spit in my face." The teacher replied, "That wasn't polite, it was rude, now get back to work, you're supposed to be doing your work-books." As they went back to work, the boy who had done the spitting said to his opponent with a grin, "I will grant you that, it was rude."

A later discussion with this teacher about her general views on moral education explained why she handled the situation as she did. In her master's thesis she had reviewed writings and research on "Middle class values in education and their application to the disadvantaged child." She said that her paper had made her realize that she was transmitting middle-class values. Nevertheless, she said, politeness was just very important to her and she was bent on transmitting it to her students. The point is that she had absorbed from educational sociology the conflictful concept that "all values are relative" and had resolved the conflict by the decision to support the "middle-class" value of "politeness," which was emotionally central to her. The result was that she attempted to avoid moralizing, but, when she finally did moralize, she perceived the moral issue in terms of the superficial "middle-class" value of "politeness" rather than the deeper and more universal value of human dignity. The boys themselves recognized that some deeper value than politeness was involved, as the smiling "I'll grant you that, it was rude" indicated. I do not presume to advise the teacher as to what she should have said in this situation. My point is that the teacher must resolve the issues involved in moral relativity more systematically if she is to carry out her moral-educational activities in a positive fashion.

When confronted with uncertainty about the relativity of ethical principles, the customary resort of the teacher is to retreat to a committee or group. Uneasy about her own arbitrary authority, she passes this authority over to the group, a good strategy for nonmoral policy decisions within the democratic process, but not a strategy for arriving at valid ethical principles.

The teacher just mentioned had gathered together suggestions of the class in the form of a moral code put up on a poster at the back of the class. The code had the following commandments: 1 Be a good citizen; 2 Be generous by helping our friends; 3 Mind your own business; 4 Work quietly; 5 No fighting; 6 Play nicely and fairly; 7 Be neat and clean; 8 Be prepared; 9 Raise your hand; 10 Be polite. Even if some of us feel that the original Ten Commandments could stand restatement, I doubt if these ten would be considered an improvement.

Now, we shall claim that this teacher's problems arise because of faulty thinking about ethical relativity which she shares with all the writers we have so far quoted or discussed. In this section I will present evidence that the factual assumptions made by theories of ethical relativity are not correct; that there are in fact universal human ethical values and principles.

In this section I will also present evidence which leads us to question a second common assumption closely linked to the assumption of ethical relativity. This is the assumption, accepted by all the writers quoted, that morality and moral learning are fundamentally emotional, irrational processes. Durkheim (1925) and Dreeben (1968) assume that learning to accept rules and authority is a concrete nonrational process based on repetition, emotion, and sometimes sanctions. The child is assumed to be controlled by primitive and selfish drives which he is reluctant to give up, and the steady experience of authority and discipline is necessary for his learning to live with rules. This conception of moral learning contrasts with that of Dewey (1925) and Piaget (1932), who hold that the child learns to accept authority genuinely when he learns to understand and accept the reasons and principles behind the rules, or more generally that "ethical principles" are the end point of sequential "natural" development in social functioning and thinking. (Kohlberg 1969, Kohlberg and Turiel 1971). This is a very different point of view from that taken by most teachers who either, like Durkheim, assume that "ethical principles" are the accepted rules of their own nation and culture, which should be taught to children by the teacher's deliberate instruction, example, and discipline, or else, like Neill, assume that "ethical principles" are relative and arbitrary. It will be our contention that ethical principles are distinguishable from arbitrary conventional rules and beliefs and that the stimulation of their development is a matter quite different from the inculcation of arbitrary cultural beliefs.

Before presenting our evidence, it is important to note that the value-relativity issue is not solely one of fact. As usually held by adults, value relativism is both a doctrine that "everyone has their own values," that all men do not adhere to some set of universal standards, and a doctrine that "everyone ought to have their own values," that there are no universal standards to which all men ought to adhere. Thus, the value-relativity position often rests on logical confusion between matters of fact, what "is," and matters of value, what "ought to be."

To illustrate, I shall quote a typical response of one of my graduate students to the following moral dilemma:

In Europe, a woman was near death from a very bad disease, a special kind of cancer. There was one drug that the doctors thought might save her. It was a form of radium that a druggist was charging ten times what the drug cost him to make. He paid $200 for the radium and charged $2,000 for a small dose of the drug. The sick woman's husband, Heinz, went to everyone he knew to borrow the money, but he could only get together about $1,000 which is half of what it cost. He told the druggist that his wife was dying, and asked him to sell it cheaper or let him pay later. But the druggist said, "No, I discovered the drug and I'm going to make money from it." So Heinz got desperate and broke into the man's store to steal the drug for his wife.

Should the husband have done that? Why?

Part of her reply was as follows: "I think he should steal it because if there is any such thing as a universal human value, it is the value of life and that would justify stealing it." I then asked her, "Is there any such thing as a universal human value?" and she answered, "No, all values are relative to your culture."

I quote the response because it illustrates a typical confusion of the relativist. She starts out by claiming that one ought to act in terms of the universal value of human life, implying that human life is a universal value in the sense that it is logical and desirable for all men to respect all human life, and that one can demonstrate to other men that it is logical and desirable to act in this way. If she were clear in her thinking she would see that the *fact* that all men do not always act in terms of this value does not contradict the claim that all men *ought* always to act in accordance with it. Because she has this confusion, she ends up denying the possibility of making a judgment of should or ought going beyond the self.

Very typically, the doctrine of relativity is used as an argument for tolerance. When the relativist says "everyone has his own bag," he means "everyone ought to be allowed and encouraged to have his own bag," which is a postulation of liberty as something which ought to be a universal human value. Frequently, however, the desire to postulate the principle of tolerance as an ideal leads to a postulation of the factual claim that there is cultural relativity, a complete logical confusion.

If the relativist could clearly separate the question "Are there universal moral values?" from the question "Ought there to be universal human values?" he could get an affirmative answer to both questions. Let us take the "is" question first.

For twelve years, I have been studying the development of moral judgment and character primarily by following the same group of 75 boys at three-year intervals from early adolescence (at the beginning the boys were 10 to 16 years of age) through young manhood (they are now 22 to 28 years of age). This study has been supplemented by a series of studies of development in other cultures, and by a set of experimental studies, some designed to change the child's stage of moral thought, some to find the relation of an individual's moral thought to moral action.

The first assumption behind our approach has been that the key to understanding a man's moral conduct or "character" is to understand his moral philosophy, that is, the assumption that we all, even and especially young children, are moral philosophers. By this I mean, in the first place, that the child has a morality of his own. Adults are so busy trying to instil in children their own morality, that they seldom listen to children's moralizing. If the child repeats a few of the adult's clichés and behaves himself, most parents think he has now adopted or "internalized" parental standards. A great deal of anthropology and psychology makes this assumption, which can only be made if we fail to talk to children. As soon as we do, we find that they have lots of standards which do not come in any obvious way from parents, peers, or teachers.

A consideration of somewhat more advanced moral philosophies leads us to stages defined in Appendix 1. We have defined these stages by means of the analysis of responses to hypothetical moral dilemmas, deliberately "philosophical," some found in medieval works of casuistry. (A more complete treatment of the dilemmas and sample responses to them can be found in Kohlberg and Turiel 1971). When I first decided to explore development in other cultures by this method, I did so with fear and trembling induced by predictions by some of my anthropologist friends that I would have to throw away my culture-bound moral concepts and stories and start from scratch learning the values of that culture. In fact, something quite different happened. My first try was a study of two villages – one Atayal (Malaysian aboriginal), one Taiwanese. My guide was a young Chinese ethnographer who had written an account of the moral and religious patterns of the village. When he started to translate for me the children's responses, he'd start to laugh at something at which I had laughed when I first heard it from American children. Cultural differences there are, but they are not what made him laugh. To illustrate, let me quote for you a dilemma, similar to the Heinz dilemma on stealing (see p. 33 above), adapted for the villages investigated:

A man and wife had just migrated from the high mountains. They started to farm but there was no rain and no crops grew. No one had enough food. The wife got sick from having little food and could only sleep. Finally she was close to dying from having no food. The husband could not get any work and the wife could not move to another town. There was only one grocery store in the village, and the storekeeper charged a very high price for the food because there was no other store and people had no place else to go to buy food. The husband asked the storekeeper for some food for his wife, and said he would pay for it later. The storekeeper said, "No, I won't give you food unless you pay first." The husband went to all the people in the village to ask for food but no one had food to spare. So he got desperate and broke into the store to steal food for his wife.

Should the husband have done that? Why?

Stage-2 children in the Taiwanese village would reply to the above story as follows: "he should steal the food for his wife because if she dies he'll have to pay for her funeral and that costs a lot." In the Atayal village, funerals weren't such a big thing and the Stage-2 boys would say, "he should steal the food because he needs his wife to cook for him." In other words, we have to consult our ethnographer to know what content a stage-2 child will include in his instrumental exchange calculations, but what made our anthropologist laugh was the difference in form between the child's thought and his own, a difference definable independently of the particular culture.

It is this emphasis on the distinctive form (as opposed to the content) of the child's moral thought which allows us to call all men moral philosophers.

The actual definition of our stages is detailed and is based on a treatment of 28 basic aspects of morality (moral concepts or values) to be found in any culture (Appendix 2). Appendix 3 presents one of these 28 concepts, the concept of the value of life. Appendix 3 defines and gives examples of the way this value is defined at each of the six stages of development.

The progression, or set of stages, just described implies something more than age trends. In the first place, stages imply invariant sequence. Each individual child must go step by step through each of the kinds of moral judgment outlined. It is, of course, possible for a child to move at varying speeds and to stop (become "fixated") at any level of development, but if he continues to move upward, he must move in accord with these steps. The longitudinal study of American boys at ages 10, 13, 16, 19, and 23 suggests that this is the case. An example of such stepwise movement is provided in Appendix 3. Tommy is stage 1 at age 10, stage 2 at age 13, and stage 3 at age 16. Jim is stage 4 at age 10, stage 5 at 20, and stage 6 at 24. (See Kohlberg 1963; 1969, and Kohlberg and Turiel 1971 for a more detailed discussion of empirical findings.)

Second, stages define "structured wholes": total ways of thinking, not attitudes towards particular situations. Another of the 28 different aspects contributing to stage definitions concerns the motives of moral action. As can be seen in Appendix 4, which illustrates prepared arguments for and against stealing the drug in the first dilemma described, a stage is a way of thinking, which may be used to support either side of an action choice; that is, it illustrates the distinction between moral form and moral content (action choice). Our correlational studies indicate a general factor of moral level which cross-cuts aspect. An individual at stage 6 on a "cognitive" aspect (universalized value of life) is also likely to be at stage 6 on an "affective" aspect (motive for difficult moral action in terms of internal self-condemnations). An individual at stage 6 on a situation of stealing a drug for a wife is

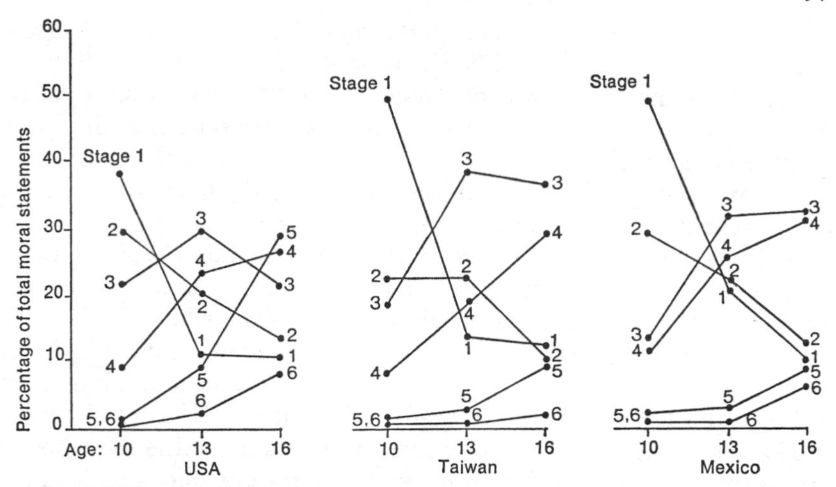

FIGURE 1 Middle-class urban boys in the U.S., Taiwan, and Mexico. At age 10 the stages are used according to difficulty. At age 13, stage 3 is most used by all three groups. At age 16, U.S. boys have reversed the order of age 10 stages (with the exception of 6) In Taiwan and Mexico, conventional (3–4) stages prevail at age 16, with stage 5 also little used. (From L. Kohlberg and R. Kramer: Continuities and discontinuities in childhood and adult moral development *Human Development* 1969 *12* 93–120 (S. Karger, Basel/New York).)

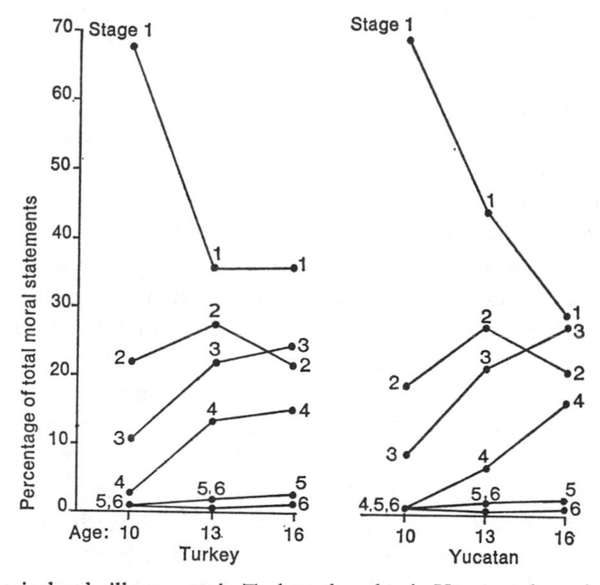

FIGURE 2 Two isolated villages, one in Turkey, the other in Yucatan, show similar patterns in moral thinking. There is no reversal of order, and preconventional (1–2) does not gain a clear ascendancy over conventional stages at age 16. (From L. Kohlberg and R. Kramer: Continuities and discontinuities in childhood and adult moral development *Human Development* 1969 *12* 93–120 (S. Karger, Basel/New York).)

likely to be at stage 6 on a story involving civil disobedience (helping slaves escape before the Civil War). It should be noted that any individual is usually not entirely at one stage. Typically, as children develop they are partly in their major stage (about 50 per cent of their ideas), partly in the stage into which they are moving, and partly in the stage they have just left behind. Seldom, however, do they use stages at developmental stages removed from one another.

Third, a stage concept implies universality of sequence under varying cultural conditions. It implies that moral development is not merely a matter of learning the verbal values or rules of the child's culture but reflects something more universal in development, something that would occur in any culture. In general, the stages in moral judgment just described appear to be culturally universal.

Figures 1 and 2 indicate the cultural universality of the sequence of stages that we have found. Figure 1 presents the age trends for middle-class urban boys in the United States, Taiwan, and Mexico. At age 10 in each country the greater number of moral statements are scored at the lower stages. In the United States by age 16, the order is reversed, so that the greater proportion use higher stages, with the exception of stage 6 which is rarely used. The results in Mexico and Taiwan are the same, except that development is a little slower. The most conspicuous feature is that stage-5 thinking is much more salient in the United States than in Mexico or Taiwan at age 16. Nevertheless, it is present in the other countries, so we know that it is not purely an American democratic construct. The second figure indicates results from two isolated villages, one in Yucatan, one in Turkey. The similarity of pattern in the two villages is striking. While conventional moral thought (stages 3 and 4) increases steadily from age 10 to age 16, at 16 it still has not achieved a clear ascendency over premoral thought (stages 1 and 2). Stages 5 and 6 are totally absent in this group. Trends for lower-class urban groups are intermediate in rate of development between those for the middle class and the village boys.

The first and most obvious implication of these findings is that many social scientific notions of "the cultural relativity of morals" are false. As Brandt's careful analysis indicates (1959), "cultural relativity in morals" has been based upon striking cultural differences in customs, but has not taken account of the meaning of such customs with regard to differences in principles or forms of moral judgment. A comparison of American college students' quaint springtime rite of sitting-in in the sixties with their quaint rites of panty-raiding in the fifties would not tell us anything about moral changes unless we looked at the way in which the students thought about the values involved in what they were doing. Our own studies are the first effort to examine this question, and suggest that the same basic ways of moral valuing are found in every culture and develop in the same order.

A second, related, fallacy is the notion that basic moral principles are dependent upon a particular religion, or any religion at all. We have found no important differences in development of moral thinking between Catholics, Protestants, Jews, Buddhists, Moslems, and atheists. Children's moral values in the religious area seem to go through the same stages as their general moral values so that a stage-2 child is likely to say "Be good to God and he'll be good to you." Both cultural values and religion are important factors in selectively elaborating certain themes in the moral life but they are not unique causes of the development of basic moral values. Our data do not indicate that all values are universal, but rather that basic moral values are universal. For example, a Taiwanese boy recommends stealing the drug "because if she dies, he'll have to pay for her funeral and that costs a lot." No American boy ever says that. But American boys will (like the Atoyal) recommend stealing the drug because otherwise "there'll be no one to cook your food." In other words, big funerals are a value in Taiwan and not in the United States. Both the value of life and a stage of instrumental-pragmatic thinking about this value are culturally universal, however.

If basic moral values are universal, the relativists' next defence is to say that the ordering or hierarchy of these values is idiosyncratic and relative. For instance, one might agree that everyone would value both life and property rights in the Heinz dilemma, but argue that which is valued most would depend upon a culturally relative hierarchy of values. In fact, however, basic hierarchies of moral values are primarily reflections of developmental stages in moral thought. Anyone who understands the values of life and property will recognize that life is morally more valuable than property. Even at stage 2 boys know that the druggist in the story would rather save his own life than his own property so that the druggist's property is less valuable than the woman's life. Appendix 3, defining the six steps or stages in the development of conceptions of the value of life, suggests these are steps not only in conceptions of life's value, but also in the differentiation of life from other values and in the hierarchical dominance of life over such values as that of property.

Another example concerning hierarchies of value is the current American problem of law and order versus justice which I have discussed in more detail elsewhere (Kohlberg and Turiel 1971). A person at stage 4 thinks law and order is justice, or as one respondent said, "If we have law and order what do we need justice for?" Governor Reagan of California thinks civil disobedience is automatically unjust. By contrast, people at stages 5 and 6 know that the purpose of law and order is the maintenance of justice. As stated in the old-fashioned terms of the founding fathers, governments are formed to protect the equal rights of citizens. Development in conceptions of justice leads to a hierarchical relation between "law and order" and "justice."

In summary, the doctrine of ethical relativity assumes that different cultures or groups hold different basic fundamental moral values or hierarchies of values, and that these different values or value hierarchies cannot themselves be judged as more or less adequate or more or less moral. When extended to individual differences within cultures, the doctrine holds that individuals, too, have different values because of differences in basic needs, and that these values also are determined by extramoral considerations and so cannot be judged as more or less adequate morally. There are two portions to the doctrine, one about matters of fact, one normative. The normative portion denies that one can *judge* or evaluate cultural or individual differences in moral judgment as better or worse. The empirical portion claims that the explanation of cultural differences in moral values is to be sought apart from a general concept of morality as such. Concretely, there have been moderate and extreme doctrines of relativity in both empirical and normative aspects. The moderate doctrine is represented by Durkheim, who holds that the concept of morality is scientifically meaningful and that an individual's attitude to the norms of his group is more or less moral, depending upon the extent to which he displays respect for, and attachment to these norms. One can characterize at least certain delinquents and psychopaths as being not moral. One cannot, however, characterize the differences in norms from one society or group to another as being more or less moral, since the essence of morality is respect for norms, and differences in the content of these norms is irrelevant to the fact that they involve the moral form (respect). As a doctrine about the empirical nature of morality, Durkheim's doctrine assumes that theories explaining differences in norms from culture to culture are not theories about why some individuals (or groups) are more or less moral (feel more or less respect) than others. As a normative doctrine, it holds that children within a culture may be judged as more or less moral and that the less moral child should be made more moral, but that cultural differences as such cannot be morally evaluated and that moral education should be one thing in one culture, another in another.

The strong form of the doctrine of ethical relativity would deny the usefulness of defining individual differences in moral terms at all. It holds that labelling individual differences as more or less moral is simply judging them from the arbitrary standards of some individual or group or making a judgment of praise or blame which has no scientific value or meaning. When the teacher labelled "putting books away" as "good behaviour" or as moral she did not add anything to the scientific understanding of the behaviour by introducing moral terminology. The extreme relativist would say the same with regard to more sophisticated efforts by psychologists to describe "moral character" (as we discuss in our final section). To label children who put their books away as more moral than those who do not, not only adds nothing to the scientific understanding of the behaviour but is not based on a moral norm of any rational validity. The extreme relativist would say the same for all discussions of individual and cultural differences in terms of morality.

In contrast to both schools of relativism we have first pointed out that there are universal moral concepts, values, or principles. As a matter of fact, there is less variation between individuals and cultures than usually has been maintained: A almost all individuals in all cultures use the same 28 basic moral categories, concepts, or principles, B all individuals in all cultures go through the same order or sequences of gross stages of development, although varying in rate and terminal point of development.

Second, we have pointed out that the marked differences which exist between individuals and cultures are differences in stage or developmental status. There are marked individual and cultural differences in the definition, use, and hierarchical ordering of these universal value-concepts, but the major source of this variation both within and between cultures is developmental. Insofar as they are developmental, they are not morally neutral or arbitrary. This means empirically that the theory which explains cultural and individual differences in values is also the same general theory of why children become capable of moral judgment and action at all. It means normatively that there is a sense in which we can characterize moral differences between groups and individuals as being more or less adequate morally.

The basic educational conclusions we shall draw from this position are that the only philosophically justifiable statement of aims of moral education, the only one which surmounts the problem of relativity, is a statement in terms of the stimulation of moral development conceived of as the encouragement of a capacity for principled moral judgment and of the disposition to act in accordance with this capacity. To support this conclusion we shall need to clarify our philosophical conception of the nature of moral principles and of the relation of moral principles to moral action. Before doing this, however, we need to go back over the research findings just presented in terms of their implications for a psychological theory of moralization. We need to do this because we believe that the only psychological theory consistent with our findings is so different from that entertained by most philosophers, educators, and psychologists, that communication is impossible without some clarification of this theory.

THE COGNITIVE-DEVELOPMENTAL THEORY OF MORALIZATION

Almost all psychology textbooks which discuss moral development treat it as the product of internalization of the norms and values of parents and of the culture through processes of identification, reward, or punishment. Our findings concerning stages obviously lead us to reject the theories of internalization which are the unquestioned "truths" of textbook social science, but also require a positive alternative explanation. Often, notions of stages are assimilated to a conception of natural biological growth and unfolding. In the area of morality, such maturational theories lead to a conception of "giving the child freedom to grow in his own way" such as was represented by our quotations from A.S. Neill. Such a maturational theory, however, is far from our own view of the implications of moral stages. Instead, we have elaborated a "cognitive-developmental" theory of moralization which attempts to explain universals and natural trends in development without assuming that these trends are the innate unfolding of the nervous system, and which specifies the kind of environmental conditions necessary to facilitate moral development (Kohlberg 1969; Kohlberg in preparation).

I have used the term "cognitive-developmental" to refer to a set of assumptions common to the moral theories of Dewey (1909), G.H. Mead (1934), J.M. Baldwin (1906), Piaget (1932), and myself. All have postulated stages of moral development representing cognitive-structural transformations in the conception of self and society. All have assumed that these stages represent successive modes of "taking the role of others" in social situations, and hence that the social-environmental determinants of development are its opportunities for role-taking. More generally, all have assumed an active child who structures his perceived environment, and hence they have assumed that moral stages and their development represent the interaction of the child's structuring tendencies and the structural features of the environment.

There are two assumptions of our theory which we shall stress here, because they are central for educators and philosophers concerned with morality. One is our second assumption, the assumption that moral development has a cognitive core. This assumption is central to any intellective approach to moral education and contrasts sharply with irrational-emotive theories of moral development such as those of Durkheim and Freud. The other assumption is of the interactional origins of morality. This assumption is central to an intellective approach to moral education as not a process of transmission of fixed moral truth but rather a stimulation of the child's restructuring of his experience.

There are two issues which require clarification in labelling our theory as "cognitive." First, the label does not imply that we consider moral judgment to be cognitive in the sense held by philosophers holding "descriptivistic" metaethical views, that is, that moral judgments describe states of the world in somewhat the same way as scientific judgments describe states of the world. (In this camp are utilitarians who believe that moral judgments describe the welfare or happiness consequence of action, intuitionists who believe moral judgments reflect immediately apprehended moral qualities of action, and Durkheimian sociological ethicists). As I elaborate in later sections, my metaethical position is "prescriptivistic" and "constructionistic" rather than "descriptivistic" or "emotive." Put differently, moral judgments and norms are to be understood ultimately as universal constructions of human actors which regulate their social interaction rather than as passive reflections of either external states of other humans or of internal emotions.

It should be noted, however, that although "descriptivism" and "objectivism" are inadequate metaethical views, they are the views of most of humanity. Below the principled stage of morality, it is simply assumed that judgments of right and wrong correspond to a right and wrong external to the judger, that "almost everyone knows right from wrong," and that "right and wrong" are the rules of society or of God. This is most patently true at stage 1. When stage-1 ten-year-old children are asked "Is there a right answer to these questions (moral dilemmas)?" they are likely to respond "you must have the right answers in the back of your book." While children at the conventional stage discriminate between moral problems and arithmetic problems, they still believe moral judgments reflect an objective "right and wrong" external to the judger. In the light of the fact that moral judgments are usually believed to be cognitions by their makers, it is psychologically correct to analyze moral judgment in terms of general principles and theories of cognitive development.

The second issue raised by the label "cognitive" is that of the role of affect in moral judgment. Discussions of cognition and affect usually are based on the assumption that cognitions and affects are different mental states, leading to the question "Which is quantitatively more influential in moral judgment, states of cognition or states of affect?" In contrast, the cognitive-developmental view holds that "cognition" and "affect" are different aspects of, or perspectives on, the same mental events, that all mental events have both cognitive and affective aspects, and that the development of mental dispositions reflects structural changes recognizable in both cognitive and affective perspectives. It is evident that moral judgments often involve strong emotional components. It is also evident that the presence of strong emotion in no way reduces the cognitive component of moral judgment, although it may imply a somewhat different functioning of the cognitive component than is implied in more neutral areas. An astronomer's calculation that a comet will hit the earth will be accompanied by strong emotion but this does not make his calculation less cognitive than a calculation of a comet's orbit which had no earthly consequences. And just as the quantitative strength of the emotional component is irrelevant to the theoretical importance of cognitive structure for understanding the development of scientific judgment, so too the quantitative role of affect is relatively irrelevant for understanding the structure and development of moral judgment. The dilemmas we present to our children are hypothetical and involve relatively mild emotional arousal. Several studies have compared stages of moral judgment in real dilemmas and our hypothetical ones and indicate a quite high correlation between moral stage in the real and hypothetical dilemmas. The example of the astronomer's calculation can be misleading, however, in that moral judgments differ from scientific judgments in the way in which they involve affective aspects of mental functioning. Moral judgments are largely about sentiments and intuitions of persons and to a large extent they express and are justified by reference to the judger's sentiments. The development of sentiment, as it enters into moral judgment, is, however, a development of structures with a heavy cognitive component. We presented in Appendix 4 six stages in the development of sentiments of fear, shame, and guilt as they enter into moral judgment. The emergence of self-condemnation for example, as a distinctive sentiment in moral judgment is the final step in a series of differentiations which, like all differentiations in development, are cognitive in nature. The sequential differentiations are defined in the parentheses of Appendix 4 (e.g., disapproval from punishment, moral condemnation from disapproval, self-condemnation from moral condemnation by others).

The series of differentiations involved in the emergence of guilt is related to the series of differentiations (presented in Appendix 3) involved in the development of human life, on the face of it not an "affective" concept. Both spring from the central differentiations involved in the stages as a whole. The fact that this is true is shown by the fact that there is a good correlation between a child's stage on the life concept and on the guilt concept. This consistency enters into "real life" measures of guilt as well. Ruma and Mosher (1966) obtained a correlation of 0.56 between real-life measures of guilt by delinquents over confessed offences and stage of moral judgment, a correlation as high as that between one measure of guilt and another. In general, then, the quality (as opposed to the quantity) of affects involved in moral judgment is determined by its cognitive-structural development, a development which is part and parcel with the general development of the child's conceptions of a moral order. Two adolescents, thinking of stealing, may have the same feeling of anxiety in the pit of their stomachs. One adolescent (stage 2) interprets the feeling as "being chicken," "being afraid of the police," and ignores it. The other (stage 4) interprets the feeling as "the warning of my conscience" and decides accordingly. The difference in reaction is one in cognitive-structural aspects of moral judgment, not in emotional "dynamics" as such.

The exact psychological meaning for moral judgment of the contentions just made has been clarified by several empirical findings. Maturity of moral judgment is correlated with cognitive maturity but is clearly distinguishable from it. Among children of a given age, the correlations between IQ and moral maturity are 0.35 to 0.50 in various samples, accounting for about one-fourth of the variation in moral judgment. In large part, older children are more mature in moral judgment because they are in general more cognitively mature. This is true to an extent greater than is suggested by the correlations with tests of IQ. IQ tests are poor tests of maturity of reasoning processes in moral judgment, processes more adequately measured by Piaget's tests of reasoning. Piaget's tests predict maturity of moral judgment independently of the relation of both moral judgment and Piaget reasoning to IQ. Furthermore, the empirical relations between general cognitive maturity and maturity of moral judgment are both greater and less than is suggested by these correlations. The correlations are not one-to-one but of the order that a certain level of cognitive maturity is a necessary but not sufficient condition for a given level of moral judgment. In other words, all morally advanced children are bright but not all bright children are morally advanced (or, all intellectually dull children are morally retarded but not all bright children are morally advanced). Moral maturity requires cognitive maturity but it also requires further features of development.

To summarize, our view implies that cognitive-structural features are the core of moral development, but moral judgment is not simply the application of intelligence in the sense of logical-technological thought to moral situations and problems. Our theory implies the untestable hypothesis that a child deprived of all moral-social stimulation until adolescence might perhaps develop "principled" or formal-operational logical thought in adolescence, but would still have to go through all the stages of morality before developing moral principles. If this were not so, it would be difficult to explain invariant sequence within the moral domain. Our notion of the cognitive-structural as broader than the usual conceptions of "knowing" and of "rationality" becomes evident when we consider the sense in which higher stages are more adequate than lower stages. Both psychological and philosophical analyses suggest that the more mature stage of moral thought is the more structurally adequate. This greater adequacy of more mature moral judgments rests on structural criteria more general than those of truth-value or efficiency. These general criteria are the *formal* criteria developmental theory holds as defining all mature structures, the criteria of increased differentiation and integration. These formal criteria (differentiation and integration) of development fit the formal criteria which philosophers of the formalist school have held to characterize genuine or adequate moral judgments.

From Kant to Hare, formalists have stressed the distinctively *universal* and *prescriptive* nature of adequate moral judgments. The increasingly prescriptive nature of more mature moral judgments is reflected in the series of differentiations we have described, which is a series of increased differentiations of "is" from "ought" (or of morality as internal principles from external events and expectations). As I elaborate later, this series of differentiations of the morally autonomous or categorical "ought" from the morally heteronomous "is" also represents a differentiation of the sphere of value-judgments.

Corresponding to the criterion of integration is the moral criterion of universality, which is closely linked to the criterion of consistency, as formalists since Kant have stressed. The claim of principled morality is that it defines the right for anyone in any situation. In contrast, conventional morality defines good behaviour for a Democrat but not for a Republican, for an American but not for a Vietnamese, for a father but not for a son.

The way in which these criteria are embodied in our stages is indicated by Appendix 3, the moral worth of human life. The series approaches prescriptivity because the moral imperative to value life becomes increasingly independent of the factual properties of the life in question. First the person's furniture becomes irrelevant to his value, next whether he has a loving family, and so on. (It is correspondingly a series of differentiations of moral considerations from other value-considerations.) In parallel fashion it is movement towards increased universality of the moral value of human life. At stage 1 only important persons' lives are valued, at stage 3 only family members, at stage 6 all life has equal moral value.

These combined criteria, differentiation and integration, are considered by developmental theory to entail a better equilibrium of the structure in question. A more differentiated and integrated moral structure handles more moral problems, conflicts, or points of view in a more stable or self-consistent way. Because conventional morality is not fully universal and prescriptive, it leads to continual self-contradictions, to definitions of right which are different for Republicans and Democrats, for Americans and Vietnamese, for fathers and sons. In contrast, principled morality is directed to resolving these conflicts in a stable, self-consistent fashion.

In this way a psychological explanation of why the child moves from stage to stage converges with a philosophical explanation of why one stage is "better" than another. A series of studies (Turiel 1966, Rest, Turiel, and Kohlberg 1968, Rest 1968) indicates that children and adolescents comprehend all stages up to their own, but not more than one above their own. The material in Appendix 4 was taken from one of these studies (Rest 1968). Adolescents were asked to restate each of the statements in their own words and to rank the statements in order of how good they were (Rest 1968). Statements at stages two or more above the subject's own were restated in terms of lower-stage thinking. Stages below the subject's own were disapproved or ranked low. Statements more than one stage above the subject's own are typically liked, but usually assimilated to the subject's own stage or the one above. Subjects prefer the stage one above their own to their own stage or to all the lower stages because, in developmental jargon, it represents a better equilibrium, because it is more differentiated and integrated than a lower stage.

What we have said suggests some of the reasons why the developmentally highest stage is not universally recognized as the most adequate mode of moral thinking by either the common man or philosophers. We shall assume that most philosophers, unlike the common man, have little trouble comprehending stage-5 or 6 reasoning. They still may not recognize it as most adequate, however, because they often evaluate such moral reasoning by philosophical criteria of rationality imported from nonmoral domains. The greater structural adequacy of the developmentally more advanced, of the more prescriptive and universal, is not something that is established in terms of either scientific truth criteria or means-ends efficiency. We have said that moral judgments are not true or false in the cognitive-descriptivist sense. A higher conception of the value of life or a higher conception of moral emotion (as internal self-judgment rather than fear) is not directly truer than a lower conception. Neither can higher moral conceptions and judgments be said to be more rational by technical-economic criteria of efficiency of means to ends, that is, as better means to maximize the happiness of the self or of society.

The "natural" processes of development entail progressive organization of moral structure resolving concrete moral problems. In the context of a given dilemma it may be quite apparent that stage 6 is a more adequate, equilibrated moral solution. Stage-6 reasoning may not, however, be based on a philosophically more adequate metaethical position or even on a more elegant or "rational" formal normative ethic. Accordingly, a philosopher may judge stage 6 to be no more adequate than lower stages because it is not more scientifically true, it is not more instrumentally efficient, it need not reflect more metaethical or epistemological sophistication, and it need not reflect a tighter or more parsimonious set of normative-ethical postulates. It is, then, only the philosophical formalist who views morality as an autonomous domain with its own criteria of adequacy or rationality who is likely to evaluate moral arguments by formal moral criteria and hence to clearly recognize stage-6 reasoning as more adequate than the reasoning at lower stages.

What we have said so far provides an explanation for the fact that movement in moral thought is usually irreversibly forward in direction, an explanation which does not require the assumption that moral progression is wired into the nervous system or is directly caused by physical-natural forces. It also helps explain why the step-by-step sequence of stages is invariant. The sequence represents a universal inner logical order of moral concepts, not a universal order found in the educational practices of all cultures or an order wired into the nervous system. Since each new basic differentiation at each stage logically depends upon the differentiation before it, the order of differentiations could not logically be other than it is.

We have tried to show how our first basic assumption that moral judgment has a cognitive-structural core explains why there is a universal directed sequential progression in moral judgment. We shall now consider the implications of our second basic assumption, the assumption that moral stages represent the interaction between the child's structuring tendencies and the structural features of the environment. The basic set of findings explained by the assumption are that variations in the child's cognitive and social environment affect the rate and terminus of moral development, but do not define the stages as such. In contrast to this interactional assumption, it at first seems possible to explain moral growth as resulting from exposure to higher stages of thinking presented to the child by significant figures in the child's environment. Because children reject examples of thinking lower than their own, and because they fail to comprehend examples more than one stage up, they only assimilate or take over presented messages one stage above their own (Turiel 1966, Rest 1968, Rest, Turiel, and Kohlberg 1969). If a child's parent is at the principled level, the child reaches the conventional (and principled) stage of moral judgment more rapidly than he would if his parent were at the conventional level (Holstein 1968, 1969). Passive exposure to the next stage of thinking is, however, probably neither a necessary nor a sufficient condition for upward movement. The amount of change occurring in the Turiel and Rest studies of passive exposure was extremely slight. Even where contact is presumably intense, as in the family, passive exposure does not directly account for a child's stage. If it did, conventional-stage parents would be as successful as principled-stage parents in bringing the child to the conventional level of thought. One reason why exposure is not a sufficient condition for upward movement is because a child at a given stage does not necessarily comprehend messages at the next stage up. Rest (1968, 1969) found that the only children who comprehended messages one stage above their own already showed substantial (20 per cent) spontaneous usage of that stage of thought, and it was these children who accounted for all of the learning or assimilation of models at one stage up. Presumably, then, movement to the next stage involves internal cognitive reorganization rather than the mere addition of more difficult content from the outside. Following cognitive-developmental theory in general, Turiel (1969) postulates that cognitive conflict or imbalance is the central "motor" or condition for such reorganization or upward movement. To test this postulate, Turiel is conducting a series of experiments presenting children with varying combinations of contradictory arguments flowing from the same-stage structure, as illustrated by the examples in Appendix 4. These studies should provide concrete evidence for the general notion that stage change depends upon conflict-induced reorganization.

We have so far contrasted environmental influence by passive exposure to external examples of higher thought with environmental influence by the induction of conflict leading to internal reorganization, the latter clarifying our assumption of interaction. The effects of non-moral structural features of the environment upon the child's moral thought further clarify the interactional concept; these effects are best explained by our postulate that the social-environmental determinants of development are its opportunities for role-taking. Piaget's theory (1932) has stressed the peer group as a source of moral role-taking, while other theories stress participation in the larger secondary institutions or participation in the family itself (Baldwin 1897, Mead 1934). Research results suggest that all these opportunities for role-taking are important and that all operate in a similar direction by stimulating moral development rather than by producing a particular value system. In studies in three different cultures, middle-class children were found to be more advanced in moral judgment than matched lower-class children. This was not because the middle-class children heavily favoured a certain type of thought which corresponded to the prevailing middle-class pattern. Instead, middle-class and working-class children seemed to move through the same sequences, but the middle-class children seemed to move faster and farther. Similar but even more striking differences were found between peer-group participators (popular children) and nonparticipators (unchosen children) in the American sample. Studies underway suggest that these peer-group differences partly arise from, and partly add to, prior differences in opportunities for role-taking in the child's family (family participation, communication, emotional warmth, sharing in decisions, awarding responsibility to the child, pointing out consequences of action to others). In particular, Holstein (1968) found that the amount of parental encouragement of the child's participation in discussion (in a taped "revealed differences" mother-father-child discussion of moral-conflict situations) was a powerful correlate of moral advance in the child.

Why should the existence of environmental opportunities for social participation and role-taking be basic for moral advance? The answer to this question also helps answer the question "Why are there universal features of moral judgment in all societies?" or "Why are the same thirty categories of moral judgment found in all cultures?" The answer is that there are universal structures of the social environment which are basic to moral development just as there are universal structures of physical environment basic to "pure" cognitive development. All of the societies we have studied have the same basic institutions: family, economy, social stratification, law, and government. In spite of cultural diversity in content, these institutions have universal transcultural functional meanings. Although the detailed prescriptions of law vary from nation to nation, the form of "law" and the functional value of its importance and regular maintenance are much the same in all nations with formal law.

When we try to define the universal core structures of morality, the problem is not that societies have too few core institutions in common but that they have too many. In general, when theorists attempt to extract the culturally universal essence of morality, they turn to (1) rules, (2) sympathy or concern for welfare consequences to others, and (3) justice. Developmental theory's conception of role-taking embraces all three, in the sense that all morally relevant rules and institutions are conceived of as interpreted through processes of role-taking directed by concerns about both welfare and justice. All institutions and societies are alike in the sheer fact of being societies, that is, in being systems of defined complementary roles. The primary meaning of the word "social" is the distinctively human structuring of action and thought by role-taking, by the tendency to react to others as like the self and to react to the self's behaviour from the other's point of view. Essentially each of our stages defines (or is defined by) a new cognitive-structural mode of role-taking in conflict situations. To understand the development of role-taking we must consider not only the principle of empathy or "welfare," considering the effects of action upon the others involved, but also the principle of "justice," that is, of reciprocity and equality in human relations.

When we move from role-taking to the resolution of conflicting roles, we arrive at the "principle" of justice. A moral conflict is a conflict between competing claims of men: you versus me, you versus him. The precondition for a moral conflict is man's capacity for role-taking. Most social situations are not moral because there is no conflict in role-taking between the expectations of one person and another. Where such conflicts arise, the principles we use to resolve them are principles of justice. Usually expectations or claims are integrated by customary rules and roles. The principles for making rules and distributing roles (rights and duties) in any institution from the family to the government are principles of justice or of fairness. The most basic principle of justice is equality: treat every man's claim equally, regardless of the man. Equality is the principle of distributive justice, but there is another form of justice – commutative justice or reciprocity. Punishment for something bad, reward for something good, contractual exchange are all forms of reciprocity, which is equality in exchange. Arguments about what is just are either arguments about the relative claims of equality (everyone deserves a decent minimum income) and reciprocity (only those who work hard should get the rewards of hard work) or arguments about equal liberty or opportunity versus equal benefit.

The psychological unity of role-taking and justice at mature stages of moral consciousness is easily recognized. In Tillich's words "contemporary ethical theory has strongly emphasized the person-to-person encounter as the experiential root of morality. In the case of nonpersonal reality man can make it into an object, dissect it, analyze it, or construct something new ... The only limit is man's own finitude ... There is, however, a limit ... in the ego-thou encounter. The limit is the other person ... All the implications of the idea of justice, especially the various forms of equality and liberty, are applications of the imperative to acknowledge every potential person as a person" (Tillich 1963, pp. 36–8).

If the psychological unity of empathy and justice in moral role-taking is apparent in the stage-6 consciousness described by Tillich, it is also apparent at the very start of the moral experience. At every stage children perceive basic values like the value of human life and are able to empathize and take the roles of other persons, other living things. Even at the start the child experiences the value of his parents' life, or of a pet dog's life, as the result of primary empathy with other living things, of the projection of consciousness into others. At the start, too, he has some experience of justice, since reciprocity, too, is part of the primary experience of role-taking in social interaction (Erikson 1950, Mead 1934; Homans 1950; Malinowski 1929; Piaget 1932). With development, however, basic social values and the role-taking behind them are increasingly organized in terms of moral principles of justice (as increasingly differentiated from morally irrelevant reasons for role-taking and choice).

For example, at the age of four my son joined the pacifist and vegetarian movement and refused to eat meat, because, as he said, "it's bad to kill animals." In spite of lengthy Hawk argumentation by his parents about the difference between justified and unjustified killing, he remained a vegetarian for six months. Like most Doves, however, his principles recognized occasions of just or legitimate killing. One night I read to him a book of Eskimo life involving a seal-killing expedition. He got angry during the story and said, "You know, there is one kind of meat I would eat, Eskimo meat. It's bad to kill animals so it's all right to eat them."

He "took the role of the seal" in the sense of empathically experiencing its predicament. This in turn implied a stage-1 sense of justice as equality, as the equal treatment of men and seals and a stage-1 sense of justice as reciprocity in the demand for an eye-for-an-eye, tooth-for-a-tooth retribution on its Eskimo hunter. Such stage-1 concepts of justice become differentiated, integrated, and universalized with development until they eventually become Tillich's stage-6 moral sense.

The concepts of role-taking and justice, then, provide concrete meaning to the assumption that moral principles are neither external rules taken inward nor natural ego-tendencies of a bilogical organism, but rather the interactional emergents of social interaction. As expressed by Piaget: "In contrast to a given rule, which from the first has been imposed upon the child from outside ... the rule of justice is a sort of immanent condition of social relationships or a law governing their equilibrium" (Piaget 1932, p. 196).

Piaget argues that just as logic represents an ideal equilibrium of thought operation, justice represents an ideal equilibrium of social interaction, with reciprocity or reversibility being core conditions for both logical and moral equilibrium. Although the sense of justice would not develop without the experience of social interaction, it is not simply an inward mirror of sociologically prescribed forms of these relations, any more than logic is an internalization of the linguistic forms of the culture. While disagreeing with the details of Piaget's interpretation of the development of justice, we agree with his essential conception of it as an interactional emergent.

THE DEFINITION OF THE MORAL

In the preceding two sections we have attempted to show that moral stages represent an invariant series with each higher stage being more adequate structurally than its predecessors. This adequacy has been discussed from a psychological perspective, characterizing later stages as "higher," "more developed," "more differentiated and integrated," and "more equilibrated." Because a pattern of thought or action is more mature, however, it does not follow that an educator ought to stimulate the pattern of thought. Even if it be granted that the more mature is in some sense more adequate than the less mature, it does not follow that an ideal pattern of thought is to be defined in terms of a natural stage of development such as stage 6. Educators do not define ideal patterns of thought about physics in terms of natural stages of thinking about the physical world, and it is not clear that they should do so in the case of moral thought.

Therefore, to move from the "is" of natural development to an "ought" or ideal of moral education, we must consider the adequacy of our higher stages in philosophical rather then psychological terms. We have already said that the greater adequacy of higher stages is not to be evaluated by criteria of scientific truth or instrumental rationality. What, then, is the basic criterion in terms of which one stage is more adequate than another? Here we must follow those philosophers who have held to the autonomy of the moral, to the irreducibility of moral thinking or moral standards to other criteria. One can only characterize a higher stage as more moral. Moral language and moral action are *sui generis*: they cannot be evaluated except in their own terms. We shall claim, however, that only stage-6 thinking or language is fully moral, that each higher stage is a closer approximation to the characteristic which philosophers such as Hare have taken as defining distinctively moral language. In this sense, we are arguing that the educational aim of stimulating moral development to stages 5 and 6 is the aim of giving the individual the capacity to engage in moral judgment and discourse, rather than the aim of imposing a specific morality upon him.

We have claimed that higher stages of judgment are more moral than lower stages in a formal sense. Regardless of our agreement with a stage-6 judgment of the action springing from it, we are able to say it is moral. For reasons we postpone until later, it is plausible to claim that a broad view of education should include among its aims the stimulation of the child's capacity to be moral in this sense. We need to make clear, however, that our claim that stage 6 is a more moral mode of thought than lower stages is not the claim that we can or should grade individuals as more or less moral. We argue elsewhere that there is no valid or final meaning to judging or grading persons as morally better or worse. Judgments of persons as morally good or bad are judgments of praise and blame are not justified by the existence of universal moral principles as such. At the highest stage, the principle of justice (or the principle of maximizing human welfare) prescribes an obligation to act justly (or to further human welfare), it does not prescribe a duty to blame the unjust or give us rules for meting out blame to the unjust. Although there are some rational grounds for punishment, there are no ultimately rational or moral grounds for blaming other people. From a moral point of view, the moral worth of all persons is ultimately the same, it is equal. Moral theory is not required to set up standards for evaluating the moral worth of persons, and the claim that stage 6 is a more moral way of thinking is not an assignment of higher moral worth to the stage-6 individual.

The reasons for this caviat are obvious enough to the educationist.

While it is a philosophically legitimate goal for the educator to raise general intelligence, as something good, and to rejoice in a child's increase in intellectual performance, it is completely unjustified for the educator to judge a child scoring higher in intelligence as of more personal worth than one scoring lower in intelligence. While only the thoughtless teacher might make this mistake in regard to intelligence tests, it would be easy to misinterpret our tests of moral maturity as justifying such unjust moral grading.

We must now clarify in a detailed way the reasons for which we consider higher stages to be more moral than lower stages. Like most philosophers, we are claiming, but on social scientific grounds, first, that the term "moral" refers to moral judgments or decisions based on moral judgments. We will argue in the last section that the primary psychological referent of the term "moral" is a judgment, not a behaviour or an affect, for example, "guilt." (The difference between fear or anxiety on the one hand and guilt on the other is provided only by a concept of moral judgments associated with the affect, not with the affect itself.) Accordingly, then, the referent of "moral" is also not sociological, for example, a rule. There is nothing in the social institutionalization of a rule that makes it moral as opposed to technological, aesthetic, etc. For one man, a prohibition of parking is a moral norm, for another a mere administrative regulation. What makes it moral is not the legislation of the rule but the individual's attitude towards it, as even the most extreme and greatest of the sociologists of morals, Durkheim, recognized.

Second, like most moral philosophers from Kant to Hare, Baier, Aiken, etc., we define morality in terms of the formal character of a moral judgment or a moral point of view, rather than in terms of its content. Impersonality, ideality, universalizability, and pre-emptiveness are among the formal characteristics of a moral judgment. These are best seen in the reasons given for a moral judgment, a moral reason being one which has such properties as these.

Third, we claim that the formal definition of morality works only when we recognize that there are developmental levels of moral discourse or judgment which increasingly approximate to the philosophers' forms. A developmental strategy of definition is one which isolates a function, such as intelligence, but defines this function by a progressive developmental clarification of the function. Intelligence or cognition as defined by Piaget is both something present from the start of life (in the infant's adaptive sensorimotor behaviour) and something whose ultimate structure or form is given only in the final stages (e.g., the formal-operational-natural thought of the adolescent as experimenter and theorist). Similarly, in our view there is a moral judgmental function present from the age of four or five onwards in judgments of "good" and "bad" and "has to" (our stage 1), but this function is only fully defined by its final stages (principled morality).

As stated by Aiken (1952), in "Levels of Moral Discourse," moral language goes on at two levels, the conventional and the principled. (Aiken, as a nonpsychologist, ignores our preconventional level of moral discourse.) At the conventional level, moral language refers to an actual expectation or rule of the group or of particular members of the group. At this level "the moral judge functions primarily as a middleman or agent; he voices the claims of society but is not the primary source of this moral authority." As Aiken points out, however, fully moral discourse does not rest on authority but consists of reasoning based on a moral attitude or point of view which claims to be autonomously moral, that is, independent of appeals to either authority or self-interest.

Our claim that only principled-stage thinking is fully moral was concretely made earlier when we said that each stage involved a differentiation, not made at the previous stage, of moral and nonmoral value; Appendix 3 illustrates this for the case of the moral value of human life.

Moral judgments are judgments about the right and the good of action. Not all judgments of "good" or "right" are moral judgments, however; many are judgments of aesthetic, technological, or prudential goodness or rightness. Unlike judgments of prudence or aesthetics, moral judgments tend to be universal, inclusive, consistent, and grounded on objective, impersonal, or ideal grounds. Statements such as "She's really great! She's beautiful and a good dancer," or "The right way to make a Martini is five-to-one," involve the good and right, but they are not moral judgments since they lack the characteristics of the latter. If we say, "Martinis should be made five-to-one," we are making an aesthetic judgment: we are not prepared to say that we want everyone to make them that way, that they are good in terms of some impersonal ideal standard shared by others, or that we and others should make five-to-one Martinis whether we wish to or not.

In similar fashion, when a ten-year-old at stage 1 answers a "moral should" question – "Should Joe tell on his younger brother?" – in terms of the probabilities of getting beaten up by his father and by his brother, he does not answer with a moral judgment that is universal (applies to all situations of this kind) or that has any impersonal or ideal grounds. In contrast, stage-6 statements not only specifically use moral words like "morally right" and "duty" but also use them in a moral way: "regardless of who it was," implies universality; "Morally

I would do it in spite of fear of punishment" implies impersonality and ideality of obligation, etc. Thus, the responses of lower-level subjects concerning matters of moral judgment fail to be moral responses in somewhat the same sense that the value judgments of higher-level subjects concerning aesthetic or morally neutral matters fail to be moral. In this sense, we can define a moral judgment as "moral" without considering its content (the action judged) and without considering whether it agrees with our own judgments or standards. It is evident that our stages represent an increasing disentangling or differentiation of moral values and judgments from other types of values and judgments. With regard to one particular aspect, the value of life, the moral value of the person in the stage-6 argument has become progressively disentangled from status and property values (stage 1), from his instrumental uses to others (stage 2), from the actual affection of others for him (stage 3), etc.

More generally, the individual whose judgments are at stage 6 asks "Is it morally right" and means by morally right something different from punishment (stage 1), or prudence (stage 2), or conformity to authority (stages 3 and 4), etc.

MORAL PRINCIPLES

Following formalist philosophers from Kant to Hare I have claimed that only the higher stages of moral thought have the formal features of distinctively moral judgment. We need to clarify and deepen our conception of these features of mature moral thought by clarifying our characterization of the highest stages as "principled." Many, although not all, philosophic treatments of morality view the central characteristic of adequate moral judgment as its derivation from "moral principles." It is evident enough that most of our value judgments are not directly based on principles. When we judge a martini or a painting or a scientific article as good, we do not attempt to derive our judgments from principle. If a bad painting is made according to principle, so much the worse for the principle. Nevertheless, the whole notion that there is a distinctively moral form of judgment demands that moral judgments be principled. We cited earlier Hare's characterization of the distinctive formal features of morality as "prescriptivity," and "universality" (the two in turn implying "autonomy" of moral choice or obligation). Hare's characterization echoes Kant who defined prescriptivity as the sense of the categorical (as opposed to the hypothetical) imperative. To be categorical, an imperative must be universal: "so act as to make the maxim of thy conduct the universal will". Empirically, we have found these two features linked, so that a stage-6 judgment of a right which is prescriptive or independent of the inclinations of the self and the beliefs of others is also a judgment of a right which is right for all mankind. When an effort is made to formulate a judgment which is prescriptive and universal, the judgment almost of necessity will be made in terms of a moral principle. To understand stage-6 morality, therefore we need to understand the nature and functioning of moral principles.

A moral principle is a universal mode of choosing, a rule of choosing which we want all people to adopt in all situations. By "principle" we mean something more abstract that the ordinary rule. Rules like the Ten Commandments are proscriptions or prescriptions of action. When conventional morality chooses to be morally pretentious, it labels such rules "principles." In regard to the drug-stealing story conventional college students say; "the principle of loyalty to your family comes ahead of obeying the law here," or "the principle of honesty comes before helping your wife."

On the face of it, these students do not wish to universalize the rules. One cannot universalize the rule "be loyal to your family," to all people, since not everybody has a family. For the same reason, one cannot generalize it to all situations and also because it is doubtful that if one's uncle were Hitler one could claim loyalty to be a relevant or prima facie principle. One does not have to believe in situation ethics to realize that no proscription or prescription of a class of acts is universalizable. We know it is all right to be dishonest and steal to save a life because a man's right to life comes before another man's right to property. We know it is sometimes right to kill because it is sometimes just. The Germans who tried to kill Hitler were doing right because respect for the equal values of lives demands that we kill someone who is murdering others, in order to save lives. There are always exceptions to rules about classes of acts.

By "moral principle" all thoughtful men have meant a general guide to choice rather than a rule of action. Even our college student who talks of "the principle of loyalty to your family" means something like "a consideration in choosing" rather then a definite rule prescribing a class of acts. The strongest notion of principle is that defined by pure utilitarian doctrine prescribing the single principle of the "utilitarian maxim" (act always so as to maximize the greatest happiness of the greatest number) and by the Kantian doctrine prescribing the single principle of the categorical imperative. This "strong" conception of principle implies a single logically or intuitively self-evident or rational maxim for choice; from it one can deduce any concrete morally right action in a situation, given the facts of the situation as the minor premise of the deduction. Such a strong conception of principle is one which not only is universalizable to all men and all situations but also is absolutely definitive of right action in any situation. We have so far never encountered a live human being who made moral judgments in terms of principle in this sense. On the other hand, we do find people judging in terms of principles, if principles are conceived of in the weaker sense as illustrated in the writings of members of the principled-institutionist group such as Sidgwick and Ross.

In this weaker sense, a person may consistently hold more than a single principle of moral judgment and these principles may not be definitive of a choice in all situations (i.e., alternative choices may be derived from them). Such principles, however, are still to be differentiated from a collection of rules or "prima facie obligations." In our empirical work we have started by considering the term "principle" as referring to considerations in moral choice or reasons justifying moral action. They are answers to the question "Why is it right to do such and such?" given some answer to the question "What is it right to do?" We have found empirically that almost all these reasons easily fall into the categories outlined by principled-intuitionist philosophers, for example, Sidgewick's prudence (welfare-consequences to the self), benevolence (welfare-consequences to others), and justice (distributive equity and commutative reciprocity). The only additional category of ultimate reasons we have added is respect for authority.

Accordingly, in our detailed coding of categories of moral judgment we have the following categories of "principles": prudence (and self-realization); welfare of others; respect for authority, society, or persons; justice.

As we suggested in preceding sections, all of these "principles" or reasons are present in one form or another from stage 1 onwards, except that prudence and authority have dropped out as reasons by stage 6. From stage 1, these reasons have two characteristics. First, they are ultimate terms, they refer to states of affairs which seem right or good in themselves and are in that sense "principles." Second, they refer to states of affairs that are involved in all moral situations and are potentially relevant to all people. There is no moral situation that does not involve considerations of people's happiness or welfare and considerations of equal treatment between people.

While benevolence and justice are used as moral reasons from stage 1 onwards, they do not become genuine moral principles until stages 5 and 6. At the conventional stages, choices are made by reference to conventional rules, stereotypes, and sentiments. The reasons for conforming to these rules include considerations of benevolence and justice as well as of prudence and social authority. Where there are ambiguities, conflicts, or gaps in the rules, decisions are based on considerations of benevolence and justice. Not until stages 5 and 6, however, is there an effort to derive systematically and consistently prima facie rules or obligations from these principles or to view obligation as fundamentally directed by them, rather than by concrete rules. In this sense, the fundamental aspect of principled morality is the adoption of a law-making perspective. That welfare and justice are guiding principles of legislation as well as of individual moral action points to the fact that a principle is always a maxim or rule for making rules or laws as well as a maxim of individual situational conduct. This, of course, follows from the fact that if a principle is universalizable and reversible, there could not be different sets of rules for law-makers and law-obeyers. (This is one reason why "always obey the law" does not have the status of a moral principle.) It also points out that principles are metarules – rules for the creation and evaluation of rules – rather than first-order rules.

Now it is clear that our conception of moral principle implies that one cannot ultimately separate form and content in moral analysis.

Hare has recently argued with vigour the necessity of defining truly moral judgment and "moral principles" solely in formal terms. To do so would, of course, involve a much less controversial claim for a conception of mature morality. Kant, for different reasons, insisted on a purely formal conception of principle, but to attain such a conception he made the principled form "universality" into a content, for example, into the commandment that one universalize one's actions. When one attempts a purely formal definition of principle, however, one only ends up with the old rules of conventional morality expressed in more universal and prescriptive form. Kant's claim that it was wrong to tell a lie to save a victim from a murder is a case in point. In the formalist conception, principles are still conceived of as rules of action, that is, rules prescribing classes of acts in classes of situations.

As such, their universality is always purchased at the price of ignoring unique elements of human welfare and human justice in the concrete situation. In our conception, however, principles are guides to perceiving and integrating all the morally relevant elements in concrete situations. Neither philosophers nor all the people we have interviewed have ever come up with morally relevant elements in concrete situations which are not the elements of human interests (welfare) or human rights (justice).

Now it is clear that our conception of principle implies a "situation ethic" in the sense that it reduces all moral obligation to the interests and claims of concrete individual persons in concrete situations. We take it as the characteristic logical fallacy of conventional morality that it fails to reduce the welfare and "claims" of the group as a collective abstraction to the welfare and claims of its members as individuals. Durkheim is perhaps the greatest explicit defender of the concept of obligation as directed to the group or institution rather then to the welfare and claims of its members. From our point of view there is a logical fallacy parallel to elevating the group above its members: the fallacy of treating a principle as elevated above the individuals in the situation to which it applies. Put in different terms, most of us feel a cold chill at the notion that mature moral obligation is fundamentally directed to an abstract maxim or principle as Kant held. Moral obligations are towards concrete other people in concrete situations. The notion of a Kantian feeling obligated to the principle of the categorical imperative and so refusing to tell a lie to save a human life (i.e., refusing to modify the means for a concrete human end) is as chilling as a utilitarian Bolshevik letting 10,000,000 Kulaks starve for the greater happiness of the unborn greater number (i.e., refusing to modify the ends for the concrete human means). True principles guide us to the obligating elements in the situation, to the concrete human claims there. The case is always higher than the principle, a single human life is worth more than all the principles in philosophy to the mature man. Principles simply tell us how to resolve these concrete claims, when claims compete in a situation, when it is one man's life against another's.

Perhaps the case can be made even clearer by considering the so-called "higher moral values." Just as it is possible to elevate the Ten Commandments of authoritarian (stage-4) morality into principles, so is it possible to elevate the existence of the state, or the collective goals of the state or society into "higher moral values," or "absolutes." Said Hitler, "Our goal is that the German people should again acquire honour, again bow in adoration before its history. We recognize only two Gods; a God in Heaven and a God on earth, and that is our Fatherland." If Hilter had recognized only one God, the God in Heaven, and held that the only absolute value was the Divine Will or the coming of the Kingdom of Heaven, the structure of his thought would have been the same. So too, the structure would have been the same if he had held up "Humanity" as an absolute value, as a collective concept above the individuals involved in concrete situations, as did the Bolsheviks who let the Kulaks starve. Here is an eighteen-year-old boy who uses the "higher principle of humanity" in this disembodied and unprincipled way responding to the story about stealing the drug:

"I'd steal the drug. Whether my wife died or not, I'd feel I'd acted humanely, not just out of love, not just a personal thing between my wife and myself; I feel I'd done what I could for the principle of being human."

(Even if you weren't affectionate or close to your wife?)

"Yes. If I had to kill the druggest to get the drug, I probably would, also. Because I'd be putting value on life-right, I'd kill the druggist if I had to, if there's no other way to get the drug, and suffer the consequences. It would be a personal commitment to humanity."

No wonder many mature men and astute moral philosophers reject the notion of a morality of "higher moral principles above the law" for a stage-5 relativistic insistence on democratic law and social contract and consensus.

All the misuses of the concept of moral principle thus involve a failure either to universalize a "principle" or to reduce it to a guide to the perception of the claims of persons in a moral situation. As we shall claim in the next section, when principles are reduced to guides for considering the claims of persons in concrete situations they become expressions of the single principle of justice. The misuses of principle we have quoted immediately strike us as misuses because they are unjust, although they may be maximizations of social utility. We must now consider our rationale for reducing stage-6 moral principles to principles of justice.

THE PRIMACY OF JUSTICE

We have so far elaborated a formal conception of morality linked to principles of welfare and justice. We have not, however, differentiated clearly between stage 5 and stage 6 and the relative place of benevolence and justice in each. The core elements of stage 5 are that it is a rational legislative perspective which reduces obligations to rule-utilitarian considerations on the one hand and social contract on the other. It recognizes the arbitrary element in concrete rules and laws and derives from the obligation to rules the basic rational procedural principles for forming a society or for legislation. From our point of view, the core problem which stage 5 cannot resolve is the problem of the conditions under which it is morally right or obligatory to violate the law. The principles of welfare and social contract are inadequate to resolve this problem. Stage 6 resolves the problem by recognizing the primacy of justice over all other moral considerations, by recognizing that civil disobedience is justified if and only if it is preventing a legally condoned injustice.

Our major and most controversal claim is that the only "true" (stage 6) moral principle is justice. We shall claim that human welfare is always the core of morality but that, at the principled level, welfare considerations subsumed under the heading "justice" take priority over other "principles" for considering welfare whenever there is conflict between the two, and that there is no strong "principle" for deciding between the various welfare alternatives other then justice. The reason for this emphasis on justice becomes clear when we recognize that moral principles derive from, or are differentiated from, the lower stages of moral thought. We have pointed out that we take the word "justice" to mean a moral resolution of competing claims, that is, a reference to a method of distributing or defining claims. The basic rule of justice is distributive equality: treat every man equally. We recognize, however, that people also have special claims on the individual moral actor or upon the state. These claims are based on commutative justice or reciprocity, and include keeping contracts or trusts, undoing harm done, and showing gratitude as some return for service and effort. While there is no single accepted principle of justice which orders all these aspects, we generally assume a sphere of human rights in which equality takes priority over the special claims of commutative justice.

Other than justice, the only general principle seriously advanced by philosophers has been the principle variously termed utility or benevolence. It is important first to recognize that benevolence in the sense of "love, empathy, sympathy, human concern, humanism," and so on can never be a principle of choice. It is primarily another stage-3 virtue label, not a guide to action. While benevolence can be universalized in the sense of "everyone should care for the welfare of all other humans," when there is a conflict between welfares, benevolence can provide no criterion except that of quantitative maximization.

The content of moral concerns and claims is always welfare, but maximization is not a true moral principle. Concern for welfare consequences characterizes each of our six stages; my son was concerned about "the greatest good of the greatest number" but included seals and men equally in his calculations. A clearer example is Tommy, whose complete response to the story about stealing the drug follows. I cite it because I defy a utilitarian to distinguish a fundamental formal difference of principle between this stage-1 response and that of stage 6.

"His wife was sick and if she didn't get the drug quickly, she might die. Maybe his wife is an important person and runs a store and the man buys stuff from her and can't get it any other place. The police would probably blame the owner that he didn't save the wife. That would be like killing with a gun or knife."

(Would it be all right to put the druggist in the electric chair for murder?)

"If she could be cured by the drug and they didn't give it to her, I think so, because she could be an important lady like Betsy Ross, she made the flag. And if it was President Eisenhower, he's important, and they'd probably put the man in the electric chair because that isn't fair."

(Should the punishment be more if she's an important person?)

"If someone important is in a plane and is allergic to heights and the stewardess won't give him medicine because she's only got enough for one and she's got a sick one, a friend, in back they'd probably put the stewardess in a lady's jail because she didn't help the important one."

(Is it better to save the life of one important person or a lot of unimportant people?)

"All the people that aren't important because one man just has one house, maybe a lot of furniture, but a whole bunch of people have an awful lot of furniture and some of these poor people might have a lot of money and it doesn't look it."

Tommy thinks always in terms of the actual utility consequences of action, even to the point of ignoring intention completely. How bad it is to let someone die for lack of a drug depends on the importance of the person and has nothing to do with the inhuman attitude of the person withholding the drug. The value of the act is determined by maximizing utility. It is true that important people count for more than unimportant people, but it is all appraised in a maximizing or utilitarian fashion. Only one thing is amiss – the worth of a person's life is essentially determined by how much furniture he owns. The moral maxim seems to be the greatest furniture of the greatest number. Appendix 3 indicates the reasons why Tommy's failure to differentiate the value of a person's life from the value of the furniture he owns is scored stage 1.

Our point is that concern for the welfare of other beings, "empathy," or "role-taking," is the precondition for experiencing a moral conflict rather than a mechanism for its resolution. The moral question is "Whose role do I take?" or "Whose claim do I favour?" The working core of the utilitarian principle is the principle of justice, "consider each person's welfare equally," not the maximization principle. Finally, as everyone knows, and as our studies document, the utilitarian principle of justice, "consider everyone's happiness equally," is not a working principle of justice. Our conception of justice dictates that we consider every man's moral claims equally, rather than considering every man's happiness equally. Our stage-6 subjects will say "Steal the drug for anyone, whether it's his wife or not, every man has a right to live." But they do not advocate treating the happiness of wife and of stranger equally. Furthermore, they do not rationalize the preference for their wife's happiness on "rule-utilitarian" grounds. Instead, they speak of a marriage tie or "contract" or relationship of reciprocal trust and love, that is, a claim of commutative reciprocity, not one of utility.

At this point, I shall summarize my argument for justice as the basic moral principle. The argument involves the following steps:

1 Psychologically, both welfare concerns (role-taking, empathy, or sympathy) and justice concerns are present at the birth of morality and at every succeeding stage.

2 Both welfare concerns and justice concerns take on more differentiated, integrated, and universalized forms at each step of development.

3 However, at the highest stage of development only justice takes on the character of a principle, that is, becomes something that is obligatory, categorical, and takes precedence over law and other considerations, including welfare.

4 "Principles" other than justice may be tried out by those seeking to transcend either conventional or contractual-consensual (stage-5) morality but they do not work because either A they do not resolve moral conflicts, or B they resolve them in ways that seem intuitively wrong.

5 The intuitive feeling of many philosophers that justice is the only satisfactory principle corresponds to the fact that it is the only one that "does justice to" the viable core of lower stages of morality.

6 This becomes most evident in situations of civil disobedience for which justice, but not other moral principles, provides a rationale which respects and can cope with the stage-5 contractual legalistic argument that civil disobedience is always wrong.

7 Philosophers have doubted the claim of justice to be "the" moral principle because they have looked for a principle broader in scope than the sphere of moral or principled individual choice in the formal sense (that is, they have looked for a principle for a teleological "general theory of value and decision"). For example, the maximization of welfare principle is a general principle for decision outside the area of specifically moral choice. Metaethically, then, welfare is a more ultimate principle but not in moral choice. For example, maximizing social welfare would probably be the ultimate basis for deciding that it was desirable to teach morality explicitly in the school (given that it was just, or not a violation of rights, to do so). This does not contradict the facts that the highest principle of morality to be taught is justice, or that it would be morally wrong to teach justice in the schools in an unjust way.

8 Denial of the claims of justice as the central principle of morality, then, coincides with a definition of morality which has various gaps and fallacies in terms of metaethical criteria.

FROM IS TO OUGHT: THE NATURALISTIC FALLACY

Let us consider the sense in which our description of what morality is tells us what it ought to be. To begin with, there are two forms of the "naturalistic fallacy" we are not committing. We are not equating moral judgments with cognitive-predictive judgments or with pleasure-pain statements, as do the simple cognitive-naturalistic models. Our analysis of moral judgments does not assume that moral judgments are really something else. Further, we are not assuming that morality or moral maturity is part of man's biological nature, that the biologically older is the morally better. We are however, committing a third form of the "naturalistic fallacy" by asserting that any conception of what moral judgment ought to be must rest on an adequate conception of what it is. If all those who have PH.DS in philosophy showed a stage-6 concern for universal and autonomous moral principles, while all other people were Durkhemian asserters of the authority of the group or Benthamite hedonists, it would be impossible, I believe, to construct a plausible account of why men should be stage 6 or adopt a stage-6 morality. But as it turns out, neither a Benthamite nor a Durkheimian construction of what morality ought to be, based as they are on the assumptions that morality really is stage 2 (Bentham) or stage 4 (Durkheim), is viable, because both ignore the reality of what morality demonstrably is at stages 5 and 6. Every constructive effort at rational morality, at saying what morality ought to be, must start with a characterization of what it is, and in that sense commits "the naturalistic fallacy." If morality is stage 5 or 6, then what morality ought to be is either a systematized or purified version of stage 6 or else ought to be stage 7. In human history there was a time when philosophers perhaps had to create stage 6 and not just systematize it. One may argue that philosophers should be defining a stage-7 morality, but I doubt if one could find any volunteers for the task. Let me be concrete about what I mean. Rawls (1963) has taken a formal set of assumptions which I term stage 5, the assumptions that society is ordered by a constitution defined by a social contract of equals. He then shows how such a society must be based upon principles of justice or of equal rights, since these are the only principles to which rational individuals in the imaginary original position could consent. These principles in turn, then, are in a sense prior to the law and social institutions and in certain conditions justify civil disobedience. In other words, Rawls has used a formal argument to derive stage-6 morality from stage 5, and to systematize stage-6 morality insofar as stage-6 morality is defined by sociopolitical choices.

My point is that Rawls is doing by formal ethical argument what "natural experience" does in development. The doctrine of a social contract and freely chosen law which must have a universal form usually rests on reference to an existing external social consensus and political process. It contains within it, however, a latent conception of autonomous principles of justice which guide both individual morality and the direction of political change. Where law or the existing social consensus is unjust, the stage-5 individual is caught in conflicts resolvable only at the stage-6 level. Let me quote an example from our longitudinal study of someone struggling between a stage-5 and a stage-6 point of view:

"We are dealing with essentially the same situation as the beginning. We have a law that says something must be done and so in disobeying this law they are doing wrong. However, it would seem that the basic law itself is morally wrong and so from a moral point of view, the right thing to do is to disobey the law."

(Why is the law morally wrong?)

"Because it is treating human beings as animals and I said before that I do believe there is a difference.

"Here we have a situation of an individual reaching in his mind the decision that something determined by the state is wrong. Now I think this is perfectly valid that an individual can have his own feelings and opinions. However, if he makes the decision that this law is wrong and decides to disobey it, he must do so with the full realization that it is the state's prerogative to do whatever it can to uphold this law.

"I think this means that the individual must realize he is acting outside of society, so to speak, and must be prepared to take whatever consequences society is going to mete out for this."

(Would it be right to punish the people who hid the runaway slaves?)

"This is the same thing again. It is within the prerogatives of the state to uphold its laws and to punish people, again staying within the framework of the system we have now. Certainly it is right in that sense and I think you have to stop at this point. You could say it is morally wrong because in breaking the laws the people were acting in what they thought was morally right and what I would say is morally right, but nevertheless, the action was outside the bounds of society."

(What about if its laws are morally wrong? You said slavery is wrong? Or are you saying that this is your opinion that it is morally wrong?)

"Yes. That's right. All I can say is that it is my opinion. I can't speak for anyone else."

(Do you think there are things that are morally right and wrong other than what people think are morally right and wrong? That there are some actual rights and wrongs?)

"If they are I think they would be awfully hard to define.'

(So, when you say slavery is morally wrong, you are saying it is your opinion.)

"Yes."

(At the time before the Civil War when they had slavery was it right or wrong to have slavery? I guess I have asked this before.)

"I think it was wrong, but I think you would have to take it back to the framework of the people of that time. Dealing with a situation of ignorance and many people sincerely felt they were not dealing with human beings, maybe in that framework it was morally right from their point of view."

Our prediction is that next time we interview this subject he will assert stage-6 moral right which is right because it is ideally universalizable whether or not it is in fact universal. In any case, this man, unlike subjects at a lower stage, could profit from a conventional course in philosophic ethics.

I use Rawls' work as one "legitimate" ethical effort to show that principles of justice ought to be the ultimate basis of morality. It is legitimate in the sense that it works within the terms of moral discourse (stage 5) to clarify these terms and to show that within them implicitly there is a more fundamental set of terms (stage 6). In contrast, Durkheim attempts to use a nonmoral set of terms, those of social science, to show that stage 4 not only is but ought to be morality. The Durkheimian form of the naturalistic fallacy can be shown to be a genuine fallacy in the same sense as Benthamite reductionism was.

We maintain, then, that problems arise for stage 6 only when we ask questions of it which it cannot answer, for instance, if we try to justify the moral right in terms of the good, if we ask the question, "What good is morality?" or "What good is justice?" My claim that principles of justice are the highest developmentally, the most adequate or equilibrated, and most autonomously moral forms of moral judgment and decision-making, can be and is made without answering the question "What good is justice?" or saying that justice is better (in some all-inclusive sense) than any other form of morality. If we ask "What good is justice?" we shall immediately tend to answer it in "goal-seeking" or utilitarian terms, that is, we shall examine the consequences of just action for the individual actor's welfare or for the welfare of society or both. An evaluation in terms of welfare will be a naturalistic evaluation, that is, it will be a qualitative evaluation of the satisfaction of actual interests in some psychologically definable sense. The alternative is, of course, a definition of the goal-seeking in terms of self-realization or perfection of the individual or the group. The point I am making is that "What good is morality" or "What good is justice" are questions that cannot be answered by a normative ethical theory or by using moral concepts. The questions, "What good is morality?" and "Why be moral?" are legitimate questions, as are questions like "What good is art?" and "Why pursue the beautiful?" Statements of what aesthetic structure or beauty are or ought to be – aesthetic "theories" – do not directly answer this question. Similarily, a theory of formal logic is a theory of what logical inference is and ought to be but it is not a theory which answers the question "What good is logic?" or "Why be logical?" Answers to such metaethical questions are not given by a stage-6 normative ethical theory.

Now, from the educational point of view, the questions "What good is morality?" or "What good is moral development?" are extremely germane and meaningful questions, since they will determine the place we give to moral development in the definition of the aims of the school. These questions, however, are questions to be answered by "a general theory of value," not by moral theory in our sense. My own "theory of values" rests on Dewey's analysis, including an emphasis on the essential unity of scientific judgment and rational value judgment. In other words, the answer to "what good is the child's morality?" is largely a scientific statement of the functions and consequences of the child's moral development for the welfare and development of the child's personality and of his society.

In summary, my view of the various ways in which knowledge of facts and statements of value are related in the study of moral development includes the following points.

1 The scientific facts are that there is a universal moral form successively emerging in development and centring on principles of justice.

2 This Kantian moral form is one which assumes the fact-value distinction, that is, the moral man assumes his moral judgment is based on conformity to an ideal norm, not on conformity to fact.

3 Science, then, can test whether a philosopher's conception of morality phenomenologically fits the psychological facts. Science cannot go on to justify that conception of morality as being what morality ought to be, as Durkheim attempted to do. Moral autonomy is king and values are different from facts for moral discourse. Science cannot prove or justify a morality, because the rules of scientific discourse are not the rules of moral discourse.

4 Logic or normative ethical analysis can, however, point out that a

certain type of moral philosophy (e.g., stage 4) does not handle or resolve certain problems which it acknowledges to be problems that it ought to handle, whereas another type of morality (e.g., stage 5) can do so. Here factual investigation of men's beliefs must support internal logical analysis (differentiation and integration) of why the developmentally higher philosophy can handle problems not handled by the lower ones. In this way science can contribute to moral discourse.

5 Moral discourse between levels, then, is much like Plato's dialectical knowledge of the good. A higher-level conception of the good cannot be proved superior to a lower-level conception; it can only be "called out" by teaching or by natural moral conflict-differentiation-integration (Turiel 1966). If the individual can be brought to comprehend a higher level, he prefers it because he can then see his old lower level from the more inclusive framework of the higher level.

6 The scientific theory of why people factually *do* move upward from stage to stage, and why they factually *do* prefer a higher stage to a lower is broadly the same as a moral theory of why people *should* prefer a higher stage to a lower. In other words a psychological theory of why people move upwards in moral ideology is not like a psychological theory of why they move from the anal to the genital stage. It is committing the naturalistic fallacy to say that a Freudian theory of an instinctual progression is an ethical justification of why genitality is better than anality. It is here that the theory of *interactional* hierarchical stages of cognition and morality and the theory of *maturational* embryological stages are critically different in their logic, as I have discussed in detail elsewhere (Kohlberg and Turiel 1971).

7 From the moral point of view, form is absolute, the fact-value distinction is absolute, and science and ethics are different. The proper scientific study of morality must recognize this fact. The scientific study of morality, however, must include in its scope the functions of morality for the development of the individual and the group. Here the fact-value distinction breaks down in a new way, and we get a Deweyan statement of morality, not as an autonomous absolute, as in the Kantian law or the Platonic good, but as a non-absolute part of the social life of the child, whose welfare is more important than his moral status.

A CONCEPTION OF MORAL EDUCATION

I objected earlier to the current thoughtless system of moralizing by individual teachers and principals when children deviate from minor administrative regulations or engage in behaviour which is personally annoying to the teacher. I also objected to the deliberate effort to inculcate majority values. The rationale for both practices derives from the assumption of ethical relativity. Following Dewey and Piaget I shall argue that the goal of moral education is the stimulation of the "natural" development of the individual child's own moral judgment and capacities, thus allowing him to use his own moral judgment to control his behaviour. The attractiveness of defining the goal of moral education as the stimulation of development rather than as the teaching of fixed rules stems from the fact that it involves aiding the child to take the next step in a direction towards which he is already tending, rather than imposing an alien pattern upon him.

In preceding sections we have argued that the attainment of stages 5 and 6 – the stage of principled judgments – is a philosophically justifiable goal of moral education. Perhaps the strongest reasons for adopting this view of moral education in the context of the public school are "negative," that is, it does not entail the violation of the child's moral freedom, which is involved in any other formulation of moral education goals. Our first statement of the respect for the child's autonomy implied in the developmental view is political and constitutional. We have argued (following Ball 1967) that the Supreme Court's post-Schempp position makes systematic conventional moral education in the public school unconstitutional (see Kohlberg 1967, for a more detailed discussion of these issues). Ball argues that it is possible to interpret the court's decision as ruling out any form of moral or ethical, as well as religious, instruction in the school. The recent court decisions define religion as embracing any articulated credo or value system, including the "Ethical Culture" or "Secular Humanism" credos which essentially consist of the moral principles of western culture. Ball concludes that the Supreme Court is in effect prohibiting the public school from engaging in moral education since such education is equivalent to the state propagation of the religion of Ethical Culture or Secular Humanism.

Let us be concrete about the implications of what has been said. We quoted earlier the teacher who said "Don't be rude" to the child who spit in the other child's face and who had done a master's paper on the problem of social-class difference in values and the schools. She said "I know there are class differences in values. I think politeness is important. I don't care whether it is a middle class value or not." This, of course, was reflected in her labelling the child who spit in the other's face as "rude." We would agree that if she really systematically attempted to instil "politeness" into her pupils, she would be guilty of imposing "middle-class values," or rather her own arbitrary values, on the child. Politeness, hardly a moral virtue, may reflect a universal concern over propriety of behaviour, but middle-class definitions of politeness or propriety are different from ghetto definitions of politeness. Our moral objection to spitting in another child's face is not that it is "impolite" but that it is a violation of the other's dignity, of respect for the other as a human being. An advocate of "Black Power" and "Black Values" may legitimately object to a teacher's indoctrinating children with middle-class lily-white conceptions of politeness, but he cannot object to teaching respect for the fundamental rights of other human beings. His only basis for being heard in his claims for "Black Values" is the basis of regard for the equal rights and dignity of blacks as human beings.

We have said that the content of moral education must be defined in terms of justice, rather than in terms of majority consensus, if the civil rights of parents and children are not to be infringed upon by such education. These claims have been made in terms of the political philosophy underlying the school as a public institution. We have argued, however, that the "official" morality of rights in our society also represents a culturally universal principled stage of moral judgment, so that the teaching of justice is also the stimulation of moral development.

The second claim for the legitimacy of the developmental approach to moral education is that the stimulation of moral development defines an educational process respecting the autonomy of the child, whereas any other definition reflects indoctrination. The constitutional issue arises from the point of view of the child's parent, who can object to the teaching of values other than the parent's own. Respect for the parent's rights is not respect for the child's autonomy, a more legitimate concern.

We have claimed that the experiences by which children naturally move from stage to stage are nonindoctrinative, that is, they are not experiences of being taught and internalizing specific content. These experiences are listed as those involving moral conflict (in the cognitive-conflict sense) and exposure to other, higher modes of thinking than one's own. Insofar as the teacher deliberately uses such experiences as her method of moral education, she is not being "indoctrinative." Expressed differently, there is little difference, from our point of view, between effective teaching "about morality" and the teaching "of morality" in the sense of the stimulation of its development.

Again, let us be concrete about this issue. A senior philosophy class in a Newton high school was used as a vehicle for the stimulation of development of moral judgment by its teacher who was a graduate student of mine. This goal was explicitly announced and the writer's scheme of moral development was explained towards the end of the class. In order to clarify issues of indoctrination involved, a gimmick was used. The students were told that they would be post-tested on the moral judgment interview (as they had already been pretested) and that their moral level on the post-test would be used to give them a grade for the course. Only a few students objected to the procedure on indoctrination grounds. (Many did on the grounds that it was unfair because some were high levels before the course and some were not, etc.) Those who objected to this use of the test on indoctrination grounds were, needless to say, students at the principled level. The students were then encouraged to distinguish between teaching about morality and teaching of morality, in the sense of agreeing that it was legitimate to test their comprehension of stage-5 and stage-6 reasoning, but not to test their assimilation of, or acceptance of this line of reasoning. The findings of the Rest, Turiel, and Kohlberg study – that adolescents do prefer, assimilate, and "believe in" the highest level reasonings which they can comprehend – were then discussed. Our efforts to get the students to comprehend stages 5 and 6 were then tantamount to getting them to accept these stages of reasoning.

Let us now be more concrete about means of moral education in the school. It is not always necessary that the matters discussed be ones of the immediate and real-life issues of the classroom. I have found that my hypothetical and remote but obviously morally real and challenging conflict situations are of intense interest to almost all adolescents and lead to lengthy debate among them. They are involving, because the adult right answer is not obviously at hand to discourage the child's own moral thought, as so often is the case. The child will listen to what the teacher says about moral matters only if the child first feels a genuine sense of uncertainty about the right answer to the situation in question. The pat little stories in school readers in which virtue always triumphs or in which everyone is really nice are unlikely to have any value in the stimulation of moral development. Only the presentation of genuine and difficult moral conflicts can have this effect.

We have mentioned that in order to stimulate development, moral communication by the teacher should, in addition to involving issues of genuine moral conflict to the child, represent cognitive elements new to him. Effective communication also involves the important problem of the match between the teacher's level and the child's. Conventional moral education never has had much influence on children's moral judgment because it has disregarded this problem of developmental match (see Hunt's paper pp. 231–51). Although children are able to understand moralizing beneath their level, they do not seem to accept it nearly so readily as comprehensible moralizing somewhat above their level. It is obvious that the teacher's implementation of this principle must start with his careful listening to the moral judgments and ideas actually expressed by individual children.

The principles just mentioned were used by Blatt and Kohlberg (1971) to develop a four-month program of once-weekly moral discussions for a class of twelve children aged 11 to 12. Children discussed and argued hypothetical dilemmas. The teacher supported and clarified those arguments of the children which were at the average (stage 3) level, rather than those one step below that level (stage 2). When these arguments seemed understood, and could be extended to new situations, the teacher would challenge the level (stage 3) previously supported, and support and clarify the arguments of those one stage above (stage 4) the previous consensus. The children were given pre- and post-tests, using stories different from those involved in the classroom discussions (with some new stories given only for the post-test). Fifty per cent of the children moved up one stage, ten per cent moved up two stages, and the remainder stayed the same. In contrast, ten per cent of a control group moved up one stage during this period, and the remainder stayed the same. One year later the relative advance was still maintained. Similar results have since been obtained by Blatt, with classes of black and white children aged 11 and 15 in a public-school setting (Blatt 1970). The potential value of such educational efforts appears when one considers some recent longitudinal findings (on a small sample of middle-class males), which indicate that moral maturity at age 13 is an extremely good predictor ($r=0.78$ to 0.92) of adult moral maturity (at age 24 to 27). This high correlation cannot be attributed to the cessation of development of moral judgment at age 13, for such development continues past college in most of this group. For example, while none of the 13-year-olds were primarily at the principled level, 36 per cent of the 24-year-olds in this sample were at the principled level (stages 5 and 6). Those (over 15 per cent) who did not develop some of such thinking by later high school, however, did not develop to the principled stage in young adulthood. In general, then, while moral development continues into adulthood, mature 13-year-olds retain their edge in development, presumably because development is stepwise and the advanced pupils have fewer steps to go through.

MORAL ACTION AND MORAL EDUCATION

According to Aristotle, "virtue is of two kinds, intellectual and moral.

While intellectual virtue owes its birth and growth to teaching, moral virtue comes about as a result of habit. The moral virtues we get by first exercising them; we become just by doing just acts, temperate by doing temperate acts, brave by doing brave acts." Aristotle, then, is claiming that there are two spheres, the moral and the intellectual, and that learning by doing is the only real method in the moral sphere.

American educational psychology also divides the personality into cognitive abilities, passions or motives, and traits of character. Moral character consists of a bag of virtues and vices. For example, one of the earliest major American studies of moral character, conducted in the late twenties (Hartshorne and May 1928–38), included honesty, service, and self-control in the bag of virtues.

If we accept such a bag of virtues, it is evident how we should build character. Children should be exhorted to practise these virtues and should be told that happiness, fortune, and good repute will follow in their wake; adults around them should be living examples of these virtues, and children should be given daily opportunities to practise them. Daily chores should be used to build responsibility, the opportunity to give to the Red Cross should serve to build responsibility, service, altruism, and so on.

The psychologist's objection to the bag of virtues is that there is no such thing. Virtues and vices are labels by which people award praise or blame to others, but the ways people use praise and blame towards others are not the ways in which they think when making moral decisions themselves. Hartshorne and May found this out to their dismay forty years ago by their monumental experimental studies of children's cheating and stealing. In brief, they and others since have found that:

1 You cannot divide the world into honest and dishonest people. Almost everyone cheats some of the time; cheating is distributed in a bell curve around a level of moderate cheating.

2 If a person cheats in one situation, it does not mean he will or will not cheat in another. There is very little correlation between situational cheating tests. In other words, it is not a character trait of dishonesty that makes a child cheat in a given situation.

3 People's verbal moral values about honesty have nothing to do with how they act. People who cheat express as much or more moral disapproval of cheating as those who do not cheat (See Kohlberg 1963).

Once these findings were obtained, it became easy to understand the psychological mistake underlying the bag of virtues approach. Common sense tends to treat moral words as if they described reality. However, words like honesty are actually used primarily to praise or blame other people, not to describe cognitively in the scientific sense. If people used words in the same way to praise and blame themselves and to govern their own decisions, there would be no problem. As we all know, however, behaviour looks very different from the internal and external frames of reference. What is "honestly expressing your feelings" to the actor is "cruelly disregarding the other person's feelings" to the outsider. What was "conducting a scientific investigation of honesty" to Hartshorne and May was, from a different point of view, "dishonestly lying and cheating to school children" (by tempting them to cheat under the pretense of conducting intelligence tests).

What Hartshorne and May found out about honesty and the rest of the bag of virtues upsets more scientific-sounding words introduced by psychoanalytic psychology to talk about morality – for example, "superego-strength," "resistance to temptation," "strength of conscience," etc – just as much as it upsets common-sense treatments of moral words. When recent researchers have attempted to measure such "moral" traits in individuals, they have been forced to use Hartshorne and May's old tests of honesty and self-control and have gotten exactly the same results (Kohlberg 1963). Insofar as one can extract some general personality factor from children's performance on tests of "honesty" or "resistance to temptation," it is a factor of ego-strength, or ego-control, or will, and includes such traits as capacity to maintain attention, intelligent task performance, capacity to delay response, and capacity to delay gratification (Grim, Kohlberg, and White 1968). Although "ego-strength" is essential in understanding moral action, it does not take us to the core of morality or to the definition of virtue. The greatest evildoers in human history have been men with strong egos who lacked principled moral values. The capacities to pursue a goal are only positive from a moral point of view if the ego's goals are moral.

We have seen that the bag of virtues does not serve the individual very well in defining his moral goals, in spite of the obvious necessity of sometimes using virtue-labels in bringing up children. The finding that individuals do not organize their own moral behaviour around a bag of virtues should be a comforting finding, however. The plight of those who try is described by the theme song of the show, *You're a good Man, Charley Brown.*

You're a good man Charley Brown, you have humility, nobility and a sense of honor that are very rare indeed. You are kind to all the animals and every little bird, with a heart of gold you believe what you're told, every single solitary word. You bravely face adversity, you're cheerful through the day, you're thoughtful, brave and courteous. You're a good man Charley Brown – you're a prince and a prince could be king, with a heart such as yours you could open any door – If only you weren't so wishy-washy.

If, like Charley Brown, we define our moral aims in terms of virtues and vices, we are defining them in terms of the praise and blame of others, and are caught in the pulls of being all things to all men and end up being wishy-washy. Virtues and vices do have a central significance to individuals at the conventional level of morality: our praise and blame of others is based on ascribing virtues and vices to them. At the preconventional level, virtues and vices have no such significance because the individual does not care about intention. The young child is not oriented to the bad as "being selfish," "being deceitful," etc.: he is, rather, oriented to the bad as being punished (stage 1) or "not making out" (stage 2). At the stage of moral principle, the individual is oriented towards acting to create a moral state of affairs, not towards "being honest." The principled virtue, "justice," is not a "trait" like honesty; it is a concern about maintaining a just state of affairs.

What then is the place of virtues (i.e., approved "traits" of character) in defining moral education? We have said that virtues are the language of assigning praise and blame. The great believers in emotive ethics and in the irrationality of human morality – Westermarck, Freud, Nietzsche, etc. – have viewed morality as a system of blame of others (moral indignation) or self-blame (guilt and shame). The great believers in conventional morality such as Durkheim make praise and blame the core of moral education. The Russian moral education of the virtues of "self-discipline" involves the manipulation of praise and blame ("love-withdrawal") to encourage "moral character." In particular, the child is encouraged to blame other children who deviate (Bronfenbrenner 1968). The place of the virtues in moral education, then, is the place of the language of praise and blame in education.

My own uncertain answer to this question is that praise and blame are necessary parts of moral development, but should not be used to define its ends. When a child spits in another child's face, we feel it expresses a "vice" worse than "being rude." Insofar as punishment is awarded, it must be accompanied by moral blame. The "vice" of premoral (stages 1 and 2) parents and teachers is to punish instrumentally, rather then for moral reasons; they punish when there is no vice. Many a mother punishes an infant for "being dirty" (i.e., for inconveniencing the mother) with possible detrimental effects discussed elsewhere (Kohlberg 1963). Teachers who are not premoral, but conventional and thoughtless, do the same thing in less severe forms.

Praise and blame are invitable in classroom life, regardless of the teacher's moral aims. To use these methods morally, that is, in terms of conceptions of moral virtues and vices, is preferable to using them exclusively amorally, that is, to praise and blame behaviour, such as putting books away, which has no moral meaning.

What then is the place of moral action in moral education? Fortunately, moral maturity in judgment and in action are closely related. We have already said that knowledge of the good in terms of what Plato calls opinion or conventional belief is not virtue. An individual may believe that cheating is very bad but that does not entail that he will resist cheating in real life. Espousal of unprejudiced attitudes towards Negroes does not entail actual action to ensure civil rights when others have some prejudice. However, true knowledge of principles of justice does entail virtuous action. It appears that Plato's ancient doctrine that virtue is one and that is justice, because virtue is based on knowledge of the good, is to some extent true. The bag of virtues approach assumes a virtue for every moral rule (i.e. honesty for rules of cheating and stealing, responsibility for rules about completing tasks, etc.). Because morally mature men are governed by the principle of justice rather then by a set of rules, there are not many moral virtues, but one. The essential elements of justice in relation to cheating are understood by both our stage-5 and stage-6 subjects. In cheating, the critical issue is recognition of the element of contract and agreement implicit in the situation, and the recognition that, although it does not seem so bad if one person cheats, what holds for all must hold for one. In a recent study by Krebs (1967), 100 sixth-grade children were given experimental cheating tests and our moral-judgment interview. The majority of the children were below the principled level in moral judgment. Seventy-five per cent of these children cheated. In contrast, only 20 per cent of the principled subjects (that is, stages 5 and 6) cheated. In another study conducted at the college level, only eleven per cent of the principled subjects cheated in contrast to forty-two per cent of the students at lower levels of moral judgment.

In the case of cheating, justice and the expectations of conventional authority both dictate the same behaviour. What happens when they are opposed?

An experimental study by Milgram involved such an opposition. In the guise of a learning experiment, undergraduate subjects were ordered by an experimenter to administer increasingly severe electric shock punishment to a stooge victim. In this case, the principles of justice involved in the stage-5 social contract orientation do not clearly prescribe a decision. The victim had voluntarily agreed to participate in the experiment and the subject himself had contractually committed himself to perform the experiment. Only stage-6 thinking clearly defined the situation as one in which the experimenter did not have the moral right to ask them to inflict pain on another person. Accordingly, 75 per cent of the subjects at stage 6 quit or refused to shock the victim as compared with only 13 per cent of all the subjects at lower stages.

A study by Haan, Smith, and Block (1968) carries the issue into political civil disobedience. Berkeley students were faced with a decision to sit-in at the Administration building in the name of political freedom of communication. The researchers administered moral-judgment interviews to over two hundred of these students. The situation was like Milgram's. A stage-5 social-contract interpretation of justice, which was that held by the University administration, could take the position that a student who came to Berkeley came with foreknowledge of the rules and could go elsewhere if he did not like them. About 50 per cent of the stage-5 subjects sat in. For stage-6 students, the issue was clear-cut and 80 per cent of them sat in. For students at the conventional levels, stages 3 and 4, the issue was also clear-cut and only ten per cent of them sat in. However, there was another group which was almost as disposed to sit in as the stage-6 students. These were stage-2 instrumental relativists, of whom about 60 per cent sat in.

We have pointed out that advance in moral judgment seems to correlate with more mature moral action. Principled subjects both cheat much less and resist pressures by authorities to inflict pain on others much more than do less mature subjects. We do not yet know whether educational stimulation of moral-judgment advance would actually produce more mature conduct in conflict situations. In any case, in addition to stimulating the development of general moral-judgment capacities, a developmental moral education would stimulate the child's application of his own moral judgments (not the teacher's) to his actions. The effort to force a child to agree that an act of cheating was very bad when he does not really believe it will only be effective in encouraging morally immature tendencies towards expedient outward compliance. In contrast, a more difficult but more valid approach involves getting the child to examine the pros and cons of his conduct in his own terms (as well as introducing more developmentally advanced considerations) (Turiel 1966).

In general, however, the problem of ensuring correspondence between developing moral judgments and the child's action is not primarily a problem of eliciting moral self-critisicm for the child. One aspect of the problem is the development of the ego abilities involved in the nonmoral or cognitive tasks upon which the classroom centres. For example, an experimental measure of high stability of attention (low reaction-time variability) in a simple monotonous task has been found to be a clear predictor of resistance to cheating in Hartshorne and May's tests (r=0.68) (Grim et al. 1968). The encouragement of these attentional ego capacities is a task not of moral education as such but of general programing of classroom learning activities.

Ego strength, however, must be considered educationally in terms of its relation to level of moral judgment. Krebs (1967) found that if children have an amoral philosophy (stage 2), they are much *more* likely to cheat if they are high on ego strength (high in attention and IQ). If children have a conventional morality (stage 4), they are much *less* likely to cheat if they are high on ego strength. In other words, high ego strength aided the preconventional hedonists in living up to their "egoistic principles" in the face of temptation and pressure to conform, whereas high ego strength aided the conventional children to live up to their "conventional principles." If children have reached the stages of principle, high ego strength is less necessary, for even those principled children who are low in ego strength do not seem to cheat. This is not surprising because it is characteristic of conventional morality to yield to (and find excuses for) behaviour suggested by social pressures or by an ambiguous social situation. (In this sense, the basic virtue may be called "autonomy" as well as "justice.")

The fact that "living up to his principles" for a stage-2 child leads to cheating raises a fundamental issue for classroom moral education. In order to encourage the child's application of his values to his behaviour, we need to make sure that the kinds of behaviour demands we make have some match to his already existing moral values. Two major types of mismatch occur. One type, which we have already mentioned, occurs when teachers concentrate on trivial classroom routines, thus moralizing on issues that have no moral meaning outside the classroom. If the teacher insists on behavioural conformity to these demands and shows no moral concerns for matters of greater relevance to the child's (and the society's) basic moral values, the child will simply assume that his moral values have no relevance to his conduct in the classroom. It is obvious that the teacher must exert some influence towards conformity to trivial classroom rules, but there are two things he can do to minimize this sort of mismatch. The first is to ensure that he does communicate some of his values with regard to broader and more genuinely moral issues. The second is to treat administrative demands as such and to distinguish them from basic moral demands involving moral judgment and moral sanctions. This does not imply that no demands should be treated as moral demands but that the teacher should clearly distinguish his own attitudes and reactions towards moral demands from his more general conformity demands.

The second form of mismatch between the teacher's moral demands and the child's moral values arises from the fact that the teacher feels that certain behavioural demands are genuine moral demands, but the child has not yet developed any moral values that require these behaviours. This is exemplified by the fact that resistance to cheating on tests does not derive from anything like moral values in young children aged five to seven, whereas resistance to theft and aggression do correspond to more spontaneous and internal moral values at this age. Given this fact, it does not seem wise to treat cheating as a genuine moral issue among young children, whereas it may be with older children. In general, the teacher should encourage the child to develop moral values relevant to such behaviour as cheating but should not treat the behaviour as morally demanded in the absence of such values. It must be stressed that it is the over-concern with conforming *behaviour* characteristic of traditional approaches to moral education that lies behind most of the mistakes of educators in the moral realm.

MORAL EDUCATION AND POLITICAL EDUCATION

We have stressed the importance of defining moral education in a manner that avoids a myopic preoccupation with conformity behaviour in school settings. A more balanced perspective is attained when we recognize that the development of moral reasoning is central to political or social studies education. While philosophers from Plato and Aristotle to Dewey have recognized the close relations between moral and political education, our own work is the first systematic effort to unite the two in a coherent practical way. Our efforts currently involve adapting the principles of the Blatt discussion procedures to the dilemmas that form the core of the Don Oliver "Public Issues" social studies units. Our efforts are based on research by Lockwood (1970), Fletcher and Endo (unpublished), and Bane (unpublished). These findings are:

1 Public issues of the sort used by Oliver are responded to by reliably codable moral judgment statements.

2 A student's moral level on the Oliver public-political dilemmas and on the Kohlberg moral dilemmas are correlated (r=48).

3 Goodness of discussion of public issues (as rated by the Oliver

schema) is clearly correlated with moral level on the issues being discussed.

4 The goodness of discussion schema of Oliver, being itself a model of discussion based on a conception of constitutional democracy and philosophic rationality of value-judgment, is a model appropriate to our stage-5 and stage-6 subjects. When a stage-5 subject is engaged in "good discussion" by the Oliver criteria but is discussing with a stage-3 or stage-2 subject, the good discussion bounces off the low-stage subject.

The implications for moral education are as follows:

1 There is no clear line between effective social studies education and effective moral education.

2 The criteria of effectiveness are not essentially different. If "behaviour" is exaggerated as a focus in the moral education field, it is ignored in all the rest of education. The capacity to participate in the social process is the effective sign of moral and social studies education, not either "pure knowledge" or "pure behaviour".

3 The unit of effectiveness of education, insofar as it has social value, is not the individual but the group. An individual's moral values are primarily important for society as they contribute to a moral social climate, not as they induce particular pieces of behaviour. Whether people are for or against war in Vietnam has a social import far vaster than that reducible to individual "moral" acts of Hawks and Doves. A man's moral level affects the social group and institutions to which he belongs in a myriad unspecified ways which cannot be reduced to individual acts of moral self-sacrifice or self-control. Moral discussion classes such as those of the Blatt experiments are limited, not because they do not focus on moral behaviour, but because they have only a limited relation to the "real life" of the school and of the child.

MORAL EDUCATION AND THE ATMOSPHERE OF THE SCHOOL

The issue of "real life" brings us to what should be a central concern of moral education, the moral atmosphere of the school (Kohlberg 1970). To extend classroom discussions of justice to real life is to deal with issues of justice in the schools. Education for justice, then, requires making schools more just, and encouraging students to take an active role in making the school more just. Here we can only illustrate the application of our two major principles of environmental stimulation of development. The first is our conception of the enhancement of participation and role-taking opportunities. One example of the importance of social participation in moral development may be seen in the finding that children with extensive peer-group participation advance considerably more quickly through the Kohlberg stages of moral judgment than do children who are isolated from such participation (with both groups equated for social class and IQ). This clearly suggests the relevance and potential of the classroom peer group for moral education. In Russia the peer-group structure is created by the teacher (i.e., he divides the classroom into groups), and the peer group is then manipulated by punishments and rewards to impose the teacher's or the school's values upon its deviant members. If the stimulation of the moral development of the individual child is a goal, however, the role of the peer group is quite different. In the previous section we discussed the fact that classroom isolates were slower in developing moral judgment than were integrates. This suggests that inclusion of the social isolates in the classroom peer group might have considerable influence on their moral development, though not necessarily an influence of immediate conformity to teacher or school demands.

The implementation of this goal would involve various methods to encourage inclusion of isolates such as are under investigation in a research project at the University of Michigan conducted by Ronald Lippett. Some of these methods involve creating a classroom atmosphere encouraging participation rather than attempting directly to influence sociometric integrates to include isolates. Some involve more direct appeal to integrated members of sociometric groups: an appeal to the implementation of already existing social and moral values held by these children rather than the effort to impose the teacher's values upon them by reward or punishment. The process raises many important issues and these can be potentially stimulating to the moral development of the integrates as well, for they will be coping with a new situation: "Well, we were finally nice to him and look what he did." These issues provide the teacher with an opportunity to play a different and perhaps more stimulating and open role, to act as a "moral guide" rather than as an exponent of conformity to school rules and teacher demands.

While participation in the peer group is important, the ultimate issue of participation is of course that of participation in the structure and decisions of the school itself. Here the principle of participation must be integrated with our principle of stimulation by a justice-structure one stage above the child's own. We are now studying the level of justice of schools as these are perceived by students and staff. The hypothesis is that schools with atmospheres perceived by students as at their stage or lower lead to less moral advance than do schools which atmospheres perceived at higher stage.

In these terms we might summarize the difference in goals between a political education program and a moral education program as follows. The first might take as means and ends a community effectively run by majority vote or democratic agreement in accordance with our stage 5, whereas a moral education program might take as means and ends a community effectively and satisfactorily run by consensus. Let me give, as an example, the Friend's Meeting School in Rindge whose rules are made and discussed in a weekly business meeting. It is described by the brochure as follows:

The sense of community is most strongly felt in the weekly Meeting, consisting of faculty, their families and students. Decisions are made by consensus rather than by majority rule. This places responsibility on each member to struggle to see through his own desires to the higher needs of others and the community, while witnessing the deepest concerns of his conscience. The results of these decisions are not rules in the traditional sense, but agreements entered into by everyone and recorded as minutes.

In such meetings the student is forced to sift out where he should abide by the democratic majority and where he must uphold moral principles in spite of the majority. While Institutions, as opposed to persons, can never rise above stage 5, such procedures could help in the development of a stage-6 orientation.

Ultimately, then, the issue of participation raises the issue of the social structure of the school and a complete approach to moral education means full student participation in a school in which justice is a living matter. It is clear that the educator's ability to engage in this type of education is to a considerable extent contingent on the teacher herself reaching a principled level of moral judgment.

REFERENCES

Aiken, H.D. The levels of moral discourse *Ethics* 1952 *62* 235–48

Baldwin, J.M. *Social and ethical interpretations in mental development* New York: Macmillan 1906

Ball, W.B. Religion and public education: The post-Schempp years. In Theodore Sizer (ed.) *Religion and public education* Boston: Houghton-Mifflin 1967 pp. 144–63

Berkowitz, L. *Development of motives and values in a child* New York: Basic Books, Inc. 1964

Blatt, N. Studies on the effects of classroom discussion upon children's moral development. Unpublished doctoral dissertation, University of Chicago 1970

Blatt, N., Kohlberg, L. Effects of classroom discussion on moral thought. In Kohlberg and Turiel 1971

Brandt, R. *Ethical theories* Englewood Cliffs, N.J.: Prentice Hall 1959

Bronfenbrenner, U. Soviet methods of upbringing and their effects: A social-psychological analysis. Paper read at a conference on Studies of the Acquisition and Development of Values, National Institute of Child Health and Human Development, May 1968

Child, I.L. Socialization. In G. Lindzey (ed.) *Handbook of social psychology* vol. 11 *Special fields and applications* Cambridge, Mass: Addison-Wesley 1954, pp. 655–92

Dewey J. *Moral principles in education* (1909) New York: Philosophical Library 1959

Dreeben, R. *On what is learned in school* Cambridge, Mass: Addison-Wesley 1968

Durkheim, E. *Moral education: A study in the theory and application in the sociology of education* (1925) New York: Free Press 1961

Erikson, E.H. *Childhood and society* Boston: W.W. Norton & Co. 1950

Grim, P., Kohlberg, L., White, S. Some relationships between conscience and attentional processes *Journal of Personality and Social Psycholoyg* 1968 *8* 239–53.

Haan, N., Smith, M.B., Block, J. Moral reasoning of young adults: Political-social behaviour, family background, and personality correlates *Journal of Personality and Social Psychology* 1968 *10* (3) 183–201

Hartshorne, H., May, M.A. *Studies in the nature of character:* I *Studies in deceit;* II *Studies in self-control;* III *Studies in the organization of character* New York: Macmillan 1928–30

Holstein, Constance Parental determinants of the development of moral judgment. Unpublished doctoral dissertation, University of California, Berkeley 1968

Homans, G.T. *The human group* New York: Harcourt, Brace 1950

Jackson, P.W. *Life in the classroom* New York: Holt, Rinehart & Winston 1968

Jones, V. *Character and citizenship training in the public schools* Chicago: University of Chicago Press 1936

Kohlberg, L. Moral development and identification. In H. Stevenson (ed.) *Child pyschology*. 62 Yearbook of the National Society for Studies in Education. Chicago: University of Chicago Press 1963

Kohlberg, L. Moral and religious education and the public schools: A developmental view. In T. Sizer (ed.) *Religion and public education* Boston: Houghton-Mifflin 1967

Kohlberg, L. Stage and sequence: The cognitive-developmental approach to socialization. In D.A. Goslin (ed.) *Handbook of socialization theory and research* Chicago: Rand, McNally & Co. 1969

Kohlberg, L. The moral atmosphere of the school. In N. Overley (ed.) *The unstudied curriculum* Monograph of the Association for Supervision and Curriculum Development, Washington D.C. 1970

Kohlberg, L., Turiel, E. *Moralization research, the cognitive developmental approach* New York: Holt, Rinehart & Winston 1971

Krebs, R.L. Some relationships between moral judgment, attention, and resistance to temptation. Unpublished doctoral dissertation, University of Chicago 1967

Lockwood, A. Relations of political and moral thought. Unpublished doctoral dissertation, Harvard University 1970

Malinowski, B. *The sexual life of savages* New York: Hilcyon House, House and House 1929

Mead, G.H. *Mind, self and society from the standpoint of a social behaviorist* Charles W. Morris (ed.) Chicago: University of Chicago Press 1934

Neill, A.S. *Summerhill: a radical approach to child rearing* New York: Hart Publishing Co. 1960

Piaget, J. The moral judgment of the child (1932) Marjorie Gebain (transl.) New York: Collier Books 1962

Rawls, J. The sense of justice *Philosophical Review* 1963 *72* (3) 281–305

Rest, J. Developmental hierarchy in preference and comprehension of moral judgment. Unpublished doctoral dissertation, University of Chicago 1968

Rest, J., Turiel, E., Kohlberg, L. Relations between level of moral judgment and preference and comprehension of the moral judgment of others *Journal of Personality* 1969

Ruma, E., & Mosher, P. Relationship between moral judgment and guilt in delinquent boys *Journal of Abnormal Psychology* 1967 *72* 122–7.

Tillich, P. *Morality and beyond* New York: Harper 1963

APPENDIX I

Definition of moral stages

I PRECONVENTIONAL LEVEL

At this level the child is responsive to cultural rules and labels of good and bad, right or wrong, but interprets these labels in terms of either the physical or the hedonistic consequences of action (punishment, reward, exchange of favours) or in terms of the physical power of those who enunciate the rules and labels. The level comprises the following two stages:

Stage 1 *punishment and obedience orientation* The physical consequences of action determine its goodness or badness regardless of the human meaning or value of these consequences. Avoidance of punishment and unquestioning deference to power are valued in their own right, not in terms of respect for an underlying moral order supported by punishment and authority (the latter being stage 4).

Stage 2 *instrumental relativist orientation* Right action consists of that which instrumentally satisfies one's own needs and occasionally the needs of others. Human relations are viewed in terms similar to those of the market place. Elements of fairness, of reciprocity, and equal sharing are present, but they are always interpreted in a physical pragmatic way. Reciprocity is a matter of "you scratch my back and I'll scratch yours," not of loyalty, gratitude, or justice.

II CONVENTIONAL LEVEL

At this level, maintaining the expectations of the individual's family, group, or nation is perceived as valuable in its own right, regardless of immediate and obvious consequences. The attitude is one not only of *conformity* to personal expectations and social order, but of loyalty to it, of actively *maintaining*, supporting, and justifying the order and of identifying with the persons or group involved in it. This level comprises the following two stages:

Stage 3 *interpersonal concordance or "good boy – nice girl" orientation* Good behaviour is that which pleases or helps others and is approved by them. There is much conformity to stereotypical images of what is majority or "natural" behaviour. Behaviour is frequently judged by intention: "he means well" becomes important for the first time. One earns approval by being "nice."

Stage 4 *"law and order" orientation* There is orientation toward authority, fixed rules, and the maintenance of the social order. Right behaviour consists of doing one's duty, showing respect for authority, and maintaining the given social order for its own sake.

III POST-CONVENTIONAL, AUTONOMOUS, OR PRINCIPLED LEVEL

At this level there is a clear effort to define moral values and principles that have validity and application apart from the authority of the groups or persons holding these principles and apart from the individual's own identification with these groups. This level again has two stages:

Stage 5 *social-contract legalistic orientation* Generally, this stage has utilitarian overtones. Right action tends to be defined in terms of general individual rights and in terms of standards that have been critically examined and agreed upon by the whole society. There is a clear awareness of the relativism of personal values and opinions and a corresponding emphasis on procedural rules for reaching consensus. Aside from what is constitutionally and democratically agreed upon, the right is a matter of personal "values" and "opinion." The result is an emphasis upon the "legal point of view," but with an emphasis upon the possibility of changing law in terms of rational considerations of social utility, (rather than freezing it in terms of stage-4 "law and order"). Outside the legal realm, free agreement, and contract is the binding element of obligation. This is the "official" morality of the United States government and constitution.

Stage 6 *universal ethical-principle orientation* Right is defined by the decision of conscience in accord with self-chosen *ethical principles* appealing to logical comprehensiveness, universality, and consistency. These principles are abstract and ethical (the Golden Rule, the categorical imperative); they are not concrete moral rules like the Ten Commandments. At heart, these are universal principles of justice, of the reciprocity and equality of human rights and of respect for the dignity of human beings as individual persons.

APPENDIX 2 Universal aspects of morality

	Categories	
	Modes	
Judgments of obligation Right Having a right Duty Responsibility	Judgments of moral value Blame Punishability	Supportive judgments Justification Nonmoral value Descriptive and definitional
	Elements or principles	
Teleological elements Prudential Social welfare	Attitudinal elements Love Respect	Relational elements Justice as liberty Justice as equality Justice as reciprocity
	Issues or institutions	
Norms Social rules of norms Personal conscience Roles of affection and welfare	Relations and roles Authority Civil liberties Contractual reciprocity Institutions of punishment	Values Life Property Truth Sexual
	Levels	
Judgment of acts	General judgments of rules	Judgments in situational conflict Sociopolitical judgments Normative and metaethical theory judgments

APPENDIX 3

Six stages in conceptions of the moral worth of human life

Stage 1 No differentiation between moral values of life and its physical or social-status value.

Tommy, age 10 (III Why should the druggist give the drug to the dying woman when her husband couldn't pay for it?): "If someone important is in a plane and is allergic to heights and the stewardess won't give him medicine because she's only got enough for one and she's got a sick one, a friend, in back, they'd probably put the stewardess in a lady's jail because she didn't help the important one."

(Is it better to save the life of one important person or a lot of unimportant people?): "All the people that aren't important because one man just has one house, maybe a lot of furniture, but a whole bunch of people have an awful lot of furniture and some of these poor people might have a lot of money and it doesn't look it."

Stage 2 The value of a human life is seen as instrumental to the satisfaction of the needs of its possessor or of other persons. Decision to save life is relative to, or to be made by, its possessor. (Differentiation of physical and interest value of life, differentiation of its value to self and to other.)

Tommy, age 13 (IV Should the doctor "mercy kill" a fatally ill woman requesting death because of her pain?): "Maybe it would be good to put her out of her pain, she's be better off that way. But the husband wouldn't want it, it's not like an animal. If a pet dies you can get along without it – it isn't something you really need. Well, you can get a new wife, but it's not really the same."

Jim, age 13 (same question): "If she requests it, it's really up to her. She is in such terrible pain, just the same as people are always putting animals out of their pain."

Stage 3 The value of a human life is based on the empathy and affection of family members and others towards its possessor. (The value of human life, as based on social sharing, community, and love, is differentiated from the instrumental and hedonistic value of life applicable also to animals.)

Tommy, age 16 (same question): "It might be best for her, but her husband – it's a human life – not like an animal, it just doesn't have the same relationship that a human being does to a family. You can become attached to a dog, but nothing like a human you know."

Stage 4 Life is conceived of as sacred in terms of its place in a categorical moral or religious order of rights and duties. (The value of human life, as a categorical member of a moral order, is differentiated from its value to

specific other people in the family, etc. Value of life is still partly dependent upon serving the group, the state, God, however.)
Jim, age 16 (same question): "I don't know. In one way, it's murder, it's not a right or privilege of man to decide who shall live and who should die. God put life into everybody on earth and you're taking away something from that person that came directly from God, and you're destroying something that is very sacred, it's in a way part of God and it's almost destroying a part of God when you kill a person. There's something of God in everyone."

Stage 5 Life is valued both in terms of its relation to community welfare and in terms of being a universal human right. (Obligation to respect the basic right to life is differentiated from generalized respect for the sociomoral order. The general value of the independent human life is a primary autonomous value not dependent upon other values.)
Jim, age 20 (same question): "Given the ethics of the doctor who has taken on responsibility to save human life – from that point of view he probably shouldn't but there is another side, there are more and more people in the medical profession who are thinking it is a hardship on everyone, the person, the family, when you know they are going to die. When a person is kept alive by an artificial lung or kidney it's more like being a vegetable than being a human who is alive. If it's her own choice I think there are certain rights and privileges that go along with being a human being. I am a human being and have certain desires for life and I think everybody else does too. You have a world of which you are the centre, and everybody else does too and in that sense we're all equal."

Stage 6 Belief in the sacredness of human life as representing a universal human value of respect for the individual. (The moral value of a human being, as an object of moral principle, is differentiated from a formal recognition of his rights.)
Jim, age 24 (III Should the husband steal the drug to save his wife? How about for someone he just knows?): "Yes. A human life takes precedence over any other moral or legal value, whoever it is. A human life has inherent value whether or not it is valued by a particular individual."
(Why is that?): "The inherent worth of the individual human being is the central value in a set of values where the principles of justice and love are normative for all human relationships."

APPENDIX 4

Motives for engaging in moral action*

Stage 1 Action is motivated by avoidance of punishment and "conscience" is irrational fear of punishment.

*Source: Rest, 1968

Pro – If you let your wife die, you will get in trouble. You'll be blamed for not spending the money to save her and there'll be an investigation of you and the druggist for your wife's death.

Con – You shouldn't steal the drug because you'll be caught and sent to jail if you do. If you do get away, your conscience would bother you thinking how the police would catch up with you at any minute.

Stage 2 Action motivated by desire for reward or benefit. Possible guilt reactions are ignored and punishment viewed in a pragmatic manner. (Differantiates own fear, pleasure, or pain from punishment-consequences.)

Pro – If you do happen to get caught you could give the drug back and you wouldn't get much of a sentence. It wouldn't bother you much to serve a little jail term, if you have your wife when you get out.

Con – He may not get much of a jail term if he steals the drug, but his wife will probably die before he gets out so it won't do him much good. If his wife dies, he shouldn't blame himself, it wasn't his fault she has cancer.

Stage 3 Action motivated by anticipation of disapproval of others, actual or imagined-hypothetical (e.g., guilt). (Differentiation of disapproval from punishment, fear, and pain.)

Pro – No one will think you're bad if you steal the drug but your family will think you're an inhuman husband if you don't. If you let your wife die, you'll never be able to look anybody in the face again.

Con – It isn't just the druggist who will think you're a criminal, everyone else will too. After you steal it, you'll feel bad thinking how you've brought dishonor on your family and yourself; you won't be able to face anyone again.

Stage 4 Action motivated by anticipation of dishonor, i.e., institutionalized blame for failure of duty, and by guilt over concrete harm done to others. (Differentiates formal dishonor from informal disapproval. Differentiates guilt for bad consequences from disapproval.)

Pro – If you have any sense of honor, you won't let your wife die because you're afraid to do the only thing that will save her. You'll always feel guilty that you caused her death if you don't do your duty to her.

Con – You're desperate and you may not know you're doing wrong when you steal the drug. But you'll know you did wrong after you're punished and sent to jail. You'll always feel guilty for your dishonesty and law-breaking.

Stage 5 Concern about maintaining respect of equals and of the community (assuming their respect is based on reason rather then emotions). Concern about own self-respect, i.e., to avoid judging self as irrational, inconsistent, nonpurposive. (Discriminates between institutionalized blame and community disrespect or self-disrespect.)

Pro – You'd lose other people's respect, not gain it, if you don't steal. If you let your wife die, it would be out of fear, not out of reasoning it out. So you'd just lose self-respect and probably the respect of others too.

Con – You would lose your standing and respect in the community and violate the law. You'd lose respect for yourself if you're carried away by emotion and forget the long-range point of view.

Stage 6 Concern about self-condemnation for violating one's own principles. (Differentiates between community respect and self-respect. Differentiates between self-respect for general achieving rationality and self-respect for maintaining moral principles.)

Pro – If you don't steal the drug and let your wife die, you'd always condemn yourself for it afterward. You wouldn't be blamed and you would have lived up to the outside rule of the law but you wouldn't have lived up to your own standards of conscience.

Con – If you stole the drug, you wouldn't be blamed by other people but you'd condemn yourself because you wouldn't have lived up to your own conscience and standards of honesty.

CHAPTER 2

Ethical pluralism and moral education

KURT BAIER

I HAVE been asked to examine the problems created by ethical pluralism for those who would devise a program of moral education, and to discuss whether these problems can be solved by emphasizing in such a program procedural methods rather than substantive ethical principles.

As a philosopher, I can best contribute to the clarification and solution of these problems by formulating as clearly as possible what are the proper aims of moral education. By itself, this will not help those trying to design programs of moral education, but it will at least yield criteria on the basis of which to assess alternative programs. A second thing I can do as a philosopher is to explain what ethical pluralism can legitimately mean, what special problems it creates for stating the aims of moral education, and how they might be overcome.

SOCIAL TRAINING, MORAL TRAINING, AND MORAL EDUCATION

Before saying anything about its aims, I must try to distinguish moral education from two things with which it may be confused: social training, and moral training. Social training is the process that prepares each child for full membership in a community, that is, a group of men regarding one another as fellows. Part of that training is coming to know and accept the restrictions insisted on by the community in the choice as well as the pursuit of individual ends. These restrictions are formulated in social rules whose content each youngster learns in the course of his social training. He also learns that he must comply with these rules. His complying with them includes his willingness to extend to fellow members assistance when needed, co-operation in those more complex enterprises whose accomplishment requires the co-operation of several people, the fellow-feeling and trust due to a fellow member, and obedience to those holding positions of authority. When the trainee himself becomes a full member, he in turn receives these same benefits which result from other members' compliance with the social rules.

Of course, no amount of social training is wholly successful. Most or all members will at some time or other feel that other members have violated some social rule, and their feeling will sometimes be justified. Communities, therefore, devise complaint procedures for use against one another for the investigation of these complaints, for adjudication on them, and for some form of settlement, involving adjustment or penalty.

Moral training is analogous to social training, except that it prepares a child for full membership in a moral community, that is, a community with a morality. A community has a morality if and only if it looks upon all or some of its social rules in a certain way. That way can be characterized by saying not merely that some sets of social rules are preferable to others but that this set of rules must be good enough to be acceptable; and to be acceptable it must meet certain requirements. Of course, for a group to have a morality it is not necessary that all members of the group (or indeed any) be completely clear or agreed on what these requirements are. However, ideas such as the common good, the public interest, natural rights, social justice and universalizability are very common and generally known (albeit notoriously vague and unclear) ways of formulating them. Most of these ideas, in one way or another, embody the same two central ideas: that the restrictions should prevent or minimize harm and promote or maximize good, and that they should do so for everyone alike.

Thus, we can say that the morality of a community is that subset of its social rules which in that community is taken (at least by and large) to satisfy these requirements and so is acceptable to every rational member (at least by and large). If among a community's social rules there is no such subset, then the community does not have a morality, although it may have a religion, customs, or taboos. Of course, a group's having a morality does not mean that the social rules of which it is composed actually do satisfy these requirements, but only that they are taken to do so.

Traditionally, the demand that a morality should be acceptable to everyone alike is expressed in the demand for an answer to three questions. The first is the question, "Why should there be any restrictions by social rules at all?" The second is the question, "Why should they be these social rules rather than others?" or "Show me that what this community requires of its members is what it should require of them," or "Show me that what is thought right and wrong in this community really is so." The third question is "Why should a person follow these rules even when he can break them with impunity?" A morality is acceptable if there are answers to these questions.

It is easy to see how this way of looking at social rules arises and that it is completely in accordance with reason. For the imposition, through social rules, of restrictions on a person's ends and his ways of attaining them is felt by him as a serious interference in his life and he therefore demands a justification. This can be provided by showing that such restrictions are necessary for the attainment of what any rational being, aiming at the best possible life for himself and those dear to him, would want to attain.

The difference between moral training and moral education is that moral training is the process whereby a child acquires the morality of his community, whereas moral education is a deliberate activity, carried on primarily by professional teachers, for the purpose of fostering moral excellence in the young.*

Moral education thus necessarily has two features which moral training may lack. The first is that it is a deliberate activity, with a definite aim, and carried on by professionals, capable perhaps of assessing the merits and demerits of their program, possibly capable of improving it. The second is that the aim is not just to inculcate the morality of the community, but to foster moral excellence in the pupils. This involves not merely teaching them the morality of the group but also showing them the respects in which it falls short, and how it may be set right. Moral educators must aim at teaching a morality which allows one to answer the three central questions of ethics. For, otherwise, the prevalance of the morality taught will appear to the pupils, not as a necessary condition of the good life, but as an unnecessary evil.

THE THREE ABILITIES MAKING UP MORAL EXCELLENCE

How, then, would we tell, in regard to two alternative programs of moral education, which one was the better? Obviously, we need to have two kinds of information. The first concerns the criteria of excellence of a program of moral education. The second concerns the results we get by using these programs of moral education in the process of giving a moral education to those for whom they are designed. Only the first is information a philosopher is qualified to give.

*I say "primarily" because it may well be possible to devise such programs for use by parents in the education of their children, perhaps even for use by adults in their own further self-improvement. But I ignore such possibilities here.

If I am right about moral education, then its aim is to produce not adult conformists, but adults who are moral beings, who understand what morality is, why it is needed, what the basis of its rules is, and who, because they understand all this, are willing to do what is morally required of them, even when this is contrary to their inclinations and best interests. A program of moral education is therefore the more effective, and so the better, the more successful it is in turning premoral youngsters into moral beings. Of course, there will be the usual other criteria of excellence: the time it takes to accomplish its results, the effort and cost involved, the range of personality types for whom it is effective, and so on.

What, then, is it for someone to have reached the status of a moral being? We should call someone a moral being, if he has acquired the disposition to do what is morally required of him because he knows or thinks it is so required. To have this complex disposition, he must have three distinguishable but connected excellences, the knowledge of what is morally required of him, the ability to do whatever is morally required of him, and the willingness to do whatever he knows or thinks is so required.

Take first the most important excellence to be produced by moral education: knowing what is required of one. This involves in the first place knowing what the group morally requires of one. At the most unsophisticated level, this is simply having learnt the types of conduct to which the group attaches what might be called the negative moral sanctions. Moral sanctions are forms of community pressure designed to ensure a high degree of conformity with moral requirements. Negative moral sanctions are pressures in support of the minimal requirements of morality. They have two primary aims: to bring home to the culprit that he has not played his part in the communal co-operative organization for the good life, and to let others know of it. Whereas social sanctions generally consist in the threat of the imposition of certain hardships or burdens whose object is to deter potential rule-breakers, the threat underlying moral sanctions is temporary or permanent exclusion from membership in the moral community. The imposition of the moral sanction is not merely the imposition of the burden of disapproval, condemnation, or indignation, but the loss of trust, assistance, co-operation, and fellowship which is involved in loss of membership. Where burdens such as imprisonment, fines, hard labour, or flogging are imposed as punishment, they are imposed as "expiation," as the price of renewed membership. Forgiveness and pardon are not simply remissions of the penalty, they are the victim's and the community's reacceptance of the culprit as a member of the community. It stands to reason that this is more appropriate and more readily done if he shows signs of repentance, that is, an understanding of the error of his ways and a resolve to mend them.

I said that the negative moral sanctions were concerned with the minimal requirements of morality. They are that part of a morality, conformity with which is a condition of full membership. Therefore, failure to comply brings into operation permanent expulsion or suspension of membership until expiation has occurred (that is, until the person has undergone treatment designed to make him willing to conform). A morality usually also contains other directives which go beyond what is required of the individual. These directives concern the things the community appreciates its members doing, the so-called deeds of supererogation. Failing to do what is morally required is doing wrong, and for doing wrong the community imposes the negative moral sanctions. Doing more than is required – by giving aid, cooperation, and benefits to others under difficulties and at cost to oneself – is doing what is supererogatory, and for doing it the community imposes what might be called the positive moral sanctions: expression of approval, praise, commendation, admiration. Such conduct earns an individual the gratitude of the community. The positive sanctions give him not only the pleasure of the community's approval but, by letting others know of his deeds, give him a blank cheque on the good will of the community, on which he can draw when he is in need.

Now, if we were concerned not with moral education but with moral training, that is, with turning a child into an adult conformist, then teaching him what his community morally requires of him would be all he would need to *know* about what is morally required of him. And knowing that the community calls "wrong" the sort of conduct to which it attaches the negative moral sanction would be all he would need to know about the meaning of "wrong."

But, since we are here concerned with moral education and not merely moral training, knowing the morality of the group is not enough, for it falls far short of knowing what *is* wrong and what *is* supererogatory. I believe that the following additional points must be known to a person before he can be said to know or even to believe that something is morally required of him, that is, that it is wrong not to do it. He must know that we apply the negative moral sanctions because we believe a course of action to be wrong, and not vice versa. He must know that we believe certain actions wrong because we believe them to be of certain types, though he need not know all of the relevant types. But he must know at least one of them, namely, actions which are cases of harming others, or of having harmful consequences, or of not doing what would prevent or diminish harm to others. He must also know that, since actions may be believed to be of these types when they are not, some actions may be believed wrong when they are not. He must know that the morality of his group, since it may contain false moral convictions, may not be wholly sound. And lastly, he must know that, therefore, what his group feels to be morally required of him may be different from what *is* morally required of him.

Knowing what is morally required of one is therefore a complicated and difficult matter. It involves knowing what one's group feels to be morally required of one as well as knowing whether one is morally required to do that or something else. Persumably, it is only when the morality of one's group is very unsound that one is morally required or even permitted to do something else. The problems here are analogous to those of civil disobedience. Just as it would seem to be wrong prima facie to break the law, so it would seem to be wrong prima facie to ignore the morality of one's group. But more about this later.

In the absence of any established or even agreed findings by moral philosophers on these topics, the most one can expect of a moral being is that he have a thorough knowledge of the morality of his group, that he appreciate the uncertainly about the soundness or unsoundness of many of its rules and precepts, and that he attempt to acquire as sound a belief of what is morally required of him as is possible in these circumstances.

A second excellence required in a moral being is the ability to do what he knows or thinks is morally required of him. (This ability has to be inculcated also in the course of moral training.) We are here dealing with a special case of the ability to act in accordance with what one takes to be the best reasons applicable to the situation. In this special case, the best reason is a moral reason, namely, that there is a course of action which is morally required of one. This ability is of a highly sophisticated type. The behaviour involved is a form of goal-directed behaviour (unlike reflex action, such as the knee-jerk, or yielding to an irresistible urge, such as taking a breath after one has held one's breath) in which a person's goal has been determined by a reason, not just a desire. In other words, his goal is determined by some consideration, that is, by some supposed fact which he thinks should or may move him to adopt a certain goal and a certain suitable (and otherwise unobjectionable) means to its attainment, even if he has no desire to attain it or actually an aversion to attaining it, as when he decides that his best interest requires that he take a course in speed-reading or join a health club or shake his cigarette addiction. Of course, a fact – for example, that he is hungry – may be a reason for adopting the very same goal – to find something to eat – which would normally be "determined by" that desire, hunger. What, then, we may ask, is the difference between a goal determined by desire and one determined by reason? We would say that someone's goal was determined by a reason, if he thinks the (known) fact that he is hungry a reason for adopting that goal and if he has found it *an adequate* reason in the circumstances, that is, if he has found no stronger reasons either for refraining or for doing something else altogether. It is determined by desire if it is determined "blindly" (without the belief that being hungry is a reason for finding something to eat) or in the face of reasons to the contrary.

The ability to act in accordance with what one takes to be the best reasons comprises two distinguishable sub-abilities: the ability to engage in practical reasoning and the ability to decide (and act) in accordance with the outcome of practical deliberation. The latter ability is a form of self-control. It is called strength of will or strength of character when it is displayed in circumstances in which acting in accordance with the best reasons involves overcoming difficulties of various kinds, such as hardships, suffering, loss, or temptations. Clearly, this general ability, though important for moral education, is not peculiar to it, but is presupposed in all rational conduct. Whether the inculcation of this ability forms part of a program of moral education or some other part of a person's training, therefore, depends on the educational curriculum as a whole. However, the role of moral reasons among other kinds of reasons should be made clear in the course of moral education and pupils in such a course should certainly acquire enough strength of will and character to be able to act in accordance with moral reasons when these conflict with strong desires, whether hedonistic or egoistic.

The third excellence required is willingness to do whatever moral reasons point to as the morally required course. This willingness, often called the good will, must be distinguished from the ability, discussed in the previous section, for a person may be willing, without being able, to do what is morally required of him, and vice versa. This willingness comprises two propensities: the propensity to engage in moral deliberation before action, that is, the habit of checking whether one's inclinations are in accordance with what is morally required of one, and the propensity to use the ability to decide in accordance with the outcome of practical deliberation, and so to treat moral reasons as superior to (as overriding) other kinds of reason and also inclination, when there is a conflict between them.

Summing up, we can say that the aim of moral education, as opposed to moral training, is to produce adults who do not simply conform to the morality of their group, but are full moral beings, that is, persons who do what they believe is morally required of them. To produce such adults, moral education must foster in those to be educated three excellences. The first is the knowledge of what the group feels is morally required of one, together with beliefs as sound as possible of what is sound and what unsound in the group's morality, and what deviations from the group's morality are therefore morally permitted to, or required of, one. The second is the ability to do what one believes or knows is morally required of one. And the third is the willingness to do it.

Clearly, the ends of moral education are to produce group and individual moralities which are sound, to produce individuals who can correctly determine what is morally required of them, and who will tend to do what is so required of them. And the underlying idea is that the fulfilment of these requirements by the members of the group is necessary for the good (or best possible) life for its members. It is also clear that no program of moral education can be expected to be completely successful with all of its pupils and that some of its failures will have to be corrected by the negative and positive sanctions. However, it is equally clear that if moral education fails very seriously, whether in the task of ensuring that the morality's requirements upon its members are sound (acceptable), or in the task of inculcating in them an understanding of the need for and the value of the restrictions the morality imposes, or in the task of inculcating in its members a willingness to play their part in the co-operative enterprise of accomplishing the good life, a very great, perhaps intolerable, burden will be placed on the moral sanctions. Where moral education has failed seriously, the moral sanction, instead of producing remorse, repentence, contrition, and resolutions to mend one's ways, will produce resentment, resistance, alienation, or rebellion.

The upshot of our discussion so far is that one of the most important tasks of moral education is fostering a certain intellectual excellence, namely, the ability to determine whether what the morality of one's group requires of one is what it should require of one; and if it does not, to determine what is morally required of one, in such a case; whether to obey under protest, disobey and suffer, or disobey and try to escape the moral sanctions, or perhaps to find some other alternative. It can be said, I think, without fear of contradiction, that there is no agreement among philosophers, sociologists, theologians, or any other group of specialists, about how this is done. How, then, can we hope to devise a program designed to foster this excellence? It may be suggested that ethical pluralism is the best way, perhaps the only morally legitimate way, of coping with this situation. It might be said that, in the absence of agreement on these matters, it would be wrong for the state to introduce uniform programs of moral education. In fact, it may be said, a healthy dose of moral scepticism is precisely what is needed to loosen up our moral conservatism and intolerance and to introduce those moral changes which, in this otherwise rapidly changing society, are overdue.

ETHICAL PLURALISM AND TOLERANCE IN MORAL MATTERS

What, then, is ethical pluralism? Clearly, there are many degrees of ethical diversity, not all of which amount to pluralism. We should hardly speak of ethical pluralism simply on account of diversity of social stations, roles, and corresponding duties, for the fact that businessmen, officers, policemen, teachers, priests, and politicians have different tasks determined by their different roles is quite compatible with all of them agreeing that it is a moral duty to perform the tasks of one's station or role, whatever these may be.

Nor would we want to speak of ethical pluralism simply because there is culturally determined ethical diversity. For the fact that different cultural groups at one and the same time, or one and the same group at different times, subscribe to opposing moral convictions is compatible with all members of the same group at the same time agreeing on what is morally required of them.

However, we can speak of ethical pluralism the moment such ethically diverse groups come into close social contact with each other, as when they engage in trade with each other, intermarry, or participate in common economic or cultural activities. What differentiates ethical pluralism from mere ethical diversity is the fact that the activities regulated by these different moral convictions are co-operative or competitive and therefore impinge on the lives of those engaging in them, which is not so in cases of mere ethical diversity. The main problem created by ethical pluralism therefore arises even when the groups with opposing moralities are not parts of a social or political whole, such as a multi-nation state or a state comprising a great many ethnically diverse groups as long as they do not live in conditions of total apartheid.

The main problem raised by ethical pluralism can be explained by contrasting societies characterized by ethical pluralism and societies characterized by ethical monism. Even in an ethically monistic society there will usually be a diversity of roles and duties. Members of such a society will frequently have role conflicts, since it will be virtually impossible for them not to play more than one role: husband, father, uncle, son, employee, member of a trade union, citizen, home owner, tax payer, and so on. And even within the same role there may be conflicts of duties. The duties of teaching may conflict with the duties of research, with the duty to participate in wider educational activities, and with other duties. But, typically, these duties are regarded as merely prima facie duties capable of being overridden by other stronger duties and rights. In other words, there are available to us higher-level moral rules telling us how to settle conflicts of duties within a given role or between different roles. And these rules in turn are formulated on the basis of very general principles, such as those of the common good, equality, justice, human rights, and freedom. By contrast, ethical pluralism is a state of affairs (or the doctrine advocating it) in which opposing moral convictions are regarded not as convictions concerning conflicting prima facie duties and rights, to be settled by higher rules or principles designed to resolve such conflicts, but as convictions concerning duties and rights *all things considered,* and to be left unresolved.

Ethical pluralism may take a less radical or a more radical form. In the less radical version, opposing moral convictions might in principle be capable of settlement, but are not in fact thus capable, given the present state of knowledge of the relevant facts and moral principles. Suppose one group considers it wrong for an unmarried girl to yield to the amorous entreaties of an eligible young man and another wrong for her not to yield without good reason. In such a case, we simply lack knowledge of the principles we should employ in settling this difference of view, and of the facts (mostly the consequences of adopting either practice) which would be made relevant by the adoption of the appropriate principles.

In the more radical version, such opposing moral convictions form part of opposing moralities which are based on different and autonomous, that is, not mutually corrigible, aims and standards.*

MORAL TOLERANCE IN MATTERS OF PUBLIC AND PRIVATE MORALITY

The problem created by both versions of ethical pluralism is, of course, that on neither of them can there be an agreed settlement for such

*Compare, for example, W.B. Gallie, Liberal morality and socialist morality. In Peter Laslett (ed.) *Philosophy, Politics, and Society* Oxford: Basil Blackwell 1956, 116–33, especially p. 132.

conflicts and disagreements. It may perhaps be argued that the problem is not serious since there will not be disagreement on all moral matters and, where there is disagreement, the disagreeing parties can simply agree to differ. Communities that have adopted ethical pluralism could simply require moral tolerance of their members just as they require religious tolerance and tolerance in matters of taste and custom. However, I do not think that this is an acceptable solution for all, including the most important, cases of disagreement.

I think tolerance can work well in those moral matters which belong to what might be called "private morality," but it would not be adequate for "public morality." Private morality is that part of the morality of the group to which *only* "the private moral sanction," whether negative or positive, attaches (i.e., the self-condemnation and self-disapproval or the self-congratulation and self-approval (moral pride) of those who have engaged in conduct which is wrong or supererogatory). Public morality is that part of the morality to which private *and* public moral sanctions attach. As I explained, the public moral sanction is the condemnation or commendation, the disapproval or praise, of certain types of conduct (those generally thought wrong or supererogatory) by whoever comes to know of instances of such conduct, and quite irrespective of whether or not he is directly affected by it. What belongs to public morality is protected also by the private moral sanction, at least for those who have had a proper moral upbringing. For they know that if they do wrong, even if their conduct is not known and so not followed by the appropriate public moral sanction, they *deserve* the negative public sanctions, and so feel guilty; and if they do what is supererogatory, they *deserve* the positive public sanctions, and so feel morally proud.

As far as private morality is concerned, therefore, ethical pluralism poses no serious problem. We can all agree that, in matters of merely private morality, each person may apply the private moral sanctions as he sees fit. It is nobody else's business whether one feels guilty or morally proud on account of such conduct. Mutual tolerance in matters of private morality need cause no trouble.

Could we not, then, perhaps advocate that *all* contentious moral matters be relegated to private morality and ask for general moral tolerance in such matters? It is clear that this would be a very drastic solution in the case of the radical version of ethical pluralism, for the whole range of first moral principles would then have to be relegated to private morality. Tolerance would require us to say, for example "if some think that everyone has a right to life, let them respect that right, but let them be tolerant of those others who do not think so."

Even for the less radical version of ethical pluralism, the solution is rather unhelpful. Suppose a university department has to decide whether to admit certain Negro students who have applied for admission. Jones thinks that Nego students ought to be admitted in preference to white students with the same qualifications and even when they have qualifications inferior to those at the cut-off point. Smith thinks that admissions qualifications should be the same for black and white students. Robinson thinks that black students should be admitted only if they have substantially better than the minimal qualifications and not at all if there are sufficient white applicants. Roberts thinks that no black students should be admitted at all. Given that there are qualified Negro applicants, it will be impossible to devise an admissions policy in conformity with the moral convictions of all these staff members. Relegation of this matter to private morality is no help, for there is not only the question of what each faculty member should think the right policy, but also the question of what is to be done.

Or suppose that Jones thinks it wrong to use birth-control methods and his wife thinks it wrong to have more than the six children they already have and so wrong not to use birth-control methods. In this case, also, the requirements of their married life make it impossible for them to act in ways compatible with both their moral convictions – unless they are prepared to give up sexual relations altogether. Tolerance of each other's views is clearly not enough. There has to be a method of arriving at a common policy. Even where the moral conflict is not insoluble, relegation to private morality is not a satisfactory solution. Suppose the wife does not think it wrong either to use or not to use birth-control methods, but would *like* to have no more children, and, therefore, would like to use birth-control methods. Then there is a solution to their problem: she can agree not to use birth control and so risk having more children. In cases where the moral conflict is not insoluble, tolerance of each other's private morality makes a difference to practice: it favours the most restrictive morality. But this raises anew the question of whether this is desirable and should be encouraged or permitted. And that surely is a question of public morality.

What exactly is it that makes it undesirable to relegate to private morality all matters on which there is moral disagreement? The answer is that in some matters an interpersonally valid decision is required if anything is to be done at all. Applications for admission have to be decided on in one way or another. Sexual intercourse has to be performed with or without birth-control aids. Advocating tolerance of moral views in such matters is advocating the irrelevance of moral views to what is the best decision. And this is surely contrary to what we take to be the point of a morality. Thus, although there may be matters which are properly matters of private morality, such as the much-discussed issue of homosexual relations in private between consenting adults,* there are others which are properly matters of public morality and whose relegation to private morality would deprive us of that service, conflict resolution, which we require in such matters. Where we need authoritative interpersonal conflict resolution, we require a settlement by public morality. Relegation to private morality therefore does not meet our needs. Hence ethical pluralism in such matters is undesirable.

THE DISTINCTION BETWEEN PUBLIC AND PRIVATE MORALITY VERSUS THE DISTINCTION BETWEEN LEGAL AND MORAL SANCTIONS

I believe this point is frequently overlooked by moral philosophers because of an important confusion (hailing perhaps from Kant) between two kinds of distinction: (*a*) the distinction between private and public morality, and the connected distinction between private and public moral sanctions; (*b*) the distinction between moral and legal sanctions. If we fail to keep these two distinctions clearly apart, we shall be apt to confuse two sorts of issues: those for which public morality should provide a uniform solution as well as public moral sanctions, but to which legal sanctions should not be attached (honesty, promise-keeping, adultery); and those for which there need be no uniform moral solution and no public sanction, of either kind, legal or moral (smoking, self-indulgence, timidity).

TOLERANCE OF MORAL BEHAVIOUR VERSUS TOLERANCE OF MORAL OPINIONS

It might, however, be argued that in a pluralistic society ethical pluralism cannot be avoided and is perfectly harmless, for although ethical pluralism involves moral tolerance, it need not involve behavioural chaos. Moral tolerance implies only tolerance of opposing moral views; it need not involve the permissibility of behaviour in accordance with all such conflicting moral views. After all, in a

*See the recent discussions of this matter by Lord Devlin and Prof. H.L.A. Hart: Lord Devlin, *The Enforcement of Morals* Oxford University Press 1959, Oxford: and H.L.A. Hart, *Law, Liberty, and Morality* Stanford: Stanford University Press 1963.

pluralistic society we all demand and receive political tolerance, yet although the laws are often made by and in the interests of our political opponents, we do not expect to be allowed to ignore the law. Similarly, it might be argued, where there is disagreement in a matter of public morality, we must be tolerant of each other's moral views, but if there also is need for a common course of action, we must accept a procedural, formal, content-independent method of arriving at such a common course of action, even though this must mean that some at least will have to act in opposition to their moral convictions.

Against this it must be said that just because such methods are content-independent, they must be regarded as arbitrary, and therefore must seem out of place in moral matters. Such methods are of course quite appropriate in matters in which there can be no rational settlement of disagreements, for example, in matters of taste, or in matters of conflicting interests where there are no relevant moral considerations, as when two people simultaneously "find" the same ten-dollar note. Such a method is clearly unsuitable in all matters of opinion, whether factual or moral, where the evidence is necessarily inadequate and there is not likely to be argeement among different people. It is unsuitable when we wish to determine who is responsible and so liable for the damage someone has incurred, even when it is extremely difficult to give a cogent judgment on this and when different judges might well arrive at different conclusions. In none of these cases would it seem appropriate to toss a coin, to have the matter settled by bargaining between the parties concerned, or even by a majority vote of those affected. And it would seem no more appropriate to do this in matters of divergent moral opinion, as when the group has to decide whether polygamy, birth control, drinking, or integration of public transport, public schools, hotels, and restaurants should be permitted, forbidden, or required.

FOUR LEGITIMATE AIMS FOR MORAL EDUCATION IN A PLURALISTIC SOCIETY

Must a pluralistic society, then, abandon the idea of devising a program of moral education suitable for all of its members and all of its schools? Or must it design a universal program which has the support of the majority? And must it allow the teaching of any moral views which any of its subgroups wishes to inculcate in their children?

I believe there are at least four major aims we can justifiably pursue in a universal program of education, and quite irrespective of whether these aims have the support of the majority or not. For, morally speaking, they *ought* not to be opposed by anyone. Further, we may justifiably urge the prohibition of any educational program that prevents children from being exposed to a program of universal moral education with these minimal aims.

Good will

The first aim is to produce in our pupils what is generally called good will. It seems to me that in this society too many young people, including college students, grow up without much respect for, or even interest in, morality. They are not even, like Glaucon and Adeimantus, sceptical about what is really right and wrong – they care too little to be troubled by doubts. Nor are they, like Thrasymachus, cynical about the worth of morality, for they never acquire a belief in the great worth of morality. One reason for this is that they have not learned to think of morality as a rational enterprise. If they care about rationality in practical matters, they think of it as an individual or social *strategy* for attaining, in a partly co-operative but largely hostile environment, the best possible life for the individual or society employing the strategy. If they have yearnings beyond this, they rely on their better instincts or on some message preached at them by an attractive teacher or prophet. If they think of morality as rational, they will identify it with a strategy for self-fulfilment. If they think of morality as going beyond that, they will think of it as nonrational, as an essentially personal ideal to which they are committed and to which they may attract converts, but about which there can in the end be no telling arguments, correct or incorrect conclusions. For them, moral convictions will be on a par with matters of more or less idiosyncratic taste.

Thus, in teaching our pupils to respect morality and the willingness to follow its precepts, we must stress that, although it involves burdens and sacrifices, it is essentially rational, that is, the burdens and sacrifices are not pointless or futile. Of course, putting it simply in this form is not likely to be successful. For it is wholly empty until we have spelled out the content of these restrictions and how they are arrived at.

An understanding of the nature of a public morality

Our program of moral education should, therefore, have a second aim, namely, to give the pupil an understanding of the nature and purpose of a group's and an individual's morality and their place by the side of the various other systems of social control. This will at least help the pupil to grasp what it is that he is supposed to respect. He will not then hold that respect for other systems of social control with which he may tend to confuse it and which do not deserve that respect.

Concerning this second aim, we can now draw together the various points made earlier. A group's morality is its *public* morality. It consists of a moral code and the public moral sanctions, negative and positive, which support it. The negative public moral sanctions vary in seriousness from expression of moral disapproval to permanent exclusion from membership in the moral community. Every well-trained member of such a moral community also imposes on himself private moral sanctions when he engages in conduct to which the public moral sanctions are attached – except, of course, where his own morality differs from the morality of the group, as frequently happens in an ethically pluralistic society. Leaving aside these cases, these private moral sanctions tend to keep a moral man in line even if he expects that his immoral conduct would not be discovered and the public moral sanctions not imposed. A group's morality is therefore an effective moral order, a form of social control.

The private moral order is significantly different from the public moral order. It consists of an individual's private moral code to which he attaches the private moral sanctions. This private code must not be confused with that part of the individual's public moral code that diverges from the group's code. The difference is that the individual does not regard his private moral code as the right code for everyone, whereas he does so regard that part of his public moral code which diverges from the group's code. Thus, what makes a moral code public is simply the fact that the individuals whose code it is regard it as the right code for the group, and so they consider it appropriate to apply the public moral sanctions to anyone who violates this code. As we have seen, one problem created by ethical pluralism is to find a way of construing opposing moral convictions as both belonging to public morality and not involving the imposition of the public moral sanctions.

An understanding of the need for some public moral order

Once this much is clear about moralities, it is also clear that the existence of such a moral order imposes considerable restrictions on what a person may be inclined, or may have good reasons, to do. Since this is prima facie objectionable, it calls for justification. Therefore, a third thing which must be made clear in the course of moral education is both the need for, and the benefits resulting from, such a moral order. For, in the absence of such a justification, the members of the moral community will rightly feel that the moral order is tyrannical. They will suspect that it imposes unnecessary restrictions on all. Or they will harbour the Marxist suspicion that the group's morality is the means by which its ruling class imposes on the whole society restrictive rules advantageous only to itself.

The first step in such a justification of a morality is the simple demonstration of the need for a compulsory social order holding in check desire and self-interest. The outlines of such a demonstration are contained in Hobbes' *Leviathan* and in Hume's *Treatise of Human Nature*, and they have been amplified and restated many times recently. The nerve of the argument is the natural scarcity of those things which men need for their survival and for a life truly worth living. The only known way, perhaps the only way, to remedy that scarcity is within a social order, in which, through the division of labour and the creation of, and individuals' assignment to, special roles with corresponding duties and rights, these scarce necessities and luxuries of life are socially, that is, co-operatively, provided. A second and no less important element in such a social order is the creation of a secure climate of life by the establishment of clear rules for the distribution among the members of the group of these things co-operatively produced. This has the effect of channelling people's energies away from wasteful fights for scarce goods, and into their production. The third, and traditionally most prominent, element of such a social order are the rules which explicitly forbid conduct intended or likely to inflict harm or suffering on others and enjoin the prevention of harm or suffering threatening others. The need for and the advantage of such a social order is best explained by showing the consequences of the absence of effectively enforced rules of these three kinds. I need not here repeat this well-known story. It seems to me that this part of the demonstration can be made out and should form part of a general moral education. It demonstrates that a social order consisting of effectively enforced rules overruling desire and self-interest is necessary if a situation disastrous for all is to be avoided, and a life worth living for any is to be achieved.

However, as it stands, the demonstration is inadequate. It shows that (almost) *any* social order is better than none. It does not sufficiently discriminate between social orders with different sets of rules. The fact that an effective order is necessary does not show that every such order is equally acceptable. By the "morality" as opposed to the "mores" of a group, we mean its social order in so far as it purports to be *acceptable* from the point of view of all its members. It is clearly important that a social order should be thus acceptable, if for no other reason than that otherwise some members may have no adequate stake in the social order, and so no adequate reason for shouldering the burdens and making the sacrifice which the social order imposes on them. In that case, they will not recognize an obligation to obey the rules of the social order. In so far as the order purports to be moral, they will reject it. Ennui and alienation would seem to be natural results of such a situation.

An understanding of the criteria of acceptability for particular provisions of a public morality

A fourth aim of some importance in our program of moral education is therefore a clear understanding of the criteria of acceptability which any social order purporting to be a moral order must satisfy. For this purpose, we can usefully distinguish three areas of a morality, depending on the manner in which interpersonal relations are regulated. One way of regulating interpersonal relations is to attach rights and duties to the roles created by the social institutions of the group: father, employer, trade unionist, policeman, teacher, general, politician, architect, doctor, and so on. Another way of regulating behaviour is through establishment of obligation-creating directives by those authorized to do so: an official's order, a legislator's law, a businessman's contractual undertaking. By these directives, conduct which is not obligatory becomes so temporarily and for those so directed. Lastly, there is a completely general way of regulating moral behaviour which applies to all normal adults. In this group belong those moral precepts which we should normally treat as paradigmatic: thou shalt not kill, thou shalt not lie, and others.

For the last group, the criterion of acceptability is whether the precepts governing these relations are designed to regulate behaviour so that it keeps the infliction of harm and suffering at a minimum.

For the first group – institutional morality – the criterion of acceptability is distributive justice, the requirement that the social institutions allocate burdens and benefits equally among members except where members have more or less than average desert, in which case burdens and benefits are to be modified according to desert. A person with greater than average negative desert deserves a greater than average burden, and a person with greater than average positive desert deserves a correspondingly greater than average benefit. What counts as positive, what as negative, desert, should itself be determined with a view to lightening the total burden and increasing the total benefit. Labour, effort, skill, are obvious candidates for a measure of desert.

For the second group, the criterion of acceptability is that the users of these obligation-creating devices should not be free to use them except within the limits set by precepts of the first and third groups.

Summary

I have outlined four aims for a program of moral education: the inculcation of good will, the understanding of the nature and purpose of a morality, the demonstration of the need for and the advantage of a compulsory social order imposing necessary constraints on individuals' desires and the promotion of their own best interest, and lastly the explanation of the criteria of acceptability, those which any social order claiming to be a moral order purports to satisfy and which are therefore the criteria of soundness of a moral order. I believe that these four aims are not called into question by ethical pluralism. It seems to me not only that there is not in fact any real disagreement on these aims in our society, but that it is possible to show that if there were such disagreement it would be misguided. If we are concerned, as I take it we are, with a rational organization of society, then these four aims can be conclusively supported, for we must grant that for any individual it is in accordance with reason to impose on his impulses and desires the discipline of long-range self-interest. It is also in accordance with reason for individuals to seek the good life in co-operation with others. To do so requires social organization and, therefore, the imposition of a social order, implying the occasional over-ruling not only of desires but also of self-interest. But for reasons already given, this justifies the demand for the shaping of the social order in accordance with the requirements of morality, that is, the criteria of acceptability.

Concerning the problem of how to deal with opposing moral convictions in an ethically pluralistic society, the points just made suggest the following solution. Opposing moral convictions must be construed as alternative moral hypotheses – hypotheses about whether the incorporation of the one or the other moral conviction in the public morality of the group would satisfy the criteria of acceptability. But since a social order is necessary, and since the existing social order lacks justification only if it fails to satisfy the criteria of acceptability, it would seem to be reasonable to hold that the onus of proof is on those who claim that the existing social order does not satisfy these criteria. I believe that in many of the current moral controversies this onus can now be discharged. There seems to be no doubt that, in the controversy over birth control, those who argue for the moral permissibility of birth control can demonstate that the opposite view is mistaken, and that any prohibition by law is therefore without moral basis. I believe the same is true for the controversy over whether homosexual relations between consenting adults are morally wrong.

It seems to me not only that there is no justification for prohibiting such conduct by law, but that there is no case for including such a prohibition in the public morality of the group. Of course, there can be no objection to anyone including it in his private morality. It goes without saying that a program of moral education need not contain any conclusions on such controversial matters. However, the program should aim at enabling the student to master the method by which, together with the relevant factual information, he would be led, if he is not yet committed or immobilized by emotion, to the same conclusions.

Lastly, it is perhaps worth mentioning that one way of teaching the criteria of acceptability would be to devise partly co-operative and partly competitive games, in some of which the rules conform to, in some of which they violate, the criteria of acceptability. This might help to drive home to the players the unsatisfactoriness of certain ways of conducting such competitive–co-operative activities, and at the same time make clear what is needed to make them acceptable.

PART TWO

Moral action: some analyses and their implications for moral education

CHAPTER 3

Moral education and moral action

A. I. MELDEN

IN THIS essay I sketch a theory of moral action and understanding in the light of which I present some views concerning the development of moral understanding. I begin with topics that may appear remote from questions having to do with moral education, but their relevance will, I trust, become clearer as the argument of the essay develops.

BODILY MOVEMENT AND ACTION

Compare the quick reflex kick of the leg with someone's flipping of a switch by which the lights in a room get turned on. On one familiar conception there is very broadly an important parallelism. The leg jerked. Why? Because of the stimulation of the muscles produced by a blow on the tendon below the knee. The finger moved. Why? Because of the occurrence of certain desires and thoughts. The "because" in both cases is a cause, or else why should the occurrence explained have taken place at all? And the items cited in the second case, while each qua cause may be, as Prichard once thought it was, a butting into the causal order in the physical world by events of quite a different kind, nonetheless involve the same sort of causal explanation that is possible for the reflex movement of the leg.

I do not accept this view of the matter at all, and for reasons that I can hardly begin to explore in any detail. Such a picture of the proceedings can hardly do justice to the multifarious items that are commonly cited in explanation of what people do. These may well be desires and thoughts, but they can hardly be construed as interior objects or events. But there are also feelings, emotions, wishes, hopes, and even reasons that are not only the reasons *that* agents do what they do, but also the reasons that agents *have* for what they do, reasons that, if good and sufficient, do much more than explain how it came to pass that the agent did what he did, since what they show is that what the agent did was reasonable and right. Perhaps, too, what may cause A to punch B on the nose was the fact that he hates him or that, poor fellow, A is mad. But so far at least there is not the slighest indication that A had any cause for doing what he did – cause, not merely in the sense that it explains how it came to pass that he did what he did, but as a reason that shows that what he did was fully justified. "Reason" and "cause" are blanket terms, and any account of human action that trades on the mere matter of verbal fact that either term (with, of course, suitable modification of the surrounding sentence structure) can be invoked to cover not only the reflex movement of a limb and the hurt that one person inflicts on another, but even the moral action of a conscientious agent, in order to argue for a common pattern of explanation (one might say a lowest common denominator of explanation) for all of these incidents, will surely impoverish our view of the broadly varied and enormously complex field of human action.

But, in addition, this picture of the proceedings simply leaves out of account the status of the person. It is not enough that there should be a desire and a thought, for the desire and thought cannot be idle but, in general, must be relevant somehow to the concerns and interests of the agent. And these concerns and interests are intelligible, not as self-contained interior events, states, or dispositions but as concerns *with* and interests *in* matters taken by the agent to be related to the external circumstances in which he is situated. Surely we need here not the conception of an "agent" who is merely programmed to respond to the input of information with the motion of his bodily parts, or the conception of a self whose function it is merely to provide the housing for interior mental events, but, rather, the flesh and blood notion of a human being who has acquired the ability through training and instruction, to recognize the situations in which he goes about his affairs for what they are, and who understands the relevance and appropriateness of his actions to the concerns and interests he has acquired in the process of his development. We need to invoke, not the picture of desires and thoughts as causes of actions (this locution is a philosopher's barbarism), but rather the more perspicuous view of an agent's desires and thoughts, including those that are cited as reasons justifying him in what he does, that cause *him* – the kind of person he is – to respond as he does to the familiar situations he has learned to recognize and to manage without hesitation or hazard.

Correlative with this notion of a person is the concept of a human action, not as a bodily movement, which is intelligible simply as an event produced by an interior act of volition, but as a doing by the kind of agent he is. There are, to be sure, minimal and limiting cases of action, for example, the idle flexing of one's finger or the pursing of one's lips – Why? – No reason at all. Here no doubt there are physiological events that can be cited in explanation of the bodily movements that take place; but occurrences of this sort are also doings that are of minimal import if they are explicable simply as unwitting performances that merely indicate the agent's ability to move the relevant parts of his body at will. But the flexing of one's finger might also be intentional, if, for example, it is done in order to relieve an annoying muscle cramp, in entering a bid during an auction, in calling for a card during a game of poker, in signalling one's partner during a game of bridge, or ... The possibilities are endless.

THE PERCEPTION OF ACTION

The very same motion of the finger may occur in any of the last-mentioned performances, for the very same motion may be involved in the agent's moving his finger in each of the cases mentioned. And *in* moving his finger in such-and-such a way (which may be the same in all of these cases) the person will be doing quite different things; relieving one's cramp, bidding, calling for a card, or signalling are quite different sorts of actions. But what makes them quite different sorts of actions are the surroundings. It would be folly to suppose that one could discover the character of the action by attending more closely to the character of the bodily performance. Equally, it would be a mistake to suppose that it is simply the differences in the causal orders in which the same event is involved that makes for the differences in the actions performed, so that to say that in the one case one is calling for a card and in the other signalling information is merely to offer causal information. Even if one could obtain information concerning causes and effects from the observations of these two actions, one would not be stating this information in stating that the actions had been performed. For what is relevant to these actions qua actions is the situation, the complex and rule-governed activities in which persons engage. Let it be that the effect upon others of my calling for a card is to raise eyebrows, and that the effect of my signalling information to my bridge-partner is to ostracize myself; still it is my signalling the information, as such and not my ostracizing myself, that is cheating; and it is my calling for a card, not my raising of others' eyebrows, that is, as such, legitimate, even if unwise. They do their own ostracizing and they do their own eyebrow-raising.

There are, then, bodily movements involved which can be called "moving such-and-such a bodily part." But there are many different actions that may get done *in* moving such-and-such a bodily part, depending upon very widely different sorts of circumstances, and many different sorts of things we bring to pass – the effect of our actions upon others, the results we achieve and the consequences of what we do – *by* doing what we do in moving such-and-such a bodily part. Generally our interest lies not in the minutiae of the bodily movements that take place or that we execute, but in the things we do *in* moving such-and-such a bodily part and in the things we bring to pass *by* what we do. That this is so is shown, among other things, by our uncertainty about the precise ways in which we move our bodily parts when we perform quite familiar sorts of actions, by the fact that if asked how precisely one moves such-and-such a limb in doing x we might well hesitate and attempt to find by doing x or by imagining ourselves doing x and then noticing how, in fact or in imagination, the limb in question gets moved. For our interest normally is no more in the bodily movements we execute than in the fact that we have these very interests. We are interested, rather, in matters that are external to ourselves, in the ways in which, in moving our limbs as we do, we deal with these matters in the situations in which we carry on our affairs.

In this connection it is particularly worth commenting on the fact that what we see, when we take notice of the actions of others, is by no means confined to bodily movements. It is not that we see the movement of a limb and interpret it as a case of someone raising his arm, or, if when in doing this he is signalling or voting, that we interpret the motion of the arm as a signal or a vote. Neither is it the case that what we see are certain physiognomic changes in the face and that, in Cartesian fashion, we interpret these as smiles or frowns by inferring the presence of certain mental states. We see people, and we see them act in various ways. We hear the sounds and noises they make, but we also hear what it is that they say. Interpretation, far from being involved generally in the observations we make with respect to other persons, holds only in the special cases of opacity, in which there is hesitation, surmise, or conjecture involved as we read, see, and hear what others do.

But how is it possible to see what others do, the movement of an arm as a case of a person who is signalling, voting, bidding, or whatever, the marks on a printed page as sentences that lie before him, the noises he hears as the statements made by a person? For there is a difference in our experience when we do not know what to make of the strange bodily movements of another person, the strange printed marks on a page, or the sounds made by a person speaking in a foreign tongue. Here the answer, clearly, is training. It is in the course of the training we receive, in our commerce with others, that we come to see others as persons and their doings as the actions they are, whether these be utterances in the form of declarations, observations, questions, requests, commands, and so on, or the very many different sorts of things that they do in moving their bodily parts, in the games they play, or the social and moral activities they carry on with their fellows. The view that training leaves our visual or auditory experiences quite unaffected, but merely adds to our interpretative repertoire, is as dubious a bit of epistemology (and perhaps similarly motivated by an obsessive preoccupation with retinal and other sense-organ phenomena) as the view, advocated confusedly by Locke and clearly by Berkeley, that we never really come to see depth at all.

THE PROTO-EXPERIENCES OF THE INFANT

It is, however, with the effect of training upon our conduct and our thought that we are here concerned, to the end of obtaining a clear understanding of some of the main features of our moral education.

Now, training can be very many different sorts of things. Some training is designed to impart skills, and these again may be of various sorts, ranging all the way from the skill involved in swinging a golf club to the skill involved in the art of politics. Some training is designed to impart habits or patterns of thought and action, ranging all the way from the eating habits we acquire while very young to the habits of mind imparted to us during the course of our formal education. And some training consists in nothing more than exercise designed to put one in proper physical condition.

It is surely false that the ability we do have to move our limbs at will is a skill or an ability acquired through training or by any sort of self-instruction. Excepting manifestly unusual cases, for example, the rehabilitation of those who suffer temporary paralysis, there are no activities in which we engage normally, and as the result of which we succeed in moving our arms and legs. There are no interior levers that we pull or acts of will that we perform to bring about the movements of our arms or legs. No doubt some interior physiological mechanisms need to be in order if one is to be able to move one's arm at will; but there are no levers there for us to recognize and to manipulate in the knowledge that this will bring about the bodily movements we want. The supposition that this is what transpires is too absurd to warrant detailed refutation; yet it is not without some attraction, since it assimilates what is indeed obscure to us – the development in the infant of the ability to move its bodily parts – to those relatively familiar and, precisely because they are sophisticated, *for us* intelligible acquisition of skills through training and instruction. We learn as youngsters to turn the knob and then pull – thus getting the door to open. But there is nothing that parallels this in the acquisition by the infant of the ability to move his bodily parts. Training presupposes but cannot itself establish – from what could it get started? – the primitive ability of the infant to move his limbs and, only with this ability, the apprehension by him of the things in his surroundings in which in some rudimentary way he manifests the earliest forms of interest. It is maturation, not training or education, that provides the earliest forms of awareness and response.

It is difficult indeed to resist the temptation to misapply the common terms that we employ in talking about the incidents in our own lives in our effort to comprehend what takes place in the lives of the very young. The vocabulary we employ in talking about ourselves, our thoughts and our conduct, is at home in what Wittgenstein called "language-games" – the forms of life in which our utterances are part of characteristic sorts of activities in which we engage; but, in the case of the very young, language games are present only in a rudimentary form, if at all. And, in dealing with the case of the very young infant who has barely matured enough to grasp a bauble suspended above his crib, we tend to misread what transpires in his life if we employ our language with its rich conceptual schema in describing the sorts of experiences he has. There is no booming such as you and I hear, no buzzing such as you and I ever notice, and no confusion such as that in which on occasion you and I are plunged, in the booming, buzzing confusion of the very young infant's experience. And when we speak of the infant being able at will to move his arm or clench his fist, it is only in a rudimentary or truncated sense that we can ascribe will to him, and so too with terms like "interest" as well as with the whole range of epistemic terms that we apply without qualification and unproblematically to ourselves.

Students of the *Philosophical Investigations* will recall Wittgenstein's account of his builders in §2 whose whole language consists of the words "block," "pillar," "slab," "beam," which a builder A calls out so that his assistant B brings him the corresponding stones. What are we to make of this? That A *orders* B to bring him a block when he says "block"? But if "order" has a place here, so does "obey" and "disobey." But B disobeys only if he refuses to bring A a block when he hears A call out "block," even at the cost of A's displeasure, abuse, or punishment. But here all we have is this: A repeatedly has called out "block" and B has "got it" – who knows how? – so that on now hearing A call, B fetches him a block. Has he associated the word with a particular object? Surely not the word with blocks he has already fetched for these are now buried in the wall. In any case how can he be said to have associated the word "block" with this particular block, since he has never seen *it* before – it has just come into view after the stones under which it was lying were removed. So if there has been association, he must have connected "block" with *any* block, that is, he must have got the idea that "block" means a certain kind of stone. But is this what is intended by the word "corresponding" when we are told that when A says "block," B fetches the corresponding stone? This, unfortunately, is too sophisticated an importation from *our* language game into the language game of the builders that, we are told, is completely given in §2. But all we are given there is the fact it comes to pass that A says "block" and B fetches a block – how, we can only wonder. Somehow a connection is made between a word and a stone, so that A's saying "block" leads to B's fetching him a block. There is a curious quality about the whole performance of A and B, who behave as if in a trance, as if they were mere automata.

Some have found this account of the language-game in §2, for these and similar reasons, obscure and therefore objectionable. But the obscurity – the resistance to our efforts to understand – lies not in the text but in those incomplete forms of human existence and experience out of which develop the comprehension we do have and through which the details of our own experience are set forth in sharp and intelligible relief. For the point of Wittgenstein's story of the builders is that language is to be understood as part of an activity in which language is woven with our conduct and our concerns into the fabric of a certain form of life. And if we need tacitly to invoke surroundings, of which there is no mention in the story of the builders, in order to make sense of the communication that takes place during the course of their labours, this is not to impugn but rather to reinforce the point that is being made.

So it is with our understanding, which goes hand in hand with the conceptual structure embodied in our discourse: we who attempt to understand the experiences of the very young infant must bring to bear upon those experiences concepts that *we* have but which are alien to it, since it is entirely innocent of the forms of life in which, by virtue of *our* own training and education, *we* have come to share with each other. It is for this reason that these experiences resist our efforts to comprehend them – only obliquely can we give expression to what they are like, whether we use James's locution of a booming buzzing confusion, or, indulging our own fancy, think of these "experiences" as formless auguries of what has not yet fully come into being.

THE DIMENSIONS OF TRAINING

But, given the acquisition by the child of its ability to move its arms, legs, and fingers, which happens, not passively, but only as, increasingly, it becomes aware of the things about it to which, with greater and greater discrimination, it responds, the way lies open for training. But training is no mere reflex conditioning, however automatic the responses of the child may come to be as a result of it. Neither is it the repeated input of data in order somehow to fix the requisite neural circuits, however much it may be that the child comes increasingly to recall and to attend to features of its environment as neural circuits are in fact being established. The training of the child, when successful, is manifestly complex and increasingly so as it comes to be a party to the language of its elders, and as verbal instruction plays a role in guiding the child's development. But the objective is the development of an individual who, hopefully, some day will be a moral person; for the training of the child, if successful, has as its objective the development of a being who shares with his fellows and his elders certain concerns, interests, and experiences, no less than certain patterns of behaviour. The child may, like Pavlov's dog, salivate when he hears the dinner bell, but his training is designed, not to make him salivate, but to inform him of what to expect, and not thereby to give him idle information, to be stored in his cerebral memory bank, but, given the condition into which he has been brought through the training he has received, to prepare him for the event so that he may conduct himself before and during the dinner in accordance with accepted rules of good behaviour. It is as a being who is interested in food but concerned to respond to its announcement in ways that are correct and proper, that the child is put on the alert by the sound of the dinner bell. In short, in being trained the young are not being merely conditioned, nor are they being programmed. Rather, they are being developed into the sorts of persons who, however extensively they differ from and with others, share with them much of the substance of their lives including a sense of what is proper and appropriate in the manner in which they go about their affairs. Theycome to share a language and with it a way of living.

In these last remarks I have been emphasizing some of the so-called subjective factors that operate in a person's life: his concerns and interests. And I have remarked upon the way in which these are engaged in a very simple case and the ways in which they are manifested in what one does. I have, of course, emphasized only some of the so-called subjective factors – there are others too – the whole range of feelings, emotions, attitudes, expectations, and beliefs that colour our experiences, and shape our conduct. These, no less than the mere externals of performance – the bodily movements executed by an agent – are brought into play in the language games we come to master; the very many different sorts of activities in which we engage and within the context of which language operates as a vehicle of communication.

Mention was made of the simple case of a child responding to the call to dinner and behaving throughout in conformity with socially accepted rules of conduct. The force of acquired habit no less than the skills involved in the use of the knife and fork are obvious in such cases; but there is much more than this involved in the understanding of the child's performance at the table. For the child acquires not only a set of habits, but the recognition that what it does habitually and without reflection is a transaction in which it engages with its dinner companion – moving the salt cellar from, roughly, here to there (but will tossing it to him do?) is passing the salt. Here a rule of etiquette appears to define an action of a certain sort, for to be trained to conform to such a rule is to recognize what one is doing in moving the salt cellar from one position to another. But socially accepted rules of conduct also provide norms of desirable conduct. To pass the salt may of course be altogether unreflective and as much a matter of ingrained habit as the pressure of the foot applied to the brake pedal on seeing a car suddenly loom in one's path as one is driving on the road; but it may also be a considerate act, one's acknowledgment of one's companion's wish, and as such not only socially acceptable but socially desirable. To witness the consideration being shown in such a simple matter as the passing of the salt (or acceding to the special preferences of others in offering one's dinner companion a morsel that he relishes, and out of consideration for him) is to see much more than moving a salt cellar from here to there (or handing someone a platter of food), however skilfully the task may be performed. It is rather to see the action of beings who are attentive to each other's desires and who are behaving as they do in response to them. It is, in its own small and trifling way, to see actions performed under the form of humanity, as the human responses to human beings. One would quite literally fail to see what a person was doing, fail to understand what was taking place, if one did not recognize that these simple acts were invested with this kind of human import.

THE CONDITIONS OF MORAL DEVELOPMENT

I have emphasized the fact that when we acquire the ability to move our limbs, we do so in responding to the things in our immediate environment, and, increasingly as we develop, in responding to others whose interests engage our concerns. We acquire habits and skills, but, most important of all, we come to share with others, through the training and education we receive, the very character of the lives we lead, without which we would not be the human beings that we are and would not recognize and understand what it is that we and they are doing during the course of our traffic with one another. To see human actions in this way is to see them within the context of our human ways of life as the human events that they are – the actions of human beings with their concerns including the concern which they do have to conduct themselves rationally in getting what they want, reasonably in their attention to the interests of others, and responsibly in their regard for whatever moral proprieties may be in order. It is not by looking for a lowest common denominator of explanation, applying both to the reflex movement of the leg and, say, to someone's flipping of a switch, that we can elucidate the notion of a human action. Rather, we must take the opposite, nonreductive, approach and view an action against a complex and conceptually enriching background of human activities and experiences. A man may, of course, flip a switch – Why? – No reason at all. But the fact that it makes sense to ask for a reason – and a reason of a kind that, were it forthcoming would relate this act to the concerns, interests, and intentions of an agent – marks the difference between this event, freighted or not as it may be with any intention or purpose that gives it its character, and the purely reflex kick of the leg to which none of this is applicable in principle.

Our objective in this essay is to set forth some of the salient features of moral education. And here it is that the notion of rule – moral rules – will occur to some as being of the very greatest importance. For, as in the case of the example discussed in the previous section – a child learning to behave properly at the dinner table – it may seem that what is most important in the moral development of the child is that he learns to observe moral rules in mastering the language game of morality just as he must learn to observe the rules of etiquette in mastering the language game – the activities – of the dinner table.

There are, however, serious pitfalls involved in this suggestion, fostered by the contemporary preoccupation with rules, not only in the elucidation of the concept of human action, but also in the account of moral understanding and justification. The effort of some philosophers to assimilate our familiar moral maxims or precepts, for example, that one ought to keep one's promises, to the rules of etiquette or the rules of the road or to the constitutive rules of a game like that of chess, are, it seems to me, doomed to failure.

That there is such a rule of the road as that traffic is to move on the right is dictated by the need for establishing a uniform custom or practice. There is no intrinsic merit in driving on the right, but it is very useful to have everyone driving a car keep to the same side of the road. No doubt, as Hume pointed out, it is very useful for people to keep their promises, for it is very convenient to have an arrangement whereby one is able to obtain some benefit now in exchange for a future benefit with which one can quite conveniently reciprocate later on. But even Hume recognized that this is not the whole of our common-sense thinking on the subject, since he recognized that we do think somehow that there is an obligation built into a promise, which, not being able to make intelligible, he could only put down to an impossible fiction of the imagination. In short, while any rule of the road (or rule of etiquette, for that matter) may be useful, for whatever reason this may be, and can, therefore, be thinkably different from what it is – a moral maxim or precept, if the one pertaining to promises is taken as paradigmatic – would appear to be in some way a priori. It seems difficult indeed to think of a morality in which promise-keeping, truth-telling, etc., was not held at a premium, but it is easy enough to think of a society in which driving on the right or eating peas with one's fork is not favoured at all.

But if, now, in order to preserve the conceptual connection between promising and its entailed obligation, we employ the model of a constitutive rule such as a rule of a game of chess, for example, one that stipulates that the bishop move diagonally on the board, then problems of still a different sort break out. For surely the moral maxim or precept that promises are to be kept does not define or elucidate "promise" in the way in which the bishop-rule defines the bishop. Besides, this model could only succeed in drawing the connection between "promise" and "obligation" much too tightly. It is not legally possible in chess to move one's bishop straight across the board of play; but it is not only permissible but, on occasion, morally required that one break one's promise. In any case, those who regard the moral maxim as a defining rule that is also employed in justifying particular acts by subsuming them under it, confound justification with definition or conceptual elucidation. For even if one were to accept the analogy with chess, it is clear that we do not justify moving the bishop as one does during the course of play, by citing the bishop-rule – for that only tells us that one has made a legal move, not whether the move made is the wise or right one to make in the particular circumstances. If there are general statements relevant here, they are, surely, the principles of chess, which are not the constitutive rules of the game but are, rather, the rules or principles pertaining to strategy, tactics, gambits, defences, etc.

In any case, does the suggestion carry the implication that there are special skills required in mastering the language game of morality just as there are special skills acquired by one who learns to obey the rules of traffic or etiquette? And, are we to suppose that the talk about a language game of morality carries the implication that morality is just one more activity in addition to others with its own special vocabulary and brand of discourse in the way in which this is true of chess or cricket?

Consider the first point. Are we to suppose that just as we learn to handle knife and fork at the dinner table, or to drive an automobile in traffic without deliberation or reflection about every move we make with pedals, steering wheel, etc., so we learn to tell the truth, keep our promises, etc.? Is doing the latter sorts of things a new kind of habit we learn; and just as we know quite well what it is to hold one's fork in one's left hand, one's knife in one's right, but until we have acquired the requisite skill, are unable to do so with dispatch, so we know what it is to tell the truth, promise, show consideration to one's parents, but lack the skills with which to bring off these tasks until we have practised doing so? So that just as some children are good at handling their knives, forks, and spoons, so some catch on quickly and are good at morality, and others never quite get the hang of it and are never good at it at all, either because the thing is beyond their ability or because they lacked the requisite practice? Surely this is absurd. One may be good at chess, good at driving a car, or good at handling a knife and fork; but "good at morals" sounds queer, to say the least. We are not drilled in morals as we are in executing a manual-at-arms or in being put through our paces by our driving instructor. Nor are there special dexterities or skills that we need to develop in order to acquire the art of morals in the way in which this is necessary for the driver in traffic or the player during a game of chess. So to think of the moral properties is to think of them either as the done things or the things done in a certain artful or skilful way; but why the done things should be done at all, or done in whatever way they are done is, if we take this line seriously, a mystery. And it will not do at all to argue for some efficiency, orderliness, predictability, or utility which these ways of doing things make possible. for what has this got to do with the obligatoriness of what is done?

As for the second point, it is surely a grave error to suggest that morality is just one more practice and, like any other that has its own vocabulary and its own rules, that it is one into which, since it pleases us to do so, we initiate the young at a certain stage of their development (in the way in which in some societies the young are initiated into the mysteries of adulthood), and from which, should it please them, they can withdraw into their former nonmoral condition. Morality is not a game from which one can withdraw as one can from a game of chess, just as it is not the superficial and external matter of "behaving oneself" either in order to conform to socially accepted practices or in order to obtain certain desired efficiencies or utilities. It is not a new skill, a new practice, a new departure; it is, rather, continuous with and a deepening of the child's understanding of matters of human fact which it begins to acquire as soon as it is able to deal with its fellows and, in its dealings with them, whether in play or in any other kind of activity, to recognize them as human beings and to deal with them accordingly.

There is not, then, first a nonmoral stage of comprehension and later, because of new activities and a new form of discourse to which the child is introduced, the beginnings of its moral education. To the extent to which the child takes account of his fellows in his dealings with them and learns how to respond to them as the human beings they are, in whatever form of activity in which he is engaged with them, to that extent he has already the opportunity to undertake its moral development. For here the recognition can and, normally, does begin that it is persons with whom he interacts, beings whose hurts and happiness affect him whose affection and regard are his concern, and with whom he must deal fairly and, if at all possible, openly, without guile or dissimulation. What I am saying is that the child, as soon as he begins to master any language game in which he interacts with others, begins to take his first moral steps, however faltering these may be.

THE UNDERSTANDING OF MORAL PRECEPTS

But how could one fail to recognize others as persons except by failing to distinguish between persons and nonpersons? And how can one fail to respond to them as the persons they are except by being impossibly imperceptive; perhaps by confounding people with posts, or something absurd like that? Alternatively, if recognizing and responding to them as the human beings they are does as such involve us in moral dealings with them, are there not norms exhibited in these relations that we have with them? And, if so, is it not possible to say what these norms are by means of general principles we can impart to the young during the course of the moral instruction we give them, in order to guide them in the way in which they are to think about and interact with others?

No doubt, during the course of the instruction we give the young, we employ moral precepts in guiding, advising, and training them. Forcefully, and in one way or another, we impress upon them the importance of telling the truth, obeying their parents, sharing their things with others, and so on. And we initiate them at an early age, into the practice of promising, impressing upon them the great importance that we attach to their keeping the faith that others repose in them. And part of the training surely consists in establishing firm habits and attitudes, getting them by means of various persuasive devices to share with us a sense of the importance of being for the sorts of things of which we approve and against the sorts of things we consider objectionable. But we shall not have achieved our objectives if our prohibitions and admonitions have only this consequence, that we succeed only in conditioning and habituating the young, not in providing them with the resources they need in order for them to exercise their own judgment in determining how best they are to conduct themselves. Nor will it do, in order to assist our efforts, to construe moral precepts, the importance of which we are concerned to convey to the young, as airtight directives, to be followed, whenever they are applicable, as unhesitatingly, as unreflectively, and as blindly as are military orders by well-drilled soldiers. "An order is an order" may make good military sense, but "a promise is a promise," if its import is, correspondingly, that one is never justified in refusing to keep a promise, is morally disastrous. It is bad moral pedagogy to begin the moral instruction of the young by dwelling upon what it cannot yet understand, in this case that the fact that a promise has been made may not be decisive in determining what one ought to do, for that strategy might convey the quite erroneous idea that our moral precepts merely tell us what, generally, or in most cases, we ought to do. What we seek to obtain is the recognition that comes with some measure of moral maturity that "a promise is a promise" has a good use: that whether or not the fact that one has promised is decisive in determining what one ought to do, given that one has the ability and opportunity to keep it, that fact is nevertheless, and necessarily so, a relevant consideration, a reason that one may not brush aside. The fact that an action is a case of the keeping of a promise is, as such, a good reason for performing it. And so with the various sorts of doings that are the subjects of our moral precepts: truth-telling, honouring one's parents, and so on. There are indeed norms of good conduct, for there are moral precepts or general principles of good behaviour by which one is in fact guided in one's conduct; and these we need to impart to the young. But what also needs to be imparted is some sense of how these are to be employed. And what must be avoided is the Kantian aberration that they are universal imperatives – as if it even made sense to speak of commanding reason or conscience or to say that, merely by obeying a command, a person was achieving moral responsibility.

How then are such precepts or norms of conduct employed? Here what is relevant is the fact that in behaving as one does in some activity in which one is engaged with one's fellows, a person is not merely moving this or that limb in such-and-such a manner, but, depending upon what is involved in the language game in which one is involved, doing X, Y, or Z. In playing a game of chess, a person is not merely pushing an object of such-and-such a shape from this square to that one, but is moving his bishop, defending his queen, preparing to castle, gaining command of the centre of the board, or checking his opponent's king, etc. Here not only the constitutive rules of the game, but the player's intentions, tactics, strategy, are relevant to the determination of what it is that the player is doing. And if, for example, in moving his bishop as he did he captured a pawn but with consequences that were shortly to be fatal, because he abandoned the command he had enjoyed of the centre of the board, he would have violated an important principle of chess. To learn to play this game is to learn that one ought to command the centre of the board; but it would be obtuse indeed to suppose that one ought to command the centre of the board *no matter what*. To be reminded that one ought to command the centre of the board, as one is prepared to relinquish it in capturing a pawn, is to be given a reason, which only a person who has learned to play the game can recognize as a reason, for not capturing the pawn. And, in that situation, it is in fact to see more clearly what in fact one was prepared to do. So it is in our ordinary affairs with each other. We are interested, normally, not in the bodily movements we execute when we transact our business with each other, but in the transactions of whatever sorts they may be, in which we engage with each other in the home, office, classroom, factory, store, garden, and so on. In our conversations with each other we not only make sounds and in so doing utter sentences, but we voice our fears, hopes, intentions, and expectations, as we make ourselves known to each other; we warn, guide, and assist each other as we work together; we instruct youngsters in the classroom; we ask for information; we request favours, give promises, enter contracts, bargain with customers or tradesmen, etc., etc., etc. There are *countless* things that we do, by virtue of our upbringing, in uttering words and in moving our limbs. But not all cases of things that we do are manifestly transactions in which we engage with each other. My nose itches, and I rub it – in the solitude of my study. Or, I feel like taking a walk; so I put on my hat and coat; and leave the house for a stroll around the block. I do these things, and they concern no one else – usually. And when I fancy the tie I see displayed in the window of the store and I go in to buy it, that concerns no one except myself and the storekeeper – usually. But, like the chess player who may not be mindful of what he is doing in capturing a pawn, we are not always perspicuous about what it is that we are doing. And, like the bishop in the story, who tells the company he has just joined – after one of them has announced proudly to the others that he was the first man to give his confession to the priest who was to become their bishop – that the first man to give him his confession was a murderer, we are not always aware of the circumstances of our actions which bear upon their consequences. In this story we would not say that the bishop *told* his listeners who the murderer was, for he did not identify him at all. Rather, this was done by his listeners who made the inference, given the two bits of information imparted to them. Perhaps, were the story suitably filled out, we might even say that the bishop could not have been expected to know what had been said before he joined the company, since he had no reason to believe that the confessor was still alive and in that company. There are cases in which wholly unexpected and unforeseeable events make a difference to what our actions bring to pass, the ways in which they affect others. But there are other cases in which there is genuine thoughtlessness, and a lack of proper perspicuity about what it is that we are doing, and where, given the foreseeable consequences of what a man does, we surely do not hesitate to describe the action more fully and in a way that involves an explicit reference to consequences. Thus, in purchasing a neck-tie, a man may well spend his last dollar, and in doing that, make it impossible for him to feed his hungry children. And a man in writing his name on a rectangular piece of paper may be signing a check and, in doing that, be overdrawing his account, thus incurring a debt he cannot discharge. Or, a man seeking to please others or to obtain a position of employment he greatly desires may not merely utter what he knows is not the case, but misrepresent himself to others (i.e., lie) and attempt to conceal it even from himself by telling himself that he was only trying to please others, or only trying to get a job. Here, of course, the fuller description of what the person does may involve no reference to consequences. Or, to take one last implausible example, a man may rub his nose in the privacy of his study and this normally is a matter between himself and his nose, but if he is the subject of a medical experiment and has agreed not to touch his nose for a specified period of time except on pain of disqualifying himself as a proper subject, he might through sheer thoughtlessness or even the temptation induced by an itch, give in, rub his nose and in doing so break his promise. It is in these sorts of cases, endlessly varied, and paralleling the chess example, that we are perhaps thoughtless, perhaps wilful, and perhaps unperspicuous, perhaps weak willed, and then often defensive about what it is that we are doing.

In such many and varied cases what function or functions are served by the reference to moral precepts? Surely, as in the case of our chess example, one of the functions of an appeal to a moral precept or principle is to remind the person to whom it is addressed of what it is that he is doing in order to enable him to gain a more perspicuous view of what in fact he is doing. A person craving something may be trying to get what he craves, and in that state shut off from his view the implications of the way in which he undertakes to get what he wants, by lying, false promising, or whatever. And for the young, especially, it is all the more difficult to surmount the temptation to adopt a tunnel-vision view of what they are doing in their craving for the things that excite and interest them. Moral education, in no small measure, consists in getting the child to acquire the habit of viewing his own actions not merely in the light of his own desires and impulses – momentary or not – as the actions of getting what he craves, desires, and enjoys, but as the more fully described actions that they are, given the context of his relations with other human beings. To see such actions as inconsiderate actions, actions involving deception, lying, the breaking of promises, failure to heed one's parents, etc., is to adopt a more perspicuous view of what one is doing. "One ought to tell the truth" addressed to someone who has said nothing invites the retort "So what?" From someone who lies in order to get what he wants such a reply normally would be made only if he wilfully refuses to face up to what he is doing and, thereby, refuses to see what he is doing in the common light of our moral concerns with each other.

But thus to see what one is doing in the case just cited is, at the same time, to see good reason for *not* doing what one has done. The moral precept is stated positively, but the corresponding prohibition, not to lie, is in the offing. For "one ought not to lie," properly understood, is not the universal negative imperative "never under any circumstances tell a lie," but a precept that specifies a reason that, in the vast majority of cases to which it is relevant, is decisive in establishing in those cases that the action in question is impermissible. It would be a mistake to suppose that what it *states* is that the vast majority of cases of lying are impermissible. One might well know this but not know how to establish that a given case is one of this majority. If moral precepts simply provided that information, they would not seem to inform us of the reasons that operate in any of our deliberations about what it is that one should do or refrain from doing, and in the cases of so-called conflicts of duties they would leave us in a hopeless state of indecision.

But how do the considerations specified by our moral precepts function as reasons? If we explore this question, we shall at the same time see reason for dismissing as frivolous indeed the first of the objections posed at the beginning of this section.

THE RECOGNITION OF OTHERS AS PERSONS

Whatever the neurophysiological mechanisms may be and however they may be involved, a child comes to recognize human beings as human beings. He comes to be concerned not only with the things that interest him and with getting the things he wants, but, as he develops and learns to engage with others in various sorts of activities, he comes normally to take account of their interests and desires as a matter of concern to him. In learning that others are human beings, he acquires not merely (if at all when any clarity first emerges in his awareness of others) information about others, but how, in the context of the activities in which he deals with them, to take account of them. A playmate, or a mother, is not a curiously shaped, noise-emitting material object that changes its place and changes the relative positions of its bodily parts; it is rather a being with whom he plays and to whose cries of pain and gurgles of satisfaction and pleasure he responds spontaneously with sympathetic cries and gurgles of his own. The child takes account of things as things to be dealt with in some way, a bauble as something to put in his mouth, a playmate as somebody to play with and to respond to in his own limited way, and his mother as a being from whom he derives his creature comforts, to whom he may look for the things he wants, and with whom he can play in security and comfort. But as he grows and develops and learns increasingly sophisticated forms of language games with others, he acquires new ways of living with others. He recognizes in more sophisticated ways the sorts of beings with which he communicates and interacts. He acquires, in the process of his development and instruction in the various activities in which he engages – talking, writing, dressing, eating at table, playing rule-governed games, etc. – a whole complex pattern of life, with all of the various interests and desires that figure in these many different kinds of activities. With all of this, a child learns as he is trained, admonished, cajoled, instructed to treat human beings as beings who, like him have interests and desires of their own and whose own interests and desires are matters to which he is not indifferent. Without this enduring way in which he is concerned with others, the admonitions he receives that he is to deal with them in ways that are considerate and concerned, that he is to share his goods with others, that he is to speak openly and truthfully, without guile or pretence, that he is to show particular regard for those with whom his life is most intimately involved, would appear as wholly alien in inception and of no matter to him except insofar as they pose possible frustrations to him. Given this enduring way in which the child is concerned with others, he can be brought to recognize that what he is doing, when thoughtlessly or wilfully he goes after what he wants, is in his particular way what he, as the kind of human being he is, is to abstain from doing. To say that he is to do this, or that he is to avoid doing that, is to say that which he, with the enduring concerns he has, can recognize as the way in which, as such a being, he would wish to act. In short, the normative character of our regard for and our talk about each other and ourselves has this as its logical substratum – the concerns that we have with and for each other within the common ways in which we live with and are able to deal with each other. Given this, it is hardly necessary to explain why it is that we prize truth-telling, considerateness, etc.; why it is that the moral precepts we address to children present them with reasons for various sorts of doings and abstentions. And it must surely seem frivolous, given this way in which we recognise and deal with each other, to object on the ground that only an impossibly imperceptive person would fail to distinguish or discriminate between persons and nonpersons. For so to recognize others as human beings is not merely to classify them out of curiosity or for some theoretical purpose; it is, rather, to see them in the light of that normative status we have, which derives from our common forms of life within which we share concerns with each other. Without this substratum in which you and I participate, you and I could not understand each other or any normative talk in which either of us might engage about what it is that you or I or anyone else ought to do.

What I have been saying can be expressed in terms of the language of rights. To learn as we do to recognize persons as the human beings they are is to recognize their moral status with respect to us, as beings endowed with the rights that they have simply as human beings. And this is to imply that the term "person" is in fact a normative term or, as Locke once put it, "a forensic term" that we apply to beings who are "concerned and accountable" (*Essay,* Bk II, XXVII, 26).

MORAL PRECEPTS AND THE MORAL CONCERN

Normally one does not deliberate about what it is that one ought to do: whether or not to tell the truth or to keep one's promises. And when, for one reason or another, one fails to do the right thing, the remedy is usually clear enough, however reluctant the agent may be to adopt it. But there are cases where citing a moral precept is not enough to remind the person of what it is that he is doing and to give him a good reason for altering his conduct, for the situation in which one finds oneself turns out, on occasion, to be unexpectedly complicated: one can meet one responsibility only by failing to meet another. More than one precept applies to one's situation, and we can no longer be guided simply by them since they support different and incompatible courses of action. What does one do when faced with such choices? Are there not higher moral principles in the light of which the validity of our common moral principles must now appear to be problematic? And if there are such higher moral principles for the resolution of such conflicts, should we not disclose them to the young, in order to complete the moral instruction we give them?

Inevitably these questions must arise in any discussion of moral education. The search for higher moral principles is as old as moral philosophy itself. And the problems it poses are much too complex to be discussed in any detail within the compass of a single essay, which is already long enough. Any comments that can, therefore, be made here may well appear to be dogmatic. However, they are not unrelated to, but are in fact suggested by, the previous account of moral action.

I have been at pains to emphasize that it is within the context of our everyday lives, in which we carry on our affairs with each other and share one another's concerns, that morality is the intelligible enterprise that it is. Without such common forms of life in which each of us achieves his normative status as a person whether this be human being, mother, father, son, or daughter – we could not understand each other as persons, we could not understand our doings as moral actions, or our utterances as the moral utterances they sometimes are. Whatever sense can be found in our efforts to appraise the force and relevance of our common moral precepts, can only be the sense that is to be found in such lives, as lived by such beings. Here we must follow the advice of Wittgenstein, to turn back to the language games in which moral discourse operates, rather then that of Plato, to engage in a hunt for metaphysical snarks, which terminates in an appeal to an intuition completely cut off from the lives we live; but it is only within these lives that anything can be intuited or make any normative sense of any sort.

It is as moral agents that we are able to recognize moral reasons as the reasons they are. And it is as such agents that we are called upon to weigh reasons presented by competing moral precepts. But suppose that one were unable to compare the force of such reasons, not merely in a single hard case but, generally, whenever one had to contend with reasons presented by competing precepts. In that case such precepts would present themselves in the guise of airtight directives and, instead of functioning as a responsible agent, one would be merely submitting to or following precepts as one would the edict of one's superior in a military organization. No doubt children often so regard moral precepts or principles; but to the extent to which they do, moral instruction is nothing more than indoctrination. And the consequence of this unthinking obedience is not a responsibility achieved by the agent but helplessness when faced by conflicts of duty. But moral precepts and the reasons they provide an agent, whenever they apply to his situation, are addressed to agents who are concerned and accountable, concerned to maintain moral relations of mutual trust and respect with others as they go about their affairs with one another, and accountable – subject to measures of praise and blame, and even to punishment – for actions that impair or destroy these relations of mutual trust and respect. If, then, we are to be guided in our conduct by a good moral reason, it cannot be in such a way that we succeed thereby only in destroying the bonds that unite us as members of a moral community. It is this overriding concern with the preservation and even establishment of such a moral community with those affected by our conduct that provides the overriding condition to be satisfied by a responsible moral agent.

There is then no difficulty in recognizing why it is that one may be required to break one's promise, for a promise is a solicitation of trust; it binds the promiser precisely because of this underlying mutual trust that exists between promiser and promisee, without which the promise utterance could not be used to promise. Hence it is that an immoral promise – a promise to do what is morally objectionable – is self-defeating; it functions as a promise only because of the presumed common moral concern of the parties involved, at the same time that it is designed to defeat that very concern. And, in a different but no less self-defeating way, the keeping of a promise that involves recognizably the doing of what is wrong – keeping a promise to return a book with the full knowledge that this involves failing to save the life of one's critically injured child – is, in Butler's phrase, "a breaking in" upon that moral nature of ours that provides the very basis of the promise itself. It is one's status as the morally concerned person one is, no less than the obligation that one has to care for one's child, that requires that one break one's promise and, if need be, to reconcile the promisee, not by an apology but by an explanation.

But this holds equally well in other cases too. We owe it to others to tell them the truth and they, trusting us, fully expect it from us. Without this, how can we learn to communicate and how can we, unless we are open and frank with each other, successfully conduct ourselves with each other out of concern for each other's interests? So, too, with what we owe our parents and with what they have every right to expect from us. But it is only as concerned and accountable persons that we are, when we are, required to tell the truth; and it is as such beings that we are, when we are, required to withold it. We do not, in short, merely compare precepts in the abstract, attempting to discover some hidden order of relative stringency, as we can do easily when we are faced with the conflicting commands of our sergeant and our lieutenant. Our precepts do not present us with a heap of independent, unrelated obligations or reasons. Each of them provides a reason for a moral agent, and we measure or weigh them, in the specific situations to which they apply, in the light of our continued concern to maintain moral relations with others. There is no fixed order of relative stringency of precepts, in the way in which, no matter what, it is fixed that the orders of the lieutenant take precedence over those of the sergeant. What is fixed is this overriding moral status and concern of the agent; and this is why, given varying circumstances, truth-telling may or may not be preferable to promise keeping, depending upon the specific nature of these circumstances. For this determination, not a formula but only good judgment will do, and it is this that we hope to achieve in the moral education and training of the young.

But in morals, alas, it is not always easy to come to an agreement between agents about what should or should not be done, given the competition of reasons. In most cases there is no dispute and there is no deliberation: Why shouldn't one fail to keep an appointment with a student, who wishes merely to chat, in order to save the life of one's stricken child by rushing her to the hospital? But there are cases where the choice is not that simply made and where, despite differences, mutual respect is maintained. This too needs to be learned: morality is not like mathematics where the dispute over the correctness of a proof in Euclidean geometry is itself proof that at least one of the disputants is incompetent. And there is at least one more lesson, and a very difficult one, that one needs to learn: not all of our choices are merely choices between this or that act; they may be the choice between the sorts of life we shall live and they will require, therefore, that we live with the choices we make. Whether it be to pull up stakes in one city in which one has lived for many years, leaving old friends and old responsibilities that have coloured and moulded one's life, in order to begin elsewhere, and, in so doing, radically alter the lives of one's spouse and one's children; or whether it be, as in Sartre's example, to leave one's aged mother to her own uncertain fate in order to take up arms in defence of one's country, the question of whether one has done the right thing goes far beyond any single performance, but relates to the whole character of the life that, in effect at least, one has chosen for oneself and decided for others. These are extreme cases and their extremity may well involve the impossibility of deciding whether choices and decisions so made are unmistakably right rather then wrong. Perhaps all we can demand of those who must face up to them is that they recognize full well the full import of their undertaking. To be able to do this is a considerable achievement in moral understanding and a mark of the kind of moral maturity we strive to make possible for our children.

CHAPTER 4

Moral action and moral education

DAVID P. GAUTHIER

THIS PAPER is divided into two principal sections. The first provides the negative moment of my argument. It suggests that the human child appears as an *agent* and as a social being interacting with his fellows, before he develops either his conceptual capacity or his moral capacity. It suggests further that these two capacities are also independent of each other, so that the child's moral development may begin without the use of language, and may fail to occur even though the child learns to interact with his fellows verbally as well as nonverbally.

The positive moment of my argument, in the second part of this paper, is a sketch of moral development, resting on the account of human action, interaction, and conceptual development presented in the first part. This sketch provides the basis for an accompanying outline of the principal characteristics of moral training and moral education. It will be shown that moral education involves training in ways of interacting with one's fellows, and in reflecting on this interaction. Both the capacity for interaction and the capacity for reflection are presupposed; the aim of moral education is to help direct their exercise.

I

A small baby, lying on his back in his cradle, smiles at his mother. Human babies, like other animals both infant and adult, are agents. Their repertoire of actions is, of course, limited in comparison with that of adult human beings, or even adult dogs. But babies, like adult human beings and unlike adult dogs, smile. No doubt the fond parent may take facial contortions caused by wind to be premature smiles. But the practised parent learns to distinguish the effects of wind from the effects of will.

"The effects of will" is a metaphor. But it is the appropriate metaphor; the infant can smile at will, which is to say that he can smile when he wants to smile. He cannot adopt a policy with respect to smiling. He cannot smile on principle, or on command, or on demand. He cannot smile to dissimulate – a baby is not one who can smile and smile and be a villain. But to say all this is to say only that an infant cannot perform many actions which adult human beings can perform, and which can be related to smiling in various and important ways. Most emphatically it is not to say that babies cannot smile, and smile in just the way that you and I do. Within his limited repertoire, the infant is every bit as much an agent as you or I.

If you do not understand French, you cannot smile at amusing French stories. But this does not mean that you cannot or do not smile in just the way a Frenchman does.

An infant smiles, but does he know that he smiles? A baby cannot perform speech acts; he cannot say that he is smiling. Nor can a baby perform acts of reflection; he cannot think that he is smiling. On these grounds we may want to argue that a baby cannot know that he is smiling. But it is essential to distinguish the knowledge that one is acting in a certain way from the knowledge of what one is doing. Knowing *that* is conceptual, theoretical knowledge; knowing *what* one is doing is practical knowledge.

A slightly older baby, crawling determinedly across the floor after his ball, knows what he is doing. A dog, who barks at the door to be let out, and then runs directly to the garden and digs up its bone, knows what it is doing. Practical knowledge of this kind is not restricted to human beings. But in human beings it is a necessary condition of the theoretical knowledge that one is acting in a certain way. The human adult is able to exercise his linguistic capacities to say what he is doing only because he already knows, without benefit of language, what he is about.*

There is a philosophic temptation to confuse action with knowledge of action, and to confuse practical knowledge with theoretical knowledge. Those who fall into this temptation are led to suppose that only an animal capable of conceptualizing, of saying what it is doing, and reflecting on what it is doing, is really capable of acting. And so the doings of dogs and infants are seen as pale shadows of adult human behaviour, lacking the conceptual nourishment which would make them full-blooded actions.

*My remarks here are suggested by a somewhat different distinction between practical and theoretical knowledge drawn by D.S. Shwayder *The Stratification of Behaviour* London 1965, especially pp. 71 ff.

Let us now return to our baby, smiling at his mother. The baby does not just smile, nor does he smile at any object that may happen to catch his attention. He smiles at his mother. In smiling at his mother he shows that he recognizes her as something quite different from the other objects in his environment.

It is usual for a smile to be the infant's first exercise in interaction with his fellows. And of course the smile occurs long before his first exercise in linguistic interaction, which is frequently saying "Mama" or "Papa." Indeed, by the time at which this linguistic interaction begins, the baby has passed through stages essential to his development as a human and social being. Deprived of simple human relationships in these early months, he will fail to develop normally. Before he can speak, he must acquire – or forever lack – some of his basic responses to fellow human beings.

A baby learns first to recognize and respond to his mother. Later he learns to talk to his mother. Later still, the child, no longer a baby, learns to talk about his mother. At this third stage the child is aware of himself as engaged in human interaction. He is not only an agent, but a conscious agent. But even at this stage of his development, his moral capacities may not – and probably will not – have manifested themselves.

The young child requires the affection and sympathy of other human beings. He invites them to share his moods and demands that they attend to his needs. But he may show no sign of recognizing in these fellow human beings independent centres of wants and needs that demand his attention, requiring him to modify his pursuit of his own satisfaction. Rather, he wants what he wants, and if his immediate gratification is refused, he shows anger or bursts into tears. The inconvenience which the gratification of his wants would cause to others moves him not at all.

Human interaction provides the raw material for the development of our moral awareness. But our recognition of others as human beings precedes and does not require our moral recognition of their wants, needs, desires, and aims as providing us with grounds of action. Our recognition of others as human may be only to demand of them and to respond to them in distinctively human ways. No doubt there is something lacking in the person who does not come to consider the demands of others on him as parallel to his own demands on them, and who does not take this reciprocity of claim as the ground of a moral relationship. But what this person lacks is not the capacity for human interaction, or the capacity for reflection on that interaction.

Few children show moral awareness without giving it verbal expression. Indeed, the child typically learns to verbalize in a moralistic way before he displays in his actions that conscious concern for others which, in my view, lies at the core of morality. Nevertheless, we may see the beginnings of moral behaviour in the child's spontaneous desire to please his fellows, and in his sympathetic responses to the joys and sorrows of others. And these need not be associated in the child's speech or thought with conceptions of a clearly moral character. Thus the moral growth of the child, in its earliest stages, neither requires nor is required by the child's conscious understanding of himself as a human person among other human persons.

I have argued that there are three clearly distinguishable aspects of conscious moral behaviour. The first is action itself, which requires only practical knowledge or practical awareness of what one is doing and of those with whom one is interacting. The second is conceptualization, which provides theoretical knowledge about what one is doing and about those with whom one is interacting. The third is moral awareness, which involves an appreciation of what one is doing and a responsiveness to those with whom one is interacting in terms of their aims and their claims. Our question now is to consider how this third aspect develops, and how it may be elicited by moral education.

II

The first stage in moral development is the acquisition of certain dispositions to action. These dispositions are traditionally known as virtues and vices; together, they comprise our moral character. The virtuous man is disposed to act in ways that on reflection secure moral approbation; the vicious man is disposed to act in ways that on reflection secure moral condemnation. But the dispositions themselves are quite independent of this reflection; they are acquired by the child before he is able to recognize their moral significance. Thus, a child learns to behave courageously, if he learns this at all, before he becomes reflectively aware of the moral value of courage. He learns fairness in his dealings with others, if he does, before he becomes reflectively aware of the moral significance of fairness. Let me emphasize that this is only the first stage in moral development – first, both temporally and logically. The virtuous man is not the fully moral man. But virtue is the condition of morality; the human being who is not disposed to virtuous behaviour may come to gain a reflective understanding of morality, but his own moral behaviour will be at best forced and artificial, rather than natural.

Contemporary moral philosophers, following Kant, have often

considered morality as practical rationality. The morally praiseworthy man is the man who acts on the best of reasons. The problem for the moral philosopher is to determine what these reasons are. And so it is natural to suppose that the problem for the moral educator is to teach people these reasons. But this last step in the argument is an oversimplified and partial truth. Human beings form many of their dispositions to act before they come to appreciate reasons for acting. And so one major task of the moral educator is to train people to act in those ways that will receive their reflective approbation, when they come to consider their actions in the light of the best reasons for acting.

There is nothing distinctive in the training used to develop moral dispositions to action in the young child. The principal techniques – exemplification of the desired behaviour by the adult and imitation by the young, praise and reward for success, admonition for failure or inattention – are employed not only in developing other human dispositions that lack moral significance, but also in developing the dispositions of other mammals. Consider a mother tiger training her young to hunt.

Of course human beings employ language, where no other animals do not. And special language may be used when adults consider that their training has moral significance. The response of an adult to the child's moral incapacity may differ from his responses to the child's other incapacities. And this difference may then alert the child to something about the acquisition of moral virtues which distinguishes them from the other talents and abilities he develops. Yet there is no clear, sharp line of demarcation. The child may acquire what we consider morally significant reactions, such as guilt and shame, more in connection with soiling his pants than with timid retreat from threatening situations. Yet courage is, and bowel and bladder control are not, considered moral capacities.

As with other dispositions, some children are more easily trained than others in the moral virtues. Some get the hang of courage, or fairness, or for that matter truth-telling and promise-keeping, more easily and naturally than others. Yet we do not readily admit that some children are better at morals than others. This is, I suggest, a matter of policy on our part. We wish to convey the impression that morals is something which everyone (or almost everyone) can do successfully, so that those who muff it have only themselves to blame. And as policy this may be entirely sensible, for if it is really important that people learn something, it is best to allow them the fewest possible excuses for failure to learn it. Nevertheless, our policy here does tend to blind us to the perfectly evident fact that children differ in their capacities to acquire the moral virtues.

The primary problem which confronts us in moral training is to determine just what dispositions will in fact receive reflective moral approbation. In a relatively static, unchanging world, it may be relatively easy to determine which traits of character are morally useful, and deserve the name of virtue. But in our world the problem may be appallingly difficult.

Let me first illustrate the problem with a nonmoral example. Prudential training, like moral training, consists in developing the dispositions of the young, and the prudential virtues are those that on reflection secure prudential approbation, as determining actions which do in fact satisfy the over-all interests of the agent.

At one time thrift was clearly a prudential virtue. The thrifty man possessed an invaluable asset in maintaining his interests in an economically insecure environment. But, in modern Canadian or American society, it is by no means evident that thrift is prudent. The thrifty man may indeed deprive himself by his thrift, for his savings may be depleted by inflation, and he may in the long run enjoy both less of this world's goods, and less peace of mind as he contemplates his dwindling resources, than his spendthrift brother.

Now consider moral dispositions. Is courage still a virtue? Or does it lead only to needless risk of life, in a world endangered at every level by excessive violence? Is loyalty a virtue? Or does it only reinforce particular attachments, in a world in which survival requires that concern for all mankind must replace devotion to a race, a class, a country, a faith, a corporation, or a university?

The question we must pose to the moral educator then is: what dispositions should we cultivate, so that our children will have those characteristics which they will later learn to recognize as morally valuable? In our world this question has no easy answer.

At the second stage in moral development, the agent formulates a *policy* of action. At this stage conceptualization, and so verbalization, are required.

An animal can act to satisfy its own wants and desires without being able to reflect about those wants and desires. What it cannot do without the capacity to speak and to think about what it does is to adopt the prudential policy of maximizing its own satisfaction. Similarly, an animal can respond to the wants and desires of other animals, and act to satisfy them, without reflection. Awareness of what another wants, just as awareness of what one wants oneself, is essentially practical, and not conceptual or theoretical. But an animal cannot, without the capacity to speak and to think about what it does, adopt the moral policy of maximizing the well-being of all.

We might say that to adopt a correct moral policy is to attain practical wisdom. In this way we should suggest the Aristotelian distinction between moral virtue and practical wisdom, but we should draw the distinction somewhat differently. For Aristotle, moral virtue is related to character, and to dispositions to act, and in this we have agreed with him. But, for Aristotle, practical wisdom concerns the choice of the right means to the right end, whereas, in our argument, practical wisdom, or goodness of policy, is a reflective awareness of the proper ends of moral behaviour.

This awareness is distinct from our responsiveness to persons as persons, although it develops from this responsiveness. It is not only the psychopath who fails to acquire practical wisdom. The non-psychopathic egoist, who takes the maximization of personal satisfaction to be the final guide to policy, the religious devotee who takes obedience to God to be the ultimate requirement, the man who sets some ideal or some cause as the final arbiter of what he should do – all these fail to show true awareness of other persons as genuine objects of concern, and so fail to achieve practical wisdom.

Now of course egoism, or religion, or idealism – each taken in moderation – may be compatible with practical wisdom. Concern for oneself, or for a God, or for a cause, does not rule out concern for other human beings. But we are all too familiar with those in whom concern for self or deity or ideal does obliterate awareness of the wants and needs of individual persons. Such men may be eminently virtuous, but their virtue is directed towards the wrong goal.

Moral development requires that persons develop a policy based on reflective awareness of their goals, and true moral development requires that this policy be based on treating others as objects of concern. Reflective awareness is not distinctively moral, but it is distinctively human, and rests on those rational processes which require language for their expression. Only a language-user can understand why his actions are morally right – or morally wrong.

How does the moral educator instruct the child in the formation of a moral policy? Reflective awareness itself is not something which is taught. The educator may make use of it, but he does not instil it. And policy is not taught directly as a set of rules or precepts. To teach a policy is to teach the way of *valuing* on which it depends. To suppose that one ought to display concern for others is to suppose that what has real value has value as being satisfying to some person. To suppose on the other hand that one ought to obey God is to suppose that what has real value has value as conforming with the divine will.

A way of valuing is not a subject fit for formal instruction. We learn to value by being in a community of valuers, and we learn to value first of all as they value, and secondarily by reflection on how we and they value, in the light of other aspects of our experience. These other aspects of experience demand and deserve further attention, for they concern the third stage of moral development. At this stage education, as distinguished from training, is of primary importance.

This third stage presupposes both moral virtue and practical wisdom. What it requires is that we learn to bring our moral sensitivity to bear on all those areas affected by our activities. The difficulty in doing so is that many of these areas are remote from our actual experience. If my activity is producing, or helping to produce, napalm, then unfortunately it may easily happen that I shall be unaware of the effects of the use of napalm. Too often, the napalm, my awareness, and my feeling of responsibility, pass from my hands (or my factory) together.

This suggests a point of some significance for moral educators. It is sometimes supposed that if moral instruction is to be given a suitably scientific base, it is necessary to inquire into the causes or explanations of human action. But in fact very little gain can be expected from such an inquiry. Our common-sense explanations of our actions are sufficient for our common-sense educational procedures, and it seems to me that at this time we cannot expect more. However, everything depends on the effects of human action, on what human actions explain, for in this area our information is sufficient to provide us with an awareness and an understanding far exceeding that which we actually employ in educating people about what to do. The moral educator should therefore focus his attention, not on the causes of human actions, but on what human actions cause.

Moral education, as opposed to training in the right habits and in a way of valuing, must be education in the consequences of what we have done, are doing, and can do. And much of the emphasis must be on "we" rather than "I" – must be on the effects of social policies, which become independent of our individual intentions and aims.

The condition of the black man in America or the red man in Canada is not primarily the effect of deliberate racism, although it is easy enough for racists to have their way. Rather, these conditions result from social policies which have not brought the resources of society effectively to bear on the transformation of the material and social environment which now makes the black man and the red man the actual social inferiors of the white man – which makes racist falsehoods into social truths. And these social policies are not so much the policies of racists as the policies of the indifferent, of those whose moral sensitivity has not been directed to the real consequences of what they do.

Moral education is – paradoxically but obviously – not moral at all in one sense. It is not an inculcation of moral precepts or a teaching of moral attitudes. This Sunday-school approach produces Sunday-school results: children who mouth the appropriate platitudes on demand but who go about their weekday affairs without a moment's concern for the implications of their actions. Moral education involves simply showing people what they are really doing. And it is aimed, not at those who lack practical wisdom or moral virtue, but at those who, possessing these characteristics, nevertheless fail to do as they ought because "they do not know what they do."

Moral education is not preaching; it is muckraking. It concerns neither the conclusion nor the major premiss of the practical syllogism, but the minor premiss – "This is dry food" (to give the Aristotelian example), "This leads to higher rents and substandard living accommodations for poorer persons," "This leads to the defoliation of food-producing areas in Vietnam."

Of course, muckraking may not be popular. People do not always wish to know the consequences of their action, especially if that knowledge will oblige them to change their behaviour at some inconvenience to themselves. It is easier and safer to teach children facts that have no relation to values, and values that have no relation to facts. The former is successfully accomplished in many school courses that describe themselves as social studies; the latter usually comes under the heading of religious instruction. What I am proposing would require a radical rethinking of many aspects of our present educational curriculum.

My conclusion is quite simple: what moral education requires is moral courage on the part of the educators. Or if you like: moral education will result only if the educators engage in moral action.

CHAPTER 5

*The contribution of schools to moral development: a working paper in the theory of action**

JAN J. LOUBSER

WHEN A sociologist turns his attention to moral education he is likely to ask questions about the effects of social structural arrangements in society, and schools in particular, on the acquisition of moral values and moral development in general. Perhaps he is even more likely to pose the problems in terms of the transmission of social and cultural values and moral codes than in terms of the individual and his socialization and moral development. In focusing on the educational system he would probably want to examine the effects of teacher-student relations, the social organization of the school, the authority structure of the school and educational system, and the relation of the school system to the community and society as a whole. In the present paper I try to discuss some of these problems, with no intention of identifying and analyzing all the important issues that remain unresolved. It is a working paper with the relatively limited purpose of laying the groundwork for later work in this area.

The first part of the paper attempts an analysis of moral action in abstract terms, constructing an ideal type of moral action. The ideal-type construct is an analytical concept, not descriptive of empirically observable moral action. It defines, in analytical terms, moral action as a type of action, distinguishable from other types of action. For this purpose moral action is defined as action in which primacy is given to considerations of the "rightness" or "goodness" of the action, whether or not the actual outcome of the action is good or bad, moral or immoral, from the point of view of any particular morality. The term "moral" is thus used as a generic term, including both moral and immoral, and should not be confused with the former of these two

*I want to thank Martha and Rainer Baum, Andrew Effrat, and Rondo Wood for helpful comments on earlier drafts of this paper.

terms, which are strictly applicable only within the framework of a specific morality. I am not concerned with any specific morality, but with the analysis of moral action as a phenomenon, looking at it from the vantage point of an abstract conceptual framework within which it can be described and compared with other nonmoral phenomena.

An ideal type of moral action developed in this way is useful in the analysis of moral action or the moral aspects of other types of action. In the present paper the ideal type is used as a hypothetical statement of the end state of full moral development in the individual. This end state may not exist anywhere on any significant scale; few individuals in any given society may actually achieve such full development. In this sense, it can be expected that all concrete moral action will fall short of the ideal type and will approximate it differentially. The most developed concrete moral action approaches the end state asymptotically. In theory, it can be fully reached only under conditions where all inhibiting circumstances are absent, conditions seldom obtained.

The circumstances conducive to or inhibiting moral development may be cultural, social, psychological, or biological, but I shall assume here that they are mainly cultural and social, and that social structural arrangements, as they embody cultural values, are the most important factors in determining the outcome of moral development. The second section of the paper discusses certain features of the social structure of schools, suggesting how they might contribute to or inhibit moral development. Some implications of these hypotheses for education and modern society are indicated.

This paper is frankly speculative, aiming at some advancement of theory in this area rather than at a review of existing findings. It is a working paper representing a first intuitive step towards a goal that can be reached only by further intensive empirical research and theoretical work.

THE NATURE OF SOCIAL ACTION

Before we can define moral action we have to develop a conceptual framework within which such a definition can be understood. We need an analytical definition of moral action that distinguishes it from other types of action. The distinctions can be drawn in terms of a few analytical variables that serve to define all types of action. These variables are assumed to be logically dichotomous for the purpose of generating a typology of action types. Different types of action can then be distinguished in terms of different combinations of the values of the variables employed in the conceptualization of action. The types are developed by selection of pure types from among all the logically possible types in a matrix containing all the variables in terms of which social action was defined.

Action, as here defined, involves an actor in a situation, and the flow of motivational energy of the actor in the direction of a goal state in relation to the situation.* In the course of the action the actor has to make a series of choices that operate as control mechanisms regulating the flow of energy or effort towards the goal state. The following series of choices are seen as determining the direction of the flow of energy as well as its scope and strength.

A choosing the appropriate orientation to be given primacy in the situation

B choosing the relevant features or modalities of objects, in relation to the goal state, to be controlled either as means or as goal objects

C choosing a definition of the situation relevant to the action

D choosing the appropriate scope of the action in terms of the actor's involvement

Each of these choices may involve more than one variable but I shall assume that for each there is a *critical* variable that is of special importance in the patterning of action choices. Similarly, by treating the choices on this critical variable as logically forced or dichotomous, the assumption is that there is a dividing point or watershed on the continuum of values of the variables that is critical for the patterning of action. These assumptions permit the construction of hypothetical types of action based on patterns of combination of values of the four choice variables.

Action is defined as social when it takes place in relation to and involving other actors in the situation. Social action is not synonymous with interaction, which involves the social action of more than one actor in relation to each other actor, and considered together. Social action can be analyzed taking any one of the interacting actors as point of reference and does not necessarily have to involve the action of the others. In order to apply the series of choices to the social case, we can focus on a situation involving two actors with one of them considered as actor and the other as a social object in the actor's situation. Let us follow the convention of calling them ego and alter, respectively, and describe the four choices ego has to make in acting in relation to

*See Parsons and Shils (1951) and Parsons et al. (1961) for a statement on the action frame of reference.

alter. I shall utilize the familiar pattern-variable scheme developed by Parsons to describe these choices.*

1 Which orientation should be given primacy? The basic problem for ego is to choose between an orientation to the immediate gratification of his own needs and impulses and an orientation to take into account the consequences of his action. In relation to alter, ego has to decide whether to take the consequences of his action for alter and alter's needs into account. The choice to act on impulse without regard to other considerations we can call *affectivity*, and its opposite, the choice to control impulse in the interest of other considerations, we can call *affective neutrality*. The control involved in the latter choice may serve different purposes, but its imposition is a condition of the intentionality of action. Intention implies consideration of consequences; in this sense affective or impulsive action is nonintentional.†

2 Which features of modalities of alter are revelant to this particular act. Ego has to decide whether he is interested in certain qualities alter possesses or in certain things alter does, whether it is a *quality* or a *performance* of alter that is of primary significance to him. Action in relation to alter implies some measure of control over the relevant features of alter, the nature and measure of control depending on the nature of the act. Without such control over what is a component of his action, ego would be unable to consummate his action. Analytically it is important to make the problem of control over object features explicit, however complex the empirical ramifications might be.

3 How should the nature of alter's relation to ego be defined? Should alter be defined in terms of the class of objects to which he belongs or should he be defined in terms of his particular relationship to ego. The choice here is whether or not to establish a boundary of the ego-alter relationship that would set it off as a system from an environment containing all other actors. The choice to draw such a boundary, to define alter in terms of his particular relationship to ego without regard to his membership in a general class of objects, is called *particularism*. The choice to define alter in terms of the class of objects to which he belongs, without regard to his particular relationship to ego, is called *universalism*.

4 What should the scope of the relation with alter be; to what extent

*The following analysis represents an adaptation of the familiar pattern variables for the purposes of this paper. For fuller conceptualization and theoretical sophistication, see Parsons and Shils (1951, pp. 76–91) and Parsons (1967, pp. 192–219).

†The formulation of this choice as one of impulse control or expression does not conceptualize adequately other very important aspects of affectivity. Perhaps the element of expression of affect should be built in here, but I have treated it as secondary, that is, involving a further choice.

should ego become involved with alter? Here ego's choice is between limiting the scope to the specific purpose of the interaction occasion, or not setting any limits in advance. His relation with alter can be characterized by *specificity* or by *diffuseness* depending on whether the scope is limited or not. The choice of diffuseness implies that the scope is unlimited except in so far as it is limited by contextual exigencies. The choice of specificity implies that the relation is limited to the particular purpose of the interaction. The choice of specificity also implies that whether or not ego is involved with alter in other contexts is irrelevant to this particular interaction. In this sense diffuseness implies involvement of wide scope; specificity, noninvolvement or involvement of narrow scope.

The first two of these four choices involve aspects of the actors involved in the social action, namely, ego and alter. Looked at from the perspective of the social act as a whole, they are both components of the units involved, or unit components, for short. The other two choices are both concerned with aspects of the relation between the actors, the nature and the scope of the relationship; I shall refer to them as relation components when I speak of them from the perspective of the act or action system as a whole.

I suggest that at the level of a single act, taken in the abstract from any given aspects of the total action or the situation, the order in which these choices have been listed above forms a natural sequence. That is, ego first decides which orientation he should take, then the features of alter relevant to his orientation, then what the nature of his relationship to alter should be, and, finally, what the scope of the relationship should be. With each choice the meaning of the situation and the type of act ego is likely to perform become more determinate. The logic of this sequence is strictly analogous to the value-added process as Smelser (1962, pp. 13–20) defines it. Although a choice can occur out of sequence, its value is added only in sequence, and it does not combine in the process until those choices preceding it have been made and their values added in sequence.

The four choices are treated as analytically independent, that is, a certain choice on one variable does not in and of itself imply a certain choice on any of the other variables. However, empirically these variables are expected to show a certain degree of interdependence or association in a given direction. These associations* are such that those

*These associations are not all in the same direction as those postulated by Parsons (1967). I suspect the difference derives from the fact that my formulation here applies to the unit act taken in the abstract, whereas Parsons was concerned with the action system level of analysis. The difference is not critical and cannot be fully discussed here.

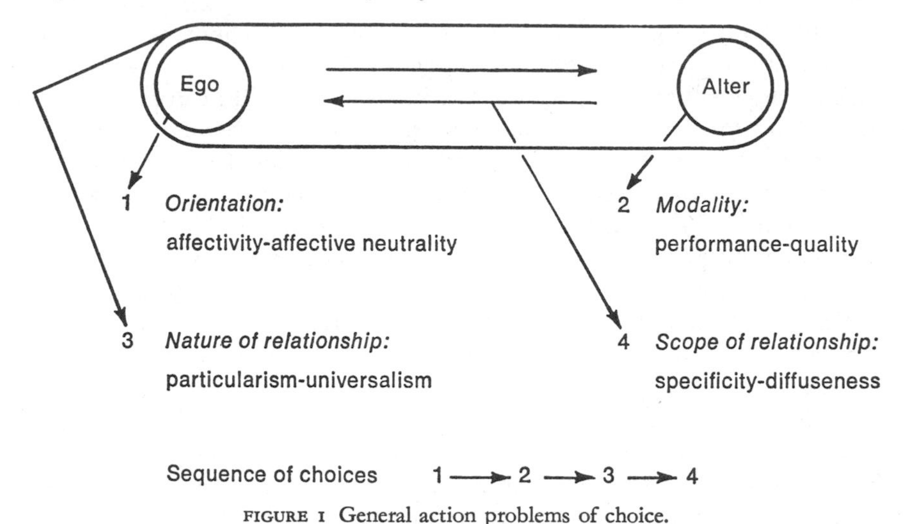

FIGURE 1 General action problems of choice.

values of the variables listed first in Figure 1 are considered choices in the same general direction and those listed last, choices in the opposite direction.

The above is an abstract analytical statement of the choices any actor faces when interacting with another. In the concrete interaction situation of two people the paradigm would of course apply to both; both have to make these choices. Whether or not a social relationship develops between them and persists depends on the degree to which their choices are compatible.

Social relationships established in this way become patterned on the four choice variables described, hence the name "pattern variables." The pattern consists of combinations of choices on two or more of the variables. The four dichotomous variables provide a matrix of 16 types of patterns in which each type varies on at least one variable with each other type. Although 16 types are logically possible, the degree of association among the choices is such that one can distinguish four "pure" types of patterns, each differing on two of the variables from the others. This ideal typology is derived in the following way: although there is a first-level association among all four variables so that a choice on each one is associated with a particular choice on each of the other three, the association is rather weak. There is a second level of association which suggests stronger associations between the two unit-component variables, affectivity-affective neutrality and performance-quality, and between the two relation-component variables, particularism-universalism and specificity-diffuseness. The direc-

	Affectivity particularism	Affective neutrality universalism
Specificity performance	Expressive action (goal attainment)	Instrumental action (adaptation)
Diffuseness quality	Supportive action (integration)	Moral action (pattern maintenance)

FIGURE 2 Ideal types of action.

tion of the association is in the order listed, that is, affectivity with performance and particularism with specificity.

To generate a matrix of types the associated variables have to be separated and cross-tabulated on the X and Y axes of the matrix. Before these processes can be carried out for both pairs, it is necessary to postulate a further, third level of association cutting across the unit-relation distinction. Of the four possible associations of the two unit-component variables with the two relation-component variables there are two that are more important for the development of the pure types: A the association of the orientation variable, affectivity-affective neutrality, with the scope of the relation variable, specificity-diffuseness, and B the association of the modality variable, performance-quality, with the nature of the relation variable, particularism-universalism. These associations are such that a choice of affectivity is more closely associated with specificity and a choice of performance more closely with particularism. The last two levels of association are therefore of primary significance for the development of pure types of action and render the fourfold typology of ideal types of action patterns shown in Figure 2.

These four ideal types of action correspond to the four functional problems that have to be solved at the system level of action organization. The cognate functions are entered in parenthesis in the boxes. The four functional scheme provides therefore a further rationale for the particular combinations of variables constituting the typology, which we originally derived from the associations among choices.*

*It is not necessary for the purpose of this paper to define these functional problems in more detail. Nor does it seem necessary to try to explain how these types of action relate to the functional problems. The rather vague sense of fit is sufficient since the analysis of moral action does not rely on the application of the functional paradigm (see Parsons 1967).

Without going into too much technical detail, it may be noted that the theoretical line of derivation would probably run from the choices to the functions to the patterns. That is to say, starting with the propositions about the associations among choice variables, it could be argued that these associations given rise to the salience of the four functional problems; that the solutions of these functional problems require specific combinations of choices; and that the ideal typical action patterns represent, therefore, typical solutions to the functional requirements of systems of action. It should be noted that these ideal types of action were not derived from the logic of the functional paradigm but from the associations among choices, which in turn were postulated on the basis of the intrinsic nature of these choices at the level of the unit act. That there is a fit between the pattern-variable paradigm and the functional paradigm is, therefore, not the result of logical circularity but an independent confirmation of the sound derivation of both paradigms.

THE COMPONENTS OF MORAL ACTION

Now that we have derived an ideal type of moral action in terms of a certain combination of values of the pattern variables, it is necessary to examine these values more closely to try to determine why these choices characterize moral action, in what sense their combinations provide an adequate definition of moral action, and in what way they combine to constitute the functional components of moral action.

At the outset it is necessary to define clearly what is meant by the word moral in conjunction with action and other words in this paper. It is always used as an analytical term designating a type of action or components of such action that can be distinguished from other types of action – expressive, instrumental, and supportive action, as seen above. It is the first term in a binomial nomenclature defining a genus in the species of action. It should, therefore, not be confused with the use of moral as distinguished from its opposite, immoral, in the evaluation of action or conduct from the point of view of a particular morality. From the point of view of any particular morality, there are moral and immoral ways of acting in *each* of the four types of action. For example, any such morality is likely to define certain instrumental acts as immoral and others as moral. Similarly, moral action as defined here would include both moral and immoral conduct as defined by a particular morality.

This clarification should be carried one step further. The following analysis of moral action tries to keep two levels of analysis separate, since to confuse them would mean missing the entire purpose of the analysis. The components of moral action are defined in abstract analytical terms, in terms of the pattern variables as combinations of choices. This formulation should not contain any specification of substantive morality of any nature. Such a formulation is difficult in the sense that the ideal type implies a certain way of acting that is sometimes hard to distinguish from the action itself. But this analysis of the pattern elements or components of moral action implies only that alternative choices represent *non*moral action, not *im*moral action.

The second level of analysis is present in rather sporadic indications of the content of an ethic in which the pattern elements of moral action become specified or applied to the human condition. This specification is done because humanity constitutes the most universal community of reference in human social action.* It represents a fixed point on which all universalizing tendencies, including those of moral action, tend to settle. To the extent that components of a substantive humanist ethic are identified, they are derived from the application or specification of the analytical concepts to the human community. This position is theoretically justified because the human community as a stable reference point is a given or constant at the theoretical level.

Moral action, then, is characterized as involving the following choices:

A affective neutrality over affectivity as orientation choice
B quality over performance as modality choice
C Universalism over Particularism as nature of relation choice
D diffuseness over specificity as scope of relation choice.

Let us follow the value-added sequence of choices that constitute moral action and then see how it fits into the functional breakdown of a system of moral action.†

Step 1. Orientation choice: affective neutrality

Affective neutrality, involving the choice to impose control rather than to gratify one's impulses or desires, is the orientation choice typical of moral action. The point is not that the satisfaction of desires is immoral but that moral action presupposes the restraint of evaluating one's action in the light of conceptions of what is right or good, whatever the nature and sources of these conceptions. When gratifica-

*For the sake of simplicity, I am deliberately excluding across-species interaction or social action.

†It is impossible to do more than spell out in some detail the definition of moral action. A full justification of this definition in terms of theoretical considerations and empirical evidence will have to await further work. I should like to emphasize again the tentativeness of these formulations.

tion is deferred for the purpose of taking consequences in terms of conceptions of good and right into account, the ensuing action is moral in the analytical sense. Whether it is moral or immoral depends on a subsequent choice by the actor with respect to the consequences themselves, and varies with the particular morality in terms of which it is evaluated. Nor does it imply that all affectively neutral choices are made for moral reasons; they may be made for strictly instrumental reasons without any regard to moral questions. This fact is reflected in the fourfold typology of action patterns where both moral action and instrumental action are characterized by an orientation choice of affective neutrality.

In the moral case, affective neutrality implies foregoing immediate gratification for the sake of a felt obligation to consider the consequenses of an act according to certain conceptions of what is right or good. It signifies the acceptance of a commitment to evaluate the moral implications of one's action. Hence it should not be interpreted as implying moral neutrality, that is, an affectively neutral orientation to moral obligations and commitments themselves. On the contrary, it can be seen as an indication of being morally concerned. The choice controls motivation to act without regard to moral considerations so that affect can be vested in the latter; as such it constitutes a control mechanism in the cybernetic sense by which the flow of affect could be regulated and directed into moral channels. Capacity for moral action depends on the acquisition of this choice mechanism. By itself, however, it cannot ensure moral action without combination with the other components. In turn, the other components cannot result in moral action without affective neutrality as orientation pattern.

Step 2. Modality choice: quality

Moral action in relation to other actors as objects requires that quality rather than performance be considered the relevant modality. Such objects are moral agents, but moral action in relation to them is not contingent on their performance as moral agents.

In one sense, moral action is not contingent on the modalities of the object at all, but on the orientation of the actor. The implication, then, is that the object is taken as given, for what he is, without any further consideration of either qualities or performances. This choice relates to the goal of moral action to achieve a sense of integrity or moral worth on the part of the actor. If the achievement of this goal, or the obligation to strive towards it, is contingent on the performance of others, ego would lose control over his own sense of moral worth or integrity. Hence the modality of the object of moral action is quality rather than performance. Moral action means respecting the object for what he is, not what he does. In the social situation moral duties are not abrogated by the failure of others to act in accordance with them.*

The quality modality also implies that control over alter's performance as a moral agent is not required for moral action on the part of ego. This choice implies that the moral autonomy and moral liberty of alter should not be infringed. As such it provides stability in moral commitments on the parts of both ego and alter.

The requirement of a quality modality choice distinguishes moral action from instrumental action, which is characterized by performance. It acts as a control mechanism to prevent the impingement of instrumental considerations on moral action, particularly the infringement on the moral liberty of others and the denial of moral obligations for expedient reasons.

The combination of affective neutrality and quality constitutes, therefore, an essential component of moral action. At the level of the moral action system, this combination defines the adaptive component, moral reasoning, in terms of which moral problems are resolved, as is more fully developed below. This combination of unit components is distinctive of moral action, setting it apart from instrumental action with which it shares the neutrality component and from supportive action with which it shares the quality component. Expressive action is, of course, characterized by the opposite choice combination.

Although this choice combination sets moral action apart from the three other pure types, it does not ensure that moral action will occur. Other combinations at the other steps in the value-added process, which would lead to something different from pure moral action, are logically and empirically possible.

Step 3. Nature of relation choice: universalism

The third component, universalism, is one that is so intrinsically related to moral action that it would be belabouring the obvious to discuss it at length. It implies that in moral action the particularistic relationship of the object to the actor is completely irrelevant, that the commitment of considered moral consequences is confined to objects who stand in a particularistic relation to the actor or belong to a class of such objects. But it is important in other respects than the requirement that objects of moral action be treated on the basis of universalis-

*This point is hard to grasp if the analytical nature of the term moral is not kept constantly in mind. These statements do not imply that to do otherwise is to act immorally; rather they imply that to do otherwise is to act in a nonmoral way.

tic standards. Universalism also implies that the authority of moral principles extends over all actors. A truly generalized moral principle must be such that all moral agents can adhere to it and would accept it, by their own moral judgment, as binding for their action.*

Universalism as a choice implies a refusal to draw boundaries, to exclude others because they lack a particularistic relation to the actor. The moral community most consistent with this component is mankind as a whole. Universalism is especially important in moral action because of the relevance of the quality modality to this type of action. It serves to generalize the respect for moral agents and to prevent the intrusion of particularistic qualities typical in supportive action. Hence it serves as a critical agent in the "diffusion of libido," as Slater (1963) calls it, to a more and more inclusive moral community.

The combination of universalism with quality is important for moral action since it sets it apart from supportive action. The pattern also distinguishes moral action from instrumental action where objects are characterized by performance universalism. Quality universalism is the pattern of choices defining objects of generalized moral respect. The universalistic component reinforces the meaning of moral objects, particularly as moral agents, and generalizes it to all objects of moral action. The combination of quality with universalism rather than diffuseness as the relation component is necessary since the latter pattern would not distinguish moral action from supportive action.

Step 4. Scope of relation choice: diffuseness

When a moral obligation is involved, the scope of the relationship between ego and alter is typically diffuse. Moral obligations cannot be confined to specific situations, but rather they are obligations without prior specification of the context in which they would be binding. Moral relationships are characterized by diffuseness in the sense that they involve the obligation to act morally regardless of the context in which the action takes place. If moral action were confined to specific contexts the integration of the relationship would be contingent on the fluctuating situation of action. Diffuseness eliminates these contingencies and permits the stabilization of the relationship, or moral action system, independent of situational factors. Although the relationships involved in moral action are diffuse in scope, all diffuse relationships are not moral.

It is of special importance in the structuring of the moral action system that universalism becomes firmly combined with diffuseness.

*This point is similar to Kant's categorical imperative, but not the same, and does not necessarily imply acceptance of the Kantian position.

The pattern of diffuseness-universalism represents a combination of the two relation components that anchor moral action in two directions. Most important is the elimination of instrumental considerations that would confine a relationship to specific contexts. Diffuseness thus sets moral action apart from instrumental action, which is characterized by specificity-universalism. Universalism, on the other hand, protects against particularistic considerations from supportive action, which involves diffuseness-particularism. Diffuseness thus adds its value to the universalism of the relationship to ensure the generality and stability of moral principles by eliminating choices that would tend to negate these principles.

Diffuseness also adds its value to neutrality and performs very much the same functions in relation to it as it does in relation to universalism. When diffuseness combines with affective neutrality, when ego acquires the capacity for generalized commitment in action in relation to alter, the requirements for moral action are met. On the one hand, the combination of diffuseness with affective neutrality sets moral action apart from instrumental action, which involves specificity; in fact, we might say that it is not until the value of diffuseness is added that affective neutrality becomes distinctively moral. On the other hand, the combination of these two values sets moral action apart from supportive action, which involves diffuseness but is characterized by affectivity.

Diffuseness constitutes the last control mechanism in the flow of motivational energy in the direction of moral action. It prevents the diversion of energy into instrumental directions resulting from the limitation of the scope of relationships to specific purposes. It ensures moral involvement with others as whole persons. Combined with affective neutrality, it constitutes a generalized capacity for action on the basis of diffuse moral commitments. Combined with universalism, it constitutes the pattern component of general moral principles.

It should be noted that the sequence of combinations follows at least two steps behind the sequence of choices. The first combination can take place only after the choice in step 2, and the last two combinations have to await the addition of the last step in the choice sequence (see Figure 3).

The internal structuring of a moral action system involves, therefore, a *new* set of combinations of the component variables, a cross-tying of associations in order to meet the functional problems of this type of action. At each step a new combination adds its value to make an outcome of moral action more determinate and to eliminate choices associated with other types of action. By following this sequence we

	Choice sequence		Combination sequence
Step 1	Neutrality		
Step 2	Quality		
		Step 1	Neutrality-quality
Step 3	Universalism		
		Step 2	Quality-universalism
Step 4	Diffuseness		
		Step 3	Universalism-diffuseness
		Step 4	Diffuseness-neutrality

FIGURE 3 Comparison of sequence.

have derived four patterned components distinctive of moral action. The sequence involves an order of combination of unit and relation components that should fit with the logic applied in the generation of the four ideal types of action. This is indeed the case. The same set of patterns can be generated by forming a matrix on the basis of the strength of the association between the relevant unit components and relation components which was discussed earlier. Figure 4 shows the complete fit between these two ways of deriving the pattern elements of moral action. It can be shown that the same logic produces the typical pattern elements of the other three ideal types of action.

The related content of moral values specified to the human social condition is given in parentheses for each component. The meaning of these content components has been indicated briefly above and need not be spelled out further for present purposes. It should be repeated once more that this is an ideal type of a system of human moral values. It is also a deterministic statement, a prediction of the end state in the evolution of moral value systems, given the stable reference point

	Neutrality (unit)	Univeralism (relation)
	A	G
Quality (unit)	Moral reason (flexibility)	Moral autonomy (liberty)
Diffuseness (relation)	Moral commitment (involvement)	Moral principles (inclusiveness)
	L	I

FIGURE 4 Moral action system.

of the human condition. In the case of the individual actor, the implication is that the moral action of the mature adult is more likely to approach the ideal type than is that of a child. Put differently, the closer a person's moral action approximates this ideal type, the more developed he is morally. In the case of any given moral system it implies that its later stages, assuming evolution, will come closer to the ideal type than earlier stages. In a population of historical moral systems the same tendency will be observed. In short, there is a developmental tendency in the direction of the ideal type, in individuals as well as in societies and cultures.*

THE SCHOOLS AND MORAL DEVELOPMENT

We can use this construct of a moral action system as a yardstick against which to measure moral development in any system, whether it be social, cultural, or individual. We can also use it in discussing the contribution made by various institutions and socializing agencies in society to the moral development of the population of the society or of mankind in general. Hence we can focus on the schools, for example, and ask: What do schools contribute to the learning or acquisition of the norms and values constitutive of this type of action? How do social structural arrangements in the schools contribute to the development of capacity for social moral actions?

An attempt to answer these questions should, however, be cognizant of the complexities of the role of the school in modern society. It might be unrealistic to consider the school as having as its main function the moral development of the child. Traditionally, the school came much closer to giving primacy to the cognitive development of children. Even where the emphasis has been on the development of the whole child, it is probably true to say that the cognitive aspect received greater emphasis than other aspects of development, certainly more than the moral. In this section, I argue that various aspects of the structure of schools are not conducive to moral development, but, in fact, inhibit and retard it. The critical question is: Is this a legitimate criticism of the school, granted that the primary function of the school in society is not moral development? The crux of the matter seems to be whether one can argue that these same structural characteristics of schools are necessary and optimal for the primary function of the school, assuming that his function is the cognitive development of

*See Parsons (1964a) and Bellah (1964) for the kind of analytical evolutionary theory that should prove useful in developing these ideas further. It is not possible to do more than simply mention the tendency here.

the child. Only if this were the case, would it seem justifiable to assert that it is unrealistic to expect that these aspects of schools could and should be changed to optimize moral development.

The assumption that the primary function of the school is cognitive development must now be defended on other than traditional grounds. It has to be shown why in modern society schools should give primacy to cognitive over moral development if the requirements for these two aspects of development are incompatible. If they are not incompatible, some of the structural features discussed below may also be inhibiting cognitive development in the same way as they do moral development. The position I am taking here is that these structural features of the school are not optimally related to its socialization functions with respect to moral development, that these features have not been demonstrated to be functionally related to cognitive development, and that the question of the primacy of the one development or the other is therefore not critical.

The problem of primacy of function of the education system, or any other subsystem of society for that matter, can be looked at from another point of view. It is in the very nature of such subsystems that they develop, become differentiated and specialized in some function to which they give primacy. This primacy to some set of subvalues or functions does, however, give rise to the problem of the integration of the society as a whole. This problem is largely taken care of by the cultural moral values that provide a grounding for the order of society as a moral community (see Parsons 1966; Parsons and Shils 1951). Cultural values vary, of course, in pattern and content and these variations can be described employing the same set of concepts of pattern variables as is utilized above. The critical point here is that whatever the primary function of a subsystem of society, or whatever the set of subvalues to which it gives primacy, this primacy has to be bounded by the broad limits set by the moral order of the society. All subsystems are in this sense governed by the moral order of the society as institutionalized through its various control mechanisms.

At least one of the functions traditionally attributed to schools is the transmission of the cultural values in which this moral order of society is grounded. This transmission in itself, it is argued below, has been a factor inhibiting moral development in the individual and in society in general. In the moral sphere, as in the cognitive, the mere transmission of content, of a set of givens, whether they are values or knowledge, must be seen as totally inadequate. In this section, I am concerned with the conditions for the development of moral capacities that would facilitate the development of new, more inclusive, more flexible, more general, and more human moral orders, and ultimately the development of a moral order for the global human community or society. These requirements are not necessarily inconsistent with the moral orders of all existing societies based on nation-states, or other exclusive bases of organization. In any event, the moral order most compatible with the ideal type of moral action used in this analysis is an order characterized by institutionalized moral individualism, which allows for a great variety of substantive moralities; it is basically pluralistic and provides full scope within the limits of its moral order for the exigencies of a highly differentiated, complex modern society.

We can now turn to the questions we posed at the beginning of this section. I shall try to relate specific structural features of schools to specific pattern components of moral action. The discussion is based on the assumption that participation in certain types of activities, social relationships, and structural arrangements has a socializing effect on participants to the extent that certain patterns of action are reinforced with some degree of regularity and consistency. No attempt is made to assess empirical evidence for the validity of this assumption. Although it seems plausible it should be clearly recognized as an assumption. A careful examination of the evidence and further research would have to be carried out to verify the empirical generalisations presented here in hypothetical form.

Moral involvement

As we have seen, social moral action requires the capacity and disposition to accept the discipline of moral duties and obligations, and to associate with others for purposes of expressing and implementing moral values. This disposition is probably developed through involvement in issues and engaging in efforts to resolve them. Acceptance of moral discipline or moral commitments (affective neutrality-diffuseness) implies the flow of affect or motivation in the direction of moral action regarding any situation in which the actor finds himself. The opposite is withdrawal of affect from moral concerns, apathy and alienation, or escape into utopian enclaves where moral action is simple and easy.

The opportunities for such moral engagement in modern society are not many. Although the adult-role models in the family can be of critical significance, the family hardly provides the structural setting for such involvement. Religious organizations, voluntary associations, and the mass media often provide channels for the expression of moral concern but more often than not these are of a do-good variety that bears very little relation to the real issues. Even the churches, with few exceptions, have for centuries taken the position that they should not really become involved in this world but seek salvation for it elsewhere. The social-organization vehicles for the generalization and enhancement of moral involvement in society have been few and far from effective.

Traditionally the school has been seen as transmitter of moral and other values, but seldom as involved in moral issues, as an agency for shaping reality closer to what ought to be. The most common conception of the school is that of an asylum for youth for the purpose of education. The school should be insulated from involvement in community and other social issues. Youth is almost by definition the age of irresponsibility. Excused from responsibility in the current affairs of their society, they are given a moratorium during which they inherit the problems of the past, and, as a result of this insulation in the school, are prevented from acquiring the capacities to deal with them.

The teacher as role model fits this picture. The ideal is noninvolvement. Teachers are expected to stay aloof from social and public issues and problems, to concentrate on the tasks of teaching. Those who deviate are likely to be dismissed, and, if they do not violate the ideal, those who are disposed to become involved eventually leave this role. The result is that the school both in conception and in personnel becomes a bastion against moral involvement in contemporary society. This fact does not mean that there is no moral discipline in the schools. Rather, as we shall see later, it means that discipline is oriented to conformity with the "bag of virtues," which contains very few incentives to engage in moral issues in society.

The schools do, of course, make an important contribution to the acquisition of capacity for affectively neutral choices, for the acceptance of control rather than immediate gratification. But this socialization takes place mainly in the context of specific task performance, emphasizing hard work, excellence, and competitive advantage. It is specific rather than diffuse and instrumental to later gratification rather than in the interest of moral obligations to others as persons. This kind of control does not become readily generalized to moral issues. There is nothing in the organization of schools that would indicate a concern for the moral development of children remotely comparable to its instrumental orientation. In fact, schools in modern society have become increasingly factories of the instrumental competence required in the highly differentiated occupational structure of society. The acceptance of this role by the school is in itself used as a justification for the moral insulation of the school, since involvement is presumed to interfere with the instrumental aims.

If moral involvement is a component of moral action and a requisite for moral development, the very existence of the school as a separate, isolated, protected haven for youth constitutes a social structure inhibiting such development. It has often been said that schools in their present form inhibit learning and might better be abolished and replaced by more flexible arrangements conducive to education. If there is some element of truth in this statement as far as cognitive development is concerned, it is much closer to the mark with respect to moral development. Proponents of incidental education might overstate their case when it comes to the acquisition of generalized learning capacities; with respect to the development of capacities for moral action, incidental education does make more sense since the conventional schools seem to be achieving even less.

In this, as in their instrumental emphasis, the schools are doing only what they are expected to do by society. This analysis does not imply that if one changed the schools everything would be fine with moral development. The point is rather that the school's insular structure and the values it emphasizes reflect the expectations of the parents, the local community, and the larger society. Change in the role and position of the school would have to take these expectations into account. Yet there would seem to be considerable room for initiative on the part of the school to become involved in current issues. Many subjects would undoubtedly be more interesting and stimulating to children if their relevance to moral issues were discussed freely and students were given an opportunity to become involved in these issues. The school could also encourage extracurricular activities of a voluntary nature that would enhance moral involvement with others and with society. In many ways the school provides a structural setting more conducive to moral involvement than most occupational roles and employing organizations; the sanctions are somewhat less direct and less calculated. There is great structural flexibility and more room for individual initiative and freedom of movement on the parts of teachers and students. Hence, although the school as it exists today inhibits moral involvement and development, it occupies a structural position in society that could be highly conducive to such involvement. But this role would require a major change in current normative conceptions of the role of the school, recognizing the obligation of the school not to insulate the child from moral involvement but to present him with opportunities for such involvement. Involvement with others in moral issues is a requisite for moral development.

Moral inclusiveness

The component of universalism requires that the moral community be all-inclusive; the component of diffuseness implies the general force of moral rules or codes independent of the specifics of situations. The pattern resulting from the combination of these two components expresses moral universalism both in the inclusiveness of the moral community and in the generality of moral principles of conduct. It signifies the requirement that a general principle should apply to all, both as objects and as moral agents. When specified to the human condition, the pattern implies the recognition of humanity as an all-inclusive moral community, which in moral action is more important than any subcommunity. Commitment to human moral principles should transcend and be given priority over those derived from any less-inclusive moral community and the codes of such less-inclusive communities should be consistent with the principles of the human moral community. As such it requires awareness of, and commitment to, involvement in human moral issues. When specified to all living beings, the content of the pattern is even more inclusive and, of course, different. Vegetarianism, to the extent that it is inspired by the principle that killing any living being is wrong, is an example of moral content at this level. In examining the contribution of the school to the development of this component of moral action, I deal first with the human content and then with the pattern as such.

Human moral inclusiveness is not easily attainable. In spite of the professions of the major religions, no society or civilization of significant scale has ever established a moral order of this nature. There have been utopian experiments and there are rudimentary developments in some societies and in the United Nations. A good example of the difficulties encountered is Christianity with its concept of the brotherhood of all men. The *brotherhood* of all men symbolizes both the diffuseness of the moral obligation and its universal inclusiveness. Christians have seldom implemented this ethical universalism, except in short-lived utopian communities and in special ventures such as missions where it tended to become marred by the kind of paternalism that tainted even the work of Albert Schweitzer. Christian emphasis on moral universalism has more often than not become fixated on the community of Christians at best, and even more often on some subgroup in that community such as Protestants or Catholics or the presumptively elect within a group of Protestants. Thus the force of a universalistic ethic can become deflected by identity boundaries, which often constitute rigid barriers against the consonant moral action.*

The basic problem derives from the human condition itself and its implications for the socializing experiences of the human child. The few exceptions that experimented with functional alternatives to the family as the initial large-scale socializing agent have only confirmed the fact that the human infant has to start his socialization process in a very small group. His initial identity is shaped by this group and at the outset it constitutes his only moral community. If it were not for his capacity to create symbols, that is, if he had to rely solely on actual experience for the extension of the boundaries of this moral community, man's moral capacities would indeed be extremely limited. And yet, the fact that these capacities are so underdeveloped in spite of the quite elaborate symbolization of the human community signifies that the creation of symbols alone is not enough if it is not supported by experience.

In most societies the school takes over from the family and, with other agencies such as religious organizations, it serves through socialization to extend the boundaries of the moral community for the child. His family, local community, ethnic group, religious denomination, region, country, the world, represent concentric circles around the child as centre. Each one of these concentric circles presents a potential boundary to the identity of the child beyond which his identity may never be extended. Hence his identity can be extremely narrow and local or wide and cosmopolitan. Each boundary represents a potential barrier to further identity extension, depending on the nature of the socialization agencies, the content of symbol systems, and the kinds of contacts the child is able to experience. Empirically it seems plausible to say that the wider the boundary of identity the greater the obstacles presented by social structure to the extension of identity to that boundary. In most societies, for example, the achievement and maintenance of a societal moral community in the face of lesser moral communities is a difficult functional problem (Geertz 1963, Parsons 1966). And yet the problems seem negligible in comparison with those posed by societal communities, often encrusted in the nation-state, for the emergence of a world-wide community as an effective moral community.

What contributions do schools make to this extension of the boundaries of the moral community? Leaving aside curricular content and the

*Judeo-Christian monotheism has operated historically against the generalization of ethical universalism to nonbelievers. The particularistic relation of a people to a personalistic god has been expressed in identity concepts such as the "chosen people," the "elect," the "religious," "Christians," and so forth, all to the exclusion of the rest of mankind.

variable degrees to which it might contain symbolization of the human moral community, the first observation is that education everywhere is organized within the framework of a nation-state or its equivalent. Every society has or aspires to have its own educational system or systems; nowhere does an education system transcend the societal community. This statement is true even of private educational systems, for example, the Catholic educational system. Both the Church and its schools reflect national boundaries, in organization at least. Catholic schools in the United States are probably more like United States public schools than like Catholic schools in other countries. Universal public education has been recognized as one of the great builders of national identity, purpose, and pride, and of national sources of manpower and citizenship. An insignificant proportion of schools in any society transcends national boundaries in curriculum, personnel, student body, or professed aims.

Almost everywhere education is organized in such a way that it fails to provide children with multicultural or multinational experiences that would contribute to the extension of their moral community. International or supranational educational systems have emerged only in rudimentary form at the higher education level and there seems little reason to hope that they will have much greater development even at that level. At the lower levels, secondary and elementary, it is virtually inconceivable that educational systems will ever overcome their confinement within national boundaries as long as they are organized as *school* systems. As long as schools are fixed localities and facilities to which population has to flow, the obstacles would seem insurmountable. Even when it becomes technologically more feasible than at present to bring all means of education to the population in their homes or elsewhere, it would be difficult to overcome the constraints that the limited physical mobility of any given population imposes on their exposure to other populations. In spite of the technological possibility of the "global village" and the considerable increase in communication that it permits, the overwhelming proportion of the experience of any human population will be local and parochial rather than cosmopolitan. The removal of the existing political and economic barriers to the free movement of population might increase the cosmopolitan nature of urban areas of the globe enough to tip the balance in favour of the development of a global moral community, but this possibility already presupposes the disappearance or weakening of national boundaries. Schools, therefore, as long as they are organized as they are now seem unlikely to make a significant contribution to the development of an all-inclusive human moral community.

When we examine the organization of education within a society the same strictures seem to apply. Everywhere schools are tied to the local community and very often they are also controlled by local boards or bureaucracies. There are, of course, exceptions, for example, France and West Germany. However, the local communities and agencies consist most often of homogeneous populations with very little variety of the major factors stratifying human societies, such as language, class, religion, race, or ethnic group (Coleman et al. 1966). Consequently, children are seldom exposed regularly and consistently to significant ranges of variation across several strata of humanity to develop an awareness of a common humanity and moral involvement with people as people. The homogeneity and localism of the school, which it shares with its parent community, deprive the child of the kinds of experiences that would extend his moral community, and inhibit the generalization of the standard of universalism. These observations should suffice to establish the plausibility of the hypothesis that the social structural conditions of schools, as they are most frequently organized, are not conducive to the development of inclusiveness of moral community. In fact, in most societies their structural position inhibits the development of even a national or societal moral community.

The other aspect of the development of this component of moral action is the acquisition of the pattern of universalism-diffuseness, of the capacity for diffuse universalism. Parsons (1964b, pp. 141–2) and Dreeben (1968, pp. 74–84) have analyzed the role of the school class in the learning of universalism but both tend to link it to specificity. These analyses imply that it is mainly a matter of the child acquiring the capacity to treat others on a universalistic basis in specific contexts, particularly task-performance contexts. These are the contexts within which the child mostly experiences universalistic treatment in the school. The universalistic standard for the treatment of others tends to be tied to specificity and to be of primarily instrumental significance. The implication is that the child already has the capacity to relate to others in diffuse ways, a capacity acquired in the family. The point that is not recognized is that, in the family, diffuseness is closely connected with particularism in providing the integrative standards for supportive action.

The problem of socialization is not simply to acquire the capacity to act on the opposite, instrumental pattern of specificity-universalism. Equally important is the acquisition of the capacity to act on the basis of diffuseness-universalism, the integrative standard of moral action. It is not only a problem of learning specificity but of generalising diffuseness to categories of people defined universalistically rather than particularistically, as in the family. This, I submit, is a much tougher learning problem. The extent to which the school's emphasis on task-performance standards contributes to the learning of specificity-universalism would seem to overshadow any contribution it might be making to diffuseness-universalism. Certainly the occasions on which the child is exposed to treatment in terms of the latter standard are less conspicuous than those in which he is subjected to the former. The opportunities for learning to bind together these two components, to act in relation to others as whole persons on a universalistic basis, seem to be rare in the typical relationships obtaining in schools between teachers and pupils, and among pupils. Although there is some reason to expect that the universalism learned in specific contexts might become generalized to diffuse contexts, it can hardly be expected that this generalization will be sufficient and pervasive enough to contribute significantly to the development of a capacity for moral universalism.

A detailed examination of the school class for positive evidence of contexts in which children are exposed to treatment in terms of diffuse universalism is impossible here. In comparison with the case that can be made for the contribution of the school to the learning of specific universalism, there seems to be little evidence that the school plays an equal role in this respect. In fact, the strength of the former case might be additional evidence that it inhibits rather than promotes this aspect of moral development.

Moral autonomy

Similar considerations to those raised above in the discussion of the acquisition of the capacity to relate to others in terms of a diffuse universalistic standard apply also to universalism-quality as a pattern of object modalities in moral action. Parsons (1964b, pp. 129–54) and Dreeben (1968, pp. 70–4) presented their most convincing argument for the contribution of the school class to the learning of universalism and performance. One can assert fairly that the entire case rests on the considerable evidence of the emphasis on performance criteria and the application of universalistic standards in evaluating performance in the school. The pattern of performance-universalism constitutes the type of object modalities most appropriate when the action goal is instrumental, or oriented to task-performance. We face, therefore, the same problem: In the light of this evidence, what can be said about the contribution of schools to the learning of quality-universalism, the typical pattern of object modalities in moral action?

The analysis has to follow essentially the same lines. The emphasis on the combination of performance-universalism tends to leave the opposite pattern, quality-particularism, intact. Universalism becomes so closely associated with performance contexts that its generalization to quality contexts is neglected. The performance context is, of course, as Parsons and Dreeben both show very well, extremely important for the development of the adaptive capacities and resources of a modern society. In addition to its importance in the supportive sector of society, the quality context is also of crucial importance in the moral sphere. In this latter respect it requires radical generalization, a combination with universalism rather than particularism as in the supportive sphere. The generalization resulting from a "spill-over" from the emphasis on universalism in the instrumental sphere is not likely to be significant, especially since it is tied to performance criteria. In other words, what is required for moral development is not the elimination of quality considerations in object choices, as in the instrumental sphere, but universalization of quality modalities.

It may be argued that schools by their strong emphasis on performance universalism in task-oriented settings tend to foster the elimination of quality considerations in action, including the treatment of others as human beings and respect for the intrinsic value of less universal quality differences than those based on religion, race, sex, class, or culture. Opportunities for learning to treat these differences universalistically, that is, as objects of moral respect, are very rare. The result is a general degrading of quality modalities and a failure to develop the capacity to treat them universalistically. This degrading is reinforced by the fact that quality differences are often, as a result of historical situational circumstances, associated with differential performance capacities. Hence the application of performance-universalism tends to emphasize the negative aspects of quality differences in instrumental contexts. In other words, the fact that cultural and economic deprivation result in lower capacities to perform, and hence in lower achievement when judged on a universalistic basis serves to degrade the quality differences by association and to reinforce the negative stereotypes and prejudices in the community. The school, therefore, instead of providing redemption from this vicious circle, tends to reinforce it further by its heavy emphasis on performance-universalism (for evidence that tends to support this viewpoint, see Spady, 1967).

In addition, the emphasis on performance-universalism has a latent dysfunction for moral development in that it tends to spill over into all roles, including membership roles. Racist ideologies often justify the exclusion of the devalued races on the basis of its alleged inferiority and incapacity to perform as well as the superior race. Even in task-oriented contexts it often leads to the treatment of others as objects of utility rather than as objects of respect. It breeds a kind of Machiavellian manipulation of human beings as pawns in the name of some overweening instrumental concern such as bureaucratic efficiency. In the structure of the school class, in the entire educational system, we find little evidence of mechanisms that would serve to inhibit these tendencies. A careful analysis of the latent functional consequences of the school would probably show that it also inhibits the development of quality-universalism, or the disposition to treat others as objects of respect.

The most important consideration in this regard is, however, the disposition to treat others, not only as objects of respect, but as objects having moral authority for their own action. Dreeben (1968, pp. 66–70) has shown how the emphasis on performance and universalism is combined with insistence on independence in task-performance, on the capacity to perform without assistance by others. The parallel of independence in the instrumental sphere is autonomy in the moral sphere. As we have seen earlier, quality-universalism in moral action implies the treatment of all moral agents as having equal moral authority and autonomy with respect to their own moral action. The implementation of moral values depends therefore on the contributions of individual actors, on their autonomous decisions to act morally. In moral action, authority is universally dispersed and the modality of objects most directly relevant is their moral authority, or autonomy.

Socialization during the first five years of life takes place almost exclusively in the family, which typically involves a very great authority differential between parents and children. Moral autonomy, that is, the treatment of all members of the family as having equal moral authority, is extremely difficult to realize. During this early period it is probably necessary to argue that complete moral autonomy on the part of the child is impossible, except on the assumption that human babies are born moral agents. Parents, of necessity, exercise some form of control over their children. This control varies with respect to mode and degree among families in the same society as well as in different societies.

The mode of control, rather than the degree of control, is the critical variable. The degree of control seems to contribute optimally to the development of autonomy if it stays within a certain range of variation, not too little and not too much. The mode of control, however, seems to be more directly related to the development of moral autonomy. The more indirect the control, that is, the more it is exercised by means of appeals for a decision by the child, assuming the child's capacity to make moral decisions, the more it would seem to contribute to autonomy (Hoffmann 1963, Peck and Havighurst 1962, chap. 5). The more direct in the sense of actually making the decision and expecting conformity, the less conducive it seems to be to the development of autonomy. The significant variable seems to be the extent to which the child is given the opportunity to experience the necessity of control and to exercise this control himself (Maccoby 1968, pp. 249–51). Piaget and others have pointed out that there is an asymmetry in parent-child relationships that always tends in directions undermining or obstructing the development of a sense of autonomy on the part of the child. Even so, the family constitutes in this connection a crucial influence on both the level of autonomy and the potential for developing autonomy with which the child enters school (Maccoby 1968).

The importance of authority differentials in moral development is also evident in Kohlberg's (1969) theory of the stages of development of moral judgment. The very first stage in Kohlberg's theory is one in which the child is oriented in his moral judgment to obedience and punishment. Although he goes through a stage of egoism and exchange, stage 3 is characterized by efforts to please others and to conform to their moral expectations and stage 4 by a tendency to base moral judgment on moral rules handed down by authority. Except for stage 2, therefore, authority and conformity represent the major elements in the development of moral judgment in its first four stages.

This fact might be interpreted positively as evidence of the crucial importance of authority differentials in the dynamics of the process of socialization, especially by adult-role models becoming internalized and forming the basis for further development of the personality and moral judgment of the child (Parsons 1964b, pp. 78–111). But the main impact of authority on moral development seems negative to the extent that it inhibits the development of moral autonomy. Kohlberg's finding that the moral judgment of very few people develops beyond stage 4, that is, the stage where moral judgment is based on the dictates of some external authority, supports this interpretation. The dynamics of superego development, and the evidence on the types of family background underlying dispositions to compulsive conformity and authoritarianism, also indicate that authority differentials are of crucial significance and support the interpretation of the dysfunctional role of excessive authority with respect to the optimal development of moral autonomy. Authoritarianism has been shown to relate very closely to a family structure in which authority differentials are very great and authority looms large as a factor in the socialization of children (Adorno, Frenkel-Brunswick, Levinson and Sanford 1950, pp. 337–89).

Authority differentials in teacher-pupil relations in the schools are also often so great that they are likely to inhibit the development of moral autonomy. Teachers are typically older than their pupils and the assumption of superiority, and hence differential authority, at least with respect to task-performance, is built into the relationship. The teacher ought to know more than the pupil, so much so that he ought to know what is best for the pupil, who is presumed to be incapable of judgment with respect to curriculum content. With respect to moral matters teachers are most often considered *in loco parentis* and presumed to be guardians of morals. They have moral authority over pupils and this authority varies, as in the family, in mode and degree. Friedenberg (1963) is probably describing a common situation in schools when he says, "Schools are permitted to infantilize adolescents and control pupils by reinvoking the sensations of childhood punishment, effective because it was designed, with great unconscious guile, to dramatize a child's weakness in the face of authority" (p. 48). Authority in the school, especially when there is much of it and it is direct, is more likely to be experienced as arbitrary and alien than it is in the family, since it lacks the legitimation of the particularistic affective relations between parents and children. In addition, it is seen as oriented to the achievement of school-system goals, which are largely arbitrary and instrumental from the student's point of view. The imperatives of co-ordination and discipline in schools as presently organized make the elimination of arbitrary authority virtually impossible, although in most situations it could probably be greatly reduced and exercised less directly. This built-in authority differential in schools constitutes one of their most serious structural obstacles to moral development.

How does this situation fit with the emphasis on independence which Dreeben points out? The school's concern with independence is confined to the performance of tasks required or authoritatively expected by the teacher. The pupil can choose neither whether or not he will perform the task, nor whether he will do it himself or rely on someone else; he is expected to do it himself and effective sanctions are used to ensure compliance. With respect to moral judgments the pupil is seldom if ever placed in the comparable position where he is required to make the judgment autonomously. Schools make deliberate efforts to prevent independence in task-performance from spilling over in areas of moral and social responsibility. The emphasis on independence in performance contexts is combined with an expectation of submissiveness and conformity in authority relationships and moral matters. This combination probably contributes much to the alienation among students as well as to recurrent restlessness about participation in the decision-making process in the schools. Hence the emphasis on independence does not contribute to the development of moral autonomy except by means of generalization, which is also inhibited by the authority arrangements in schools.

Schools provide very little experience in the exercise of moral autonomy. By maintaining moral surveillance *in loco parentis* or on behalf of society they perpetuate the notion that moral goals can be achieved by enforcement. By not recognizing the moral autonomy of pupils and not insisting on independence in this sphere as in the instrumental sphere, they inhibit the development of a universalistic approach to moral authority, the generalization of respect for others as moral agents, and ultimately the institutionalization of moral liberty as a value of society.

Moral reason

The last component of moral action is characterized by the pattern affective neutrality-quality. It constitutes the symbolic medium through which the moral action system adapts to variations in its environment. The adaptive problem is one of ensuring the stability of meaning of moral words or symbols in the face of fluctuations in the environment. The fluctuations are mainly of two types: variations in the performance of moral agents and variations in the gratification significance of moral acts. If a moral action system is to be stable it is imperative that it develop a generalized mechanism for dealing with these fluctations in an adaptive fashion. This generalized mechanism I call moral reason, for lack of a better term. Its two components are the two unit components of moral action combined in a pattern that provides stability in relation to both kinds of fluctuation. Affective neutrality provides stability in the face of fluctuations in the gratification significance or implications of moral action, and quality provides stability in the face of the varying performance of other moral agents.

Moral reason then is the mechanism by which the specific action implications of a general moral principle are derived for a given concrete situation. General moral principles do not contain detailed specifications of right action in all situations that are concretely possible. Situational exigencies have to be taken into account in determining the right course of action given a certain moral principle. The requirement is for a means by which two or more autonomous moral agents, accepting the same moral principle, can arrive at the same conclusion about the right course of action in the same situation or, if not at the same conclusion, at conclusions that are equally valid and compatible with the moral principle. Moral reason based on the pattern of affective neutrality-quality provides such a mechanism.*

The role of moral reason in moral action implies that what is moral in a given situation cannot be prescribed in advance. The reasons are not only that situations vary over a wide range and contain unforeseeable contingencies and complexities. We have seen that the components of moral action are such that every situation requires an independent moral decision or judgment on the part of an autonomous moral agent committed to universal moral principles. Given the constraints imposed by these components of moral action, there is no other way to secure compliance with a moral principle except by moral reasoning. Any attempt to impose a particular morality is inherently counter to the very nature of moral action. The resulting conformity, if it is secured, may have the appearance of moral action but is actually a travesty and denial of it.

It seems hardly necessary to discuss the contribution schools make to the development of moral reason. Schools in which moral issues are freely discussed and where the right course of action is always dictated by reasoning must be few indeed. Even at Summerhill there are limits to the free sway of moral reason. The typical school is of course much closer to the opposite extreme, where the law is laid down arbitrarily in authoritarian fashion and a particular morality rather than moral action is the main concern. Given the school's general tendency to insulate itself from social issues and problems, to avoid moral involvement, it deliberately restricts opportunities for the exercise of reasoning about such issues. Since reasoning assumes equal authority of participants in determining the outcome, the authority structure of the school also inhibits the development of moral reason.

The development of this component is perhaps the most critical for the development of the moral action system as a whole. Recall that it is the component formed in the first step of the value-added sequence by which, we hypothesized, the moral action system becomes constituted. The combinatorial logic of the value-added sequence implies that without this component the other components cannot develop and

*Hare's (1952) analysis of the characteristics of moral words and, by implication, moral reason boils down to the same two components. What he calls the "prescriptivity" of moral words is essentially the same as affective neutrality and his "universalizability," in spite of its terminological similarity with "universalism," has approximately the same meaning as quality. Since these are the only two characteristics Hare isolates they probably should be seen to contain also the other two elements, diffuseness and universalism.

combine to constitute a system. Moral reason is the mechanism by which moral autonomy, moral principles, and moral commitment develop and become integrated into a coherent system. This pattern seems to fit what is generally known about psychosocial development and moral development in particular. It also suggests one reason why social participation and involvement are related to moral development (see Kohlberg 1969, Parsons and Bales 1955).

To the extent that schools are organized in ways that minimize participation and involvement and rely on regimentation as a means of education, they restrict the operation of this mechanism and inhibit moral development severely. Rebellion in the school is a healthy if ineffectual and pathetic reaction, a symptom of a serious structural flaw in the school. It is so weak and ineffectual, not because the problem in the school is not serious, but because it is perhaps even more serious in the families in which the children are raised and in society in general. The moral backwardness of mankind and modern society should not be blamed entirely on the schools; neither should it be used to justify the status quo in the schools. If the schools are concerned with moral education in the sense of the development of capacity for moral action as it is defined here, they clearly have a responsibility to improve their own capacity to contribute to this development. Since schools are about learning and are organizations specially designed for the promotion of learning, they might be in a more favourable position to promote moral development, especially the development of moral reason, than would be any other agency in society. But it will require major changes in the structure of the school and its relation to the larger society, the community, and the family.

The development of public education has meant the emancipation of schools from religious surveillance, from the obligation to inculcate a particular religious ethic or morality. Where the principle of separation of church and state has been carried furthest in its application to education, as in the United States, religion and moral education have been removed from the school curriculum. But this removal has not led to the emancipation of the school or education in general from the surveillance of public authority in the interest of public morality. Schools, almost universally, are expected to inculcate public morality and respect for public authority. The progressive movement in education, independent and experimental schools, represent important, yet, in terms of their impact on the educational system as a whole, relatively inconsequential efforts to achieve greater moral freedom. Through a better understanding of the nature of moral action and of the factors contributing to the development of capacity for moral action, educational systems might be able to emancipate themselves from public morality and, in doing so, increase the probability that they will have a significant impact on the moral development of their population and hence on public morality.

Conclusion

Perhaps the hypothetical nature of this analysis should be stressed in conclusion. The theoretical part is clearly a hypothetical construction of an ideal type derived from a certain set of assumptions and theorems. The empirical generalizations about schools and the dynamics of moral development are equally hypothetical in that they are not based on codified research findings. Such documentation would be possible in a full-length monograph. It will without doubt introduce countless qualifications and perhaps even many reversals in the generalizations. But the broad strokes in which the picture was painted are enough to elucidate the main outline of the argument, which I contend would survive closer scrutiny.

In essence, the argument is that if we accept the ideal-type concept of moral action as developed in the first part of the paper, it is evident that the social structural arrangements in most schools inhibit the development of the components of moral action. Schools, by default or design, tend to obstruct rather than encourage the development of:

A moral commitment and moral involvement with others as whole persons and with moral issues

B universal moral principles and the inclusiveness of the human moral community

C moral autonomy, respect for others as autonomous moral agents, and moral liberty as a value in society

D moral reason and the generalized capacity for moral flexibility.

Space does not allow discussion of the implications of these observations for educational policy. They are fairly obvious but it should be equally apparent that there is no panacea. There should be many practical ways in which moral reasoning can be promoted, and authority, localism and insulation be reduced in schools.

REFERENCES

Adorno, T.W., Frenkel-Brunswick, E., Levinson, J., Sandford, R. (eds.) *The authoritarian personality* New York: Harper 1950

Bellah, R.N. Religious Evolution *American Sociological Review 29* 1964 358–74

Coleman, J.S. et al. *Equality of educational opportunity* Washington, D.C.: U.S. Government Printing Office 1966

Dreeben, R. *On what is learned in school* Reading, Mass.: Addison-Wesley 1968

Friedenberg, E.Z. *Coming of age in America* New York: Random House 1963

Geertz, C. The integrative revolution: Primordial sentiment and civil politics in the new states. In Geertz (ed.) *Old Societies and new nations* New York: Free Press 1963

Hare, R. M. *The language of morals* Oxford: Oxford University Press 1952

Hoffman, M.L. Parent practices and moral development: Generalizations from empirical research *Child Development* 1963 *34* 295–318

Kohlberg, L. Stage and sequence: The cognitive-developmental approach to socialization. In D. A. Goslin (ed.) *Handbook of socialization theory and research* Chicago: Rand McNally 1969.

Maccoby, E.E. The development of moral values and behaviour in childhood. In J.A. Clausen (ed.) *Socialization and society* Boston: Little, Brown 1968 pp. 227–69

Parsons, T. Evolutionary universals in society *American Sociological Review* 1969a *29* 339–57

Parsons, T. *Social structure and personality* New York: Free Press 1964b

Parsons, T. *Societies) Evolutionary and comparative perspectives* Englewood Cliffs, N.J.: Prentice-Hall 1966

Parsons, T. *Sociological theory and modern society* New York: Free Press 1967

Parsons, T. On the concept of value-commitments *Sociological Inquiry* 1968a *38* 135–59

Parsons, T. Interaction. In *International encyclopedia of the social sciences* New York: MacMillan and Free Press 1968b, pp. 429–41

Parsons, T., Bales, R.F. *Family, socialization and interaction process* Glencoe, III.: The Free Press 1955

Parsons, T., Shils, E.A. (eds.) *Toward a general theory of action* Cambridge, Mass.: Harvard University Press 1951

Parsons, T., Shils, E.A., Naegele, K, Pitts, I.R. (eds.) *Theories of society* New York: Free Press 1961

Peck, R.F., Havighurst, R.J. *The psychology of character development* New York: Wiley 1962

Sears, R.R., Maccoby, E.E., Levin, H. *Patterns of child rearing* Evanston, III.: Row, Peterson 1957

Slater, P.E. On social regression *American Sociological Review* 1963 *28* 339–64

Smelser, N.J. *Theory of collective behaviour* London: Routledge and Kegan Paul 1962

Spady, W.G. Educational mobility and access: Growth and paradoxes *American Journal of Sociology* 1967 *72* 273–86

PART THREE

Some psychological processes in moral development and moral behaviour

CHAPTER 6

Some problems for a theory of the acquisition of conscience

JUSTIN ARONFREED

I HAVE been interested for a number of years in the problem of understanding how the social experience of children produces internalized control over their conduct – the kind of internalized control that psychologists ordinarily attribute to the presence of conscience. There are a number of different ways in which this problem can be approached. One of the ways that I have found most instructive is to examine the durability of the behavioural effects of the various rewards and punishments to which children are exposed. These effects raise a number of issues which are important to a theory of the development of conscience. The issues can perhaps be best illustrated if we take as our primary example, for the purpose of this symposium, the effectiveness of punishment learning in producing internalized suppression of punished behaviour.

In some of the experimental paradigms of socialization which have been devised for the study of the internalization process under the control of punishment, the culmination of an experimental sequence is a test situation in which a child remains alone for a period of time, under circumstances which are carefully designed to convey that he is entirely free of any risk of external surveillance. The child is confronted with two small toys on a table at which he sits. One of the toys is highly attractive, and children find it extremely difficult to resist the opportunity to handle it. The other toy is relatively unattractive and nondescript. In a training paradigm that immediately precedes the test situation, the child has been exposed to punishment in the form of verbal disapproval and deprivation of candy, whenever he chooses the attractive toy within any of a number of pairs of toys which are set out on successive trials. During both the training and the test for internalization, all of the toys are small replicas of real-life common objects.

Among the experimental paradigms of the type outlined above, there are certain ones in which groups of children are individually trained without any verbal explanation or rationale for the application of punishment to their choices. They are simply punished when they make the wrong choices. The adult experimental agent of socialization, who administers the punishment, gives them no explicit cognitive structures or dimensions with which they can evaluate their potential or committed transgressions. When the entire experimental session is completed and the children are questioned about their behavioural choices during both training and test, almost all of them will be unable to verbalize anything that even approaches an evaluative standard in accounting for their behaviour – despite the fact that they range from eight to ten years in age. The children uniformly respond with little more than reference to the danger of external punishment during the training phase (when the agent was present). During the test for internalization, however, when apparently no other person is present to observe the child, our observations clearly reveal not only the attractiveness of the potential transgression, but also the internalized power of the behavioural suppression that can be induced by the punishment during training. When the punishment has been administered under appropriate conditions of timing, the majority of the children may show no evidence of transgression at all. Other children may transgress only after they have been exposed to temptation for the better part of the test period.

The procedures and results of this type of experiment are described in greater detail elsewhere (Aronfreed 1966, 1968a; Aronfreed and Reber, 1965). The main point that I wish to emphasize here is that the experimental paradigms appear to have produced some internalized control over the children's behaviour, even though the children have not been given and cannot verbalize any evaluative standards for their behaviour. The paradigms that have been outlined thus far are in fact designed to examine the efficacy of Pavlovian conditioning mechanisms in the attachment of anxiety to internal monitors that can mediate changes of affective state in the child. These internal monitors may take the form of behavioural cues, which are directly inherent in the child's overt punished actions, or they may take the far more interesting and important form of a number of modes in which the child can give cognitive representation to his punished choices. But even when the child's cognitive representations monitor his internalized control of behaviour, the child may not always have the capacity or the information that is required to place these representations on evaluative scales or dimensions.

It turns out that the punishment, which the child receives during training, is most effective in the maintenance of behavioural suppression during the test for internalization, when the punishment has been given early in the course of the initiation and commitment of each punished act. This result follows from the expectation that the strength of the internalized suppression of punished behaviour will be proportionate to the intensity of the anxiety that has become conditioned to the precursors of the behaviour – precursors which may have the form, for example, of either motoric orienting actions or cognitive representations (such as intentions) which are associated with the incipient behaviour. The inference that anxiety becomes directly attached to the intrinsic behavioural or cognitive correlates of a previously punished act makes it possible to understand, of course, why incipient commitments of the act may be suppressed even on subsequent occasions when there is no longer an objective external danger of punishment. The rationale of this conception also requires, however, that nonpunished alternatives to a punished act have acquired some intrinsic anxiety-reducing (reinforcement) value during the training.

These experimental paradigms and their behavioural effects have some rather obvious parallels in the naturalistic socialization of children by their parents. Their relevance to the development of conscience is immediately visible. Yet they also demonstrate the extent to which the control of conduct may be internalized in the absence of any significant dependence on evaluative standards. The results of such experiments confront us, then, with the problem of an account of how the cognitive substance of evaluative thought enters into the mechanisms for internalized control of the child's conduct, when it is clear that the mechanisms do not necessarily require evaluative thought. This problem can be engaged by focusing our attention in turn on the place of moral values in the broader arena of socialization, on the consideration of how any type of evaluative scheme (regardless of its moral status) might acquire control over the child's conduct, and on the requirements for a more general conception of the acquisition of values.

That punishment without cognitive structure can produce internalized control of behaviour will hardly seem surprising to even a casual observer of socialization. We all know that the preverbal child who can walk or even just crawl has certain behavioural dispositions which endanger himself and must be eliminated by socializing agents – for example, he may be intrigued by the opportunity to handle electrical outlets or connections. We also know that these behavioural dispositions often can be effectively suppressed either by explicit punishments or by more subtly aversive outcomes which are transmitted in the reactions of socializing agents. Moreover, the suppression may hold even when the agents are no longer present, if the previous outcomes of the suppressed behaviour have been sufficiently aversive. But a child of the age that is being used in this illustration will not have any concept of the nature of electricity. Nor will he have a standard of judgment about the desirability of touching electrical outlets. These commonplace observations remind us that human beings are animals, that animals are highly conditionable, and that morality has very little force in vast repertoires of internalized control over social conduct. On the other hand, the capacity for moral judgment reminds us that human beings are a very special kind of animal, and that they are able to use cognitive structures of great complexity for the representation and evaluation of their behaviour and their environment.

Some conceptions of the development of conscience assume a developmental sequence of qualitatively distinct stages which transform the mind of the child in an increasingly unifying or integrative manner until he attains (if he is properly nurtured) one or another cognitive structure which identifies him as a creature of a particular moral status. From this point of view, socialization and moral development are essentially synonymous. They move together towards an end state (sometimes defined as "maturity"), and the stage of their evolution is judged from criteria of the form, complexity, and substance of the child's values. This point of view characterizes not only Piaget's (1948) classic formulation of developmental shifts in children's moral judgment, but also the rather more sophisticated description of stages of moral thought in Lawrence Kohlberg's recent work (1963, 1971).

From the viewpoint of a psychologist who is interested in the broader range of behavioural and cognitive dispositions which children acquire in a social environment, moral judgment must always be a rather special and not a central phenomenon. It is interesting not so much for itself, but rather for what it reveals about the full requirements for a general theory of the developmental origins of social conduct. Moral judgment may be both a desirable and a powerful determinant of some forms of conduct. But it can hardly be supposed that moral decision-making processes enter extensively into very much of social behaviour. Certainly, moral thought cannot contain the conceptual resources that are needed for an understanding of the total spectrum of the processes through which socialization occurs. It might better be thought of as a singular and complex function that must be subordinated theoretically to a less specific and constrained view of the mechanisms that govern internalized control of behaviour.

The organized structures of value that appear in the development of children's moral thought do not begin to suggest the range of cognitive and affective resources that must be taken into account as determinants of the child's capacity for internalized control over his overt social conduct. Nor does the mere description of such structures provide us with an understanding of the transformational processes of acquisition or change that bring them into existence. The larger question that must be answered for these purposes is: How do the effects of social experience become represented in such a way that the child acquires internalized control over his behaviour? A secondary though still important question is: How does moral judgment enter into the internalization process? Such questions can be answered only by adequate theories of learning. Both conduct itself and the evaluative operations of conscience are acquired as a result of the child's contact with human society. It is true that theories of learning have tended to be concerned primarily with paradigms of conditioning and training, which are addressed to the control of relatively simple forms of behaviour. These paradigms cannot be extended with any elegance to the acquisition of values or of other kinds of cognitive structures – even when we add to their power some recent advances in our understanding of imitation and other forms of observational learning (Aronfreed 1969, Bandura and Walters 1963). Nevertheless, other recent developments in the study of the cognitive and linguistic acquisitions of children at least suggest that these phenomena also may be susceptible to theoretical models of a learning process.

Before we elaborate this point of view any further, it should be pointed out that the dimensions of value that are included in contemporary conceptions of conscience are far more extensive than the dimensions that usually have been at the focus of moral philosophy. Western moral philosophy has a strong tradition of orientation towards principles of conduct that can be used to evaluate the goodness or rightness of an act in terms of its beneficial or harmful consequences for others. It is these principles that conventionally have been associated with the concept of conscience. But the domain of conscience also has been greatly expanded by rather different conceptions, which are embedded in the recent emergence of the behavioural sciences. The cultural relativism of social anthropology, the emphasis of social psychology on normative standards and interactions, the psychoanalytic notion of the superego – with its stress on irrational and unconscious internalized control – and the tendency of behaviouristic learning theories to focus on the generalized mediating function of cognitive processes have all contributed to a dilution of the moral connotations of conscience. Investigators of conscience today often describe moral standards of conduct in much the same fashion as they describe the standards that are appropriate to sex role, to achievement, or to other relatively personalized areas of behaviour. Conscience is presumed to embrace values that support self-denial of pleasure, effort in the face of adversity, and other components of the "Protestant ethic." Child-rearing surveys of the antecedents of conscience examine not only the socialization of the child's aggression – an area of social behaviour that would easily lend itself to moral evaluation – but also the socialization of the child's dependency, its toilet habits, and its explorations of the environment. The question of what constitutes moral judgment is, of course, partly a question of definition. But it may be useful at least to recognize that moral judgment, in its more traditional sense, is only one sector of the extensive value systems which we now tend to subsume under the concept of conscience.

With this expanded concept of conscience in mind, what can we say about the relationship between conduct and conscience? The first thing that we can say is that internalized control of conduct does not presuppose the operation of conscience. The vignette of the preverbal toddler who learns not to touch electrical outlets and the brief summary of experimental inductions of internalized behavioural suppression in older children are illustrations of the fact that internalization without evaluative resources is possible and common. It seems clear that internalized behavioural control is often elicited even among adults with a mechanical immediacy that could hardly depend on evaluative decision-making processes. We know too that it is possible to train dogs or cats not to rest on the sofa in our absence. Internalized control of behaviour as a consequence of punishment training has been explicitly demonstrated with dogs in the animal laboratory (Solomon, Turner, and Lessac 1968). It also has been possible to show, in experimental studies of the origin of self-criticism, that a child will reproduce a verbal component of the punishment of a socializing agent (the label "blue"), and will use the component in describing his own transgression, even when he has been given no cognitive or behavioural dimension along which the verbal component may have an evaluative significance (Aronfreed 1964).

It is conversely true that conscience does not insure internalized control over conduct. Knowledge of the standards of conduct to which a child subscribes often does not permit accurate prediction of his behaviour when external sanctions are not imminent. I have reviewed elsewhere (Aronfreed 1968b) the history of attempts to find correlations between children's verbal expressions of conscience and overt behavioural indices of their actual conduct. In general, the results are not very impressive. Many studies have tended to confirm the original finding by Hartshorne and May (1928) that there is frequently little apparent relationship between a child's actions and his knowledge of common standards for the evaluation of the actions. Moreover, the increasingly internalized orientation of conscience which children display with advancing age does not appear to be paralleled by increments in the effectiveness of their internalized control over their conduct (which seems to become relatively stable at about school age). It is possible to draw the inference that children acquire a certain amount of capacity for internalized control of their conduct during the earlier years of socialization, and that this capacity for behavioural control remains relatively constant across changes in the structure and complexity of its cognitive foundations. However, it seems unlikely that conduct and conscience would be divorced from one another to such an extent. And there is other evidence to suggest that a child's characteristic orientation of conscience does enter into the control of his overt behaviour.

Recent and more sophisticated assessments of the operation of conscience – particularly those that have been conducted by Lawrence Kohlberg (1971) – indicate that the expressions of conscience which are verbalized by both children and adults may bear some relationship to cheating in situations of temptation or to resistance to obedience under external pressure to harm another person. The assessments of conscience which show this predictive value with respect to behaviour go beyond the individual's knowledge of common standards. They require the individual to give the rationale for the application of various schemata or principles to the evaluation of particular actions and their consequences in specific situations. Unfortunately, however, it is extremely difficult to assess actual behaviour in situations that have a variety and specification equal to those situations that can be presented hypothetically as elicitors of the child's verbal expression of values. And there are a great number of reasons why respondents who are capable of more complex and abstract principles for the evaluation of conduct – the kind of principles that sometimes have been offered as evidence of "higher levels" of moral judgment – would also show a more internalized orientation towards the control of their behaviour in a temptation or conflict situation. It need not necessarily be true that their choices of action are informed by a more moral viewpoint. It is equally possible that a sheer cognitive advantage of intelligence makes them more perceptive of the covert external devices and purposes of an experimental situation that is designed for the manipulation and surveillance of their behaviour.

Perhaps I can illustrate the basic theoretical problem that is posed by the control of values over conduct with a concrete episode that once occurred between two of my children. My then five-year-old daughter had just received what she took to be an affront from her younger brother, who was perched precariously on the ottoman. She drew back and positioned herself to push him off the ottoman, unaware that she was under observation. Then she hesitated and removed a sharp-edged toy from the area of floor on which it was clear he would fall. She was then about to carry through her original intention, when she became aware of my presence and sheepishly withdrew. A few minutes later, she casually brought up the incident once again. She spontaneously verbalized the thought that she ought not to have wanted to push her brother off the ottoman, because he might have been hurt and because she was supposed to take care of him.

Apparently, my daughter was quite capable of pushing her brother off the ottoman in the absence of any higher authority. Yet her verbalization clearly revealed the presence of conscience and the essence of moral sentiment. She criticized her contemplated act both in terms of its potentially harmful consequences and in terms of its violation of a specific obligation or attachment to her brother. She did not therefore lack conscience. Nor did she lack one of its possible connections to conduct, as we can infer from her removal of the sharp-edged toy. But she was dependent on external mediation of its other possible connections to conduct. The anxiety that was generated by her evaluative resources was not yet sufficient to motivate her internalized suppression of the incipient transgression. But the necessary intensity of anxiety could be elicited by external social cues (such as the presence of her father).

There is nothing extraordinary, of course, about this entire incident. It merely captures the obvious point that children (and adults as well) have many resources of moral knowledge which often are not reflected in their actions. The discrepancy between conscience and conduct reveals the importance of the affective correlates of cognitive structures. The placement of a potential act on a cognitive dimension or standard of conscience does not in itself give an assignment of value. Values have certain irreducible *affective* components. It is the nature and strength of these affective components, and not merely the cognitive substance of values, that permit the values to exercise control over overt behaviour. Inconsistencies among the findings of different investigators who have tried to establish the relationship between conscience and conduct may be largely attributable to the fact that the affective linkages between thought and behaviour are both complex and highly variable across different situations. An understanding of these linkages may derive considerably more from close theoretical and experimental analysis of their mediational properties than it will from attempts simply to correlate behavioural and cognitive indices of internalization. Affectivity is the final common path between evaluative control of conduct and purely "conditional" control. Recognition of the affective properties of conscience allows us to see also that conscience may govern conduct in ways that are lawful but not necessarily rational.

The importance that evaluative cognition may have in the control of the child's conduct, as well as some indication of the role of affectivity in the exercise of that power, can be seen in the results of certain extensions of the punishment training paradigms, which were described earlier. It will be recalled that children showed the most suppression of prohibited behaviour, during the test for internalization, when they had been previously punished at the point where they had just initiated transgressions. That finding was obtained in a training situation in which the children were given no verbal rationale for the occurrence of punishment. The finding can be accounted for rather well by Pavlovian mechanisms for the conditioning of anxiety. But a broad conception of these mechanisms must make allowance for the possibility that variation in the timing of punishment attaches anxiety to the child's *cognitive representations* of a transgression at points of corresponding variation in the sequential components of intention, initiation, and commitment of the transgression. Moreover, there are strong reasons for supposing that the precise timing of punishment will be less crucial, in producing internalization of the child's suppression of punished actions, when agents of socialization transmit a cognitive structure for *evaluation* of the actions.

The child's representation of an act on an evaluative standard will be relatively mobile – that is, it will be potentially independent not only of the behavioural cues which are inherent in the child's actual performance of the act, but also of the child's more immediate cognitions of the components of such an overt performance. Accordingly, even though evaluative standards may originally have been verbally transmitted to a child in connection with punishment that occurs well after a transgression has been completed, the child's evaluative representation of the punished act can easily be activated at the point of a subsequent incipient transgression. And the anxiety that has come to be directly associated with the evaluative representation, as a result of the child's earlier experience of punishment, can then be mobilized at that point to motivate suppression of the act, even though the child may not be under external surveillance or risk of sanction.

The power of a verbal medium in the socialization of children's evaluative control over their own conduct is suggested by the generally formidable effectiveness of the punishment that occurs in the natural setting of the home. The behaviour of parents is in many respects quite effective in the induction of their children's internalized suppression of socially defined transgressions. Yet parents rarely have the opportunity to punish a child's incipient transgression before it is committed. In order to examine the sources of this effectiveness, different types of cognitive structures were injected, through the verbalization of the experimental agent of socialization, into punishment training paradigms in which the timing of punishment was delayed to a point that was well beyond the child's completion of the transgression of choosing an attractive toy (Aronfreed 1968a). For example, a number of children were trained under a paradigm in which they received a cognitive structure that focused on the relative ease or difficulty of telling about the two classes of toys. It was not explicitly stated that the attractiveness of the toy was correlated with the difficulty of talking about its function. But it was made clear that certain toys were "hard to tell about" and therefore appropriate only for older children. This cognitive structuring was used during the initial instructions and also in conjunction with punishment each time that the child committed a transgression during training.

Children who were given a cognitive structure of ease versus difficulty for their choices showed much more prolonged suppression of handling of the attractive test object during the test for internalization, which followed punishment training, than did the children who originally had been trained without the provision of cognitive structure under the same delay in the timing of punishment. When the basic cognitive structure of ease versus difficulty was further elaborated to focus on a child's intentions – for example, the child was told that he was being punished for *wanting* to pick up a toy that was "hard to tell about" – the punishment during training was extremely effective in producing internalized suppression during the test. Children who were exposed to this cognitive focus on their intentions, in direct conjunction with their experience of punishment after a committed transgression, showed internalized suppression of a strength comparable to that shown by children who originally had been trained under a paradigm in which punishment had been given immediately upon initiation of a transgression (but in which there had been no cognitive structure). The effectiveness of a focus on the child's intentions is especially interesting, in view of the emphasis that has been placed on intentionality in some conceptions of moral development (for example, Piaget 1948).

Certain other variations of these experimental paradigms produced striking evidence of the role of affective mechanisms in the control of the children's conduct by evaluative cognitive structures. For example, it was found that the facilitative effect of the agent's verbalization of cognitive structure on the children's internalized suppression of their punished behaviour was considerably diminished when conditions were arranged so as to disrupt the temporal contiguity between the verbalization and the occurrence of each punishment during training. When the verbalization of cognitive structure was given well after the administration of punishment on each trial in which the child committed the transgression of choosing an attractive toy, instead of being given in direct conjunction with punishment, the cognitive structure had only a modest facilitative effect on the strength of suppression during the text for internalization. Similarly, variations in the precise temporal placement of punishment, with respect to the different behavioural components of a transgression (picking up an attractive toy, describing its function, etc.), were a significant determinant of the effectiveness of a verbalized focus on the children's intentions during training, in accordance with whichever behavioural component was structured as the aim of their intentions. Both of these findings indicate that the children's representational and evaluative cognition controlled their internalized suppression of punished behaviour in proportion to the extent to which their cognition has acquired the capacity to induce anxiety – in turn, a function of the contiguity in time between their experience of punishment and the agent's verbal transmission of the relevant cognitive structures. Evidence of the affective mediation of cognitive control, in the socialization of children's internalized monitors of their conduct, is by no means unique to the behavioural suppression that results from punishment. Corresponding evidence has been obtained from other experimental paradigms of socialization, which have been designed to study the respective contributions of conditioned affectivity and cognitive representation to the origins of children's altruistic and sympathetic behaviour (Aronfreed and Paskal 1965, 1966).

We can now turn our attention to the question of whether there is a developmental progression in the types of evaluative cognitive structures that become available to children for the control of their conduct. As an introduction to this question, it will be useful if we first examine somewhat more closely the concept of internalization itself. At an initial and fairly simple level, we might consider conduct to be internalized to the extent that its reinforcing consequences are intrinsically mediated and not supported by external outcomes such as rewards or punishments. Such a concept of internalization would be analogous to the concept of resistance to extinction, which is used quite extensively in reference to the persistence of many forms of learned behaviour in both human beings and animals. Actually, any substantial persistence of acquired behavioural dispositions, in the absence of reinforcing external outcomes, is relatively unusual in the conventional laboratory paradigms of learning for which animals are so extensively used. Yet such persistence appears to be very common in the social conduct of human beings, when we consider the large repetoires of conduct which seem to be maintained with little or no direct external reinforcement, and which often are resistant to change even though they are subjected to strong countervailing external pressures.

The criterion of internalization that we have examined thus far defines the internalized status of an act by reference to whether the choice of the act has direct external consequences for the actor. However, it does not make the full range of distinctions that we need to make in order to develop the concept of internalization. Nor does it allow us to see how the socialization of the child produces internalized monitors which have such long-term effects on behaviour. Resistance to extinction in the absence of external reinforcement is not an adequate criterion of internalization. A vast part of the internalized control of human conduct is mediated through the cognitive operations of conscience. Conscience enables a child to represent and evaluate his actions and their consequences in a variety of ways. These representational and evaluative functions vary in the concreteness or abstraction of their reference to external outcomes of conduct, and also in the directness or immediacy with which outcomes are translated into their value for the individual. In a general conception of the internalized control of conduct, it is therefore necessary to consider cognitive determinants of conduct as well as the maintenance of the conduct by observable external outcomes.

I have suggested elsewhere that a number of different kinds of cognitive schemata for the control of conduct may profitably be thought of as lying along a continuum of *internal versus external orientation* (Aronfreed 1968c). For example, although there may be no immediately rewarding or punitive consequences of a child's actions, and even no objective surveillance of his actions, certain forms of conduct may be maintained by the child's anticipation of the potential consequences of alternative behavioural choices, or by his cognitive representations of the past reactions of socializing agents. There are also many less externally oriented schemata for the representation and evaluation of alternative actions, which can control a child's conduct without reference to the direct external consequences of the actions for the child. Children become capable of evaluating their actions with respect to the standards or practices of those whom they hold in esteem or authority. And, as their cognitive capacities expand, they may begin to make more abstract evaluations of how their actions affect the welfare of others or fit into their own conceptions of obligation or contract. They may sometimes apply even broader principles which they perceive as rules for the determination of the intrinsic rightness or goodness of an action. These different evaluative schemata might be considered to represent increasing degrees of independence of the control of conduct by its external social outcomes. They would also have different implications for the impact of various kinds of social influence on the stability of conduct.

It is a matter of very considerable interest that certain cognitive shifts in the evaluative structure of conscience are found quite regularly among children in western societies. These shifts are correlated with age to an extent that suggests the presence of a developmental progression. The shifts include not only transitions among the different evaluative schemata, which are outlined above, but also a number of other changes in the components of moral judgment. All of the shifts might be described roughly as movement from a more externalized to a more internalized orientation. For example, as the child advances in age, he becomes less inclined to evaluate actions by reference to their concrete consequences for the actor, and he becomes more inclined to evaluate actions by reference to more abstract principles of conduct which themselves show some evidence of differentiation and sequence (Kohlberg 1963). Piaget's (1948) classic formulation suggests other developmental regularities of change in children's moral conceptions: (1) movement from judgment of a transgression in terms of harmful consequences to judgment in terms of intention; (2) movement from the perception of punishment as impersonally ordained "immanent justice" to the perception of punishment as the consequence of the disruption of a relationship between the transgressor and others; (3) movement from the interpretation of rules as fixed and absolute to their interpretation as reciprocal social agreements which are relative to individuals and situations; (4) movement from the judgment of appropriateness of punishment in terms of its severity to judgment in terms of reciprocal or restitutive relationship to transgression.

These sequential transitions in the basis of moral judgment, which are correlated to advancing age, have led some theorists to take the view that socialization serves merely as a catalyst for developmental changes in the structure of moral thought. One serious limitation of such a conception can be exemplified in the incident that we examined earlier. A five-year-old girl, who was clearly quite capable of physical violence towards her brother, nevertheless showed unmistakeable evidence of having subjected her potential actions to the moral scrutiny of conscience. She verbalized her understanding of an obligation not to harm her brother. It might be said that she had only the rudiments of a moral decision-making apparatus. Nevertheless, her grasp of a moral principle of conduct can hardly be in question. Of course, she will acquire more complex moral rules as she gains increasingly abstract cognitive structures that will enable her to take into account many different aspects of an act and its consequences. But that increasing complexity will be part of a broader development, which will make her more complex in many ways – in her language, in her comprehension of the physical world, and in her cognitive representation of her social environment. If greater complexity is to be equated with greater capacities for differentiation as well as for abstraction, then it is the very nature of development that the child becomes more complex. However, if we also equate that increasing cognitive complexity with increasing morality, when it happens to have the substance of moral thought, then we have already made the assumption that nature provides moral judgment. And there do not seem to be any further questions of much interest that we can ask. In fact, the young lady in question is already moral, although she may not be complex, because her thought shows some of the fundamental properties of moral value. We have no reason to assume that her moral judgment is the product of the sequential unfolding of a natural order. We would do much better to suppose that her moral conceptions are the result of rather specific forms of social experience.

Another limitation of theories of moral judgment that presuppose an evolution from lower to higher stages is the absence of any specification of the processes of transformation. Although there sometimes appears to be a vague implication that social treatment is a determinant of the evolution, the central theme of such conceptions clearly is that of Rousseau's *Emile*. The assumption is that patterns of conscience necessarily evolve, through a fixed sequence of qualitative transformations, in the direction of what is considered to be socially desirable or "mature," provided only that certain common catalytic forms of social experience are available to the child. Failure of the sequence to reach its terminal point must be regarded as an arrest of the natural order of development.

There are many serious factual problems for such an evolutionary view of moral development (Aronfreed 1968b, chap. 10). For example, the findings of a great many studies indicate that the age shift from an external to an internal orientation does not occur with equal force among middle- and working-class children in western society. The shift sometimes appears to be quite negligible in comparison to large and fairly stable differences between the two classes. In societies other than western society, the externally oriented components of conscience do not show the same decline with age. The findings of some cross-cultural investigations in fact suggest that these components are the end result of acculturation in some societies. Among college students in our own society, a number of investigators have demonstrated great differences of moral orientation among individuals who differ in their commitment to various political, religious, or other social institutions and ideologies. Developmental stage theories of conscience also leave us without much understanding of socially induced changes of value, which may be quite radical and yet not occur over developmental time – for example, the kinds of changes that sometimes occur in concentration or prisoner-of-war camps.

Finally, a much broader issue for the validity of stage conceptions of conscience may be found in the nature of the evidence that is given the greatest weight in analyses of children's verbalizations of their evaluative thought processes. One may ask whether changes in these verbalizations may not reflect the changing complexity of the child as a verbal creature who is responding to the inquiries of an adult, without the implication of any fundamental change in the substance of the values that continue to determine the performance or suppression of specific acts of conduct. The distinction that is implied in this question applies also to whatever evidence there may be of cross-cultural uniformities in the development of conscience. It may well be the case that such uniformities are entirely localized in the form or structure of the cognitive operators that the child's capacity permits him to impose on underlying substantive dimensions of moral value – the same operators that can be imposed on many other systems of representation that have no moral content whatsoever (for example, the child's representations of time and space). In contrast, the representational *substance* of moral values may be highly variable from one society to another. Such a contrast would mean that a developmental progression in children's verbal expressions of conscience would reflect much more general shifts in cognitive capacity rather than inherently moral stages of development.

The arguments presented in this paper point, then, to the conclusion that the child's acquisition of conscience is a continuous representation of social experience, even though it may also have cumulative and structural features. The basic problem in an account of the acquisition of conscience remains the one of specifying how social experience produces both the substance and the transformations of conscience.

REFERENCES

Aronfreed, J. The origin of self-criticism *Psychological Review* 1964 *71* 193–218

Aronfreed, J. The internalization of social control through punishment: Experimental studies of the role of conditioning and the second signal system in the development of conscience *Proceedings of the Eighteenth International Congress of Psychology* Moscow 1966

Aronfreed, J. Aversive control of socialization In W. Arnold (ed.) *Nebraska symposium on motivation* volume XVI Lincoln, Neb.: University of Nebraska Press 1968a

Aronfreed, J. *Conduct and conscience; The socialization of internalized control over behaviour* New York: Academic Press 1968b

Aronfreed, J. The concept of internalization. In D.A. Goslin (ed.) *Handbook of socialization and research* Chicago: Rand-McNally 1968 c, Chap. 4

Aronfreed, J. The problem of imitation. In L.P. Lipsitt, H.W. Reese (eds.) *Advances in child development and behaviour* Vol. IV New York: Academic Press 1969

Aronfreed, J., Paskal, V. Altruism, empathy, and the conditioning of positive affect. Unpublished manuscript, University of Pennsylvania 1965

Aronfreed, J., Paskal, V. The development of sympathetic behaviour in children: An experimental test of a two-phase hypothesis. Unpublished manuscript, University of Pennsylvania 1966

Aronfreed, J., Reber, A. Internalized behavioral suppression and the timing of social punishment *Journal of Personality and Social Psychology* 1965 *1* 3–16

Bandura, A., Walters, R.H. *Social learning and personality development* New York: Holt, Rinehart, and Winston 1963

Hartshorne, H., May, M.A. *Studies on the nature of character* vol. I *Studies in deceit* New York: McMillan 1928

Kohlberg, L. Moral development and identification. In H.W. Stevenson (ed.) *Yearbook of the National Society for the Study of Education* part I *Child Psychology* Chicago: University of Chicago Press 1963, pp. 277–332

Kohlberg, L., Turiel, E. *Moralization research, the cognitive developmental approach* New York: Holt, Rinehart, and Winston 1971, in preparation
Piaget, J. *The moral judgment of the child* Glencoe, Ill.: Free Press 1948 (first English edition: London: Kegan Paul 1932)
Solomon, R.L., Turner, L.H., Lessac, M.S. Some effects of delay of punishment on resistance to temptation in dogs *Journal of Personality and Social Psychology* 1968 *8* 233–8

CHAPTER 7

Psychology's undervaluation of the rational components in moral behaviour

DAVID P. AUSUBEL

THE MAIN purpose of this paper is to examine various ideological trends in psychological thought that in general reflect the prevailing tendency to undervalue rational components in moral behaviour. This undervaluation has largely expressed itself in four ways: (1) a tendency to place undue emphasis upon the affective mechanisms involved in moral conduct – both developmentally and in the contemporaneous process of translating moral judgment into actual behaviour; (2) a tendency to overemphasize the subjective, arbitrary, metaphysical, and unverifiable aspects of moral values, and hence to adopt an amoral or ethically neutral stance in psychology that relegates moral judgment beyond the pale of relevant and legitimate concerns in the behavioural sciences; (3) a species of psychological determinism that regards behaviour as essentially determined by forces that are not subject to rational volitional control, and thus exempts human beings from moral accountability for wrongdoing; and (4) a variety of cultural relativism that views moral standards as wholly arbitrary and idiosyncratic expressions of particular cultural traditions, and thus disallows both the possibility of cross-cultural moral values and the legitimacy of cross-cultural value judgments.

In opposition to these perceived trends I shall argue A that rational processes are crucial in the development of conscience and in the decision-making operations that enter into moral conduct; B that certain aspects of moral values are objective and verifiable, and hence both that moral judgment is an integral part of any behavioural assessment and that behavioural considerations are relevant and essential in formulating moral values; C that except in the case of psychotic persons, effective and rational inhibitory controls can typically be applied in most moral choice situations, thereby rendering the individual accountable for his moral lapses; and D that generic moral values and value judgments can be formulated on a cross-cultural basis.

I shall attempt to consider these issues solely from a psychological point of view and shall make no attempt whatsoever to take into account current philosophical positions or relevant material from the history of philosophical thought. This is not because I believe that philosophers have nothing to contribute to a discussion of these problems, but rather because it would be highly presumptuous of me to lay claim to the philosophical competence that such an analytical approach obviously presupposes.

I should also point out that my approach to the aforementioned issues will be substantive rather than historical in nature. That is, I shall not attempt to survey in any systematic fashion the views of my psychological predecessors or contemporaries. Rather, I shall attempt merely to set forth my own position on these issues, largely without reference to the views of others. This is not because I wish to repudiate my intellectual debt to my colleagues, but because there really is not sufficient time to do both jobs – historical and substantive – adequately.

RATIONAL ASPECTS OF VALUE ASSIMILATION, MORAL OBLIGATION, AND MORAL DECISION-MAKING

Beginning in late childhood, with the onset of desatellization from parents, and further abetted by the emergence of truly abstract cognitive functioning in preadolescence and adolescence, rationality becomes a progressively more potent determinant of moral conduct vis-à-vis affective mechanisms. This trend is manifested in at least three different ways: (1) in the bases on which moral values are selectively internalized; (2) in the basis on which feelings of obligation to abide by these values are interiorized; and (3) in the actual processes of reaching an action decision in behaviour involving moral issues.

Developmental trends indicative of greater rationality in the assimilation of values

Because of the child's social inexperience, his satellizing orientation to value assimilation, and his inablility to appreciate cognitively the functional basis of moral law, the organization of conscience during early and middle childhood is necessarily authoritarian and absolutistic. The internalization of moral values hinges on implicit acceptance of parental values, personal loyalty, and dependence on derived status. Rules are highly specific and possess an axiomatic, "sacred," and self-evident rightness that tolerates no exception regardless of what extenuating circumstances may exist (Lerner 1937a, Piaget 1932). Hence, infractions of rules (consequences per se) are perceived as inherently evil regardless of the intentions of the wrongdoer, and punishment is conceived of as automatic and as inherent in the external world as are the consequences of physical antecedents (Piaget 1932).

Normative shifts that occur in conscience development during late childhood, preadolescence, adolescence, and early adulthood (Kohlberg 1958, 1963a,b; Lerner 1937a; Piaget 1932) reflect gains in both cognitive maturity and age-level alterations in personality organization. All of these qualitative changes in conscience development – although reflective of personality as well as of cognitive determinants – are indicative of a more rational and critical basis of selectively internalizing moral values. In the first place, even though residual elements of the satellizing orientation remain, the child's motivational orientation towards value assimilation shifts from implicit acceptance on the basis of personal loyalty to acceptance on the grounds of objective equity and ego enhancement. Thus, in interiorizing new values, such considerations as logic, fairness, status, and prestige become more important than parental approval or loyalty to parents; and the satisfaction of these considerations obviously demands much more critical and rational scrutiny than is the case when the satellizing orientation prevails.

Second, the individual's conceptions of rules and punishment also become less absolutistic. He interprets them more as man-made functional contrivances based on mutual consent that are designed to facilitate social interaction than as axiomatic and unmodifiable givens emanating from an external authority (Piaget 1932). When the rules per se are perceived as less sacrosanct, he can place more weight on intentions than on consequences and can recognize the necessity for sometimes departing from the letter of the law in order to preserve the spirit (Piaget 1932). The number of things "thought wrong" (Pressey and Robinson 1944) as well as unequivocal condemnation of lying and stealing tend to decline with increasing age (Slaght 1928, Stendler 1949, Tudor-Hart 1926). He gradually becomes less concerned about egalitarian fairness predicated upon identical rights and punishments for all, and accepts the idea that these should be related to the varying needs, abilities, and maturity of the individual. Not only is more account taken of extenuating circumstances, but concessions are also made to prevailing standards of moral laxity and expediency, for example, willingness to steal from corporations or as long as there is no possibility of apprehension (Stendler 1949). There is less tendency to identify as wrong either what is punished or what is labelled as wrong

(Kohlberg 1963a, Piaget 1932). Finally, with increasing age, concepts of good and bad that were formerly confined to discrete situations become organized on a more abstract basis and hence acquire greater consistency and generality (Gesell and Ilg 1946, Hartshorne et al. 1930, Havinghurst and Taba 1949).

Determinants of change in basis of value assimilation

The foregoing changes in the basis of moral value assimilation can be largely attributed to an interaction between particular kinds of personality and cognitive maturation – desatellization and the accompanying liberation from the attitude of axiomatically and implicitly accepting parental norms, on the one hand, and the emerging ability to grasp and manipulate for the first time truly abstract moral ideas in the realm of interpersonal and social relationships, on the other. Significant personality factors include alterations in dependency relationships, the need for acquiring more status on the basis of competence and performance ability (as the result of increased parental and social expectations along these lines), and resatellization from parents to peers, teachers, and other adult authority figures. Significant cognitive factors include increased capacity for perceiving social expectations and the subtle nuances and attributes of social roles, and increased ability to discriminate, generalize, formulate, and manipulate abstractions, and take multiple perspectives. In addition to enabling the individual to function cognitively on a much more sophisticated and abstract moral plane, such growth in intellectual ability sustains the shift in value orientation from implicit interiorization of parental values (on the basis of dependent identification and personal loyalty) to the more critical and rational approach implied in the logical and objective weighing of considerations of social and interpersonal equity. Growth in self-critical ability and in capacity for a less egocentric approach to values belong in both categories of determinants.

As the preadolescent and adolescent begins to lose his volitional dependence upon parents and to become more concerned with acquiring an earned status, his satellizing orientation to value assimilation becomes increasingly less serviceable for the satisfaction of his ego needs. Since the inherent sacredness of moral standards also depends in part upon a perception of parents as infallible and omniscient beings, it begins to break down as the child enters the school and community and discovers that there are other authorities, various moral alternatives, and different versions of the truth. The more he comes into contact with the variable moral beliefs of the culture at large, the more his parents' early monopoly on moral authority is challenged, and the less axiomatic their values become for him. The adoption of a more rational orientation to the assimilation of moral values during the desatellizing stage is also greatly facilitated by the opportunity of following objective evidence and principles of equity to their logical conclusions without incurring such heavy burdens of guilt and disloyalty, and without being so concerned about the possible loss of derived status.

Reflective of this shift in the basis of value assimilation is the increasing sensitivity of children to the disapproval of such authority figures outside the home as the school superintendent (Bavelas 1942), the decreasing importance of the parents as emulatory models (Ugurel-Semin 1952), and the replacement of the latter by glamorous, historical, and public figures (Havighurst, Robinson and Dorr 1946, Hill 1930). As shown by the steadily diminishing correlations during the years from 10 to 16 between children's reputations for various traits and the closeness of affectional ties in the family (Brown, Morrison and Couch 1947), parents become increasingly less influential than other socializing agents in determining children's values. Values acquire a wider social base as increased exposure to new social environments, coupled with less subservience to parental views, enables the older child to perceive the standards of his home as merely special variants of subcultural norms. Hence, with increasing age, his values tend to become more typical of the culture at large and less typical of his own family.

The changing nature and organization of peer-group experience also promotes developmental changes in moral behaviour. A primary function of the early peer group is to provide a supplementary source of derived status; and the child accepts its authority on the same unilateral and absolute basis as he does his parents'. Prior to the age of eight he also operates in small, isolated, and informally organized groups in which roles are poorly differentiated and a lack of functional division of labour exists. Later, groups become larger, less isolated, and more stable. Children experience membership in several different groups exhibiting a variety of rules, practices, and values, and begin to improvise their own rules to meet new situations. As individual roles are differentiated, the need for co-operation and mutual obligations increases. The older the child becomes, the more he looks to the group as a source of primary status and the more the group tends to supplant parents as the source of moral authority.

However, it is mostly in heterogeneous urban cultures that values (during preadolescence and especially adolescence) tend to acquire a wider social base and peers tend to replace parents as interpreters and inforcers of the moral code. But neither phenomenon is indispensable for the maturational changes in moral organization that occur at this time. Repudiation of parental authority and of filial ties is *not* necessary for the acquisition of mature conceptions of moral responsibility and culpability based on intention, interpersonal needs, and reciprocal obligations. All that is required from a personality standpoint is a change in status and dependency needs and sufficient social experience to appreciate the functional basis of existing authority relationships. In the first place, in a population of boys from 5 to 14 in our own culture, it was found that neither the extent of parental control nor the internalization of parental requirements decreases with age (MacRae 1954). Second, there is impressive evidence of the development of mature and rational conceptions of moral law both in a particular American Indian culture where only a single moral standard prevails (Nichols 1930) and in a Chinese-American community where traditional emphasis is placed on filial piety (Liu 1950). Thus, when parental authority continues in undiminished force during preadolescence, adolescence, and adult life, its underlying basis evidently changes: the parent becomes less of a personal authority figure and more of a symbol of the moral authority of society.

Acting conjunctively with personality factors in bringing about desatelizing changes in moral development are the various aforementioned facets of cognitive maturation. Increased ability to generalize and to think in more logical and abstract terms makes possible a more objective and integrated approach to moral issues. Much normative change in moral conduct can similarly be attributed to the fact that, with increasing age, as he becomes more able to "take multiple perspectives extensively, flexibly, and abstractly" (Strauss 1954), the child's perceptions of social roles become more accurate (Lerner 1937b, Strauss 1954), for "built into role conceptions are the justifications of motivations for behaviour appropriate or inappropriate to enactment of roles" (Lerner 1937b). With increasing age, children also tend to adopt a less subjective approach to values. They consider them from a less personal and more detached point of view, show greater ability to argue from the standpoint of a hypothetical premise, and think more in terms that transcend their own immediate experience. A corresponding trend in value assimilation is a decline in egoism and an increase in altruism (Ugurel-Semin 1952, Wright 1942). Children become more aware of the needs, feelings, and interests of others and more able to consider a situation from another's point of view. For example, the reason offered for the unacceptability of stealing tends to shift from fear of apprehension and punishment to the perceived injury it causes others (Eberhart 1942). Finally, intellectual development, in conjunction with the decline in egocentricity and subjectivism, enhances self-critical ability, making possible both the perception of finer discrepancies between precept and conduct and the judgment of one's own moral behaviour on the same basis as that of others.

The foregoing account of moral development (Ausubel 1952, 1954, 1958), along with Kohlberg's conceptualizations (1958, 1963a,b), are relatively alone both in stressing cognitive determinants of developmental changes in the basis of value assimilation and in insisting that significant changes in the mechanisms underlying conscience development occur during and beyond the adolescent period. Far from indicating that the individual's structure of values is wholly dependent upon such affective mechanisms as satellization or dependent identification and is virtually complete by the age of seven, they imply that his value structure undergoes significant change well into adolescence and early adult life, and is eventually organized largely on a rational basis.

It is true, of course, that relatively few adolescents and adults, as both Havighurst and Taba (1949) and Kohlberg (1958, 1963a) have shown, acquire moral beliefs and reach moral judgments by formulating a generalized and self-consistent code of conduct or by invoking logically universalizable and consistent ethical principles. This largely reflects the prevailing climate of moral expediency in the wider culture, the ubiquitous tendency in the adult world to solve moral conflicts by appealing to platitudinous slogans and dogmatic doctrine, and "the fact that the teaching of what is right and wrong is done with reference to isolated, concrete acts of behaviour; relatively little effort is made to help them develop a coherent moral philosophy" (Havighurst and Taba 1949). However, we can hardly conclude that, because most North American teen-agers and adults, unlike European intellectuals, do not have an explicitly formulated moral Weltanschauung, their moral values operate on an unconscious and purely affective level. In the light of the previously cited developmental data, it seems more plausible to suppose that a subverbal set of rational principles is operative on an implicit basis. But even when an individual *can* identify the rational principles underlying his moral decisions, the influence of Freudian tradition on psychological thought is so strong that they are usually discounted; the argument here is that the simultaneous identification of motivation for a given theoretical position, belief, or course of action ipso facto either invalidates its logical basis or rationale or renders it irrelevant.

Rational aspects of moral obligation and decision-making

Concurrently with overvaluing the affective basis on which moral values are interiorized, psychologists have tended to overvalue the affective and to undervalue the rational bases of moral obligation and decision-making. Before this point can be demonstrated, however, it is necessary to distinguish between moral values and moral obligations in the structure of conscience, since these two conceptually distinct aspects of conscience are often treated as if they were one.

The term conscience is an abstraction referring to the cognitive-emotional organization of an individual's moral values, to the feeling of obligation to abide by these values, and to other psychological processes involved in keeping conduct compatible with internalized moral standards. It presupposes, first, that he is able to assimilate certain external standards of right and wrong or good and evil and accept them as his own. The assimilation of moral values, however, does not necessarily mean that these values will influence conduct in any stable and systematic fashion until a sense of *obligation* evolves to conform to them in his own personal behaviour and to feel accountable for lapses therefrom. The sense of obligation is itself a moral value and must undergo internalization; developmentally, however, this step occurs *after* the interiorization of other ethical values. That is, the child believes that certain actions are good or bad and applies these designations to *other* persons' conduct before he feels that he ought or ought not do them himself. But, unlike other values, moral obligation has the regulatory function of compelling adherence to all internalized norms of behaviour. Hence, it is the core value of his moral system which not only makes possible the implementation of other values but also welds them together into an organized system of behaviour. It gives generality and genotypic consistency to moral conduct by entering into every moral decision he makes. For example, the disposition to refrain from committing an act of dishonesty depends on more than the strength of the value of honesty in a given context. The total inhibitory control that can be exercised in this situation is rather the strength of the particular moral value (honesty) weighted by a general factor represented by the strength of the moral obligation to abide by all internalized values.

Now, while it is true that feelings of moral obligation during the satellizing period are undoubtedly unilateral in direction, and are derived both from feelings of loyalty to parents and other authority figures and from the belief that a lapse in moral obligation is wrong because it injures these authority figures, significant changes occur with desatellization. In the first place, although a residual affective basis in personal and group loyalties typically remains, feelings of moral obligation and accountability are characteristically placed on a societal rather than on a personal basis and are referred to more abstract principles of justice and responsibility. Concurrently the notion of unilateral obligation and respect for the adult gives way to a concept of reciprocal obligations based on voluntary co-operation and mutuality of consent (Piaget 1932). As a member of particular groups and of society at large, and as a consequence of his feelings of belongingness, the individual, on rational as well as affective grounds, feels that he is obligated to abide by the rules of these groups and of society because of the mutuality of obligations involved, the reciprocity of their application, and their implied reversibility and universalizability. It is largely on this basis that the Soviet system of group-oriented moral training, predicated on Makarenko's teachings, builds a sense of obligation in the young group member to respect the laws of the group and of society (Bronfenbrenner 1962). Added to this are purely intellectual or philosophical loyalties to one's moral values or belief systems that make one willing and anxious to conform to them. It is in itself a central principle of equity to abide by other principles of equity, which one has internalized – even if this is opposed to narrowly defined self-interest; this principle, after all, is the essence of what is meant by intellectual conviction. In some individuals moral obligation is also buttressed by religious convictions, that is, by feelings of obligation to the deity to honour divinely prescribed and sanctioned values and prohibitions.

Perhaps more self-evidently than in the internalization of moral values and of feeling of moral obligation, rationality enters into the processes of moral judgment and decision-making. Such rational processes are involved in invoking relevant moral principles, in applying them convincingly and logically to particular moral problems, and in balancing the claims of competing principles. Their use is admittedly inhibited by the traditional paucity of explicit moral principles among North American adolescents and adults and by their lack of training and experience in reaching moral decisions by explicitly applying general moral principles and strategies of moral problem-solving to everyday ethical problems.

At this point it should be noted that psychologists who overemphasize the influence of affective factors and mechanisms in the internalization of moral values and obligations are not alone in psychology's undervaluation of rational components in moral behaviour. Social learning theory, growing out of a tradition of habit training, behaviourism, reinforcement theory, and learning by imitation has de-emphasized the rational aspect of moral conduct by stressing the automatic, nondeliberate, and nonreflective properties of positive habit strength (based on prior reward), of generalized habits of inhibition (based on prior punishment and anticipated fear of punishment), and of imitation and prestige suggestion. The cogency of the social-learning view, of course, has been undermined largely not only by the foregoing considerations regarding the rational basis of value assimilation, moral obligation, and moral judgment during and after the desatellizing stage of personality development, but also by the evidence supporting identification theory – evidence both of its primacy during the satellizing stage and of its residual influence thereafter (Kohlberg 1963b). In addition, there is strong evidence that suggestibility in children decreases as a function of increasing age (Messerschmidt 1933; Reymert and Kohn 1940).

Anthropological overvaluation of the affective basis of moral behaviour

Symptomatic of the overpsychologizing of moral conduct in our culture is the overvaluation by various social anthropologists (Benedict 1946, Leighton and Kluckhohn 1947, Mead 1950) of particular affective and noncognitive determinants of guilt behaviour. These anthropologists have advanced the paradoxically ethnocentric view that guilt is not universally present or prominent as a sanction in mediating and sustaining the culture. They contend that in some cultures "sensitivity to shame . . . largely takes the place that remorse and self-punishment have in preventing anti-social conduct" in western civilization (Leighton and Kluckhohn 1947). Instead of acknowledging that guilt behaviour can occur whenever and wherever an individual internalizes moral obligations and can exercise sufficient self-critical ability to perceive his own wrongdoing, they lay down three indispensable criteria for the development of guilt behaviour. First, the child must accept the parent as omniscient and as the source of all moral authority. Second, genuine guilt feelings can exist only when shame and other external sanctions are not operative. Third, guilt must be characterized by conviction of sin and need for atonement. Behaviour that does not conform to these requirements is categorized as shame.

If we accepted the first criterion, there could be no guilt behaviour in the numerous cultures in which children do not regard parents as omniscient and in which the authority for moral sanctions is derived laterally or from the group as a whole. However, actual examination of the moral behaviour of children and adults in such cultures (e.g., Navajo) does not confirm this proposition. The same criterion would also deny the observed occurrence of guilt among adolescents and adults in our own culture who accept the peer group and society (rather then parents) as the source of moral authority, and among nonsatellizers who never accept the moral authority of parents, but who nevertheless interiorize moral obligations on the basis of abstract principles of equity. The second criterion ignores the fact (*a*) that guilt (a negative self-judgment for violating moral obligations) is invariably accompanied by shame (a self-deprecatory reaction to the actual or presumed judgments of others), and (*b*) that at all stages of development internal sanctions are reinforced by external sanctions. Hence, although shame and guilt are distinguishable from each other, they are neither dichotomous nor mutually exclusive. The third criterion is peculiarly specific to certain religious doctrines and beliefs about the original nature of man that prevail in cultures adhering to the Judao-Christian tradition, and hardly applies to peoples like the Japanese who nevertheless show striking evidences of both guilt and shame in their moral behaviour.

The discounting of moral beliefs

A widely prevalent opinion consonant with the moral confusion and cynicism of our times is that there is little or no relation between moral beliefs, on the one hand, and moral behaviour on the other. This view is in accord with current psychological emphasis upon drives, motivations, and emotions as causes of behaviour with a correlative devaluation of the significance of cognitive processes. In part, it is also a reflection of moral relativism, since it proceeds from the assumption that moral behaviour is simply a matter of passive adaptation to and assimilation of prevailing group norms. It is presumed that an individual will believe as the social class to which he owes allegiance believes, and that he will act in accordance with the behavioural expectations of this same group; and if there is little social-class expectation of correspondence between belief and behaviour, he will presumably manifest the same type of discrepancy. Although this view is quite plausible in some respects and is supported by several empirical studies, it obviously simplifies the issues involved.

It is my contention that there is a very high correlation between *true* moral beliefs on the one hand and moral behaviour on the other. The apparent discrepancy between the two can be explained on the following grounds: (1) It is often assumed that moral belief is synonymous with moral *knowledge*; (2) *expressed* beliefs are confused with true beliefs; (3) much of the discrepancy is an outcome of genuine moral confusion, inconsistency, and conflict rather than of deliberate or "unconscious" insincerity.

Moral knowledge is only one aspect, and a relatively minor aspect, of moral belief. It is true that a certain minimal amount of intelligence and social experience is required to learn acceptable moral values. The latter, however, become transformed into moral beliefs only when they are interiorized or invested with sufficient emotional and intellectual conviction to constitute genuine dispositions to behave in a certain way. Immoral behaviour in persons of normal intelligence who are exposed to acceptable moral beliefs is not an outcome of insufficient moral knowledge but of either lack of a feeling of obligation to conform to these values, or selective impairment of the self-critical faculty in relation to ethical aspects of their own behaviour.

The negligible significance of moral knowledge as a variable in moral behaviour is borne out by the low correlations which Hartshorne et al. (1930) found between moral knowledge and performance. There is also little difference between delinquent and nondelinquent boys in ability to identify the correct ethical alternative in hypothetical moral problems (Bartlett and Harris 1936). Curiously enough, intelligence correlates much more highly with moral conduct than it does with moral knowledge (Hartshorne and May 1930). This can be interpreted to mean that intelligence influences moral behaviour not (as might be expected) through determining moral beliefs, but in an extraneous manner, that is, intelligent children have less reason to cheat in order to do well in school work and are more apt to percieve the conditions when cheating might prove dangerous. One difference between the delinquent and the nondelinquent youth (within a given socio-economic class) is that the latter's greater mean intelligence enables him to avoid participation in illegal activities where the chances of apprehension are great.

A second reason for the seeming disparity between beliefs and behaviour is that expressed beliefs are not necessarily actual beliefs. Avowal of conventional and socially acceptable beliefs is considered to be judicious in any society although, during adolescence, youths often delight in expressing cynical and antisocial viewpoints which exceed by far their actual behavioural manifestations in this direction. On the other hand, in relation to peer-group activities, adolescents tend to be highly conforming in their beliefs.

Discrepancy between belief and behaviour may also be brought about by insincerity in behaviour – behaviour that is expedient and primarily designed by the individual to earn a good reputation despite its inconsistency with his true beliefs. This possibility raises a very difficult problem of interpretation, since it would be legitimate at this point to ask the following question: In the light of our definition of belief as a genuine conviction, as a disposition to behave in a certain way that is consonant with underlying thought and feeling, is not such expediency an indication that it is essentially the purported belief which is insincere rather than the behaviour which actually reflects the individual's true belief?

A simple unqualified answer cannot be given to this question. Certainly, behaviour in choice situations has to be regarded as a test of the sincerity of belief. A belief cannot possibly be genuine unless an individual is willing to undergo suffering, if need be, for it. However, common sense argues that some concessions to social expectations – if only in the external manifestations of behavior – are necessary for normal adjustment. It is impossible for any individual continually to challenge convention and steer his own moral course regardless of the norms that prevail in his social group. Thus, depending on the nature and extent of the compromise, the intention (e.g., legitimate self-protection or ruthless disregard of the rights of others), the degree of coercion involved, etc., it is possible for a true moral belief to result in an expression of belief and behaviour which contradicts it; they are both therefore insincere, but for understandable and justifiable reasons. However, in cases of discrepancy between belief and behaviour where such extenuating circumstances do not exist, it would be necessary to conclude that the expressed belief is insincere (i.e., not reflective of true belief) in the light of its behavioural counterpart.

A third possibility – in which neither belief nor behaviour is insincere – can also account for this discrepancy. A moral belief may be sincerely held and still give rise to behaviour incompatible with it and which cannot be excused on the grounds of self-protective conformity. In this case a genuine belief exists which is accurately reflected in expressed belief but is not translated into compatible behaviour because of the greater strength of competing motives – typically, considerations of self-aggrandizement.

In summary, then, the disparity between moral belief and behaviour that appears to arise from insincerity may exist under three different conditions: (*a*) the expressed belief is insincere, being inconsistent with both true belief and behaviour, but no real gap exists between the latter two phenomena, (*b*) the expressed belief and behaviour are both insincere and inconsistent with true belief for reasons of legitimate conformity to social norms. Hence in this instance, the disparity between true belief and behaviour is mostly phenotypic, (*c*) neither expressed belief nor behaviour is insincere for a genuine true belief does exist, but they are inconsistent with true belief only because of the prepotency of a competing motive. In all three cases, therefore, it is necessary to conclude that belief exerts a profound influence on behaviour if by belief we mean actual cognitive and emotional content as opposed to expressed verbal characteristics.

Finally we come to the third main reason why there appears to be so much discrepancy between moral belief and behaviour, namely, lack of consistency, insufficient generality, and confusion between moral beliefs. Here the issue is not that a genuine moral belief does not exist and is represented by an insincere verbal expression, or that a true moral belief is present but leads to inconsistent behaviour for reasons of justifiable expediency or the greater strength of a competing motive. The apparent discrepancy rather is an indication of cognitive limitations in logic and consistency. Granting as we must that a very large portion of the moral inconsistency manifested by any individual has to be ascribed to the various reasons discussed above, an irreducible minimum still remains which can only be explained on the basis of the lack of complete logical consistency, which to a greater or lesser extent characterizes human intellectual functioning. It is just as fallacious to ascribe *all* moral inconsistency to conflicts between motives as it is to ascribe *all* forgetting to purposeful repression.

In early childhood we see evidence of moral inconsistency on the basis of developmental immaturity in ability to generalize; and although improvement in this ability continues until adult life, it always falls short of complete perfection. Much of this inconsistency, however, should not be ascribed to inevitable cognitive limitations in logical process. There are at least two other contributing factors here: (*a*) previously discussed deficiencies in moral education, and (*b*) the objective moral confusion prevailing in our culture. Many times there are conflicts between moral values when differences between alternatives cannot be clearly discriminated. However, in a very real sense, as Havighurst and Taba (1949) point out, this outcome is conditioned by the type of moral education given in our culture.

The other extenuating factor contributing to this apparent cognitive deficiency in moral consistency is the widespread moral confusion permeating modern society. This situation, which is illustrated by the formal cultural endorsement of humility, kindliness, and helpfulness, with a simultaneous overvaluation of prestige, aggressiveness, and success, has deteriorated rapidly since the onset of the Second World War. The current generation of youth, therefore, has developed an extremely high tolerance for moral ambiguity and confusion. Because of the prestige suggestion inherent in the operation of social norms, they are assimilable by many individuals in such a way that their incompatibility is never perceived; it is presumed by the perceiver that inconsistency in cultural values is inconceivable, and, therefore, an advance "set" exists to perceive such values as consistent regardless of manifest content – even if logic-tight compartments must be constructed to prevent critical comparisons from being made. Hence, while it should be realized that assimilation of cultural norms is never a completely thorough-going or passive process, a basis for uncritical acceptance does exist.

Another type of evidence that is often advanced to support the thesis that moral beliefs do not influence behaviour comes from studies pointing to the fact that Sunday School attendance and degree of religious observance are correlated negligibly with moral conduct (Betts 1927, Hartshorne et al. 1930, Hollingshead 1949, Strang 1929). Havighurst's and Taba's (1949) data also support this proposition: "When social position is kept constant, there is a reliable tendency for those subjects rated high on religious observance to have higher character reputations than those rated low on religious observance . . . Those subjects with no church affiliation tend to have a lower character reputation than those who are affiliated with a church." This means that religious observance forms part of the total pattern of formal, socially approved behaviour that is important in determining an individual's reputation.

The important thing to bear in mind, however, is that evidence such as this proves only that formal religious observance makes for good character *reputation* but is indifferently related to moral conduct. It does *not* prove that religious *belief* itself is unrelated to moral behaviour. In fact, just the opposite is indicated by findings that Mennonite children ascribe religious values to more life situations and more moral authority to the church than do non-Mennonite children (Kalhorn 1944) and that adolescents in a particular closely knit Lutheran community have very high reputations for honesty and reliability despite relatively low social status (Havighurst and Taba 1949). It stands to reason that a person who *really* believes that moral uprightness is God's law, who feels obligated to practise the moral precepts of his religion in his everyday behaviour, and who feels morally accountable to God for his conduct, will be qualitatively different in his moral behaviour from the general run of mankind. But when religion is practised only formally on Sunday mornings, it is little more than an institutionalized form of conscience balm for the immorality practised on weekdays.

The alleged prepotency of the affective determinants of moral behaviour

Overvaluation by psychologists and psychiatrists of the affective determinants of moral behaviour has led to widespread acceptance of the proposition that there is a one-to-one relationship between the operation of such determinants and the actual content of moral conduct. Having grown up professionally in this tradition, I was therefore pleasantly surprised in the course of my own psychiatric experience by the large number of my patients who, through sheer exercise of will and rational acknowledgment of the rational superiority of certain norms of conduct, successfully managed to suppress the expression of many unfair, destructive, or socially pernicious personality trends whose existence they learned to recognize and disapprove of. Thus, I do not find it essential to believe that human beings necessarily *have* to express their affective and attitudinal tendencies overtly – or even covertly – in disguised forms which escape their own recognition. In fact, we often find that individuals, on the basis of purely rational considerations of moral principle and obligation, feel impelled to take interpersonal and social positions that are temperamentally repugnant to them or are antithetical to their personality preferences, inclinations, and self-interest. Man is not a helpless puppet of his personality traits, affective impulses, and inaccessible motives. Modern psychiatry and clinical psychology notwithstanding, he is a rational as well as an affective being.

Overemphasis on affective methods of handling guilt

The final expression of psychology's overvaluation of the affective aspects of moral behaviour with which I shall deal concerns current overemphasis on nonconscious and nonrational mechanisms of handling guilt. It is not necessary, however, to believe that all guilt feelings are intolerable and must somehow be repressed, disowned, rationalized, confessed, expiated, etc. In the same sense that there is tolerance for conscious anxiety, there is tolerance for conscious guilt, the degree of tolerance, of course, being subject to wide individual differences. Man's portrait of himself need not be free of all moral blemishes. Hence, a good deal of ordinary guilt can be acknowledged on a conscious level and taken in stride without any efforts being made towards reduction of guilt. There is reason to believe that the intrinsically secure person who is moderately self-sufficient possesses more guilt tolerance than either the insecure of the overly dependent individual.

In our culture we tend to underestimate man's capacity for moral depravity. We tend to assume that people could not conceivably be guilty of certain immoral intentions and practices because if they were, "how could they possibly live with themselves?" And if we do admit such a possibility, we reveal the impact of psychoanalytic doctrine and moral relativism on our thinking by blaming "unconscious motives," and by absolving the individual from moral accountability on the grounds that he is the innocent product (victim) of his heredity and environment and could not possibly have acted in any other way.

Several alternative explanations, however, should be considered. In the first place, most people can tolerate more conscious guilt than we are willing to concede; we have exaggerated man's need for perceiving himself as completely untainted in a moral sense. Secondly, many times when we think that a person should be experiencing guilt feelings he really is not for one or both of two good reasons: (1) no real internalization of moral obligation has taken place; or (2) self-criticism is inhibited to the point where no discrepancy can be perceived between behaviour and obligation, regardless of how flagrant the disparity may appear to others. It is necessary to differentiate this latter situation from instances in which A guilt is actually experienced but wrong-doing is still denied because of pride, inability to admit being in the wrong, and outright intellectual dishonesty; and B guilt occurs but is rationalized away without conscious awareness of distortion or misrepresentation of facts.

The mental hygiene value of keeping guilt on a conscious level parallels the advantages of dealing with anxiety on the same basis: the possibilities of evolving constructive solutions are greatly enhanced. In the case of the former, this means learning to bear and live with one's quota of guilt while taking such realistic preventive and restitutive measures as are indicated. Where legitimate compromises with moral principle are clearly necessary, the reasons for these compromises should be unambiguously perceived and acknowledged as such rather than rationalized on a more acceptable basis. In this way it is possible to retain one's moral code intact under the most trying circumstances. Unless the reasons for unavoidable moral expediency are kept clearly in mind, habituation to and corruption by acting expediently tend to occur; and what starts out as a reluctant manoeuvre under duress ends up by becoming the individuals' characteristic mode of ethical behaviour.

Children generally, in contradistinction to adults, are not capable of making this type of moral adjustment. Being unable to appreciate or evaluate the issues involved in making inescapable moral compromises, they are more likely actually to assimilate than to simulate acceptance of the inferior ethical alternative represented by the compromise. We are witnessing just such a situation today in Germany. Many adults were able to survive Hitlerism morally unscathed, whereas the children who grew up at the time remain completely indoctrinated.

THE RELEVANCE OF ETHICS FOR A SCIENCE OF BEHAVIOUR

Another way in which psychology has undervalued the role of rationality in moral behaviour has been by stressing the metaphysical and purely philosophical aspects of moral values and contending thereby that psychology must necessarily adopt an ethically neutral stance. Thus, during the past four decades or more, psychology, the science of behaviour, has attempted to evade coming to terms with ethics, the science of ends, norms, good, right, and choice. The focus of psychological concern has been on adjustment as an end in itself, the contention being that moral values are subjective and unverifiable. According to this view, moral judgments are matters of arbitrary preference and opinion beyond the pale of science; no objective psychological criterion is possible. Behaviour may be appraised by psychologists as constructive or antisocial, but never as good or evil. The purpose of psychology is to explain conduct, not to judge it; questions of accountability are held to be irrelevant in the light of psychological determinism, and hence the proper concern of jurists and philosophers only.

In reply to this line of argument I would say first that to ignore ethical considerations in appraising behaviour is to overlook one of the most significant aspects of human conduct. Whether the psychologist chooses to recognize it or not, most purposeful behaviour in human beings has a moral aspect, the psychological reality of which cannot be ignored. The goals of human development, insofar as they are determined by man and culture, are always predicated upon certain moral assumptions. Thus, the development of the individual is invariably influenced by coercive exposure to the particular set of assumptions which his culture espouses and which he himself eventually assimilates. Second, empirically verifiable ethical propositions *can* be discovered once we accept certain basic *philosophical* value judgments regarding the proper ends of development which themselves are empirically unverifiable. If, for example, we were to grant that self-realization were the highest goal towards which many could strive, it would then be possible objectively to establish which behavioural alternatives are most compatible with this goal and hence most ethical.

But even if the primary value judgments are not empirically verifiable, they must still be predicated upon empirically determined human capacities for the kind of norms that are advocated. It is futile to speak of life goals that are motivationally unsupportable or of standards of maturity that only angels could reach. The same criterion obviously applies also to principles of accountability, which must be grounded on attainable norms of moral development. Finally, moral behaviour is of interest to the specialist in child development because it has a developmental history. It undergoes orderly and systematic age-level changes and manifests psychobiological (cross-cultural) uniformities and psychosocial as well as idiosyncratic variability. In terms of the underlying psychological processes involved in conscience development, we deal with genetically determined potentialities. However, the actual acquisition of moral behaviour, the normative sequences, and the variability in development are largely determined by experiential and sociocultural factors.

It is important, therefore, that a given ethical objective or standard that rests on purely philosophical value judgments – for example, the proposition that the highest good towards which man can strive is self-realization – makes psychological as well as philosophical sense. It must, in other words, be psychologically acceptable to human beings as a possible and worthwhile goal. People must also be judged intellectually capable of defining the nature of self-realization and of acting in a manner consistent with it. Moreover, for self-realization to become a guiding principle of moral behaviour and a cornerstone of conscience, human beings must be capable: (*a*) of internalizing it as a moral value, (*b*) of acquiring feelings of obligation to promote its expression, (*c*) of developing feelings of self-dissatisfaction and remorse if they deliberately thwart its furtherance, and (*d*) of accepting accountability for violating it as a principle of moral conduct.

Moral relativism

The proponents of moral relativism, who hold that man cannot through observation, experiment, and reason discover ethical values that are comparable to other scientific truths, base their contention on four main arguments: (1) that a concept of absolute truth is incompatible with the philosophy of science; (2) that "good" and "evil" are relative to the circumstances under which an act is committed, for example, the "white lie"; (3) that moral values cannot be universal or objectively valid since they are conditioned by historical and social factors; and (4) that even if it were possible to base an ethical system on the facts of "human nature," a separate system would have to be devised for every culture and subculture, since human nature is primarily a function of cultural environment. Only the first two arguments need concern us here, the latter two will be considered in the later section on cultural relativism.

The first argument with respect to absolute truth merely confuses the issue. To be objectively valid, ethical values have to be no more "absolutely," "unquestionably and eternally true," and unrevisable than any other scientific proposition. Implicit in the modern concept of scientific truth is the assumption that any empirically derived formulation in science is tentative and approximate, that is, the truest statement that can be made in the light of available knowledge. The achievement of "absolute truth" is a theoretical, not a phenomenological reality. For every event that happens there is, in my opinion, a true or "absolute" explanation, the discovery of which must always remain a goal to be striven for rather than a goal which is attainable. After an infinite series of revisions and refinements this goal can be approached but never reached.

Secondly, if the alleged dependence of ethical judgment upon situational factors is examined critically, it will be found that the illustrations used in support of this argument represent instances in which a conflict exists between alternative moral principles. It is wrong to tell a lie, but it is conceivable that circumstances exist in which a more compelling moral duty takes precedence. However, to admit that ethical principles can operate antagonistically in the same field is not to negate the objective validity of the individual principles. Most complex physico-chemical, biological, and social phenomena represent just such equilibria between opposing forces. The outcome or resultant in these cases reflects the relative strength of the competing variables.

It can be justifiably argued that many theorists in the field of ethics could classify the position taken by the writer in this section as relativistic on at least three accounts: (1) the writer's refusal to claim a privileged status for ethical propositions in contradistinction to other empirically derived scientific principles dissociates his position from that of those moral absolutists who assert the existence of axiomatic, "revealed," intuitive, or dogmatic ethical principles enjoying exemption from the methodological considerations and rules of evidence customarily applied in science; (2) his acceptance of the need for "socially immanent ethics" represents a concession to the flexibility of "universal ethics" which many moral absolutists are unwilling to grant; and (3) his thesis that norms of ethical conduct must be related to developmental capacities for moral behaviour denies the extreme absolutistic assumptions that the moral powers of man are innately and axiomatically given, that they undergo no evolution in form, and that they must therefore be judged in relation to a single criterion of value.

If subscribing to these beliefs places him in the camp of the more relativistic of the ethical universalists, the writer is certainly not averse to being grouped with this wing of philosophical thought, especially if this will dissociate him from adherence to the commonly accepted, albeit inaccurate, stereotype of what constitutes moral absolutism. The futility of dichotomizing the proponents of moral absolutism and relativism into two polar schools of thought is further illustrated by the observation that both schools are divided on the issue of whether ethical values can ever be given the same type of empirical validation as the laws of a particular scientific discipline. In this connection, the writer's distinction between psychological and philosophical ethical values might effect some reconciliation between these two points of view.

RATIONALITY AND MORAL ACCOUNTABILITY

Still another expression of psychology's devaluation of the role of rationality in moral behaviour is its general acceptance of a doctrine of determinism, which allegedly exempts human beings from accountability for their misdeeds. Irrespective of whether affective antecedents and mechanisms beyond the individual's control are held to be prepotent in moral conduct, or whether the outcome in moral choice situations is conceptualized as an automatic reflection of positive habit strength or of the strength of generalized habits of inhibition, rational volitional restraints and considerations are obviously de-emphasized.

When Oscar Wilde wrote his famous "Ballad of Reading Gaol," decrying man's right to pass moral judgment on the actions of his fellow man, he did not realize that his position would become so widely accepted only a half century later by social scientists and philosophers concerned with human behaviour. The credo of the modern social scientist is predominantly deterministic. It repudiates the notion of free will as reactionary and unscientific, and regards the practice of passing moral judgment as abhorrent, unpsychological, and tinged with the presumption of godlike omniscience. The moral character of an individual is presumed to be shaped by forces beyond his control and, therefore, exempt from any judgmental assessment with ethical implications. Immoral behaviour is held to be no different from any other kind of undesirable behaviour. It can only be understood psychologically as a type of adjustment mechanism. Caroline Zachry's (1944) appraisal of delinquency, for example, is thoroughly representative of current nonlegal professional opinion. "To isolate certain forms of emotional disturbance and to label them with a term of opprobrium is both scientifically inaccurate and inimical to the interests of youth. It presupposes an attitude of sitting in moral judgment, of attaching blame for behaviour which should be considered as a symptom of disturbance."

My main quarrel with determinism rests on a very general premise. Contrary to Fromm's assertion (1947), the psychologist is not required to accept the view that the will is not an independent force but merely the executioner of the dominant motive impinging upon the behavioural field – that "free will" is an illusion which confounds awareness of the outcome of the struggle between conflicting forces with the power to determine the outcome. By considering the development of conscience, I have traced the gradual evolution of a generalized sense of moral obligation. In association with its executive arm of inhibitory self-control, this feeling of obligation constitutes a more or less consistent system of behaviour with considerable generality of function that is implicated in every moral decision. The outcome of the latter is not merely a reflection of the relative strength of a given moral value and its opposing motive, but also of the strength of the generalized sense of obligation to abide by *all* moral values and the vigour of its associated volitional counterpart.

The writer is aware of the fact that a genetic theory of conscience not only provides a basis for ethical conduct and moral accountability, but also establishes a basis in the past for immoral behaviour which *was* beyond the individual's control when it impinged on his ethical development. This fact is undeniable and is frequently used as an argument for determinism. In the past history of every individual can be found events which explain his failure to behave morally in certain situations and enable one to predict how he will act in the future. However, the possibility of explaining and predicting an individual's moral lapses on the basis of his developmental history bears no relevance to the problem of moral accountability which requires a judgment with respect to the present situation. Regardless of past events beyond his control, if he can presently recognize a moral obligation and is physically and psychologically capable of exerting inhibitory control, he is accountable for his misdeeds. If in addition a genetic explanation is available for same, it provides a nice demonstration of the fact that behaviour, like all events in nature, has casual antecedents (i.e., is deterministic). But what has this to do with moral accountability? Acceptance of behavioural determinism does not oblige one to repudiate the doctrine of responsibility for moral behaviour.

It can be argued, of course, that *current* capacity for acknowledging moral obligation and suppressing contrary motives is itself a product of psychological determinism. In terms of *ultimate* causality, this assertion is undeniable. With respect to more *proximate* casual determinants, however, it is equally undeniable that a reasonable and psychologically identifiable latitude of free choice prevails, and that the individual is therefore responsible for the ethical implications of the choice he makes.

If this hypothesis is correct, moral culpability exists whenever the possibility of exercising inhibitory control is present in an ethical problem but nevertheless fails to be exercised. If motives cannot be effectively combatted by volitional restraint because of overpowering emotion, the question of accountability obviously becomes more complicated. The defence of "uncontrollable impulse" generally means that suppression was originally possible but was surrendered to indulgence under special extenuating circumstances. In such cases, culpability is present although undoubtedly in lesser degree than in instances where more deliberate choice was possible. However, lack of awareness of the "true" motives for a misdeed is no defence as long as moral restraint can be exercised. That a murderer fails to appreciate that his hostility is a reaction against parental rejection no more absolves him of responsibility for his crime than the historical fact of parental rejection itself, although our knowledge of the latter fact makes his action more comprehensible.

It is the writer's firm contention that the vast majority of immoral and delinquent acts are committed under conditions where there is clear awareness of a moral duty. For example, in instances of criminal behaviour committed by a nonsatellizer who consciously places himself above the law, or is intellectually dishonest in failing to perceive the incompatibility of his behaviour with his professed ethical code, the decision regarding culpability should be unequivocal.

The determination of moral culpability is obviously a highly intricate process requiring considerable psychological analysis. All individuals cannot be judged by the same yardstick. For example, expediency becomes a less legitimate standard of behaviour as the degree of freedom from dependency increases. Also, considerations of expediency should become less influential to an individual when interpersonal relationships are based on human values than when relationships are predicated upon his value as a commodity to be bought and sold on the market. Thus, what ostensibly appears to be a double moral standard may when examined genotypically turn out to be a highly consistent ethical code of behaviour.

The condemnatory aspects of moral judgment to which Fromm (1947) objects so violently are inescapable if such judgment is to have any real moral significance. And condemnation inevitably implies punishment. Neither children nor adults are able to learn the limits of acceptable conduct unless they are punished when they exceed these limits. Furthermore, on strictly logical grounds, the entire notion of moral accountability – which is an essential ingredient of a sound conscience – would be completely meaningless if it did not imply liability to ethical judgment, culpability, and punishment. Also, few if any children are quite so fragile that they cannot take deserved reproof and punishment in stride. Punishment, finally, does not preclude in any way an earnest effort to discover the underlying causes of the misbehaviour, to avoid a spirit of vindictiveness, or to apply suitable preventive, therapeutic or rehabilitative measures.

If therapy alone were instituted, culpable immoral behaviour would not be distinguished in any way from other behaviour disorders. The notion of liability to punishment following misbehaviour is more than a specific product of certain forms of cultural organization. It is an inevitable component of the individual's own concept of moral value and obligation which lies at the root of his conscience formation. As a guilt-reducing mechanism, its therapeutic value should also not be minimized. The threat of social punishment, therefore, is an important regulatory mechanism in the development of conscience. It also serves a self-protective function with respect to perpetuating the moral standards of a given social order. After conscience is acquired, of course, it is no longer the main deterrent for misbehaviour, but merely serves to restrain impulsive acts of "testing the limits."

With respect to society's right to condemn and punish (without being accused of taking over godlike prerogatives), I must side with the judiciary and against Oscar Wilde and the prevailing opinion of social scientists. Holding individuals accountable for their behaviour is not only a logical extension of the belief in an objectively valid system of ethics, but is also a legitimate device necessary to society to protect its members from predatory individuals. The latter justification is also applicable to the incarceration both of culpable individuals who are dangerous and incorrigible, and of nonculpable persons whose freedom would constitute a menace to public safety.

CULTURAL RELATIVISM AND MORAL CONDUCT

Finally, psychology has attempted to undermine the viability of a psychological theory of ethics and to undervalue the rationality of moral conduct by denying that there can be a culturally universal code of nonarbitrary and verifiable moral principles transcending the idiosyncratic features of a particular cultural tradition or historical epoch. Fromm (1947) clarifies the issue by making an important distinction between "socially immanent" ethics, by which he means "such norms as are necessary for the functioning of a specific kind of society and of the people in it," and "universal ethics" or those "norms of conduct the aim of which is the growth and unfolding of man." The socially immanent ethics of a given society may conceivably embody none of the principles of universal ethics, and may even violently conflict with them, for example, the ethics of totalitarian nations. On the other hand, the specific ethical code of a given culture may represent the application of universal ethical principles to prevailing social and historical conditions.

In neither instance is the case for an objectively verifiable system of ethics invalidated. The fact that a ruthless segment of society can give its destructive ethical code the sanction of law does not rule out the possibility of a science of ethics any more than Hitler's racial edicts eliminated the possibility of a science of anthropology. And the fact that the same ethical principle may find expression in different ways, depending on the social climate, does not in any way vitiate its universality. Universal moral values can only be stated in general terms. Their implementation in a given cultural setting is a matter of social engineering. We make use of the same principle of steam pressure whether we use it to operate a locomotive, a ship, or a sewing machine.

The last argument advanced by the proponents of moral relativism is that, if we try to tie ethical values to human nature, we can have no universal system of ethics, since there are no aspects of human nature which follow from universally distributed behavioural properties and capacities of the organism. This notion can be discounted, of course, by pointing to the inevitable psychological communality that must exist among individuals in different cultures on the basis of neuroanatomical, neurophysiological, and endrocrinological similarity, on the basis of common genetic factors that limit psychological development or predetermine its sequential course in terms of process, and on the basis of exposure to similar types of interpersonal experiences.

> Man is not a blank sheet of paper on which culture can write its text; he is an entity charged with energy and structured in specific ways, which, while adapting itself, reacts in specific and ascertainable ways to external conditions ... In opposing the erroneous assumption that certain historical cultural patterns are the expression of a fixed and eternal human nature, the adherents of the theory of infinite malleability of human nature arrived at an equally untenable position. If a man were infinitely malleable [he] ... would be only

the puppet of social arrangements and not – as he has proved to be in history – an agent whose intrinsic properties react strenuously against the powerful pressure of unfavorable social and cultural patterns ... Human nature is not fixed, and culture, thus, is not to be explained as the result of fixed human instincts; nor is culture a fixed factor to which human nature adapts itself passively and completely. It is true that man can adapt himself even to unsatisfactory conditions, but in this process of adaptation, he develops definite mental and emotional reactions which follow from the specific properties of his own nature (Fromm 1947, 21–3).

REFERENCES

Ausubel, D.P. *Ego development and the personality disorders* New York: Grune & Stratton 1952

Ausubel, D.P. *Theory and problems of adolescent development* New York: Grune & Stratton 1954

Ausubel, D.P. *Theory and problems of child development* New York: Grune & Stratton 1958

Bartlett, E.R., Harris, D.B. Personality factors in delinquency *School and Society* 1936 *43* 653–6

Bavelas, A. A method for investigating individual and group ideology *Sociometry* 1942 *5* 371–7

Benedict, R. *The chrysanthemum and the sword* Boston: Houghton, Mifflen 1946

Betts, G.H. Religious attitudes and activities of university students: A report *Religious Education* 1927 *23* 917–19

Bronfenbrenner, U. Soviet methods of character education: Some implications for research *Religious Education* 1962 *57* no. 4 (Res. Suppl.) 545–61

Brown, A.W., Morrison, J., Couch, G.B. Influence of affectional family relationships on character development *Journal of Abnormal and Social Psychology* 1947 *42* 422–8.

Eberhart, J.C. Attitudes toward property: A genetic study by the paired-comparisons rating of offences *Journal of Genetic Psychology* 1942 *60* 3–35

Fromm, E. *Man for himself* New York: Rinehart 1947

Gesell, A., Ilg, F.L. *The child from five to ten* New York: Harper 1946

Hartshorne, H., et al. *Studies in the nature of character.* I. *Studies in deceit.* II. *Studies in self-control.* III. *Studies in the organization of character* New York: Macmillan 1930

Havighurst, R.J., Robinson, M.Z., Door, M. The development of the ideal self in childhood and adolescence *Journal of Educational Research* 1946 *40* 241–57

Havighurst, R.J., Taba, H. *Adolescent character and personality* New York: Wiley 1949

Hill, D.S. Personification of ideals by urban children *Journal of Social Psychology* 1930 *1* 379–93

Kohlberg, L. The development of moral thinking and choice in the years ten to sixteen. Unpublished doctoral dissertation Chicago: University of Chicago 1958

Kohlberg, L. The development of children's orientations toward a moral order I. Sequence in the development of moral thought *Vita Humana* 1963a *6* 11–33

Kohlberg, L. Moral development and indentification *Child psychology*, 62nd Yearbook, *National Society for Studies in Education* Part I. Chicago: University of Chicago Press 1963b

Leighton, D., Kluckhohn, C. *Children of the people* Cambridge, Mass.: Harvard University Press 1947

Lerner, E. *Constraint areas and the moral judgment of children* Menasha, Wisc.: Banta 1937a

Lerner, E. The problem of perspective in moral reasoning *American Journal of Sociology* 1937b *43* 249–69

Liu, G.H. The influence of cultural background on the moral judgment of children. Unpublished doctoral dissertation. New York: Columbia University 1950

Mac Rae, D. A test of Piaget's theories of moral development *Journal of Abnormal Social Psychology* 1954 *49* 14–18

Mead, M. Some anthropological considerations concerning guilt. In M.L. Reymort (ed.) *Feelings and emotions* New York: McGraw-Hill, 1950 pp. 362–73

Messerschmidt, R. The suggestibility of boys and girls between the ages of six and sixteen years *Journal of Genetic Psychology* 1933 *43* 422–37

Nichols, C.A. *Moral education among North American Indians* New York: Teachers College, Columbia University 1930

Piaget, J. *The moral judgment of the child* New York: Harcourt, Brace 1932

Reymert, M.L., Kohn, H.A. An objective investigation of suggestibility *Character and Personality* 1940 *9* 44–8

Slaght, W.E. Untruthfulness in children: Its conditioning factors and its setting in child nature *University of Iowa Studies in Character* 1924 *1* No. 4

Stendler, C.B. A study of some socio-moral judgments of junior high school students *Child Development* 1949 *20* 15–29

Strang, R. Religious activities of adolescent girls *Religious Education* 1929 *24* 313–21
Strauss, A.L. The development of conceptions of rules in children *Child Development* 1954 *35* 193–204
Tudor-Hart, B.E. Are there cases in which lies are necessary? *Pedagogical Seminar* 1926 *33* 586–641
Ugurel-Semin, R. Moral behavior and moral judgment of children *Journal of Abnormal Social Psychology* 1952 *47* 463–74
Wright, B.A. Altruism in children and the perceived conduct of others *Journal of Abnormal and Social Psychology* 1942 *37* 218–33
Zachry, C.B. Preparing youth to be adults. In *Adolescence*, 43rd Yearbook, *National Society for Studies in Education* Part 1. Chicago: University of Chicago Press 1944, pp. 332–46

PART FOUR

Some problems of methodology and practice

CHAPTER 8

Matching models and moral training

DAVID E. HUNT

The fundamental factors in the educative process are an immature, undeveloped being; and certain social aims, meanings, values incarnate in the matured experience of the adult. The educative process is the due *interaction of these forces*. Such a conception of *each in relation to the other* as facilitates completest and freest interaction is the essence of educational theory (Dewey 1902–4 my italics) ... we really know very little about ... the "match" between individual development and external stimulation at various stages of growth (Deutsch 1967, 10).

The major reason for the lack of cumulative knowledge during the sixty-five years between these two statements has been the failure to take seriously the implications of an interactive model that coordinates the effects of educational environments on particular types of learners to produce specific objectives. Individual differences are given much lip service, and even more drawer space in the form of filed tests results, yet educational planners and decision makers continue to work from models for "students-in-general." Ignoring the importance of differential student characteristics leads to posing questions in terms of the general effectiveness of educational procedures, for example "Is a discovery approach more effective than a structured approach?" with no acknowledgment of the differential effectiveness of such approaches on different kinds of learners.

The present paper takes as a basic assumption the necessity of a differential effectiveness model or, as Stern put it, "The characteristics of the student and of the educational objectives must both be employed as guides in the design of maximally effective environments for learning" (Stern 1961, 728). It is further assumed that the concept of *matching* provides a helpful conceptual device for considering the differential consequences of such interaction.

Lewin's classic formula – B = f (P, E), or "Behaviour is a function of the Person and the Environment," and Cronbach's (1957) recommendation to co-ordinate individual differences with environmental influences have been generally accepted, but specific models providing such interactive formulations have developed slowly. Probably the major obstacle to dealing with interactive effects has been the difficulty of conceptualizing and measuring both the person and the environment in theoretically comparable terms. A few approaches aimed to co-ordinate person-environment effects upon contemporaneous functioning may be noted: Stern's use of a need-press model for viewing the congruence and dissonance between college environments and students (Stern 1960); Schroder's, Driver's, and Streufert's use of an information-processing model to predict the optimal combination of environmental complexity and the integrative complexity of the person (Schroder, Driver, and Streufert 1967); Kagan's emphasis on the match between the stimulus and the schema to predict subsequent response and feeling of pleasure (Kagan 1967); and Pervin's summary of studies on individual environment "fit" to account for performance and satisfaction (Pervin 1968).

Differential effectiveness of treatment workers upon different clients has also been viewed in matching terms. For example, Sapolsky demonstrated therapist-patient compatibility to be an important determinant of therapeutic outcome (Sapolsky 1965). Warren and her colleagues have developed a very comprehensive system for panning differential treatment which consists of different kinds of treatment workers as well as different forms of treatment for delinquents at different levels of interpersonal maturity (Warren 1967).

The role of matching in stimulating development from one stage to another has been considered by Piaget (1932), Kohlberg and his colleagues (Kohlberg 1963, 1966; Turiel 1966, 1969), and D.E. Hunt (1966a) among others. Several authors have noted that Piaget has dealt with the problem only in general terms: "A fourth principle, hinted at but not quite formulated by Piaget concerns the role of the still poorly understood factor of the match between the schemata within the organism and the circumstances of the situation in determining whether accommodative modification will occur in any given encounter with the environment" (J. McV. Hunt 1961, 259).

The most relevant work for matching in the area of moral training has been done by Kohlberg and his colleagues. Kohlberg stated the problem as follows: "There is also an important problem of match between the teacher's level and the child involved in effective moral communication. Conventional moral education never has had much influence on children's moral judgment because it has disregarded this problem of developmental match" (Kohlberg 1966, 24). Using Kohlberg's theory of stages of moral development, Turiel stated: "It is thus necessary to consider what the child responds to in the environment as well as the nature of interaction with the environment which leads to change. The effectiveness of environmental influences largely depends on the match between the level of concepts being encountered and the developmental level of the child" (Turiel 1968, 99). D.E. Hunt has formulated the potential match/mismatch of certain person-environment combinations in terms of a change model as follows: "The present change model is a differential treatment model consisting of logically derived statements of the 'if . . . then' variety which are conditional upon the current conceptual orientation of the person. Knowledge of a child's present conceptual level is essential, and if we know the present level, then we can derive the specific environment most likely to produce progression toward a higher level" (D.E. Hunt 1966a, 287).

The present paper will describe a metatheoretical framework within which matching models can be considered, and will then apply it to a few selected models. In order to be relevant to guiding practical decisions, a matching model should be translatable into the general form, "What environment is prescribed for this person in order to produce this desired change?" Assuming that one issue to be dealt with in the present conference is that of planning deliberative forms of educational intervention most likely to stimulate growth in the child's moral judgment and behaviour, we will usually focus on such changes; however, the framework should be generically applicable to matching models in other domains as well.

The metatheoretical framework for considering matching models will be organized around four major dimensions of variation: desired change, conception of the person, conception of the environment, and conception of the interactive process. Since there are not now a large number of matching models, we will occasionally use an example from an approach which may come from a general rather than a differential view in order to illustrate a particular point.

DESIRED CHANGE

Matching models aim for different kinds of change: one model may aim for inducing developmental growth, whereas another may aim for producing a specific change in behaviour. It usually requires a different combination of person and environment to accomplish different objectives.

Specific objectives

Among psychologists, Kohlberg has been the most articulate advocate of the developmental approach in the area of moral education with what might be called a *genotypic* approach emphasizing the underlying processes and structural organization which determine moral behaviour. He states the objectives of moral education as follows:

> This alternative is to take the stimulation of the development of the individual child's moral judgment and character as a goal of moral education, rather than taking as its goal either administrative convenience or state-defined values . . . Each of the Kohlberg stages of moral judgment represents a step toward a more genuinely or distinctly moral judgment. We do not mean by this that a more mature judgment is more moral in the sense of showing closer conformity to the conventional standards of a given community. We mean that a more mature judgment more closely corresponds to genuine moral judgments as these have been defined by philosophers (Kohlberg 1966 19, 21).

Kohlberg, therefore, adopts moral maturity as the dimension of change in advocating development along this dimension as the goal of moral education. A person's stage of moral development is related to his moral behaviour (Kohlberg 1965), but it is assumed that the stage of moral judgment is a more meaningful unit than that of a single index of moral behaviour or of its conformity to certain standards.

In contrast to this genotypic view are approaches that take the *phenotypic* objective of producing an immediate, observable change in moral behaviour. Although not a matching model, the approach of Bandura and McDonald (1963) specified an objective of behavioural change. Following learning-theory tradition, these investigators attempted to produce changes in the person's verbal behaviour, that is, explaining an event in terms of subjective or objective responsibility.

The genotypic-phenotypic distinction, exemplified by the developmentalist and learning theorist in specifying moral objectives, can also be seen in the area of psychotherapy where some approaches aim for cognitive and affective reorganization (genotypic) while other approaches aim directly at modification of behaviour (phenotypic). The distinction can be observed in education by what has been referred to as the Piaget-Skinner controversy in which the genotypic approach aims for structural recognization and increased intrinsic motivation, while the phenotypic approach aims for the acquisition of specific, correct responses.

Having drawn the distinction in a rather oversimplified way for emphasis, it may be noted that both approaches are concerned with behaviour, but they take a different stand on the role of behaviour in defining objectives. In the area of treatment and control of delinquent youngsters, for example, one cannot ignore the frequency of reported unlawful behaviour. However, there is considerable difference of opinion among treatment approaches as to whether one should attempt to suppress directly the occurrence of delinquent behaviour or to deal with causal factors within the individual which are thought to determine such behaviour. For example, I recently attended a conference on models for providing differential treatment for delinquents (described in Warren 1966) at which one participant (who was not an advocate of differential treatment) suggested that the best procedure for reducing the incidence of one form of deliquency, in this case, car theft, was to insititute national legislation requiring wheel locks on all automobiles. This is an extreme example of the phenotypic approach, which attempts to manipulate directly the occurrence or nonoccurence of specific behaviour; programs such as those of Warren and her colleagues (to be described in a later section), which aim to change the orientation of the individual youth, exemplify the genotypic approach to the problem.

From the genotypic position, one needs several behavioural referents to infer underlying structure. Tomkins and Miner (1957) pointed out that behavioural referents vary considerably in their "nondiffuseness," that is, the degree to which they provide a direct index of an underlying characteristic. Although seemingly apparent, this point is rarely acknowledged by advocates of the phenotypic approach. In commenting on Bandura's and McDonald's study (1963), Turiel (1966) pointed out that they focused on only one (objective-subjective responsibility) of the eleven behavioural indices suggested by Piaget for heteronomous and autonomous orientations. Further, he continued: "By studying only one dimension as manifested in children's choices between two alternatives Bandura and McDonald dealt with isolated surface responses, and not with the concept of stage or mental structure" (Turiel 1966, 617).

Criteria for change

Although they should be applicable to evaluating deliberate intervention in both the laboratory and in everyday-life situations, criteria for change are especially important for evaluating the results from laboratory simulations and analogs. Sanford has recently decried the tendency in psychological experimentation towards increasingly trivial, meaningless investigations which are irrelevant to human problems (Sanford 1965). I would argue that a major reason for this tendency is the failure to adopt criteria for change that could be applied to the results of experiments which purport to produce change.

In reviewing studies which claim to increase the incidence of so-called "self-reinforcement" (considered an analog for the internalization of self-control), Katz pointed out: "Thus two criteria for judging whether a particular type of socially learned behaviour has become internalized would be (a) whether it occurs in the absence of direct or indirect surveilance, and (b) whether it occurs in the absence of any external mediation of immediate affective consequences" (Katz 1967, 155–56). He continued by noting that none of the studies up to that time that purported to increase "self-reinforcement" had met either criteria.

Following Piaget, Kohnstamm has summarized five criteria for evaluating newly acquired behaviour. Piaget had originally proposed that the newly acquired behaviour should be "(1) lasting, (22) transferable, and (3) fundamentally different from the pre-experimental level of behaviour" (Kohnstamm 1965, 4) to which Kohnstamm added (4) difficulty of acquisition (presumably on the basis that nothing that comes easily will last), and (5) resistance to extinction.

Closely related to these criteria is the view of how change occurs. Kelman has described "processes of opinion change," and his conception of change through compliance would seem to be much like the process assumed to occur in the phenotypic approach: "Compliance can be said to occur when an individual accepts influence from another person or from a group because he hopes to achieve a favourable reaction from the other. He may be interested in attaining certain specific rewards or in avoiding certain specific punishments that the influencing agent controls" (Kelman 1961, 62).

Similarly, Kelman's description of the process of internalization would seem to be the general process view accepted in the genotypic approach: "Internalization can be said to occur when an individual accepts influence because the induced behaviour is congruent with his value system. It is the content of the induced behaviour that is intrinsically rewarding here. The individual adopts it because he finds it useful for the solution of a problem, or because it is congenial to his own orientation, or because it is demanded by his own values" (Kelman 1961, 65).

To evaluate change occurring through the process of internalization thus requires more rigorous criteria of change. An investigator may or may not agree with the criteria suggested; nonetheless he should explicate whatever criteria he does use so that the relevance of his results can be more appropriately evaluated.

CONCEPTION OF THE PERSON

The representation of individual differences in matching models must be expressed in a form that will eventually be comparable to environmental differences in order to make statements about the consequences of person-environment interaction. Most models represent the person on one or more dimensions, which vary in their relative emphasis on structure or dynamics, so that such representations can then be placed in relation to corresponding environmental representations.

How is personal variation represented

The models most relevant for moral training are those which represent the individual along a single dimension of developmental stages. Theories of stages view the person's position on a single dimension in relation to some value orientation which assumes higher levels to be more desirable. Primary examples are moral maturity (Kohlberg 1963); conceptual level (Harvey, Hunt, and Schroder 1961, Hunt 1966a); and interpersonal maturity level (Sullivan, Grant, and Grant 1957, Warren 1967). Although each of these models employs one basic dimension on which to classify individuals, each also acknowledges other more complex features of individual variation. In addition to moral maturity level, "stage mixture" is considered (Turiel 1969); in addition to conceptual level, degree of openness is considered (D.E. Hunt 1966a); and in addition to interpersonal maturity level, the person is classified into a behavioural subtype (Warren 1967).

Another group of models is that which represents the person in multidimensional terms, usually either by way of a circumplex or a profile. For example, Stern (1960) represents the person in terms of thirty psychological needs organized in a circumplex, whereas Schutz (1958) represents the person in terms of three interpersonal needs (inclusion, affection, and control), which are expressed in terms of a profile. Many other systems of characterizing individuals in multidimensional terms have, of course, been proposed, but these two examples illustrate the major forms of representation which have been used in matching models.

In addition, Pervin (1968) has proposed a system which characterizes the person in terms of the relation between his present self-rating and his ideal self, and focuses on the disparity between these two dimensions as the essential ingredient for formulating the "best-fit" prediction with certain environmental encounters. Perhaps the simplest representation is a nondimensional, categorical classification into a typology, for example, dominant or submissive, and, as the examples illustrate, these types are frequently endpoints on a dimension.

Kind of personal variation considered

Although the distinction is somewhat arbitrary, most models vary in the degree to which they emphasize structural and organizational characteristics (e.g., cognitive complexity, perceptual differentiation) or dynamics (e.g., interpersonal attributes, needs, motives). The distinction is especially important because, if the person is represented in terms of structural organization, then the environmental representation should be expressed in similar, or at least comparable, terms. For example, Schroder, Driver, and Streufert (1967) described the person in terms of his integrative complexity, and developed a matching model by placing this measure of the structural complexity of the person in relation to environmental complexity. Conversely, a dynamically oriented system such as that of Stern (1960), which represents the person in terms of needs, views the interplay of these motivational systems with the environment as represented in terms of press, or potential for need gratification.

Warren and her colleagues (1966), in the interpersonal maturity-level classification, used as referents for classification indices of perceptual differentiation as well as those of independence and need for peer approval. Such an attempt to take account of both structure and dynamics make the task of environmental co-ordination more difficult, but it also holds the potential advantage of viewing the person as a unified organism consisting of both structural and motivational features.

Potential for change

In addition to representing the person's present position on one or more dimensions, it is also important to characterize his potential for change, or malleability. The belief that culturally disadvantaged adolescents are irreversibly closed to further development or change has been expressed recently by Bettelheim (1964), and challenged by Deutsch: "In other words, the older child may still be malleable, but may require a very different kind of intervention strategy in order to promote differential growth" (Deutsch 1967, 10). Deutsch's position emphasizes the importance of specifying both potential for malleability and form of environmental match required.

In the absence of measures of potential for change and evidence for their validity, the danger is that the belief in the nonmalleability of certain persons will become a self-fulfilling prophecy (D.E. Hunt 1966b). One promising avenue for approaching the potential for change is Turiel's 1969 use of the "stage mixture" concept as a basis for inferring potential for change. He implied that a high degree of mixture is an index of change potential whereas a low degree of mixture, or consistency, indicates a low potential for developmental change (Turiel 1969).

In concluding this section it should be noted that even though it would appear that the dimension on which a person is represented should be the same as the dimension on which change is desired, this need not be the case. It is important to note that one may use one dimension for representing the person who is the object of change in order to produce change in quite a different dimension. For example, it may be that a matching model based on the interaction between needs of a person and press in the environment will produce changes in moral maturity. The point may be debatable, and is of course open to empirical investigation, but it seems advisable at this point to maintain that there is no logical necessity for using the same dimension in representing the person as that along which change is desired.

CONCEPTION OF THE ENVIRONMENT

Representation of environmental variation

Pervin put the question as follows: "Should one consider the perceived or 'actual' environment?" (1968 p. 65). One may decide on theoretical grounds that the perceived environment approach is the more promising, but discover that it contains more methodological disadvantages than the absolute approach. Thus one may agree with Kagan's urging the "need for relativism" in his emphatic statement: "Man reacts less to the objective quality of external stimuli than he does to categorizations of those stimuli" (Kagan 1967, 132). Yet the question immediately arises as to how one is to measure this categorization, or what Lewin called the "psychological life space." Methods are available, however, as exemplified by the characterization of college environments in which, as Pervin (1968) pointed out, one may obtain a relativistic, phenomenological index by asking students for their perceptions of the college environment, and one may also obtain an absolute, objective index by direct observation and by examination of demographic data.

In a sense, the absolute-relative dimension of environmental variation is related to, but not identical with, the degree of responsiveness of the environment, or the extent to which the subject can modify the environment. Another way of stating this variation is in terms of unilaterality-interdependence (Harvey, Hunt, and Schroder 1961, 119). The definition of unilaterality, "subject learns to look externally for criteria to fit into absolutistic schemata," is similar to the absolute representation, whereas the definition of an interdependent environment, "subject learns to view own behaviour as causal in concept formation and information appraisal," is similar to the relativistic view. Whether or not they are identical, it would appear that the degree to which the environment is fixed, unresponsive, and absolute is an important dimension.

Environmental units vary in size from those as broad as an entire culture to those as minute as a pinpoint of light. Educational environments also vary over a dimension of size, ranging through educational institution, program approach, curriculum, mode of presentation, and specific lecture statement. Similarly, environments may take account of a variety of time-spans. Thus, one may analogically consider the psychological "climate" over a long period of time or the psychological "weather" at a specific point in time. From the point of view of matching models, the time unit during which the match is thought to operate is especially important because the model should contain some procedure for updating the state of the person so that the environment can be progressively modulated in an appropriate fashion.

Kind of environmental variation

Conceptions of the environment vary in their relative emphasis on the content presented or the mode of presentation, a distinction which is especially important in educational intervention. Perhaps it will turn out to be the case that the "medium is the message," but at this point there does not appear to be sufficient empirical evidence in the area of deliberative intervention to prevent investigations from taking different stances on the relative importance of content and mode of presentation. Few would disagree that the ultimate optimal environments will consist of a synthesis of appropriate content material presented in the most appropriate form. However, since we are nowhere near this ultimate stage, disagreement exists on how to fuse the mode of presentation with the content. Approaches such as those being suggested by Turiel (1969), which are aimed to increase level of moral maturity by systematically varying both the content (level of concept on the moral maturity dimension) and the mode of presentation (one-sided argument versus two-sided argument), seem to provide a potentially effective strategy.

Role of training agent

First, is it necessary in order to produce the desired goal that a human being radiate the prescribed environment? Very little is known about those conditions of educational stimulation that require the presentation by a person in order to be effective. However, with the enormous upsurge of computer-automated instruction, the question will very shortly become critical.

Second, is the essential ingredient in the environmental component the general style of the training agent or the specific environment he radiates? This is a particularly crucial issue because several matching models in the area of psychotherapy and psychological treatment take the characteristics of the treatment worker as the major environmental unit which varies, and is therefore seen as being matched, for certain types of clients (e.g., Palmer 1968, Sapolsky 1965). Several investigators have similarly focused on the "natural style" of the teacher as the unit to consider in terms of match/mismatch potential for certain kinds of learners (Washburne and Heil 1960, Thelen 1967). As I have noted (D.E. Hunt 1966c), much more investigation of the limits to which training agents can extend their general preferred style to other forms of approach is necessary before an adequate answer will be obtained.

CONCEPTION OF INTERACTIVE PROCESS: WHAT CONSTITUTES A PERSON-ENVIRONMENT MATCH

Once the person and the environment have been represented along comparable or indentical dimensions, one can then specify more precisely what constitutes a match between them by considering their relationship. Probably the major difference among those matching models that are sufficiently explicit to represent both person and environment in comparable terms is the degree of disparity between person and environment thought to constitute a match for the particular objectives. Or, as Stern put the issue: "But what *is* an optimal environment – one that satisfies, or one that stimulates? While it may be true that pearls come from aggravated oysters, you can only get milk from contented cows. Pearls and milk each have their uses, and people will continue to exercise their preferences for one or the other, but it would be a pointless exercise of freedom to insist on milking oysters" (Stern 1961, 728).

Variation in person-environment disparity

As the Stern quotation implies, matching models that aim for immediate functional objectives or satisfaction are likely to define the match in terms of congruence or fit between person and environment, wheeas models that aim for developmental change and growth are likely to define the match in terms of a specified degree of disparity between person and environment. An example of the former approach is illustrated by Pervin: "A 'match' or 'best-fit' of individual to environment is viewed as expressing itself in high performance, satisfaction, and little stress in the system whereas a 'lack of fit' is viewed as resulting in decreased performance, dissatisfaction, and stress in the system" (Pervin 1968, 56).

The view taken by a matching theorist on the necessity for disparity in order to produce change will obviously be related to his concept of the role of equilibrium and disequilibrium in motivation. Current motivational theory is moving towards accepting the necessity for some disequilibrium or disparity, as Kagan's statement indicates: "It appears that the act of matching stimulus to schema when the match is close but not yet perfect is a dynamic event. Stimuli that deviate a critical amount from the child's schema for a pattern are capable of eliciting an active process of recognition, and this process behaves as if it were a source of pleasure. Stimuli that are easily assimilable or too difficult to assimilate do not elicit these reactions" (Kagan 1967, 136).

Specification of the "critical amount" is therefore a problem of central importance for a matching model. Kohlberg is explicit in specifying the degree of disparity required for a match: "In fact, the developmental level of moral educational verbalizations must be matched to the developmental level of the child if they are to have an effect. Ideally, such education should aim at communicating primarily at a level one stage above the child's own and secondly at the child's level" (Kohlberg 1966, 24).

Turiel has experimentally verified this specification (as we will describe in the next section) and has explicated the nature of the process underlying the necessity for a mild degree of disparity:

> One way of inducing change in moral thinking through equilibration process is by presenting the child with conceptual contradictions that activate disequilibrium. These contradictions have to be perceived by the child in such a way that he is motivated to deal with the contradictory events. If concepts corresponding to the higher mode of thought are presented at the same time, the child may assimilate these concepts by performing new mental

operations. In summary, change occurs when perceived conceptual contradictions energize attempts to restructure by exploring the organizational properties of the higher mode of thought (Turiel 1969, 127).

As suggested earlier, those models that aim for functional goals of immediate performance and satisfaction tend to prescribe little or no person-environment disparity, whereas those models that aim for longer-term developmental change tend to prescribe a greater disparity. However, in light of Kagan's comments, it may be necessary to reconsider those models with immediate functional objectives to discover the degree of disparity necessary to acomplish their objectives. It may also be noted that the same model may be used for specifying both short-term and long-term matches. For example, in applying the Conceptual Systems change model (D.E. Hunt 1966a), certain educational environments most likely to produce functional objectives were specified, whereas a different set most likely to produce developmental growth was also suggested.

A secondary issue to be dealt with is the expected consequence of various degrees of mismatching. For example, the change model just referred to D.E. Hunt 1966a) specified the expected consequences, not only of the optimal environment for students at specific conceptual levels, but also the expected consequences of what were referred to as suboptimal and superoptimal stimulation (or what Kagan referred to as too easy or too difficult to assimilate). The consequences of mismatching may vary from a mild worsening of performance and boredom to retrogression. For obvious reasons, it is unlikely that empirical evidence will be collected on extreme cases of mismatching, but we will later consider some evidence on milder forms of mismatching.

The relation between preferred environment and matched environment

That the environment a person prefers will be identical to the matched environment is assumed generally in areas of performance (Pervin 1968, Stern 1961) and psychotherapy (Goldstein, Heller, and Sechrest 1966). However, this relation must be qualified according to the matching objectives. Gassner reported (1968) that patients who were matched with their therapists for high compatibility (Schutz 1958) were more likely to perceive their therapists as more attractive than did patients who were low in compatibility with their therapists, but the matched group showed no difference in behavioural improvement when compared to the mismatched group. In effect, the preferred environment may have matched in relation to a criterion of patient satisfaction, but not necessarily of patient improvement.

Astrove (1966) reported preliminary findings that suggested that adolescents varying in conceptual level tended to prefer educational environments that were different from those prescribed as matched environments in the change model (D.E. Hunt 1966a). For example, although the environment prescribed as developmentally matched for the lowest group (who are poorly socialized and easily frustrated) is that of a clearly organized, structured, situation, the students themselves preferred an environment with very little organization.

Findings such as these will need to be considered in relation to the earlier observations regarding the tendency to experience pleasure in mildly disparate situations so that the complex patterns of relations between the person's preference and what are regarded as optimally matched environments can be unravelled.

APPLICATION OF FRAMEWORK TO THREE MATCHING MODELS

To illustrate the potential utility of the present metatheoretical framework, we will apply it to three matching models: moral maturity, conceptual level, and Community Treatment Project. Although only the moral maturity model takes as its direct objective the enhancement of maturity of moral judgment, the other two models may also be relevant to objectives in moral training. In each case, we will consider the model according to the various dimensions we have suggested, and then report the results of at least one empirical investigation derived from each model. The three models are diagrammatically summarized in matching terms in Table 1.

Moral maturity matching model (Kohlberg 1963, 1964, 1966; Turiel 1969)

Since we have used the Kohlberg model frequently to illustrate the dimensions, its characteristics will need only brief review. The desired change is an increase in the person's stage of moral development. The person is considered along the general dimension of moral maturity segmented into six stages as follows:

Stage	CHARACTERISTICS
1	punishment and obedience orientation
2	naive instrumental hedonism
3	good-boy morality of maintaining good relations
4	authority-maintaining morality
5	morality of contract and democratically accepted law
6	morality of individual principles of conscience

(Kohlberg 1964, 400)

The telegraphic quality of this summary should be noted in that Kohlberg actually defined moral stages in terms of 25 basic aspects (Kohlberg 1966, 7). Kohlberg conceptualizes the environment in terms of its potential for stimulating role-taking at one or another of these stages. Finally, as noted earlier, he specifies the match for producing developmental progression as an environment consisting primarily of content at the next highest stage and secondarily at the child's present stage.

Turiel (1966) tested the validity of this matching predict on by hypothesizing that "an individual accepts concepts one stage above his own dominant position more readily than he accepts thoise two stages above, or one stage below" (Turiel 1966, 614). This prediction is diagrammatically represented at the top of Table 1. In the experiment,

TABLE 1

Summary of three matching models (+=matched; 0=mismatched)

MORAL MATURITY MATCHING MODEL*

Stage of person's moral maturity	Stage level of environmental stimulation					
	1	2	3	4	5	6
Stage 2	0		+	0		
Stage 3		0		+	0	
Stage 4			0		+	0

CONCEPTUAL-LEVEL MATCHING MODEL†

Predominant conceptual level	Program approach	
	Structured	Flexible
Low	+	0
High	0	+

COMMUNITY TREATMENT-PROJECT MATCHING MODEL‡

Interpersonal maturity level of youngster	Type of treatment worker		
	Type 1	Type 2	Type 3
Low	+	0	0
Medium	0	+	0
High	0	0	+

*From Turiel 1966
†From Hunt and Hardt 1967
‡From Grant, Warren, and Turner 1963, Palmer 1968

a group of seventh-grade boys were first classified according to their dominant moral stage, and then assigned to one of four treatment conditions – one below, one above, or two above their dominant stage, or to a control group. Then (except for the control group) they were exposed to role playing and discussion which centered on dilemmas at whatever level was called for by the treatment condition. Finally they were retested after one week to assess their post-treatment stage of development so that the degree of change could be inferred. Results confirmed the hypothesis, since exposure to stimulation one stage above the child's present stage produced the greatest change.

Conceptual-level matching model (Harvey, Hunt, and Schroder, 1961 D.E. Hunt 1966a)

As originally stated and applied, the objective of the conceptual-systems change model was to increase the person's conceptual level (CL). From this view, persons are dimensionalized on CL from a very concrete to a very abstract level. Position on the CL dimension is segmented into stages as follows:

Stage	CHARACTERISTICS
Sub I	impulsive, poorly socialized, egocentric, inattentive
I	compliant, dependent on authority, concerned with rules.
II	independent, questioning, self-assertive

(D.E. Hunt 1966a)

The environment is dimensionalized into degree of structure and opportunity for autonomy. For developmental objectives, the change model prescribed the following environments as matched:

Stage	*Prescribed environment*
Sub I	accepting but firm; clearly organized
I	encouraging independence within normative structure
II	allowing high autonomy and low normative pressure

(D.E. Hunt 1966a)

Experimental evidences for the conceptual-systems model has been derived from its use as a differential treatment model in evaluating the effectiveness of several summer Upward Bound programs (Hunt and Hardt 1967). Upward Bound is a pre-college enrichment program, sponsored by the Office of Economic Opportunity for culturally disadvantaged high-school students, in which the students attend special programs on college campuses for six to eight weeks in the summer. We conducted the national evaluation of this program by studying a sample of 21 of the total 214 programs. In these target programs measures were administered to approximately 1,600 students at the beginning and end of the summer so that change indices could be calculated. It should be noted that objectives of the Upward Bound programs themselves did not specifically include growth in CL, but rather were objectives related to the goals of the program, for example, motivation for college.

The matching model was used in the evaluation project in the following way: based on the rationale of the matching model in the middle of Table I, the 21 target programs were first classified into two groups – structural approach and flexible approach – on the basis of their position on the autonomy scale. These two groups were further classified into low and high CL on the basis of the predominant CL of the students in each program. Students' change scores were then considered in terms of the model in Table I by comparing the degree of change in matched programs (structured – low CL, and flexible – high CL) against the change in mismatched programs (structured – high CL; flexible – low CL). For four of the seven measures (attitude to summer program, motivation for college, possibility of college graduation, and interpersonal flexibility) students in matched programs showed significantly greater change than in mismatched programs, and for two of the remaining measures (internal control and self-evaluated intelligence), there was a borderline tendency for students in matched programs to change more. Not only did these results support the matching model, they also underlined the importance of considering differential effectiveness when evaluating program impact. In only one case was there any significant change observable when difference in program approach was considered alone. Put another way, one must consider the program in relation to the kind of student in order to understand the nature of the changes which occur.

Community Treatment project matching model (Sullivan, Grant, and Grant 1957, Grant, Warren, and Turner 1963, Warren and CTP staff 1966, Warren 1967, Palmer 1968)

The Community Treatment Project (CTP) is a very sophisticated, theoretically derived, differential-treatment model for working with adjudicated delinquents. For present purposes only a portion of the CTP model will be dealt with: that aspect which provides the basis for matching treatment workers with youths at different maturity levels. Many of the objectives of the model are complex, and differ for youths at different levels of interpersonal maturity. However, CPT is also necessarily concerned with preventing the subsequent occurrence of delinquent behaviour. Indeed, some of the most compelling evidence for the over-all CTP model is the finding that the failure rate (which included all revocations of parole, recommitments from the courts, and unfavourable discharges) after 15 months of community exposure was 52 per cent for the control group (who had been institutionalized) and 28 per cent for the group treated according to the general CTP model.

According to the formulation of Sullivan, Grant, and Grant (1957), the CTP model views persons as varying along the dimension of interpersonal maturity which also consists of the underlying organisation of perceptual differentiation. Position on the interpersonal maturity level is segmented into stages and, for purposes of treating delinquents, three stages are considered: low, medium, and high. In contrast to the first two models, an important element in environmental variation in this model is that of the characteristics of the treatment worker. The matching model between the youth's maturity level and prescribed of the characteristics treatment worker follow:

Maturity level	*Treatment worker characteristics*
Low	Type 1: tolerant, supportive, protective
Medium	Type 2: firm, conwise, alert, willing to punish
High	Type 3: wise, understanding, warm
	(Summarized from Grant, Warren, and Turner 1963)

Palmer has stated the rationale of matching as follows: "Stated in general terms, the principal goal of matching is the establishment and maintenance of relationships which can be of increased relevance to the long-term difficulties and capacities of given types of youths, and which – from the point of view of the youths – can also be of increased relevance to their more immediate investments, preoccupations, and preferred modes of interaction" (Palmer 1968, 2).

Of course, during the seven-year period CTP has been operating it has not always been possible to match the youth and treatment worker perfectly. Palmer took advantage of this state of affairs and reclassified youths in terms of whether, according to the table at the bottom of Table 1, the youth had been closely matched or not closely matched. The failure rate for the closely matched group was 19 per cent after 15 months, as compared to the group which had not been so closely matched, the failure rate of which was 43 per cent, a highly significant difference. Therefore, the validity of the matching models was strongly supported.

IMPLEMENTATION OF MATCHING MODELS

Cronbach has recently summarized ways by which programs of educational instruction can be adapted to individual differences (Cronbach 1967). Some matching models may be helpful for some of these logistical problems, for example, homogeneous classroom grouping (D.E. Hunt 1966a; Thelen 1967; Torrance 1965). However, since the particular decisions in implementation (i.e., how many should be in a group?) are situationally specific and depend on current availability of resources, it seems inadvisable to consider the issues of implementation in the present framework. We hope that the framework will, however, indicate the general utility of matching models for dealing with problem areas, and that it may be helpful for considering the differential utility of specific matching models.

REFERENCES

Astrove, G. Preference for educational environments as a function of student conceptual level. Unpublished honors thesis, Syracuse University 1966

Bandura, A., McDonald, F.J. Influence of social reinforcement and the behavior in shaping children's moral judgments *Journal of Abnormal and Social Psychology* 1963 *67* 274–81

Bettleheim, B. How much can man change? *New York Review of Books* 1964 *3* 1–4

Cronbach, L.J. The two disciplines of scientific psychology *American Psychologist* 1957 *12* 671–84.

Cronbach, L.J. How can instruction be adapted to individual differences. In R.M. Gagne (ed.) *Learning and individual differences* New York: Macmillan 1967 pp. 23–44

Deutsch, M. Social intervention and the malleability of the child. In M. Deutsch (ed.) *The Disadvantaged child* New York: Basic Books 1967, pp. 3–29

Dewey, J. *The child and the curriculum* Chicago: University of Chicago Press 1902

Gassner, S. The relationship between patient-therapist compatibility and treatment effectiveness. Unpublished doctoral dissertation, Syracuse University, 1968

Goldstein, A.P., Heller, K., Sechrest, L.B. *Psychotherapy and the psychology of behaviour change* New York: Wiley 1966

Grant, M.Q., Warren, M., Turner, J.K. Community Treatment Project

An evaluation of community treatment for delinquents. *CTP Research Report No. 3* California Youth Authority 1963

Harvey, O.J., Hunt, D.E., Schroder, H.M. *Conceptual systems and personality organization* New York: Wiley 1961

Hunt, D.E. A conceptual systems change model and its application to education. In O.J. Harvey (ed.) *Experience, structure, and adaptability* New York: Springer 1966a, pp. 277–302

Hunt, D.E. Adolescence: Cultural deprivation, poverty, and the dropout *Review of Educational Research* 1966b *36* 463–73

Hunt, D.E. A model for analyzing the training of training agents *Merrill Palmer Quarterly* 1966c *12* 137–56

Hunt, D.E., Hardt, R.H. The role of conceptual level and program structure in summer Upward Bound programs. Paper presented at the meeting of the Eastern Psychological Association, Boston, April 1967

Hunt, J.McV. *Intelligence and experience* New York: Ronald 1961

Kagan, J. On the need for relativism *American Psychologist* 1967 *22* 131–42

Katz, I. The socialization of academic motivation in minority group children. In *Nebraska symposium on motivation* Lincoln: University of Nebraska Press 1967, pp. 133–91

Kelman, H.C. Processes of opinion change *Public Opinion Quarterly* 1961 *25* 57–79

Kohlberg, L. The development of children's orientation toward a moral order: 1. Sequence in the development of moral thought *Vita Humana* 1963 *6* 11–33

Kohlberg, L. Development of moral character and moral idealogy. In M. Hoffman and L. Hoffman (eds.) *Review of child development research* vol. 1 New York: Russell Sage 1964, pp. 383–431

Kohlberg, L. Relationships between the development of moral judgment and moral conduct. Paper presented at the meeting of the Society for Research in Child Development 1965

Kohlberg, L. Moral education in the schools *School Review* 1966 *74* 1–30

Kohnstamm, G.A. Experiments on teaching Piagetian thought operations. Paper presented at the Conference on Guided Learning, Cleveland, Ohio, January 1966

Palmer, T.B. An overview of matching in the Community Treatment Project. Paper presented at the meeting of the Western Psychological Association 1968

Pervin, L.A. Performance and satisfaction as a function of individual-environment fit *Psychological Bulletin* 1968 *69* 56–68

Piaget, J. *Moral Judgment of the child* New York: Cromwell Collier 1932

Sanford, R.N. Will psychologists study human problems? *American Psychologist* 1965 *20* 192–202

Sapolsky, A. Relationships between patient-doctor compatibility, mutual perception and outcome of treatment *Journal of Abnormal Psychology* 1965 *70* 70–6

Schroder, H.M., Driver, M., Streufert, S. *Human information processing* New York: Holt, Rinehart & Winston 1967

Schutz, W.C. FIRO: *A three-dimensional theory of interpersonal behaviour* New York: Rinehart 1958

Stern, G.G. Congruence and dissonance in the ecology of college students *Student Medicine* 1960 *8* 304–39

Stern, G.G. Environments for learning. In N. Sanford (ed.) *The American College* New York: Wiley 1961, pp. 690–730

Sullivan, C.E., Grant M.Q., Grant, J.D. The development of interpersonal maturity: Application to delinquency *Psychiatry* 1957 *20* 373–85

Thelen, H.A. *Classroom grouping for teachability* New York: Wiley 1967

Tomkins, S.S., Miner, J.B. *The Tomkins-Horn Picture Arrangement Test* New York: Springer 1957

Torrance, E.P. Different ways of learning for different kinds of children. In E.P. Torrance and R.D. Strom (eds.) *Mental health and achievement*) *Increasing potential and reducing dropout* New York: Wiley 1965, pp. 253–62

Turiel, E. An experimental test of the sequentiality of developmental stages in the child's moral judgments *Journal of Personality and Social Psychology* 1966 *3* 611–18

Turiel, E. Developmental processes in the childs moral thinking. In P. Mussen, J. Langer, and M. Covington (eds.) *Trends and issues in developmental psychology* New York: Holt, Rinehart & Winston 1969, pp. 92–131

Warren, M.Q. Classification of offenders as an aid to efficient management and effective treatment. Prepared for the President's Commission on Law Enforcement and Administration of Justice, Task Force on Corrections 1966

Warren, M.Q., and Community Treatment Project Staff. Interpersonal maturity level classification *Juvenile* 1966 ed. California Youth Authority 1966

Warren, M.Q. The Community Treatment Project after five years. California Youth Authority, 1967

Washburne, C., Heil, L.N. What characteristics of teachers affect children's growth? *School Review* 1960 *68* 420–6

CHAPTER 9

Moral education: is reasoning enough?

D. W. OLIVER and M. J. BANE

MANY PEOPLE assume that some form of secular moral education should take place in the schools. But what kind of moral education? And how should the schools provide it?

In this paper, we first describe a social-studies curriculum which we believe meets the criteria for moral education defined as training in moral resoning. We then describe some of the difficulties we have encountered in teaching the approach, and our intuitions about its limitations. Primarily we are troubled by the fact that we have not dealt with nonrational moral sensitivities. In the last part of the paper, we discuss the problems of carrying on moral education in a broad sense within the existing school system, and suggest some modifications that we believe are necessary.

VALUES AND PUBLIC ISSUES

For the past several years we have been developing a social-studies curriculum directed at the clarification of public issues through the use of rational strategies within a framework of courteous and disciplined discussion.* This curriculum is based on a number of premises regarding what talk about public issues should be and what kind of people do the talking. It assumes that the people doing the talking are committed to the process of reasoned discussion as a means of resolving value disputes, and that, to some degree, they are concerned about the welfare of the broader community as well as their own self-interest.

A number of more specific assumptions are made regarding the

*Much of the material in this section is adapted from the teachers' guide to the Public Issues Series: Donald W. Oliver, Fred M. Newmann, and Mary Jo Bane *Cases and Controversy* American Education Publications 1967.

purpose and function of value concepts. We assume that when faced with a public dispute in which it is difficult to determine who is right or wrong, or when it is difficult to say whether the community or individual parties in the dispute should make this decision, one should search for general principles of eithical or moral conduct; and that the use of general moral principles allows us to develop stable and predictable ways of resolving conflicts.

We postulate, moreover, that, although the use of general values applied to social and political conduct allows us to judge public policies more reliably and consistently, these values often clash. It is our position that looking for value conflict or value tension is a more realistic approach to social controversy than searching for some overriding principle will that tell us the correct solution to any particular problem. For, although such broad principles as respect for human dignity or justice may be essential bases of judgment in a controversial situation, it is often difficult to communicate the strength of one's position on the basis of general but ambiguous principles. We believe that throughout history men have developed more specific value categories which may be thought of as both elements of and bridges to the more basic values of human dignity and justice, such values as:

the right to think, to believe, to speak, to worship as one's conscience or personal experience dictates
the right to be secure from physical attack or injury
the right to make agreements with other men and have these agreements respected
the right to have one's personal property protected from seizure and destruction.

It is clear, however, that defining some ultimate good, such as human dignity, in more specific value terms does not resolve controversy. It simply provides a public rhetoric by which the controversy might be more easily clarified. In this sense our curriculum efforts have been directed mainly at identifying the intellectual and procedural strategies that are used in talking about public controversy. It is assumed that such clarification will at least facilitate compromise, temporary accommodation of basic differences, or agreement within the community of advocates.

The basic value premise of the curriculum may be called "rational consent," the implicit agreement that controversy is to be accommodated or resolved by reflection and conversation rather than force or coercion. Specific procedures which allow the business of the community to be carried on, and the mechanics of governmental decision-making, are looked upon simply as the formal ritual which legitimizes the product of prior reflection.

An element obviously missing from this model is the whole political-process component, factional in-fighting, and the use of various kinds of semi-coercive methods and power plays within the world of real politics. While we understand the critical importance of this missing component, we have chosen to help the school do what we feel it might do best. We have little doubt that young people can best learn the principles of power politics in the real world, not in artificial simulation situations in the classroom.*

CLARIFICATION THROUGH DISCUSSION

The approach used in the Harvard Social Studies Project can be divided into three basic elements: A the analysis of public controversy in terms of prescriptive, descriptive, and analytic issues; B The use of distinct strategies for justification and clarification of one's views on such issues; and C systematic attention to the discussion process as one deals with a controversial issue.

Identifying issues

Any given situation or case can stimulate controversy in a number of directions, depending upon the type of question that concerns the participants or observers. By way of illustration, we might look at the Stamp Act controversy, a series of events which led to up the American Revolution:

In 1765 the English Parliament passed a Stamp Act which required that stamps be bought and placed on all public documents used by the American Colonists. The major purpose of the Act was to raise revenue for the continuing administration and defense of the Colonists, especially against unfriendly Indians on the western frontier. However, the Act set off a wave of protest and violence, which was completely unforseen by the English. In Boston, mobs marched through the streets, set fire to the governor's mansion, and threatened the lives of anyone who might attempt to administer the Act. An almost complete boycott went into effect; either the law was violated and public papers were given out within the stamp, or legal transactions requiring stamps were suspended. All along the eastern seaboard, any English official who sought to land, store, or sell stamps was intimidated and threatened with physical injury. Stores of stamps were burned on the New York

*For a discussion of this problem, see Fred M. Newmann's contribution to "Political Socialization in the Schools" *Harvard Educational Review 38*, no. 3, Summer 1968.

waterfront. Largely because the boycott began to threaten the prosperity of English merchants who sold goods to the Colonists, the Act was repealed.

Prescriptive issues

This historical case provokes disagreement on several levels. One level involves judgments about what should or ought to have been done, given the information available. Judgments concerned with the legitimacy or the rightness of actions and policy are prescriptive issues: Was it right for the English to impose the Stamp Act in the first place? Should governmental acts be imposed only when the people affected are adequately represented? What kinds of protests would one consider reasonable? At what point is one justified in using violence and abandoning legal methods of protest? We could further classify prescriptive issues in such categories as:

Personal conviction and conscience What should you do as an individual in the Stamp Act situation?

Public policy Should parliament have passed such an act without the consent of the American colonists?

Ethics Which value is more important: the right of the colonists to representation or the maintenance of a peaceful, orderly society?

Law Were the Americans adequately represented under the English constitutional system of the day?

These types of prescriptive issues are related. The purpose of differentiating them is simply to show ways in which we might clarify our thinking by carefully defining the issues we choose to discuss.

Descriptive issues

After identifying a number of prescriptive issues, a discussion of the Stamp Act might turn to a different set of questions. Was violence actually necessary to bring about the repeal of the Stamp Act? Did the Stamp Act seriously affect the commercial interests of the colonists? Was there a long tradition of acceptance of virtual representation by the colonists as a means of legitimizing parliamentary action? Were the motives of the troublemakers in the colonies based mainly on constitutional principle or mercenary greed? Questions like these focus on problems of fact – describing people's behaviour, interpreting what the world is actually like, or explaining why certain circumstances presumably occur.

Analytic issues

Finally, we identify analytic issues. These questions focus not on what *should* be done, or what is the actual state of affairs, but on what is the most useful meaning or interpretation of a word, phrase, or problem. In the Stamp Act situation there is clearly a definitional problem in the word "representation." A broader and perhaps more important type of analytic dispute arises over the way we interpret the issue under discussion. For example, one person may see the issue of "adequate representation" as a strictly legal or constitutional issue. He seeks to answer the question by studying English constitutional arrangements of the eighteenth century. A second person may see "adequate representation" in moral terms: to what extent should the person affected by a law have some say in the creation of the law? In order for these two people to discuss the term "adequate representation" productively, they would first have to reach some agreement on which of these issues is more important or which should be discussed first.

Although we have distinguished prescriptive, descriptive, and analytic issues as different types of problems, they usually cannot be kept separate during a discussion of an issue. The purpose of dealing with them separately here is to suggest that there are various aspects of inquiry which can be separated when a discussion becomes murky or unproductive.

Strategies of justification and clarification

The analogy

One powerful technique, which we feel is central to the clarification of prescriptive issues, involves dealing with an issue within the context of a number of related cases. Thus we might begin with a specific case such as the Stamp Act situation, identify a relevant issue arising out of the case (should violence be used as a method of gaining increased representation in government), identify another case (or analogy) that is similar in that it raises similar value conflicts (for example, student violence on the Columbia university campus), and see how we feel about a policy as it applies to the second case.

The power of the analogy is that it provokes discussants to make distinctions and qualifications that strengthen and clarify value positions. The person who supports violence in the Stamp Act situation but who denounces violence at Columbia must find some critical distinction between the two situations. (One might assert, for example, that students were voluntarily members of the Columbia community, and could withdraw if they so chose, whereas the colonists were not voluntary members of the British Empire.) Thus, one might start with a position that violence can be justified under extreme circumstances to gain representation in a group or community and move to the qualified position that violence is justified as a method of gaining representation only when the community in which you seek representation provides no opportunity for voluntary withdrawal.

Evaluating evidence

In dealing with descriptive issues, the major problems lie in accumulating and evaluating evidence, and as in understanding logical relationships among different types of evidential statements. Students can be taught various canons of reliability and distinctions such as that between associative and causal claims.

Defining terms and making distinctions

There are a number of strategies for dealing with definitional problems: using an authoritative source; searching for synonyms on the basis of common experience; searching for general criteria as they are induced from specific examples.

Discussion process

There is a subtle and important link between the analytic process by which issues are defined and positions justified, and the quality of the interpersonal setting within which discussion takes place. We have loosely called this link the discussion process. It includes being sensitive to what others are saying in a discussion, the ability to summarize where the discussion, is especially points of agreement and disagreement, the ability to challenge the direction or relevance of another individual's argument. While these may sound somewhat elementary to sophisticated adults, we have found that high-school students are lacking in such skills. Discussion is usually construed by students as catharsis or combat. As catharsis, the purpose of talking is to get something off your chest; as combat, the object is to "win" the argument. The notion that discussion might serve to clarify one's own values requires radical reorientation of classroom discussion. As we shall point out later in the paper, the heart of this issue is creating a group climate in which the student takes other discussants seriously enough to break the set of "performing for the teacher."

As should be clear from the above discussion, we assume that rational strategies used in the discussion of societal conflict provide the basis of a type of moral education. In essence of the educational process involves a subtle relationship between individual valuations and the use of moral disciplined strategies as a means of clarifying or justifying such valuations. The educational outcome is not the acquisition of substantive values, such as equality, justice, or property rights.

It is assumed that students already have these values. The outcome is presumably the student's ability to work through increasingly more complex principles of conduct as he attempts to justify his own point of view in the presence of contrary views expressed by his fellow students and teachers. The source of these complex principles is induction through rational discussion. It is also assumed that the student develops a tendency to re-examine his principles in the light of societal change, for the values themselves require constant redefinition as they are applied to new situations.

RELATIONSHIP TO MODERN ETHICAL AND PSYCHOLOGICAL THOUGHT

We see the public-issues approach as moral education, although this may conflict somewhat with the older use of that term in the social studies. The older view advocates the teaching of democratic virtues: the importance of voting, respect for "community helpers," love of country, the fostering of charitable feelings towards those less fortunate, etc.

Our own view of moral education clearly focuses on moral reasoning, and is more in line with the conclusions expressed by Benn and Peters:

Our view about morality, therefore, which we have expounded by considering the contributions of the main schools of moral theory can be summed up as follows:

i A moral rule differs from a customary one in that it implies the autonomy of the individual. A rule becomes moral by being critically accepted by the individual in the light of certain criteria.

ii The criteria can be summarized by saying that the rule should be considered in the light of the needs and interests of people likely to be affected by it with no partiality towards the claims of any of those whose needs and interests are at stake.

iii The acceptance of such criteria is implied, albeit in a minimal degree, by the notion of rationality in the sense of reasonableness.

Our contention is, therefore, that there is a sense in which moral philosophy or ethics, which is the attempt to make explicit the criteria in terms of which rules are morally justified, itself exemplifies, in a minimum degree, the acceptance of the criteria which it attempts to make explicit (Benn and Peters 1959).

If this is morality, then one might clearly describe our efforts in social studies education as moral education.

The basic definition of morality developed by such moral philosophers as Benn and Peters is also the basis of Kohlberg's approach to moral education. Kohlberg's studies of the moral reasoning of children show that as the child develops the reasons he gives for advocating a particular response to a moral dilemma become increasingly more complex. The young child is oriented towards punishment and naïve hedonism; as he grows older, he passes through a stage of conventional morality and gradually develops a more thoughtful, principled approach. Throughout this process, the concept of justice held by the child becomes more differentiated and more attuned to the rights of others, based on equality and reciprocity. Kohlberg sees moral education as the stimulation of this natural developmental process which leads to mature moral reasoning:

A definition of the aim of moral education as the stimulation of natural development appears, then, to be clear-cut in the area of moral judgment, which has considerable regularity of sequence and direction in development in various cultures. Because of this regularity, it is possible to define the maturity of a child's moral judgment without considering its content (the particular action judged) and without considering whether or not it agrees with our own particular moral judgments or values or those of the American middle-class culture as a whole. In fact, the sign of the child's moral maturity is his ability to make moral judgments and formulate moral principles of his own, rather than his ability to conform to moral judgments of the adults around him (Kohlberg 1967).

Our experience in teaching the public issues approach seems to confirm many of Kohlberg's observations concerning moral education. Our goal, like Kohlberg's, is to develop the moral reasoning abilities of our students. It seems, however, that most of our students – relatively mature high-school students of average ability – operate from Kohlberg's stages two, three, and four. Their orientation towards a controversial problem is that the major actors avoid trouble and maximize their own individual interests, unless some naturally endowed traditional authority intervenes. They hold vague notions that some things are "morally right," but tend to justify laws by traditional criteria of authority rather than by abstract legal or moral principles. They have tremendous difficulty in operating easily with our value conflict model, which we can now label a stage-five or -six conception of morality.

The results of these three streams of intellectual activity – Benn and Peters' concept of moral reflection in a democratic state, Kohlberg's notion of natural development stages leading towards increasingly mature moral reflection, and our own educational efforts to implement a curriculum and teaching dialogue centring on more complex modes of moral justification – are all based on common assumption about the nature of human discourse. All assume that man is or can be a rational animal, that he seeks greater complexity in the manipulation of verbal arguments, and that he can become engaged in abstract social and political issues in a somewhat impersonal way without such a deep investment of his own psyche that it will warp his perceptions.

PROBLEMS WITH THE APPROACH

In teaching our program, we have assumed that students can learn to carry on productive discussions about public issues under the leadership of a trained and sensitive adult. We have used various forms of discussion, from teacher-dominated to entirely student controlled, and have supplemented these discussions with didactic instruction in the analysis of argument. For "content," we have relied on various types of cases – stories, journalistic narratives, historical accounts.

We have, however, encountered various problems in using the approach in the classroom. Although students sometimes become very excited about the issues raised by the cases, they seldom seem to take the issues seriously in a personal sense. They enjoy the combat of discussion and the opportunity to express their opinions, but they are not generally sensitive to the arguments of other people. When the issue is one in which they seem personally involved, the discussion becomes a repetition of opinions rather than an attempt at clarification. When the issue does not seem particularly important, discussion becomes a game in which the object is either to second-guess the teacher and arrive at the right answer or to overwhelm the other participants psychologically. These attitudes make it difficult to carry on productive conversations in the classroom. We suspect, also, that there is very little transfer of learning to situations outside the classroom, since discussion is viewed as "another schoolroom game".

There are, of course, some techniques which might be tried within the framework of our program to deal with some of these problems. We might extend our range of concern to personal as well as public decisions. Presumably such situations would be more relevant to the students, but would, at the same time, provide an opportunity to teach strategies for making rational moral decisions.

Questions, for example, could be phrased in personal, rather than general terms: "Should *you* participate in civil disobedience in protest against the Vietnam war?" rather than, "Should peace groups use illegal means in pursuit of their aims?" Or homey examples might be used, such as the trumpet player's situation analyzed by Hare (1963). Should I, and by implication everyone, be allowed to play my trumpet in any place and at any time that I desire to do so? This question provides Hare, and could provide classroom teachers, with an opportunity to examine the relationship between individual freedom and social good and to attempt to develop general procedures for dealing with such conflicts. Or the class might consider important issues in their own lives, for example premarital sex and love, in individual and social terms.*

Efforts might also be carried out to deal more systematically with students' different levels of cognitive and moral development. This is suggested by Kohlberg's finding that people at one stage of development can understand moral arguments at one level above their own and can be trained to move to this level, but that they cannot understand or move two or more levels up.

For example, students discussing the Stamp Act case might use arguments that reflect a stage-three level of moral development: they might argue that what the Sons of Liberty did was right because "that was what good patriots did" or because the British were being "bad rulers," without being able to specify what their labels mean or imply. These students might be presented with stage-four arguments, those emphasizing preservation of authority, rather than with social contract or natural rights arguments. It might be argued, for example, that the Sons of Liberty were wrong because they were breaking laws and disrupting the legitimate government of the empire. It might be possible in this way to lead the students through the stages of moral argument without losing them along the way.

We believe, however, that although these techniques would improve the effectiveness of training students in the processes of moral judgment, they do not resolve a more general problem of moral education. The more fundamental question is whether or not most people engage in the kind of moral reasoning advocated by our curriculum, and even if they do, whether this kind of reasoning is but an insignificant part of something we might call the moral personality. One could argue, for example, that we should be more concerned with moral sensitivity than with moral reasoning. Or perhaps a sensitivity to paradox and tragedy in human nature (rather than consistency and universality in moral rules) is a far more powerful force in the expression of man's inherent humanity than the use of reasoning strategies in the development of flexible moral principles.

*See, for example, the discussion of this issue in Joseph Fletcher *Moral Responsibility: Situation Ethics at Work* Philadelphia: Westminster Press 1967, pp. 125–40.

THE LIMITS OF REASON

The bonds that tie together a moral community of men cannot rest simply on a common sense of intellectual justice. Perhaps more important than such attributes as consistency, universality, and impartiality is an intuitive notion of man's physical, moral, and intellectual limitations. And it is quite conceivable that the essentially tragic nature of man's being can be communicated only through ritualistic celebration and metaphor. Perhaps educators, philosophers, and psychologists should join with theologians and sensitive youth in a search for the kind of powerful metaphor with which our Christian heritage once provided us. We somehow need to create myths and celebrations by which we can project the common joys, sorrows, and compassion that we share simply by the fact that we are human.

We can see the limitation of rational analysis by looking more deeply into some of the great issues of life – love, work, violence. The issue of violence, for example, requires a broad conception of appropriate educational experiences. Our discussion of the Stamp Act defined the issue of violence in utilitarian terms, asking when the benefits of violence were greater than its costs. In this sense, violence is a technique that can be used for achieving important human goals after a rational decision that no other means are available. The need for violence is eliminated when justice and personal fulfilment are available to all people, and when institutions for resolving conflicts operate as they should.

It seems equally reasonable, however, to consider violence on several other levels. Man lives in a naturally violent universe. Matter is created and transformed in gigantic stellar explosions. On earth. living things kill and are killed in a dynamic food cycle. Man's violence, even though it seems to be of his own making, may merely be a reflection of his position in nature. From another perspective, institutionalized violence is sometimes identified as a symptom of a society gone mad, while individual violence may represent an appropriate response to an insane social order. On a third, more personal level, men's physical and emotional violence towards each other may reflect a psychological fact. The dark and tragic side of man exists, whether its roots are assumed to lie in original sin or in the Oedipus complex. Violence may fulfil basic needs.

The story of Christ is one of struggle and tragedy, temptation and death, agony and joy. Contemporary literature, which has few real heroes, most often reflects the paradox and the irony of human existence The world of absurd novels and drama – of John Barth, Thomas

Pynchon, Edward Albee – is not a world in which reasoned discourse leads men to justice and equality. The closest we come to popular heroes are John and Robert Kennedy. They were men of tragedy, who celebrated life with joy and zest, killed in absurd drama.

Within this context, the possibility and specific nature of "Utopia" becomes critical. W.H. Auden suggests that there are two kinds of "dream pictures of the Happy Place where suffering and evil are unknown," the Edens and the New Jerusalems:

> Glancing at a lampshade in a store window, I observe it is too hideous for anyone in their senses to buy: He observes it is too expensive for a peasant to buy.
>
> Passing a slum child with rickets, I look the other way, He looks the other way if he passes a chubby one ...
>
> You can see, then, why, between my Eden and his New Jerusalem, no treaty is negotiable.
>
> In my Eden we have a few beam-engines, saddle-tank locomotives, overshot waterwheels and other beautiful pieces of obsolete machinery to play with: In his New Jerusalem even chefs will be cucumber-cool machine minders.
>
> In my Eden our only source of political news is gossip: In his New Jerusalem there will be a special daily in simplified spelling for non-verbal types.
>
> In my Eden each observes his compulsive rituals and superstitious tabus but we have no morals: In his Jerusalem the temples will be empty but all will practice the rational virtues (Auden 1958).

Applying Auden's metaphor to our own assumptions about society, it would seem that the Happy Place which our "natural discourse" curriculum encourages students to envisage and work towards is a New Jerusalem. This is a world of the social scientist rather than the theologian, of the intellect rather than the emotions. Encouraging students to dream of Edens, to confront the tragedy and irrationality in human life, and to think metaphorically as well as analytically should also be part of the educational process, if we are to leave the questions truly open.

There is also a question of whether it is psychologically possible to separate ethical decisions and political ideology from total life style. Smith, Bruner, and White (1964) showed us how complex is the relationship between opinion and total personality; Lane found the roots of political ideology in individual styles of dealing with the world as a whole (Lane 1962). White and Lippitt speak of a "psychological core of democracy" including "open-mindedness to influence from others; self-acceptance or self-confidence and friendliness and good will in attitudes and actions toward others" (White and Lippitt 1960).

Kenniston's study of young radicals is an especially interesting illustration of the problem (Kenniston 1968). His interviews with a number of the leaders of the New Left Vietnam Summer Movement revealed that these "young radicals" were from affluent, warm, permissive homes; they were unusually intelligent, open, and honest; they were deeply committed to working towards justice and equality within the system, through nonviolent means. Kenniston also found, however, a deep-rooted concern with violence.

> Many of their earliest memories involve conflict, outer anger, and inner fear. They were, throughout their childhoods, especially sensitive to the issues of struggle within their families and communities. Although in behavior most of these young radicals were rather less violent than their contemporaries, this was not because they were indifferent to the issue, but because their early experience and family values had taught them how to control, modulate, oppose and avoid violence. Verbal aggression took the place of physical attack. They learned to argue, to compromise, and to make peace when confonted with conflict ...
>
> I have mentioned the many tensions – psychological, interpersonal, and organizational – that are related to this issue in their work. The avoidance and control of violence, whether in international warfare, political organizations, small groups, or face-to-face personal relations, is a central goal and a key psychological orientation in the New Left. Many of the problems of the Movement are related to the zealous effort to avoid actions and relations in which inner aggression or outer conflict may be evoked ...
>
> The position of the psychologically non-violent revolutionary in opposition to a violent world is paradoxical ... for all his efforts to control violence, cataclysm, and sadism, the young radical continually runs the danger of identifying himself with what he seeks to control, and through a militant struggle against violence, creating more violence than he overcomes. The issue of violence is not resolved for these young men and women (Kenniston 1968, 254–6).

This analysis suggests that violence has profound psychological implications, which should be treated in any serious discussion. It might be more appropriate to being talking about the morality of violence by considering the underlying personality dynamics than by debating the usefulness of violent strategies in the American Revolution.

We believe, therefore, that great issues of the human spirit, such as feelings and expressions of violence, must be dealt with on a level deeper than that suggested by such phrases as "justification strategies" or "moral reasoning." We believe that education should encourage people to examine the relationships of men to their societies or to the universe not only through the rational analysis of "case studies," but also through the genuine attempt to create and wonder about a profound, perhaps religious, experience.

MORAL EDUCATION AND SCHOOLS

One way to approach this in the schools is through the development of new programs in the humanities. The present trend in teaching both social studies and English is to organize them as academic disciplines patterned after those in the university and to emphasize methods of scholarly thought. Traditionally, the humanities deal with art, music, and literature largely in historical or "critical" terms, as works to be experienced for the purpose of critical analysis. We believe there is a need for more profound educational "happenings" through which one might focus on a variety of conceptions of the human condition. Certainly art, music, literature would play a part in the creation of such happenings, but so might television, movies, and drama – media which are now considered to be mainly entertainment.

We would argue that the relatively modern distinctions between work and education, religion and entertainment, prevent "humanities" teachers from dealing with some of the most powerful happenings available for education. One might ask, for example, whether *2001*, *The Graduate*, *Alice's Restaurant*, *Easy Rider*, and *Midnight Cowboy* are educational films, religious films, or entertaining films to be seen at the neighbourhood theatre? Is the time, effort, and money required to create such films spent in the interest of education, religion, or entertainment? From our point of view, such films are both educational and religious.

These distinctions were, undoubtedly useful in the development of an affluent technological society: education is preparation for work and occurs between the ages of 5 and 17; work is what happens Monday through Friday; recreation and entertainment happen on weekends and in evenings; religion happens on Sunday. We see a profound questioning of these distinctions today, especially among young people.

There is a crisis of meaning, created essentially by affluence and the accompanying cynicism of youth regarding the necessity of work as the core of man's existence. The crisis has been compounded by the inability of three major institutions, school, work, and church, to deal with the redirection of energy previously channelled into economic development.

The conventional school is still tied to the goals of "getting ahead" in vocational and materialistic terms, although the availability of so much material wealth suggests that this is no longer a pressing need. Even those schools that are making a sincere effort to provide a free and human learning environment and to develop curricula based on important questions in the humanities find it difficult to make significant changes in the perceptiveness and willingness of students to raise important social and personal questions honestly. We interpret this failure as an indication of a conflict between the goals and structure of the existing school and the goals of the humanities. Fundamental questions are most appropriately discussed in small groups of equals; the school is organized in large groups of students led by an authority figure. The humanities question the authority and structure of institutions; the school demands acceptance of authority and standard behaviour patterns in order to carry out its work. The school is therefore faced with an incescapable dilemma when it attempts to carry on serious inquiry in the humanities in the same environment where it teaches conventional knowledge.

The work institutions in general have not considered it part of their function to evaluate the society or the individual's place in it. It is unlikely that the Ford Motor Company, for example, would encourage its workers to question whether Fords should be made at all, or whether the resources of the company should be allocated to a different goal of the society. Nor are Ford employees apt to raise questions of their own position in the society – whether personal satisfaction comes from spending forty hours a week on an assembly line, or whether a flexible schedule might be a more civilized way to organize one's life.

At the same time, the world view of religious institutions whose traditional task has been the consideration of ultimate meaning is often carried forth with obsolete forms and rituals. At best, they raise social and ethical issues and promote community service, but they are outside the significant processes of life for most people.

BEYOND SCHOOLS

The problem requires a view of the educational process as a continuing experience in thoughtful self-exploration. To create conditions for this type of experience will require fundamental changes in our existing educational institutions.

We feel that the exploration of one's self, one's values, and one's personal relationships can be promoted by membership in a group of people who hold different views of reality but who are constantly engaged in a search for a truer and more personally relevant view. A group's interaction forces each of its members to respond in some way to the views of the others, whether by rejection, assimilation, or accommodation. For the group to be influential, it must be important enough to the individual that he takes seriously the thoughts and feelings of the others. The situation must be comfortable enough that each person can reveal himself to some degree to the others. The relationships must be truly open and egalitarian. No member's thoughts should be rejected out of hand, nor should any member's be accepted uncritically.

We feel that this type of group situation is vital to the examination of those deep-rooted values and attitudes formed within the intense emotional setting of the family or early childhood group. Under ordinary circumstances, personality patterns are remarkably persistent. Only in powerful, emotionally laden environments has research uncovered significant reorientations of values (see, e.g., Jacob 1957, Newcombe 1943). Although value-change in itself is not our goal, we do feel that the examination of values – which, if done seriously, implies the possibility of change – should be the primary emphasis of moral education. And we feel that this can take place only in the type of group situation described above.

This is quite different from the learning groups that commonly exist in schools. We would hope that, within our groups, adults and young people would deal with each other as people engaged in a common search for life's meaning, not as occupants of roles. Young people typically deal with adults almost exclusively in the fulfilment of obligations. They rarely have close contact with adults who represent a variety of professions, social classes, or philosophies, or with adults who have neither a parental or teaching role. The school setting is uniform and stylized. The teacher is trained to maintain a certain "distance" from the students; he can never become too personal. Conversation is usually carried on in the form of "public pronouncements" rather than tentative explorations of private feelings. Even students' views of themselves tend to be stereotyped; often, young people do not see each other in any role other than that of students.

In order to operate well, we feel that our "moral learning groups" need other freedoms not commonly part of the school, besides freedom from status distinctions. The school tends to limit somewhat arbitrarily both the topics studied by the students and the way in which they are studied. Much of the current culture – movies, TV, advertising, rock music – is ignored by the school. The student is expected to define himself and his society in terms of ideals and conventions of presentation that are at least partly outmoded. He deals primarily with written "classics" but is not encouraged to think seriously about what Simon and Garfunkle or television advertising are saying about the present human condition. Moreover, students are required to read, think, and express themselves verbally. Visual and musical expression, so much a part of the "outside" culture, are a very minor part of the school curriculum. Finally, the style of knowing in the school, as in the society generally, is heavily biased towards rational analytic knowledge. The "hippie" and existential preference for personal, intuitive knowing is seldom even acknowledged.

We feel that the schools operate within a very limited range of human experience. We would like to see them dealing with the whole gamut of modern culture, the whole range of personal feelings and perceptions, and all the forms of expression imaginable.

This philosophy raises serious problems of implementation. How can we do all this? Who is to decide on an agenda with an infinite number of possibilities? We feel that another type of freedom is demanded here. Each group, as a group, should be free to choose its own topics, its own schedules and settings, and its own procedures. Groups should have a large bloc of time, tree from other obligations, and access to all types of resources. They should also have skilled leaders to help the group get through its procedural problems without abdicating responsibility to a small group or riding roughshod over minority factions.

We feel, then, that procedural freedom and freedom from traditional status distinctions are necessary to create mutually trusting groups in which real moral education – the examination of deeply rooted and important values – can take place.

It is not easy to imagine institutional settings in which these groups could exist. We have had some experience with an intensive summer experience that met many of our criteria: a range of ages among the members, close egalitarian relationships, and procedural freedom. This seemed quite successful, and leads us to consider the possibility of summer camps or vacation schools, when group members are free from other responsibilities, as workable settings.

Another possibility is to release students from conventional studies for a large bloc of time, perhaps six or eight weeks, sometime during their high-school career. This would have the same benefit of affording complete freedom in scheduling.

We are also exploring the possibility of groups that take only part of an individual's time. We are finding that a group that meets once a week, in addition to a full school or work schedule, does not generate the necessary commitment. Perhaps releasing students from that half of their school time normally given to English, social studies, and "frills" would be adequate. We are currently trying such an arrangement.

CONCLUSION

Teaching students to handle personal, social, and political issues with more sophisticated modes of moral reasoning seems to us a legitimate goal of the public school. Our own curriculum efforts have been directed at making explicit the strategies by which value positions can be justified, largely in the context of oral discussion. We have developed case materials to provide the teacher and student with an easily accessible base from which to explore these issues. It is clear from both the work of Kohlberg and our own clinical intuitions that students operate with relatively primitive modes of justification and see conversation more as a forum for combat, catharsis, or persuasion, than as a context for the clarification of personal value premises upon which public policy issues are grounded.

Although our own efforts are presently looked upon as somewhat "radical" in the field of social studies, mainly because they are an assault on the traditional disciplines of history and the social sciences, we feel that our society's values are being questioned by too many people for teachers to continue to ignore the importance of moral analysis in the classroom. Our concern is that once a conception of "moral education" gets into the classroom, people will somehow assume that it has a significant impact on the student. Our own research indicates that this is not the case. Students may do better on pencil-and-paper tests measuring complexity of the reasoning process, but their spontaneous dialogues are little affected. Even if one assumes that we will learn how to affect the latter, it is still doubtful that much will carry over into day-to-day decision-making.

The reasons for our scepticism are numerous. The language we use describe moral reasoning directed at personal conflict or social controversy is highly analytical and abstract; the conflicts and controversies are far more complex and visceral than the structures we can apply to them. Controversy is, in fact more powerfully described through the metaphors of the dramatist, which transcend public language. Young people's growing distrust of the formal analysis of moral issues and their faith in existential or situational solutions to moral dilemmas suggests that systems for analyzing these issues not only must be based on solid philosophical ground, but also must be psychologically meaningful and relevant. And finally, we are sceptical of formal schooling as a situation in which the analysis of personal and moral issues might take place. The press of time and large numbers of students leads teachers to structure and rigidify modes of thinking, which should be open and spontaneous. Moreover, our experience indicates that the great percentage of students value reflection, not as an end in itself, but only as a means of clarifying decision and action in the real world. The schools have shown little inclination to facilitate (or even allow) students the opportunity to test the consequences of moral decision-making in the community at large.

The revolt of young people in so many spheres of human activity – politics, education, art, personal life style – is an effort to reinterpret and change traditional arrangements in society. As we see it, the great need for young people (and perhaps adults alike) is not simply the opportunity to discuss and justify personal or social decisions about events in the world. They need the opportunity to project themselves in rich hypothetical worlds created by their own imaginations or those of dramatic artists. More important, they need the opportunity to test out new forms of social order – and only then to reason about their moral implications. It is quite clear that school is not a likely place for this kind of activity to occur, and that the traditional social science disciplines provide but meagre forms of knowledge to help us imagine, act on, and interpret that world. We need new institutions which legitimize the right of adolescents and adults to spend time reflecting and planning social action. We need a broader base of knowledge from which the reflection will spring than that traditionally stressed in schools and universities. And we need to consider the fields of ethical analysis and socialization, as philosophers and psychologists talk about these fields, as but one mode of clarification, and perhaps a relatively minor one at that.

REFERENCES

Auden, W.H. "Vespers" from "Horae Canonicae." In *Selected poetry of W.H. Auden* New York: Modern Library 1958, pp. 168–9

Benn, S.I., Peters, R.S. *The principles of political thought* New York: The Free Press 1959, p. 63

Hare, R.M. *Freedom and reason* Oxford: The Clarendon Press 1963, pp. 114, 194

Jacob, P.E. *Changing values in college* New York: Harper & Row 1957

Kenniston, K. *Young radicals* New York: Harcourt, Brace and World 1968

Kohlberg, L. Moral education, religious education, and the public schools: A developmental view. In Theodore Sizer *Religion and public education* Boston: Houghton Mifflin 1967, p. 179

Lane, R.E. *Political ideology* New York: The Free Press 1962

Newcombe, T.M. *Personality and social change* New York: Holt, Rinehart & Winston 1943

Smith, M.B., Bruner, J., White, R.W. *Opinions and personality* New York: John Wiley 1964

White, R.K., Lippitt, R.O. *Autocracy and democracy* New York: Harper and Brothers 1960, p. 244

PART FIVE

Discussion

edited by Brian S. Crittenden

Introduction

BRIAN S. CRITTENDEN

SUPPOSE we are setting out to plan a curriculum in moral education. It is obvious that before we can deal effectively with specific questions about the scope and sequence of the program and the teaching-learning methods, we need to gain a fairly clear view of what is involved in moral action. Although in this respect the subject of morality may not be essentially different from physics or mathematics. I believe there are some special circumstances which give added importance to the task of clarification. It seems to me that the following are of this kind: A The distinctive notions of morality – good, bad, right, wrong, duty, obligation, and so on – enter in some form or another into the lives of most people in our society from an early age. Unlike the carefully tended concepts of a formal discipline, these terms endure the wear and tear of everyday life, and their meanings shift with all the currents of self-interest and ideology. B In addition to what the school might do, several other groups in society, particularly parents, actively engage in various kinds of moral training. C Many people still think of morality as being intimately related to religion and therefore conclude that if the principle of the separation of church and state bars religion from the school (or at least requires the school to be neutral), the same must go for morality. Others who do not confuse religion and morality may reach the same conclusion by claiming that diversity of moral belief and practice is part of the pluralism which our society guarantees. In other words, it is often thought that the public school cannot engage in moral education without practising discrimination. D Many people are inclined to equate morality with mores and taste, or with the law. In a popular usage, "morality" seems to refer exclusively to sexual behaviour. E In the day-to-day conduct of schooling, teachers, like parents, are often not very discriminating in applying the weight of moral language to what children do. F At a more sophisticated level, the chances of moral education have been damaged by a number of relatively recent doctrines: the socio-economic determinism of moral values, legal positivism, the radical separation of "facts" and "values" (or "is" and "ought"), the irrationality of moral decisions.*

Taken together these factors help to explain why the public schools have tended to neglect any systematic, direct approach to moral education. Their presence suggests how crucial it is to give attention to the general theoretical framework before plunging into the details of curriculum design. I am not suggesting that we have to wait until the last trace of theoretical confusion has lifted. In the nature of the case, such an outcome is hardly possible; and anyway, whether moral training is done badly or well, it goes on inexorably as long as society survives. However, if we must fly in something of a fog, taking care over the theory may provide us with a kind of radar. This is the aspect to which the discussion of the conference, following the main bearings given by the papers, is directed.

As a preamble to a moral education program I think that one would have to explore at least these general questions: What are the distinguishing features of moral education? What skills does one need in order to engage effectively in this kind of activity? Is there a body of knowledge to be mastered? In what way can the school directly contribute to the acquisition of the required skills and knowledge? What is known about the experience and capacity of children at different ages which might be relevant to the organization of a curriculum? In what ways does (and should) a school informally provide moral education? How are other aspects of schooling (e.g., literature, history, social studies) involved in moral education?†

*Since the Second World War there have been important changes in attitude, which create a more favourable atmosphere for moral education. For example, Nazi leaders were condemned for "crimes against humanity"; the Civil Rights movement in the United States has defended its claims and action in moral terms; moral reasons, specifically distinguished from legal, military, and other considerations, have been cited constantly in the protest against the war in Vietnam; in part the student revolt is a criticism of the universities' insensitivity to moral values (e.g., in accepting certain government contracts, in "value-free" social science, in the treatment of students, and so on); intellectuals have been urging their colleagues to accept their moral responsibility in the society. None of this seems to flow easily from the doctrines we have inherited from the past few generations. The rhetoric is warm and the conviction sincere, but I doubt whether the "new" morality has a very clear grasp of its theoretical foundations.

†However much the school may eschew a formal program of moral education or protest its neutrality on moral questions, the whole enterprise of education is profoundly coloured by moral values. In the long history of educational theory moral criteria have almost always been of primary importance in determining what the school *ought* to be doing.

Although this is not a comprehensive list, I think it marks out the boundary lines within which the discussion of the conference is located. A substantial selection of what was said has been rearranged under four main themes that are clearly central in the prefatory work to which I have been referring.

THE SHAPE OF THE MORAL DOMAIN

It would seem useful if, despite the diversity of moral systems and practices, a set of general criteria could be distilled to which any principle or decision or action would have to conform before it could be said to be moral. Granted agreement on the criteria, there would at least be genuine moral disagreement and, if the criteria were applied with sufficient rigour, some hope of enlarging the range of consensus on moral questions. Among recent efforts to provide such criteria, an important difference has emerged. Some, like R.M. Hare, claim that the conditions to be met are purely formal. In his view, a decision that one *ought* to do X is moral provided A the "ought" is used with prescriptive force, B the prescription is recognized as applying to anyone in similar circumstances (universalizability), and C the decision overrides all other considerations. If these conditions are fulfiled, the judgment is a moral one regardless of what action is substituted for X. Others, who may grant that moral discourse does have such features, argue that these features are not sufficient: that the sphere of morality is most radically distinguished by the range of issues it involves. In this view, what a judgment is about is crucial in determining whether it is moral rather than aesthetic, prudential, and so on. This is the position taken by Kurt Baier. Thus, he proposes that moral rules are the subset of social rules which is taken, by and large, to satisfy the requirements of maximizing the good and minimizing the harm of all alike.

Although both positions characterize the moral domain in a quite general way, I believe they make a significant difference to the scope and nature of moral education. At least, the two theoretical accounts and their practical bearing on moral education do need detailed examination. This broad issue was not taken up in the discussion of the conference. There seemed to be agreement among the participants that some criterion of "content" was necessary. The discussion in this first section takes its point of departure from Baier's sketch of the moral domain. It begins with a question about the logical status of criteria for what counts as "moral," then the "content" requirement is related to the more general question of acting rationally and the extent to which being rational characterizes morality, and finally a question is raised about the adequacy of the content criterion as Baier states it or of identifying morality with justice.

Does not the apparently descriptive account that Baier gives of morality itself incorporate certain moral preferences? This is the question with which Narveson begins the discussion. Baier himself claims that one can speak descriptively of different moralities, even though the notion of morality does involve reference to standards of evaluation; that estimating the advantage of one morality over another is not subject to the charge of circularity because it is not itself a *moral* judgment. It is pointed out by Scriven that "moral," like "explanation" and many other terms in our language, may be applied both to a mere claimant and to something which has justified its claim. For the purpose of moral education, he suggests, there are sufficient examples of clearly reasonable principles for it to employ without introducing dubious and distracting candidates or waiting until a decision is reached on which moral system is most rational.

Several passing references to rationality as a test of moral rules and systems are taken up explicitly by Melden. He claims that a clarification of the kind of rational procedures appropriate for resolving moral problems is more fundamental than appeal to the common good or general interest. In the comments by philosophers, which follow Sullivan's request for a more exact specification of the distinguishing features of a rational man, there is a clear agreement that logical argument, the truth and adequacy of factual claims, and so on, are integral to the making of moral decisions. However, there does seem to be this difference: Narveson is confident that the criteria and principles of rationality in the moral sphere can be worked out fairly precisely; Scriven and Melden interpret the nature and role of rational procedures in morality somewhat more flexibly. In Scriven's remarks there is a brief sketch of how morality can be evaluated on rational grounds without employing moral criteria – Baier had made a general claim of this kind shortly before. In effect, they stress the point that questions of reasonableness must be raised about the ends as well as the means of moral action.

The further comments on rationality are related mainly to the reactions of two of the psychologists. Turiel suspects that the philosophers have been preoccupied with an adult version of rationality and have ignored its uniqueness in children. He is not satisfied with the treatment of rationality as a unitary phenomenon. Perhaps logical rationality is only one kind; there might be distinctive aesthetic and moral rationalities as well. Kohlberg challenges the importance which the philosophers are attaching to rationality in examining the nature of morality. In his view, if the more mature level of morality is characterized by justice, this is not because justice conforms to a model of rationality but because some notion of justice is at the core of the earliest (irrational) stages of moral development.

There is substantial agreement among the philosophers in their replies. "The rational man" is set up as an ideal type to which people, regardless of age, approximate in their actual behaviour. Rationality cannot be treated relativistically in respect to age or developmental stages. Because a child reasons at the level typical of his age, it does not follow that he necessarily makes the decisions which are rational for the situation in which he finds himself (Scriven). Of course there are different kinds of reasoning (rather than rationalities). Kohlberg's stages provide an illustration of this variety. The important thing is that people at every age may reason well or badly, and some ways of reasoning may be better than others for the purposes of morality (Baier, Gauthier). If morality were irrational there would be no point in persevering with it as a way of organizing our life (Baier, Melden). The comments are preoccupied with the role of reason in moral judgment; rationality in translating one's moral decision into action receives some attention in the fourth main section of the discussion.

Despite the differences that Turiel and Kohlberg raise, they also agree that some form of rationality – in the sense of tracing logical connections between concepts and propositions – is central to morality. Oliver is the only participant who seems to raise a radically dissenting voice. Perhaps he is really appealing for a different version of rationality or mode of reasoning, one that is more responsive to the actual conditions under which people judge and act morally. Edel's summary refers to the papers and the whole discussion, not only to the selection reproduced here. He suggests that learning how to criticize our moral principles and value hypotheses in the light of the consequences of acting on them is a crucial part of moral education.

During the conference, the discussion of the rationality of moral judgment touched on a number of themes that were not developed. Two of these should be mentioned specifically, I think, because of their bearing on moral education.

The first relates to the question of justifying the principles we employ in support of a moral decision. A crucial assumption in offering a moral argument is that people do in fact have some concern for the well-being of others. Granted this assumption, it seems there are moral principles for which it would be absurd to require justification. The reason is that there are some assertions about what is good or bad which immediately claim our rational assent simply because they so directly involve fundamental and common human experiences. For example, we don't have to debate whether pain, malnutrition, ignorance, humiliation, loneliness, and despair are bad. But what about the assumption: is it irrational not to be concerned for the well-being of others?

The second theme is closely connected with the first. Briefly, it is that the exercise of reason in any realm of value has to be firmly anchored in the context of the feelings, desires, interests, and needs that human beings have. As Charles Taylor observes, " 'good' is used in evaluating, commending, persuading, and so on by a race of beings who are such that through their needs, desires, and so on, they are not indifferent to the various outcomes of the world-process" (Taylor 1967).

In the final part of this section the question is whether the range of morality is adequately accommodated within a subset of social rules or the notion of justice. I introduced this question at the conference because it seems to me that while securing justice, ameliorating the conflict of individual interests, and serving the good of society as a whole are central concerns of morality, they are by no means the whole of it. My reference to a "style of life" is ambiguous. What I was trying to suggest by this phrase is that morality has a special role in relation to the whole range of human values. A relatively narrow moral question is of the form, "what am I obliged in justice to do here and now?" The general moral question, which arbitrates the claims of all spheres of value, is of the form, "what is the most worthwhile thing for me to do in these circumstances?" As soon as we try to apply particular moral principles to the usually complex situations of our life, the priority values, which express the style or form of life, come into play. What counts as a reasonable application of a principle of justice, for example, is likely to vary as it is seen from either a predominantly egalitarian or libertarian perspective. Moreover, whatever stand we take on the scope of morality, I believe we are inevitably making certain assumptions about the form of life that is desirable for human beings. If this is so, an adequate moral education cannot avoid examining theories about the nature of man.

My position (at least as I expressed it at the conference) is strongly challenged by Narveson on the ground that there are precepts of conduct which can be established independently of any particular style of life and should not be confused with the personal, subjective, and often arbitrary choices involved in the latter. Baier emphasizes that he is describing the ground floor of morality – the notions which override other value demands – and not all that might be admitted to it. In his summary, Edel places the divergent views in relation to the Aristotelian stress on "good" and the Kantian stress on "ought." He concludes with the suggestion that Kohlberg might test whether there is a developmental pattern in other aspects of morality besides justice. Beck questions Kohlberg's over-unified concept of morality and his criticism of the "bag of virtues" approach. He argues that the complexity of moral action makes it necessary for us to recognize a plurality of character traits connected in a variety of ways. This is not to imply that all virtues belong to the sphere of morality. Melden broadly supports this view. Edel points out that psychologists have raised difficulties over the notion of a character trait, so that philosophers who support a theory of virtues will need to examine the psychological evidence.

METHOD AND SUBSTANCE IN MORAL EDUCATION

The fundamental topic on which the discussion in this section bears is the role to be played by the common school in a society that protects, and is marked by, a wide diversity or moral practices, beliefs, and systems. Within this context, it is useful to keep in mind the distinction, commonly used in reference to religious education, between teaching/learning *about* morality and teaching/learning *to be* moral. Although this distinction was not examined in a direct and detailed way during the conference, it clearly relates to some of the positions which are advanced in this section and to the whole theme of the fourth. Another distinction often made in educational theory does receive rather more explicit attention in the present section and is applied to the problems which moral pluralism generates for the conduct of public schools: the distinction between method and content.

It is clear that if most people agree on the formal conditions for the correct use of moral language and on the adequacy of such a formal account for depicting the moral realm, the schools may proceed to teach students *to be* moral; in the sense, that is, of teaching them the rules for using "ought" and so on as moral terms. Even if one cannot be taught to engage in moral reasoning, decision-making, and acting without the introduction of some substantive principles, there will be no difficulty for moral education in the public school provided there is some measure of agreement among the experts on what these principles are.

At the present time, however, even among philosophers in the British analytical tradition, there are serious differences over the general characterization of morality and the nature of moral reasoning. Some of them are reflected in the first section of this discussion. We may even seriously question the validity of the method of analysis which, in distilling the criteria for what are admissible as moral reasons, arguments, and so on, neglects historical and social contexts. Perhaps, as MacIntyre suggests, the "content-free" approach really reflects a highly individualistic view of society (MacIntyre 1966). If I have correctly gauged the extent of diversity, it could be claimed that public schools are likely to avoid partisanship and indoctrination only by teaching *about* moralities, or about ethical theories (although this might involve teaching students to become good at doing moral philosophy). In other words, even when morality and religion are seen as quite distinct, they may require much the same kind of treatment in public education. Possibly it is all one should expect the school to contribute towards moral development; or perhaps the state of ethical theory has been depicted in an unduly pessimistic way.

In the discussion it will be seen that Baier clearly includes teaching to be moral within the scope of moral education and that he does not restrict it to a procedure but includes the inculcating of some precepts and attitudes. He is critical of the preoccupation with the method or manner of moral decision-making to the neglect of content. Some reasons are better than others, and so some decisions are better than others; agony over a problem in which one reaches the wrong decision is no substitute for clear moral thinking. In contrast to Baier, Gauthier takes the paradoxical position that the most important contribution of schooling to moral development has no distinct moral method or content; it consists in teaching people to know and appreciate the consequences of acting in various ways. Of course, a difficulty for the teacher here is that it is often not enough simply to see what the consequences are; it is how they are interpreted that makes the vital difference (for example, is this act to be seen as cruel or heroic?). And this commonly depends on our basic attitudes, principles, and prejudices. In reference to this point, Edel stresses the variety of ways in which the consequences of action bear on the meaning and use of moral precepts.

In the second part of this section, a number of participants argue that the only admissible function of the school in formal moral education is to teach moral philosophy. This program is urged as desirable in any circumstances – not simply because it seems to be a solution to the practical problem of moral pluralism. However, in terms of the earlier distinctions, it is not entirely clear how the emphasis is thought to fall. In ethics (or metaethics) are we speaking of procedures only, or do we also include at least a few very general substantive principles? Do we simply teach students about ethical theories (perhaps with an historical dimension included)? Or do we select the ethical theory we are convinced is *the* account of morality and teach students to employ its version of methodology in moral problem-solving (along with any substantive principles it may involve)? Whatever the answers to these questions, it seems that neither Aronfreed nor Baier is content to limit moral education to the teaching of ethics. Although their emphases are somewhat different, both stress the inadequacy of merely teaching the skills of moral reasoning. It is also necessary to build deliberately the connections with moral action. This theme is central to the fourth section.

As I have already noted, questions about the place of method and content in the subject matter of moral education were raised at the conference with reference to moral pluralism. In this connection the discussion simply brings us to the threshold of a further series of questions, which are more fundamental for both philosophy and education. For example, does not the moral vocabulary draw its vitality from a certain view of man and human society and from being used within the context of a social order in which this view is at least partially applied? In part, this question was raised at the beginning of the discussion in the first section. For education the point is that this is a matter not just of recognizing the larger web of theory into which moral concepts fit, but also of attending to the moral characteristics of the school as a social group and of the wider society within which it works.

THE THEORY OF DEVELOPMENTAL STAGES IN MORAL EDUCATION

During the conference, Kohlberg's paper became a special point of reference to which the discussion frequently returned. It seems appropriate, therefore, to include a separate section in which his theoretical and empirical claims are directly discussed. At the same time, because the emphasis here is squarely on the cognitive aspects of morality, it fits well with the final section in which these aspects are related to feeling and behaviour.

Most of the comments bear on Kohlberg's claim that the empirically discovered sequence is the result of "an inner logical order of moral concepts" (see above, p. 48). In this connection, it is argued that the distinction between stages 5 and 6 is not clear (Scriven); that in terms of relevance to morality all the stages need to be marked out more precisely (Narveson); that from the point of view of sound ethical theory, there are clear conceptual links between stages 2 and 5 that do not exist between stages 2 and 3 (Gauthier); that on psychosociological as well as logical grounds a somewhat different order seems to be demanded with the possibility of more advanced stages and finer calibration within the stages (Loubser). In reference to Kohlberg's concern about the normative character of the natural developmental sequence in the bases of moral judgment, Gauthier specifically challenges the moral desirability of stage 4. He suggests that deliberate moral education should try to upset the natural order at this point so that people will not typically pass through a stage-4 orientation at all. Beck raises the more general question of the extent to which the availability of information and the opportunity for a variety of human experience might affect not only the rate of the developmental pattern but the sequence as well.

Like Piaget, Kohlberg is providing an account of changes with age in a typical style of reasoning about moral questions. The skills involved are essentially cognitive; there is no necessary connection of any stage with other skills and dispositions involved in moral action. Aronfreed raises this point in the discussion. He suggests that what Kohlberg provides are not stages in distinctively moral development, but a particular instance of the child's general cognitive development.

Even if this limitation is accepted, Kohlberg's claims are evidently of great interest for moral education (and, of course, for moral philosophy). Probably the most important of these claims for a strategy of teaching and learning in morality is that no stage in the sequence can be omitted, and thus a person at any stage can be helped to advance only by being presented with the type of reasoning belonging to the next higher stage. Paskal proposes some of the intriguing theoretical questions to which Kohlberg's findings give rise: whether, for example, the sequence is shaped by innate factors. In relation to education she draws attention to the importance of gauging each individual's readiness for the next developmental stage and of choosing the learning experiences (such as the examples used) which will predispose him to make the move to the next stage.

THE COGNITIVE AND THE AFFECTIVE IN MORAL ACTION

Franz Kafka has said that "nobody can remain content with just the knowledge of good and evil alone, he must also strive to act in accordance with it." It will be clear from the discussion of this section (and there was considerably more along the same theme at the conference itself) that Aronfreed and Oliver, in particular, are not content with a moral education which simply teaches people the skills of advanced moral reasoning; they want one that effectively influences their behaviour. The question of the connection between making a moral judgment and acting on it has of course been a fundamental one in the history of ethical theory. For the modern period, the state of the question was set in large measure by Hume – especially in his view that since moral distinctions influence our actions they are basically matters of feeling, and in the difficulty he raised over the transition from "is" statements to "ought" statements. Among contemporary theories, emotivism and prescriptivism attempt, by a mixture of logical and psychological analysis, to show why there is a necessary influence of moral language on action as Hume emphasized. The former does it by interpreting moral words simply as the expression of a person's attitudes. The latter argues from an analogy between commands and moral judgments: just as the acceptance of a command involves doing (or trying to do) what it enjoins, so the acceptance, in the moral sense, of the decision that one ought to do x involves doing x.

Much of the discussion in this fourth section is related to the position taken by Aronfreed. Unlike the proponents of the ethical theories just mentioned, he is not trying to provide an explanation for the connection between moral discourse and action by examining the nature of the former. Rather, he is making claims about the controlling factors in any individual's behaviour: that these are fundamentally affective, not rational. In the first part of the section, the devaluation of cognitive aspects in their influence on behaviour is challenged. Many of the comments refer to a single example prompted by Aronfreed's paper: the use of punishment. It is pointed out by several of the participants that a deliberate negative reinforcement does not necessarily count as punishment in the moral sense. What makes the difference both for the agent and the subject is that the deterrent is interpreted in a conceptual context marked out by the distinctive moral concepts. As Baier notes, the way we come to understand various pressures designed to control behaviour constitutes one of the differences between simply being socialized and being taught a morality.

The same general theme (the influence of the cognitive aspects of morality on behaviour) continues to be discussed in the second part, but with particular reference to Aronfreed's claim that the control of behaviour is radically located in "affective mechanisms." Narveson argues that "cognitive structures" may in fact be more fundamental determinants of behaviour in that they shape the kind of feelings we have which in turn incline us to act in a certain way. It is suggested by Kohlberg that the relation between cognition and affect in morality can be considered apart from the bearing that they both have on behaviour. He claims to have found a high correlation between moral feelings and the level of moral judgment, and agrees that the cognitive structures determine the qualitative distinctions we make between feelings. In reference to any program of moral education based on Kohlberg's theory, Paskal draws attention to the importance of the assumption that what a person thinks about his behaviour does affect it.

Both Baier and Gauthier seek to clarify whether Aronfreed holds that it is in the nature of things or simply as a matter of fact that moral reasoning does not affect behaviour. In the course of the debate Aronfreed's position does, I think, become somewhat clearer. At the beginning he seems to speak disparagingly of the rational, cognitive aspects of moral training. Later he recognizes the importance of cognitive structures, but continues to insist that of necessity they can exercise control over behaviour only through the "affective mechanisms" that become associated with them in their acquisition.

From the point of view of education, the question of whether the cognitive or the affective is more fundamental in determining moral behaviour does not seem to be particularly relevant. What is important, as all the participants recognize, is that both the cognitive and the affective are indispensable components in an integral moral education. This point is well made in the very last comment of the discussion. In order to advance the theory of moral education from this position we would need to draw on theories about the emotions. Unfortunately, in Aronfreed's opinion at least, this is where the educators at present cannot expect much light.

In the final part of the section, Oliver stresses the importance of another aspect of feeling in morality. He criticizes the practice of translating the morally demanding situations we face into formal, abstract categories of thought. In contrast, moral inquiry involves responding emotionally to people as they are in the conditions which make up the substance of the moral problem. Edel warns against the tendency to set theorizing in sharp contrast to "sensitivity." In education, as in much of the history of ethics, the ideal is a morally sensitive man who also knows the theory.

Although most of the participants seemed to recognize that cognitive elements are crucial in the development of moral feeling and that both are necessary for moral action, the discussion did not go very far in exploring the nature of these relationships, and thus in providing a more specific guide for moral education. At least, however, it showed that they need to be more closely studied.

There are some basic considerations that help us move in the direction of an adequate account. First, we should not take abstract distinctions between the cognitive and the affective too literally. The emotional response we have to any situation involves a way of perceiving and thinking about that situation; just as there are many occasions on which we cannot claim to see a thing in a certain way unless we are experiencing a particular kind of emotion. In practice, the decision is not between reacting cognitively or affectively but between one pattern of cognitive-affective response and another. Because there is such a link between the two, it makes sense to ask whether a given emotional response is justified and to talk about the education of the emotions in morality and elsewhere.

Second, we should not treat language essentially as though it were operating in a world divorced from feeling and action. People are constantly being amused, saddened, encouraged, depressed, and stirred to all kinds of action by the use of words. The distinctive language of morality is usually acquired in a particularly strong and complex network of connections with what we feel and do. Kohlberg refers to this aspect in the discussion when he contrasts our knowledge of physical and moral principles. Of course, if a person acquires words like "good," "right," "duty," "just" in the way he acquires, for example, the basic terms of Euclidian geometry, I am doubtful whether we could engage with him in a distinctively moral argument. His moral education would have to be approached from a radically different level.

Third, if we firmly locate questions of moral value in the context of human feelings, desires, interests, needs, and so on, as was suggested earlier in this introduction, the links between thought, feeling, and action are to a considerable extent already built into the processes of moral inquiry.

Throughout the conference much attention was given to rationality in moral decision-making and to the role of the emotions. Both of these aspects are, of course, vitally important in moral education. There is another aspect at this level which I believe is at least as important for morality as the others: imagination. It was mentioned incidentally at the conference, and then mainly with reference to its use in seeing a situation from the point of view of other people. I believe that imagination plays a far more pervasive role in the whole enterprise of morality. In the recent history of ethics there has been a concerted effort to turn morality into a science. Although, as several participants pointed out, the findings of social science are significant ingredients in moral education, I would want to argue that morality lies between science and art, and perhaps finally is closer to the latter. To use Northrop

Frye's terminology, morality thus employs both the language of practical skill and knowledge and the language of imagination (envisioning the world, not as it is, but as it might be). The cultivation of the latter is necessary if we are to continually test and enlarge the perspectives that shape our moral interpretations. This aspect of moral education is not directly concerned with strengthening the will or developing logical skills in the use of moral principles, but with what Hampshire calls an "enlarged freedom of thought"; as he points out, moral failure is often not so much the result of a breakdown of the will as of the narrow range of a persons' perceptions and discriminations (Hampshire 1965, pp. 208–22). Because literature pre-eminently displays the variety of imaginative vision and the extreme possibilities of good and evil, its study constitutes a fundamental part of an integral moral education. Certainly, it is as important for mature morality as a thorough knowledge of the "facts" given by social science.

Towards the end of the discussion, Loubser drew attention to the fact that moral education is not simply ethics, or psychology, or science; it is a "composite phenomenon." This brings me back to the point from which I began these introductory comments. The papers and discussion of the conference are preparatory to the actual planning of a curriculum in moral education. The participants are speaking to this task from their specialized points of view – offering clarifications, emphasizing ingredients that need to be included. What they provide are some steps towards the design of a curriculum in which reason, feeling, imagination, and the rest are drawn together in the composite phenomenon of moral education and related appropriately both to the learner and to the total educational context.

A note on the editorial procedure. As the prepared papers were not read during the conference the entire time in each session was given to comment and discussion. Over three days, all this talking yielded a transcript of approximately 330 pages. In the process of editing, a little less than half of this material has been selected. The first criterion of selection was provided by the main themes which emerged during the conference discussion itself. In addition to this, I have taken account of the need for some measure of continuity, and of relevance to moral education. Of course, a certain amount of the manuscript could not be considered because the tape recording, for various reasons, did not provide a coherent original.

In preparing the material for publication I have departed somewhat from the chronological order of the conference in favour of the thematic arrangement. Although I have made many adjustments to the text in preparing it as a written record (and some changes have been made by the participants themselves), I have tried to retain each speaker's actual expressions as far as possible. The Ontario Institute for Studies in Education provided extensive secretarial help in the task of getting the discussion into manuscript form from the tape-recordings. During this tedious phase of the work three graduate students in philosophy of education – Erwin Biener, Michael Jackson and Malcolm MacInnis – gave invaluable assistance.

REFERENCES

Hampshire, S. *Thought and action* London: Chatto and Windus 1965, pp. 208–22

MacIntyre, A. *A short history of ethics* New York: The Macmillan Co. 1966, pp. 266–8

Taylor, C. Neutrality in political science. In Peter Laslett and W.G. Runciman (eds.) *Philosophy, politics, and society* third series. Oxford: Basil Blackwell 1967, p. 55.

CHAPTER 10

The shape of the moral domain

THE DESCRIPTIVE AND THE EVALUATIVE USES OF "MORAL"

NARVESON

I would like to raise what seems to me to be a basic question about the general characterization offered by Baier of what morality is and what (in consequence) its general aims are. When we attempt to formulate a definition of the terms "moral" and "morality" we are likely to run into the problem that our definition is itself a *normative* one; not just in the general sense in which any definition is normative in that it says how a term is *to be* used, but in the specific sense that it seems to build certain *moral* standards into the use of the term "moral" itself. That is, when you say that something belongs to somebody's morality, then on this kind of definition, you are saying something good about the set of standards so characterized.

If the proposed definition is just an attempt to specify what those who employ the expression mean by it, this would seem rather anomalous; for one would suppose that a statement about what people mean by a word would be just that – a statement – and not an evaluation. Baier's characterization appears in part to have this anomalous property. A group's morality, he says, is that subset of its social rules which is "good enough to be acceptable" according to certain requirements. Interestingly (and significantly) enough, however, Baier does not precisely specify these requirements. He says rather that there would be pretty general agreement that they would "embody the same two central ideas: that they should minimize harm and maximize good, and that they should do so for everyone alike." If we ask ourselves why Baier should content himself with a rough characterization of what most people would agree to on this point (rather than a precise analytical stipulation), the answer would certainly be, as Baier implies, that there is, in fact, controversy about these very requirements. Further, I suggest that such controversy would not simply be linguistic disagreement about the proper analysis of certain terms, but would be more like moral controversy itself. For example, it has been and still is disputed whether morality must be for the good of "everyone alike." Both egoists and various kinds of racists would presumably disagree. We may wish to rule out such views as untenable from the start, as Baier's proposal would in effect do; but I think it would be better to make the discussion of just such issues a first and major item of business in our curriculum of moral education. And as to the other clause, that morality must be devoted to minimizing harm and maximizing good, even if this is not likely to be disputed as it stands (and it is unclear whether even this is so), there will plainly be extensive controversy over the question of just what is to count as harm or good for the purposes at hand.

My point is that Professor Baier's proposals do not amount to an emphasis on "procedural methods rather than substance of ethical principles," because there is already substance, so to speak, in the methods proposed. In his admirable book, *The Moral Point of View*, Baier has remarked that morality as such is not a super-morality. But it seems to me that the characterization that he has supplied of morality as such is indeed a sort of super-morality. I should make it clear in all of this that I think it is the right super-morality. That is not my point. I mean that discussion of whether it is the right one would be a moral discussion and not solely a logical one.

BAIER

I would want to argue that one could give an account of what we mean by "moral" and "morality" which simply describes, states in factual terms, what we mean by it, and find that one has built into "moral" as we ordinarily use the term an implication of its being legitimate or rational. We distinguish morality from immorality on the criterion of justice. However, we can adopt the sociological point of view and characterize the morality of other individuals, peoples, and societies without saying or implying that it has that legitimacy or rationality built into it. So we can say that such and such a morality is unsound or crude or uncivilized. It has vestiges of the pure notion left in it, but to the extent that it departs from the perfect version it should be corrected. So I think that when we talk about people's moralities, we are talking in a non-evaluative scientific-observer descriptive spirit, while at the same time implying that there is a standard against which we measure moralities. We do not need to depart from a strictly metaethical point of view in describing or characterizing the notions of morality. Of course the fact that morality has this idea of legitimacy built into it raises the question of just what that justification comes to. That is indeed an evaluative, perhaps even a normative, issue, but it is not an ethical one. It is one that simply tells us that the kind of conduct regulator we understand by morality is a beneficial one and that when we impose the modifications required by morality in a given social order this is in itself a beneficial thing to do. A society that has a nonmoral social order and does not have these modifications imposed on it is to that extent inferior – but not morally inferior. It is simply an inferior way of organizing a people's life. But this is a very difficult issue and I am not tremendously confident about it.

EDEL

I would like to see you pursue this problem because of its significance. We have here two fundamentally different ways of looking at the requirements for the account of morality. Narveson's point of view is that the requirements themselves express the moral outlook. Baier's is that they express what has been analyzed out of the notion of morality, that in part the analysis involves the kind of sociological point of view that describes the functions morality performs in a society, and yet at the same time is some kind of evaluation that is not moral but that enables us to say that one morality is better than another. It may be useful to put this issue quite bluntly. It seems to me that it is basic to Kohlberg's position, for instance, when he tries in his paper to establish a universal transcultural concept of morality that is moral but not in any sense relative. Would Narveson say that Baier is trying to have his cake and eat it too?

NARVESON

A lot of people writing books in moral philosophy are clearly addressing themselves, not to morality as distinct from the general set of propositions about what we should and should not do, but quite generally to the evaluations of conduct or behaviour, and they are not very much concerned to make distinctions in that broad class of evaluations between moral and nonmoral ones. Stevenson's work in *Ethics and Language* is a good example. As a matter of fact, Stevenson has remarked in one of his essays that he really thinks this is not a very important distinction. He says that what we really care about is what a man is or is not going to do, not whether he happens to attach the label "moral" to the reasons that he gives for this. There is some sense in this: it is inherent in the notion of morality that the moral prescriptions are those you ought to obey whatever else you may or may not obey. You can extract from this a characterization of morality that logically will be almost completely independent of considerations about social benefit, because you could simply identify a man's moral principles with his ultimate principles of behaviour, that is those principles that he acts on fundamentally. It is logically possible that a man's morals would be devoid of considerations of social benefit, etc. He may think that other people are of no interest whatever.

My view is that we need a definition of the term "moral" so that positions like this could be called moral in a sense that does not imply the opposite of immoral. If I say Jones is a very moral man, clearly I am evaluating his behaviour. But if I say of a principle that it is a moral principle, I am not using moral as an evaluative term. This is where the difference between Baier and myself comes out. Baier would say that when you call something a moral principle you are also subscribing to certain moral criteria of goodness or badness relating to that principle. I, on the other hand, am inclined to use the word "moral" here in such a way that at least logically a person's moral principles could be very immoral indeed, that they could do very poorly by these kinds of requirements.

GAUTHIER

Baier has mentioned that the moral order must be beneficial and that it must satisfy criteria of justice. Of course the mention of justice immediately introduces a further ethical term, at this stage unanalyzed in the discussion. We have to be convinced that somehow we can eliminate the apparent moral or ethical characteristics in an analysis of this term.

BAIER

For the purpose of this discussion, I will take back the term "justice" and simply say that everyone has an equal interest in having the conflicts of interest regulated in this way rather than in some other.

GAUTHIER

But we can show that a great many systems are such that everyone will have a like interest in having conflicts regulated by one such system rather than by no system at all. Very roughly we would have to employ some criterion of social optimality in the order that we develop, and social optimality is notoriously an extremely weak condition. It seems to me that the difficulty one gets into in trying to show, for example, that we can define one social-welfare function that would be obviously superior to any other, would simply recur in even greater degrees in trying to get down to a whole system that would meet your requirements.

BAIER

I am not suggesting that there is only one system. All you have to do is to take a given social order and improve it. You can start from any number of points and improve it in the direction of, for example, more fairness. I do not want to get into welfare economics, but I think one starts there from an entirely inadequate central concept, namely, that of preference.

KOHLBERG

It should clarify the issue if we considered what a moral rule is. For example, in Israel is it a moral rule not to eat or sell pork? How would Baier's criterion apply here?

BAIER

Deciding whether something is a moral rule or not involves two questions. The first question is this: on what basis do we say that a rule is a moral rule as opposed to a religious rule or a rule of etiquette or a rule of aesthetic oppreciation or what have you? And the second question – which would be the substantive moral issue – is: supposing that we have settled what the criteria of a moral rule are, does this particular rule satisfy these criteria? In your example of eating and selling pork I suppose you are more interested in the first of these questions, that is, what do we have in mind when we call it a moral rule. Suppose the criterion is that it gains you eternal life if you do not eat pork, but it gains you eternal damnation if you do. This would not satisfy our ordinary criteria because we regard it as what is normally called a prudential rule based on the belief that if we satisfy the requirement we will gain this wonderful benefit and if we do not, we will lose it, whereas one of the criteria of a moral rule is that it would be a consideration on the basis of which we accept or reject the social rules under which we live; if, for instance, there are rules concerning interpersonal relations, whether they are harmful or beneficial, or, if they are concerned with tasks or duties or roles that are imposed by our social institutions, whether they satisfy the requirements of distributive justice.

KOHLBERG

However, the orthodox Jew who manages to get a law passed that prohibits the selling and eating of pork can do so essentially on the grounds that eating pork is bad for the soul of everybody in the country. In that sense his grounds are like those for prohibiting murder or something of this kind.

BAIER

Or course a rule like this could be supported on moral grounds. One could claim that in selling pork to another person you are endangering his well-being. However, it just happens to be a claim for which there is no evidence. Since moral rules involve restrictions on people's conduct we should have only those moral rules that are supported by pretty clear evidence. And there is not any evidence whatever of the connection between this kind of a rule and the after-life, if there is an after-life.

SCRIVEN

Let us try and get back to the problem as it faces the practical man. Kohlberg, I presume, has to decide which examples he could use in his research. Oliver and I have to decide which sorts of examples to incorporate in the curriculum. We do not have to get into the issue of the ultimate rationality of the single moral system. We can say that the word "moral" has a function precisely like fifty other words in our language in that it sometimes functions to mean the preferred, justifiable, correct system, and sometimes it means any candidate for that honour. The word "explanation", for example, is used in these ways in the history of science. We have to get used to that perfectly common ambiguity of the term. So in the case of the prohibition against pork the situation is that clearly it is a candidate for morality, and this is obvious from the sanctions that are applied in connection with it. It is treated phenomenologically as a moral principle. It is equally clear that there are grave difficulties as a matter of fact in showing that it is rationally defensible. So it is not a good example to take for moral education, since you cannot achieve general agreement about its factual basis. It seems to me that in the domain of teaching or research one would want to take examples unlike this one so as to avoid the difficulty of striking somebody with different factual – in this case theological – premises, who will misclassify the rule for that reason. Instead, one picks principles like "you should not on the whole take things away from people who like them just because you like them too." There are general principles like this one, which are common to any allegedly rational morality, so that you do not have to argue about the question of whether rules like the prohibition on eating pork are really moral.

There is a section in Kohlberg's paper where the distinction between the two senses of "moral" applies. He says: "unlike judgments of prudence or aesthetics, moral judgments tend to be universal, inclusive, consistent, and grounded on objective, impersonal, or ideal grounds." This does not seem to be true, although I should add that its truth is not necessary to Kohlberg's general thesis. First, it should be clear that here he is not referring to moral judgments in the sense of "moral-aspiring," as "explanation" was used for anything which was thought to be or taken to be an explanation. I am going to use the term "moral-type judgment" for this sense, and "moral-ideal judgment" to mean something that one refers to as *the* moral position or the *right* moral position or the *real* moral position. So it is clear here that he means "moral-ideal" and not "moral-type" because, obviously, moral-type judgments are by no means consistent, not even with each other, nor even internally. But the moral-ideal system of judgment of course has to be consistent. The confusing thing is that he says that moral judgments *tend* to be consistent, and that sounds like an empirical statement about what you find people putting out as moral judgments. But of course they will not meet that criterion unless they are refined to the moral ideal.

EDEL

In the parallel with "explanation," Scriven's point seems to suggest that the moral criteria will be characterized by the kind of problems to which they are addressed rather than by being considered as a kind of answer. But if this is the case, then Baier's requirements are uneven in type. Some are answers and some characterize problems. I am referring to the five items listed in his paper (see p. 94): public interests, natural rights, and so on. Because men are organized in a community and find it necessary to have some guiding policies, the concept of the common good will appear as a part of the requirement of the notion of a morality. But there will be different answers about the content of the common good depending on the situation. Because conflict will occur over and over again in society, we are going to have a notion of the public interest. But we will not allow anything like the Marxist's theory which says that the notion of the public interest always reflects the interest of a given class. We have agreed that there are conflicts of interest, so the only notion of the public interest we can admit is one that helps us find solutions for such conflicts. What about natural rights? This will have to be changed a bit. We will need to have a notion of a system of rights, but whether they will be the natural rights of an individual or group rights of one kind or another must be part of the answer. What about social justice? Well, every society requires some pattern of distribution of burdens and gains and this is what we are going to call a system of social justice. The condition of universalizability is going to have trouble. The underlying problem is that every society has some range for which its moral rules hold, some congregation to which they apply. Because historically this has sometimes been the in-group and sometimes the family, and these have been associated with the different kinds of orders, universalizability will have to be taken out of the list and seen to be a moral answer, not part of the question. Now if we do this, I think we avoid Baier's difficulty of both having his cake and eating it. The sociological part will be the appropriate ground for making recommendations that morality be reasonably defined in a certain way by a certain set of problems. But we have to be careful not to put into the requirements any particular answer as, for instance, the universalizability thesis does.

RATIONALITY AND MORAL JUDGMENT

MELDEN

Like Scriven I find myself singularly unimpressed by the enormous difficulty about Morality and moralities, just as I am rather unimpressed by the distinction between Science and sciences such as political science, seventeenth-century science, and so on. In talking about morality what we try to do is clarify the kinds of rational procedure we employ when we are sufficiently perceptive and reasonable in addressing ourselves to practical questions, in addressing ourselves to other people and appraising them, and so on. A procedure that is essentially rational, although not so as to preclude the possibility of error, will allow for the possibility of correcting whatever errors people do make. If we are going to talk reasonably about moral education, instead of waving signals about the common good or the general interest, whatever they mean, we really must address ourselves to the character of the rational procedures employed and the matters relevant to these in the appraisal of whatever it is that arouses our concern. We need to study the kinds of procedures for making appraisals that are such that, even though on a particular occasion we may go wrong, they still enable us to correct our mistakes in a way similar to that in science.

SULLIVAN

In the present discussion I must say that I find "rational" a weasel word, particularly when people talk about "a rational member of society." I wonder what he would look like, what he would be doing, how I would recognize him, as opposed to the irrational members?

BAIER

He would have a conception of what he wants and what is good for him, and if it is pointed out to him that his conduct or the line of conduct that he proposes to enter upon does not bring this about, then he would be moved to do something else and to go in the direction that it is suggested to him will bring him closer to the accomplishment of what he is after and what he thinks is good for him.

SULLIVAN

Let us take some issue like the war in Vietnam and suppose, for example, that Johnson says "It is in our interest to use a nuclear weapon." In the long haul how would you see his action, as rational or irrational?

BAIER

Well, I don't know. The issue is so immensely complex that men who by paradigm cases are rational creatures disagree. To ask me to adjudicate in this matter is to ask the impossible.

OLIVER

What is the point, then, of appealing to rationality?

NARVESON

I would expect that an argument in morals is a good argument, or probably a good argument, if it can convince people who are able to perform the usual intellectual tasks. If you produce some paradigm examples, like syllogisms, which are clearly valid, and if a person reacts in a totally random way to them, then you can be sure that you are not going to be able to get anywhere with him morally. But if it is quite clear that he can handle language efficiently within reasonable limits and knows the kind of elementary logic that most people know and seems to be able to size things up in other areas, then he has the kind of ability we are referring to under this title of rationality. I think that we would have to add one other thing, namely, that he would have to have some idea of what he wants. People have argued about whether computers, for example, are intelligent, but few have argued that computers are rational because they do not seem to think that computers literally want something.

MELDEN

Does not a psychotic have wants, too?

NARVESON

Yes, but he would fail on the other score. He would almost certainly fail on some of the other rationality issues that have nothing special to do with morality.

OLIVER

If a man smokes forty cigarettes a day and you tell him that he is not rational, he may reply, "Well, I get tremendous satisfaction from smoking forty cigarettes a day, although I realize that there are grave risks and that it is going to contribute to enormous social problems since we do not have enough lung surgeons. I have tried to stop, but it is a great agony and I cannot quite bring myself to do it." At that point, do we cure the man of cigarette smoking or do we say that since he has given us his reason he is a rational man?

SCRIVEN

If I understand Melden correctly it seems to me that he is emphasizing the rational element in morality more than I would care to. That is, I want to include amongst moralities those in which reasoning about a matter is simply rejected. You say, "Let's reason about this." They reply, "To hell with reason; you just acted in an immoral way and off with your head." I think you probably have to loosen the definition a bit and in this morality is unlike science. But I think there is a manoeuvre that we can make that will have the same effect in a way. If you look at how the word "number" is used in mathematics and its history in mathematics, you will find that it has gradually come to be used in very different ways. Although it began meaning the integers, it was extended to include the fractions, the negatives, the irrationals, and finally the reals. Yet it was never allowed to extend to the point where the non-Archimedean numbers, so-called, were admitted. Now, if you ask an ordinary working mathematician to justify the present use, he will not give you a very good answer. He cannot reason about it, although he is sure that such and such is a number. But there is a perfectly proper procedure of justification, which is the induction from the history of mathematics of the standards to which we implicitly respond. I think that in the analysis of morality this is what we do in producing a normative definition. We react to the various things that have been called morality. Our definition has to match them to some extent, otherwise we are just not going to have morality. But we can induce from them some idea, anthropologically speaking, of the function of these systems of rules, and we can then ask the analytical question, "Which system of rules will most efficiently serve this function?" If we reserve the words "the morality," or "true morality," or "morality" underlined, emphasized, or in quotes for this, we are doing something perfectly in keeping with the search for the meaning of concepts.

Now we come to the question of the connection with rationality. It seems to me hopeless to suggest that morality is what a man taken in the midst of life will recognize, if he is rational, as what he should do. The cigarette-smoking is a very good analogy to this within the domain of prudence. If he does not have a wife and children and it is just a question of what he should do for himself, there is nothing moral about it. If a thief gets caught when he had the best of reasons for thinking he could get away with it, really no argument will suggest to him that he did something irrational in trying to steal. He had every reason to think that he was being rational. The mistake in both his case and that of the smoker is that they ever got themselves to the point where they valued such things. In the case of the smoker, what we definitely want to say is that he would have been better off if he had never got hooked, and he is not denying that. There are no grounds for thinking – and he does not suggest that there are – that he would have had a terribly unsatisfying life if he had taken to chewing gum instead of smoking. In the case of morality it seems to me that the connection with rationality is analogous. That is, you can give excellent reasons for thinking that morality is the set of values that people should adopt in the non-moral sense of "should." But for the man who has adopted another, or not adopted these because of poor education, we cannot argue that it is immediately irrational for him to behave immorally. However, from the point of view of our discussion all we need to see is that by the crudest conceptions of rationality some forms of morality are irrational and must be rejected for reasons of inconsistency or factual error.

We could restrict our concern to those systems of educating people that meet two conditions. Not only must graduates pass the basic test Narveson mentioned – that is too weak on its own. You have to make another bet: that if they passed the basic tests and then began to study morality as a group and were exposed to detailed, hard pressured argument from both sides about moral issues, there would be some communality about their agreement as they progressed up the scale. That is, you can give an inductive connection of morality with rationality, but you cannot give an immediate one. You have to say you are betting that as they go along Kohlberg's developmental stages or through Oliver's curriculum they will continue to agree about which is the rational solution. Of course, when we get to *very* difficult cases they will not do that. At least, in the beginning they will not do it, but we are betting that they will do it for *most* of the long run, just as in learning physics.

MELDEN

May I just comment that I think there are situations in the history of science where there is no simple rational argument that is air-tight and persuasive. But there is in the process a development of reasonable decision or agreement on the part of those involved. For example, the phlogiston argument: it has been pointed out again and again that no single argument was decisive in refuting this. In a similar way I do not think that a simple argument based on what a man actually wants on a given occasion will be decisive either. But there is a difference between being rational in a very narrow sense and being reasonable. That is to say, people being reasonable, taking account of facts which as far as they can see are affecting many people, will come to consensus. This is a rational procedure. And there is a way, then, of correcting the faults we make in the course of trying to take account of as much of this matter as possible. So I would agree with what Scriven said. We have to open up the notion of being reasonable so that it goes beyond simply getting adequate or efficient means for the achievement of what, on a particular occasion or in a given situation, one happened to want.

NARVESON

It seems to me that there is implicit in the notion of rationality the thought that eventually you would be able to formulate with considerable precision the things that had made the solution right. In particular, it seems to me that you ought to be able to hook those up with things like principles of logic. Think of the prudent man. You could tell that he was irrational if he gave reasons which were literally contradictory. For example, if he said, "I agree entirely that it is in my best over-all interest to do such and such," and then did the opposite without giving any further explanation. This would be a pretty straightforward criterion of irrationality. You would connect directly with the paradigms of rationality, which are the elementary forms of logic. I would hope that we would be able to do something like that in general. Kant tried to do that, and it was not a silly idea, however much he may have failed in the effort.

MELDEN

May we have one of those first principles that you are suggesting so that we can look closely at it and see if we have anything that even begins to touch the problem? I am thinking of the Cartesian mode or model. It is the natural one to go for, and yet I find that either one has something that is rather trivial because it is tautological, such as the appeal to the common good, to what is in the interest of the people (or to "universalizability" which logically can become perfectly trivial as it applies to the application of any predicate, moral and non-moral); or else one has something that is essentially a reminder of certain considerations, which may be very useful, but which do not function in that sort of Cartesian mode.

NARVESON

Yes, but the reason why these considerations are considerations and why they are important surely has to do with their internal rational properties. The Kantian requirement, for instance, is surely something like this. A necessary condition of an ultimate moral principle's being rationally acceptable at all is that it be at least possible for everybody to obey it. If it is not even possible for everybody to obey it, it cannot possibly be a morally acceptable principle, because morality is for everybody.

ARONFREED

Despite your emphasis elsewhere in this conference on the rational presentation of concepts and problems, and your belief that the child will then see the intrinsic merit of your case, you now seem to introduce essentially behavioural criteria. You say that there cannot be such a thing as a moral principle unless everyone is capable of realizing it in his behaviour.

NARVESON

No, that is not what I said. I said that it has to be logically capable of being obeyed by everybody, which does not mean that in fact everybody will be able to do so psychologically, nor does it mean that obedience to some edict is a sufficient condition of rationality. All I said was that a necessary – not sufficient, but necessary – condition of a moral principle's being a rationally acceptable moral principle is that it be logically capable of being obeyed by everybody.

ARONFREED

Well, what do you mean by being logically capable of being obeyed by everybody?

NARVESON

I just mean that from the universal proposition that everybody should do the kind of thing that is recommended, there ensues no contradiction.

TURIEL

I would like to direct a question to the philosophers. We have been continually talking about rationality and I think we have been doing this from very different perspectives, the philosophical and the psychological. It would be better, I think, if philosophers could try to psychologize about rationality as part of something that goes on in people's heads. My feeling has been that philosophers have constantly made a distinction between the non-rational and the rational, while psychologists from their developmental perspective assume that rationality exists from the beginning but that there are different kinds of rationalities. I think Piaget made a very important point for psychologists, which changed the direction of American pyschology. His point was that a very young child has a logic or a rationality of his own and that to understand adult rationality it is necessary to determine how these earlier forms lead to the later forms. This, I think, implies a certain kind of determinism as to Kohlberg's stages, in the sense that there is a basic inborn sequence that is universal. We do not see the sequence as being necessarily an innate one. We see it rather as an interactive process and perhaps this is why it becomes necessary to speak of matching models. Nevertheless, it is a form of determinism, because the sequence is seen as being universal. If the sequence must be of a certain kind for all people, this raises the general question of where it comes from. This is to some extent a philosophical question and I would like to hear philosophers talk about it as well as psychologists. However, to go back to the earlier point, I wonder if we could hear some discussion on this non-rational/rational question if possible. I have had the feeling from the discussion in this conference of the moral stages and questions about skipping stages, etc. that, like Ausubel, philosophers dichotomize man into rational man versus arational or irrational man. And perhaps they see the child as being arational or irrational as opposed to the adult who is rational.

SCRIVEN

I do not think philosophers would want to accept that view. Perhaps the best way to conceptualize what they are doing is to think of it in terms of ideal-type theory; that is, they do want to talk about the rational man, but his role is that of an ideal type – an entity who is responding to good arguments and discarding bad arguments. It does not mean that there is a slice of that entity in everybody distinct from the other slices of him or that there are any substantiations of that entity in full-blown form. It just means that there are approximations to this in the behaviour of people at particular times. Although there is some point in talking about the child having a rationality of his own, I think we might object to this way of speaking and make a useful point in doing so. It is likely to get misleading because it is likely to suggest that after all there is the child's version of rationality, then there is the adolescent's version, then there is the grown-up's version, and which one is right all depends on how old you are. Of course, which one you *use* depends on how old you are. But there is a significant advantage about ideal-type rationality, namely, that it works and the others do not – at least they work to lesser degrees. So it comes down to a straight pragmatic criterion, I think.

KOHLBERG

Is the word rationality a basically useful analytic one for moral philosophers, any more than it is for psychologists?

SCRIVEN

It is the key word, because the key question is whether there are arguments that show that a man who is concerned only with adopting a point of view that is likely to pay off, would in fact be moral.

KOHLBERG

That is a peculiar kind of question. I would take the position that it is not relevant to the development of moral thinking. The issue is that the definition of morality is not contingent on the definition of rationality.

SCRIVEN

You have to *evaluate* the development of morality. Is it adaptive behaviour or not? And this is the same question.

KOHLBERG

The adaptiveness of morality?

SCRIVEN

Yes. Long-run adaptiveness necessitates rationality.

KOHLBERG

Although some loose notion of rationality must be involved in scientific theories and scientific behaviour, the concept of the rational man is not an important concept in analyzing scientific thought or children's thought about science or anything like that. Nobody would really raise an issue about the rational man in discussing this, and I do not think any of the philosophers here would really start with the model of rationality and then construct a model of morality from it, so to speak.

BAIER

If you had to say that behaving in a moral fashion was irrational, then presumably there would be something to be said for dropping this kind of superstitious or irrational mode of behaviour.

KOHLBERG

As I have pointed out, though, irrationality is a very strong thing – to be rational as opposed to being irrational is very weak.

BAIER

Of course irrationality is very strong. But you say that rationality has nothing to do with morality. If that were one of the consequences of the analysis of morality, then it would have to be dismissed, I think, by rational beings as a crude and superseded form of behaviour control.

KOHLBERG

I have naïvely assumed that what both you and other people in modern philosophy have been doing was to construct some workable notion of morality, not to start with a model of rationality taken from outside the moral domain and then to construct some notion of what mature, adequate morality is in terms of the standard of rationality that somehow developed outside the moral domain. You always have the problem of why one should be moral, of how you sell morality to a rational egoist, that is, an amoral rational man. But the construction of what mature morality is does not seem to me to depend on some general concept of rationality. Where would that general concept come from?

BAIER

Like any concepts, it comes from our general way of talking.

MELDEN

I think the question that has been raised here is important. All philosophers, I believe, can be sorted out with respect to the kind of approach Kohlberg has just been describing, namely, with the conception and then the application of rationality. That is one approach. Another might be this: examination of moral discourse – in the way in which presumably Aristotle developed principles of the syllogism by inductively proceeding from discourse – in order to come inductively to a logic of moral reasoning. Methodologically there is an important difference between these approaches and risks either way. But the general question as to whether the conception of a rational man emerges as a result of one's investigation, whether one proceeds in an *a priori* fashion or inductively (presumably), is to be answered I think in this way: that every moral philosopher does have a conception of rationality, rational man, in the sphere of morals. If he did not think that there was a rationality here, then he would simply abandon all hope and give up the enterprise because it would not be worth fussing about.

CRITTENDEN

I want to come back to the question that Turiel began with. He spoke of a kind of determinism that seems to be involved in the stages of moral development and asked what a philosopher would have to say about it. I think this question is by no means irrelevant to the issue of rationality. I simply suggest one answer to the question. By examining moral action, a philosopher would point out the kind of thinking and reasoning which would be necessary for genuine moral action to occur. In the process he would make clear the concepts (not necessarily moral) on which an understanding of any moral argument depended. A philosopher would talk about logical presuppositions of this kind. But that is a different sort of issue, I think, from describing the sequence of stages in which human beings in fairly typical circumstances in a given society became capable of managing the logically required concepts and forms of reasoning. I do not see that the genetic and developmental aspects are specifically philosophical although what the philosopher says about the concepts that are logically involved in morality and what the psychologist says about the conditions under which they are acquired are both vitally important for moral education.

KOHLBERG

The evidence with which the developmentalist comes is that people like ourselves have some notion of a culturally universal mature morality. We may or may not call it rational but it is something like rational morality as philosophers have conceived of it. If there is also a culturally universal sequence or origin of that morality, that is extremely important in defining the rational quality of the end product. That is, the peculiar quality of moral maturity or rationality depends on its origins or sources. In the particular model that we are working with, if some conception of justice is the core of rational morality, this is because it is also the core of irrational morality or the beginning of morality. Social reciprocity is the essence of the beginning of a sense of obligation, so that the fact that social reciprocity is the precondition of social and moral interaction then becomes determinative of its rational form, which is justice. That is the theoretical contention. On the other hand, a utilitarian approach assumes another model of rationality, maximization of interests. The young child does not start out with the core of moral concepts one has in terms of maximizing interests; he starts with another core. And the eventual rational forms will be different.

BECK

If we are going to accept Melden's statement that all moral philosophers do accept a rationality position with respect to morals, I think we must qualify it somewhat. There are important differences between the types of rationality philosophers see in morals. There is a very strong tradition in contemporary British moral philosophy which says in effect, "we do employ reasoning in arriving at moral decisions day by day and this reasoning goes back a fair way, but finally it's based upon certain ultimate principles which we just accept." Now it seems to me that this is a case of wanting to have your cake and eat it. If you can somehow rationally derive your basic assumptions, that is different. But it seems we have two views of the rationality element in morals here and I think we must admit that a considerable number of contemporary moral philosophers do accept a view that I personally would say was not rational.

TURIEL

I would like to tie these isolated points together and ask some more questions. To say that we employ reasoning in making moral judgments does not get us very far, it seems to me, in explaining the moral judgment. I think that the moral judgment is a kind of reasoning in itself in some ways differing from a logical judgment. This means that we have to look at the term "rational" in a more precise way and separate it into different kinds of rationalities.

EDEL

Perhaps it would be helpful if you told us what you as a psychologist mean by rationality. Then we could compare it to the kind of thing philosophers say, despite the differences that circulate among them. Speaking for yourself, how would you use it?

TURIEL

I would say that there are different kinds of rationality. There might be aesthetic rationality, there might be a logical rationality in applying certain kinds of concepts, there might be a moral rationality that includes affective and cognitive elements. What I think we are trying to do as psychologists is find out what the processes in making a moral judgment are. I think Kohlberg's stages represent descriptions or explanations of what these processes are and I think these are necessary in understanding how an individual makes a moral decision or deals with a moral argument. This is in contradistinction to philosophers who assume that a moral argument is an entity in itself. I think that the moral argument is interpreted by the individual, and how it is interpreted is in part determined by the nature of that process, which perhaps can be described by one of the stages. The reason why that is the important concept is, I think, that we have to see how the mind in its own processes, qualitatively different from other younger or older minds, deals with what is coming to it from the outside world.

SULLIVAN

I think this is a problem for psychologists when they try to plug in what would be rational. Scriven talked about the ability to respond to good arguments. However, a good argument which in Kohlberg's scheme brings a person from stage 2 to stage 3 would not be recognized as a rational form of discourse from another perspective.

NARVESON

I should like to address myself to two or three of the matters that were raised here in connection with rationality. In particular, I want to say something on the question of whether we are to say that children are irrational or arational, whether they have a different sort of rationality from what adults have, or to take something that would naturally be associated with this, whether different cultures might have different rationalities. Probably it is no good trying to define rationality in terms of a kind of definitive canon, that is, I do not think that one would be able to say that to be rational is simply nothing more or less than to act in accordance with this particular principle or something of this sort. It does not follow from this, however, that there are a lot of different rationalities, and I want to give some reasons for thinking this. To begin with, it seems to me very probable that the term "rational" used as an adjective is, whatever else it is, a kind of critical term. This is particularly clear from the term "irrational." When I say to someone that he is being irrational this is a particular way of criticizing him. It is not equivalent to saying that what he is doing is bad or wrong, but it is to imply that there is a respect at least in which it is bad or wrong or misguided. Certainly it would not do to say, "well, I agree that what I said was irrational, but so what?" This would be a nonsensical thing to say and it indicates what the function of the word "rational" is in various kinds of criticism. Certainly it applies in this way to arguments. I should add that while it clearly does apply to arguments, it does not apply to statements taken by themselves. For example, if I say, "it is raining," this is not a statement that by itself can be said to be either rational or irrational. It is rational if it is made under certain circumstances and in the light of certain evidence, irrational if it is made in other circumstances and with other evidence. But you cannot take a particular statement by itself and say that it is rational. There must be enough structure so that you can discover, for instance, contradictions or internal incoherences in the statement.

There is what seems to me to be a misuse of the term "rational" in Oliver's position. There was a suggestion that those, let me call them, darker forces or needs of which Oliver spoke somehow had a kind of intrinsic opposition to reasoning and thereby, I would suppose, to rationality. This seems to me to be clearly not so. You can be rational in dealing with these dark forces or you can be irrational, but being rational about them does not by itself inherently imply they have to be, for instance, suppressed or ignored or extinguished. These forces – I am using the term in a slightly metaphorical sense – are not inherently irrational any more than joy, for instance, is inherently rational.

Finally, I think it unsatisfactory to think of rationality as a sort of general capacity in human nature in a way in which you may think about intelligence. You can argue about whether intelligence is an inherited capacity and to what extent it is inherited and what it is influenced by and so forth, but I do not think that the word "rationality" will work the way that the word "intelligence" does. One of the indications of this is that we all know that people can be extremely intelligent, yet extremely irrational, just as other people who are only moderately intelligent can be quite rational. To think of rationality as a kind of inherent capacity either in human nature in general or in certain individuals in particular strikes me as wrong. If we are to talk about the rationality of an individual as such, I think that we would want to say something like the following: He is frequently or always or most of the time very rational in the sorts of things that he does, in the sorts of arguments that he uses, etc. If we say that children are, as it were, less rational than adults, it would be all right provided we mean by this that their arguments are not often as good or something of this kind. But to say that children are inherently lower in their rationality level than adults in the sense that it is some kind of capacity seems to me to be very doubtful indeed.

BAIER

As always in these discussions I think the differences are largely a matter of different uses of words. Where Turiel uses different types of rationality I think he means what Narveson would mean by different types of reasoning. We could readily translate his examples of aesthetic and moral rationality into types of reasoning. The third example, logical rationality, is rather curious and I am not sure it could be translated. The stages that Kohlberg distinguishes certainly would be quite readily translatable into types or modes of reasoning. The question then is which are, from the point of view of the good life, more acceptable types of reasoning if generally practised. That is the kind of question that moral philosophers are interested in. The main thing to remember is that there is a double distinction, a double opposite of "rational." One is non-rational and the other is irrational and other forms of adjectives derived from the root word "reason." The distinction between rational and non-rational is the distinction as between creatures capable of engaging in forms of reasoning and creatures not so capable, so that "non-rational" is not in itself necessarily an evaluative term – although it can be so used. Within the range of creatures that have the capacity for reasoning we grade for performance, and the idea of doing well or badly is an evaluative distinction. I think that is what gives Turiel the idea that there is a value dichotomy – really this is a scale rather than a dichotomy. But I do not think he can get around that kind of a thing even within the different types of reasoning which he distinguishes. Within each type one can do it better or worse, and presumably this is so even for the child.

TURIEL

I think it is necessary to make clear the definition of what you mean by better or worse. What we mean as psychologists is that in some respects "better" is a higher form of development and "worse" is a lower form. That is the only way that we use the terms.

EDEL

But does not "higher" convey a more effective solution to problems of the sort you have in mind and are you not really moving to some kind of value criterion? How can you use the word "higher" if you have not some underlying idea that what is done in response to this problem in this context can be done more or less well?

TURIEL

Decisions in general can be seen as problems. The individual has to deal with this problem and it can be dealt with in different ways. I think that the person at a higher level of development deals with the problem more effectively or more adaptively than does the person at a lower level. That is a basic developmental premise. It is only a premise and I think that from what I have heard thus far the philosophers do not concern themselves sufficiently with what they mean by "more effective."

SCRIVEN

Let us look at the following two possibilities. On the basis of careful research it turns out that every child passes through a sequence of six stages. It is an indisputable empirical fact. At stage 6 they reason pretty well or they moralize pretty well or they classify paintings pretty well or whatever it is we are talking about. And at stage 1 they are very poor at it. Now we make another discovery. Stage 4 is what always happens after stage 3. And people never go to stage 5 except through stage 4. However, objectively speaking, people at stage 4 are less effective in handling their environment – they constantly say that such and such will be so and it is not – than they are at stage 3. So stage 4 is higher developmentally but it is lower efficiently.

If you think about the hard sciences which Kohlberg automatically raised as a contrast, the notion of rationality does not come in so obviously because what you need is only reality confrontation – people becoming better able to say true things about the environment. This is simply because it is a non-statistical area. The reality orientation is built into science-training. You do not talk a great deal about rationality but you do talk about whether something would work, or which of two objects is the heavier. Until students get to the point where they are able to find out which is the heavier you have not taught them effectively your mode of inquiry. When you move to statistical areas, strategic considerations are of prime concern because you are constantly going to be wrong whichever system of making bets you pick on. The only distinction is in the frequency with which you are wrong. Now you move into the area where rationality becomes the key type of criterion. Interpersonal activities is a major case of this. Rationality is a strategic methodology. It is simply the substitute for direct truth-checking, and it is a statistical or frequency substitute. It is the method of making bets that is most likely to produce the highest *frequency* of correct answers. So that is how we decide in terms of a philosopher's criterion of rationality that stage 4 is in fact lower than stage 3 on the rationality scale. There is nothing non-empirical about this, but it is a strategy-evaluation, not a responsiveness-description.

May I add one very brief point. The idea that a child starts off as rational within his tiny mind and moves on, always rational but changing in his environment and system of reinforcers, is very reminiscent of the idea that primitive religion is really rational pre-science. It is important to see that this has two bad features, or one with two aspects. It is totally relativistic, and it mistakenly suggests that as a matter of fact children do have the best strategy in terms of the world as they see it. *Per impossible* (because we discover that a stage-1 person never jumps directly to stage 6), suppose that a person at stage 1 had an overnight flash and woke up able to think like a person at stage 6. While his brain in some sense has changed in order to do this, his environment is the same. But it is obviously the case that he will now be more effective in coping with it. He would be better off if he could think stage-6, or in our sense, more rational thoughts here and now. It is not the case that the way he thinks at stage 1 is the best for his present circumstances.

CRITTENDEN

I would like to add something to these observations on reasoning. I think that we might also consider a distinction between the reasons that one gives for why he or you ought to do something and the reasons he has for giving those reasons. If someone offers a high-level principle which meets Hare's formal criteria and so on, it is probable that he would be ranked as giving a stage-6 reason on Kohlberg's scale. If you stop there, and I do not know whether Kohlberg does or not, you would assume that he is extremely mature and reasonable in his judgment. But if you ask him why it is reasonable to accept this commonly held high-order principle, he might say that he holds it in preference to some other just as a matter of decision, his temperament is that way and he finds the sort of thing the principle prescribes appealing. In terms of this kind of response he would probably be reclassified in the Kohlberg scale.

Questions of reasonableness can also be raised about the particular features of a situation which it is claimed morally justify one's action in a given case. When an individual or group is treated selectively, the question is not simply whether the alleged difference which is offered in justification of discrimination is real. More often the question is whether a real difference is morally relevant. Settling the problem of relevance is an exercise of reason in morality. Of course there are also general claims of a factual kind that enter into moral arguments. These claims are subject to the criteria of rationality appropriate to the field in which they are made.

GAUTHIER

Let me try to sort out from a philosophical point of view what I see is the issue involved in rationality in the hope that this will shed a little further light on how philosophers are trying to use this term. I should like to suggest three sorts of distinctions.

First, there is the problem of getting from the judgment one makes (and this is in the practical sphere) to the action that one takes. This gives rise to the traditional philosophical problem of *akrasia,* that is, of the man who seems to know what is best – he sets out what his judgments are as to what he ought to do – but then somehow he does something else. I think that sometimes when people talk about irrational forces in human nature what they have in mind are motivational factors which in some way impede a person from acting on his judgment. They think of him as formulating certain judgments about what is best for him to do but being driven somehow by forces beyond his control and behaving in a different way so that we do not get a transfer from rationality of judgment to rationality of action. This is one case in which one could speak of the irrational forces in human nature. But of course this sort of irrationality, although it is of great practical importance, does not itself have very much to do with moral reasoning. It is what comes after reasoning.

Secondly, there is the rationality of the reasoning process itself. Here one is concerned with getting from the rationality of grounds, whatever they may be, to the rationality of judgment. This is of course the sphere in which logic has made its main contribution. But there are, I think, still great problems over the sort of strategies to be adopted in reasoning here – in some of those areas to which Scriven referred. If you look, for example, at studies in game theory, you can see the sorts of problems that arise in trying to determine the rational strategy for, say, a man who wants to maximize his returns in getting to the judgment about what action in fact will maximize those returns in certain sorts of conflict situations. So there are still real problems here, and the problems are of an essentially technical kind.

The third area in which I think the philosopher's conception of rationality comes in is that of the rationality of the grounds themselves and it is here in the sphere of morals that great difficulties arise. One could look at Kohlberg's various stages in moral development as stages representing different views as to the relevant grounds for judging what one should do. A stage-2 person is thinking perhaps in terms of considerations of satisfaction, a stage-3 person in terms of approval of others as the grounds for what he should do, a stage-4 person in terms of the edicts of authority, a stage-5 person in terms of agreements of an equality of persons, and so on, and a stage-6 person perhaps in terms of the notion of the person and the value of the person himself as grounds for acting. I realize that this is rather a rough sketch. What moral philosophers have been very much concerned with recently is whether there are certain grounds which can be shown to be reasonable or rational grounds when judging what one should do. I think that what Beck was suggesting was that people like Hare adopt an ultimate irrationality here, that the grounds are simply a matter of decision. On the other hand, I think people like Baier want to argue that there are, as it were, grounds for holding that certain reasons for acting are better than others, that certain considerations are reasons and certain considerations are not. From a philosophic point of view I think the real problem is whether we can say that certain considerations really do constitute reasons for acting and certain considerations do not, and if we can, then what sort of arguments can we give here. This is where the dispute among moral philosophers has gone on, and perhaps these distinctions may clarify to some extent what philosophers are thinking about in terms of rationality in this context.

OLIVER

It seems to me that a precondition of acting rationally is to have some sense of what reality is. It is quite possible that Americans, at least if I use the term to mean the U.S.A., are in many areas out of touch with reality and use various psychological mechanisms, one of which is denial. They simply deny that certain things are true in order to avoid facing up to certain problems. It seems to me that one could advocate that it is useless or trivial to go on arguing about levels of moral reasoning and the process of moral reasoning when many people are in small dark rooms watching images rather than seeing what is out there. For example, the lower middle class suburban white students we have taught do not really believe that any Negro in a ghetto could not pull himself up by his own bootstraps. There is the notion that anybody can make it if he really tries. I think this myth is based to a large degree on an ignorance of just what is there (to use Gauthier's expression), of the consequences of the society's action for Negroes, and of some pretty sound social science theory regarding early childhood development, and so on. It is quite possible that it would be more reasonable to create very powerful messages that are piped to people in an effort to force them, in a sense, to face reality before you are ever concerned with what rationality means. I think that at certain points in one's life one recognizes the absurdity of the human condition and somehow reasoning in the conventional analytic sense does not seem capable of dealing with the description of that absurdity or the different kinds of absurdities. They have to be described through metaphors, symbols and so on. And I do not know whether to recognize the absurdity of the human condition is to be irrational or rational.

EDEL

May I suggest some general concluding comments on this problem of rationality. Gauthier's view of moral education as education in the consequences led to the paradox that moral education was not moral at all. But it does not have to lead to that paradox if we qualify it by asking what we want the consequences for. It seems to be quite obvious that what we want them for is not merely to carry out our moral demands and ideas, but also to test and criticize them. If it has done nothing else, surely the whole Deweyan approach has shown the extent to which this constant testing and criticism is involved. This feedback from the consequences to our value hypotheses has a central role and one might even go so far as to say that this evaluative function is the distinctive moral function. We might have avoided a lot of trouble here if we had just spoken of the evaluative process instead of rationality. Then the whole question of how much the evaluative process has the character of a particular program of rationality would have been avoided. But of course once you begin to examine the character of the evaluative process with criticism as the distinctive moral endeavour and therefore a key idea in the notion of moral education, I suppose you get inevitably, as we did, into the question of rationality.

In the papers and discussions of this conference, rationality has taken many guises. The concept has an accordion character – you can stretch it and narrow it. Whereas Narveson tended to make it narrowly logical to do all the work – and he had great hopes that he could accomplish that – Oliver was worried about whether reasoning is enough, and Ausubel seemed to pull the accordion out to the fullest. For the most part there was a consensus on rationality as a stress in moral education and confidence that the exercise of rationality was one way of teaching morality. The whole question of the anthropological contribution was not explored. What I want to say here is somewhat similar to what Scriven said on rationality and strategy. I distinguish in rationality the kinds of principles that get added as we move from domain to domain. This is somewhat in the spirit of C. I. Lewis. It can be illustrated from what goes on in science. For a man to be rational in doing physics involves more than simply the principles of formal logic. You add what at various points in various fields have become the established results – not the results on the lower level, but the results on the higher level that have been important enough for you to make a jump and put them into the picture of the method. Sometimes you make a mistake, as in the case of the problems about action at a distance, or that all forces have to be contact forces (there was a time in the history of science when a person had to accept this principle in order to be called rational). There are some fundamental issues which raise more difficult problems: for example, whether you have a concept of causality. However, if a person said, "Let's not look for the cause of this scientific phenomenon because it has no cause," it would be regarded as a kind of irrationality, I think, from the point of view of this domain of thinking.

It is similar, I think, when you get into the moral domain. Some kind of broad valuations, not necessarily outright values, get built in more and more. For instance, would a man be rational if he acted in such a way as to produce constant internal conflict for himself? At least, it is clear that because people have contradictory desires in the sense that they cannot achieve them both, the element of non-frustration gets written into the program of what a rational man is. If a person says that he is going to live entirely for the first half of his life and not the second, C. I. Lewis will call him irrational because rationality will have to imply a whole life view. Of course, one can ask why it should imply a whole life view, but the point is that things of this kind get written into rationality in the domain of morality and the concept of rationality gets developed. I do not think that philosophers have done enough of the job of analyzing what gets built into the concept of rationality, beyond the merely formal part of logic, in the practical and the moral domains. Philosophers have done their work well on the questions of the theory of science, but of course that is what they have constantly done. The notion of moral law, for example, has not been developed for the field of morality with anything like the kind of precision with which the notion of law in the field of science has been treated. So the jobs there are still to be done.

MORALITY AS JUSTICE

CRITTENDEN

Reasonableness is one of the conditions for moral decisions which has been mentioned by everyone and I certainly accept it. But it is the second limitation, which has been most commonly emphasized, that I have doubts about, namely, the attempt to treat morality as a set of rules or, more specifically, as a subset of social rules. I think that the question of reasonableness is central. However, the way you spell out the details of being reasonable really depends on whether you think that morality is to be restricted to a subset of social rules that affect whatever the common social good happens to be. It seems to me that morality is much more adequately understood as an ultimate choice about a style of life. This comes to what Gauthier is talking about in his second stage, although I do not like to see it separated from the other two. It involves things like personal ideals. This is precisely where I have a problem with Kohlberg's stages of moral reasoning. He cuts out certain reasons as morally relevant simply by his fairly limited definition of morality in terms of justice or something like that. I think that personal ideals enter into morality: in the way we think we ought to act even when the tangible public good is not directly involved, in the way we treat animals, or in resolving a conflict of values, say, between an aesthetic and an economic value. Perhaps, as Findlay claims, the moral domain is the overarching one, the one that finally arbitrates and decides the competing demands of other value domains.

BAIER

I am very glad that you have brought this up because what I have been talking about is only, as it were, the ground floor of morality. I think that I am more generous, or tolerant, than Narveson is on this, because I do not mind private morality being called morality, whereas he would like to restrict the term "morality" to public morality. I agree that one could extend this ground floor of morality in all sorts of directions by hooking on to one or other of the many-part concepts that this ground-floor morality involves. Deeds of supererogation have not been mentioned yet. Now they come in by a slight extension of the concept of morality somewhat along the lines of the distinct-tion that Scriven made in connection with the concept of number in mathematics, and, similarly, life ideals could come in in this way. Though these latter are very important, I think they are in one sense secondary, namely, in the sense that they must give way to the core of the notions of right and wrong and obligations. That is, one cannot, morally speaking, let oneself follow personal ideals, including relig-ious or aesthetic ideals, which are in contravention of the ground floor of morality. So I think "overarching" is not the right word. The ground floor of morality is not overarching but overriding. That is, it contains the notion of obligation and the notion of moral wrongness, which have a priority over other aspects of the value dimension of life – although in many other ways these latter are more significant and rewarding.

CRITTENDEN

It seems to me that when you try to show the reasonableness of any appeal to commonly accepted moral rules, such as the rules of justice, you depend on assent to a fundamental value that you prize and which forms part of the total complex of values that makes up your style of life. For example, ultimately you may get back to something like your belief in the inherent dignity and equality of all human beings as moral agents.

BAIER

I am not sure that I agree with you. While I allow each individual his style of life I believe that one has to recognize that the realization of any style of life is possible only within a community, that is, within a social order. Once you allow that move you are on the rational slope in the direction of the modification of social life in accordance with the criteria of acceptability for everyone who is a member of that community.

CRITTENDEN

I can accept the moral demands of the community because I have certain ideals about human beings and how they relate to one another.

BAIER

But whether you accepted the community or not you would want to get as close as possible to the realization of your life ideal, and the community is a necessary ingredient. Even if you were to hate every-body else, you still need them.

NARVESON

I want to go back to the points which Crittenden was addressing himself to. It seems to me that it would be a great mistake – it would be the paradigm of a mistake – for any sort of a program of moral education that is to be feasible in a non-arbitrary and non-sectarian way to generally inculcate the view that the general precepts of morality, like those of justice, for example, had foundations of exactly the same sort as those which a personal style of life has. This seems to me to be drastically wrong. It is wrong because it would inevitably give people the impression that morality is a matter of taste – ultimate taste or Taste (with a capital T) to be sure, but still taste. It all seems to come down to being a matter of the subjective needs of the individual, which strikes me as being false. What is important about the kind of general view that Baier recommends is that it shows that there are some precepts of conduct that are very substantially independent of particular styles of life and have nothing really to do with one's choice of his style of life. At the same time we ought not to give people the impression that the subject of their personal style of life is in some way trivial just because it is not a part of what I call morality. Obviously it is of the greatest importance to think about one's life and what one ought to do as an individual. But it is very important to give the individual the sense that those are the questions which are really up to him as an individual, where the consideration of what he ought to do depends on what he wants, whereas moral considerations are not, essentially and fundamentally, considerations that depend on what the individual wants. They are considerations that have a much more general and, as I think, rational basis – in particular, the general principle that other people's wants are to be respected and taken into account.

CRITTENDEN

To reply very briefly, I think it is not nearly so clear-cut as Narveson suggests. For one thing, already implicit in the program of the methodological approach to moral education as he outlines it is a commitment to quite a number of values which would be very basic in marking out a style of life. What will count as reasonable when we discuss a moral issue is itself shaped by end values to which we are committed.

NARVESON

I do not see why you should bring in that language about a style of life at all. That is my point. I am claiming that there is a radical difference between discussing something under the aegis of its being a matter of individual choice as against its not being so. The mere fact that you can find lots of borderline cases where it is not clear how we should move, simply because there are places in which these two sorts of considerations meet, does not prove that this distinction does not exist at all; quite the contrary.

EDEL

I would like to make some comments on the various views that have been expressed on the scope of morality. First, the notion of the recognition of the person that is involved in both the narrow and the wide use of "moral" has to be qualified. There are all sorts of recognitions of a person going from the mere recognition of the fact that he exists, in the sense that you do not walk into him, to engaging in co-operative enterprises with him, even though it may be for ends of your own, all the way up to the sense of the person in which we were speaking. So both phenomenologically and behaviourally, and also in terms of giving a justification, the appeal to the person is something that involves qualification; as it were, blanks to be filled in with respect to both content and manner.

Second, the issue between morality in terms of the principle of justice rather than ideals and styles of life is, as I see it, the traditional philosophical problem of the tension between the right and the good. The predominance of the idea of ought or right in the whole of modern post-Kantian philosophy has obscured the fact that there are actual, not simply conceivable, distinct models in which the notion of good as the object of man's ultimate endeavour – whether it be one good or a plurality of goods – is the way in which moral discourse is carried on and moral thinking done. This is true of a great part of ancient ethics. It is generally agreed that Aristotle did not have a concept of ought. He had other concepts that did the work. The idea of a single ought tends to be rather a modern project. Now Kohlberg who is an incorrigible oughtist cannot really appreciate this. He translates any appeal to the good as a utilitarian attempt to justify morality rather than to state its nature. He does not allow for the possibility that a person will have a conceptual framework in which this whole notion of the good is central and in which "right" and "ought" are interpreted as applicative concepts or attempts to achieve the good. This need not necessarily take just the utilitarian form. Also you will misrepresent this kind of conceptual structure if you say that it is putting morality on the scale to see what it is good for. It is not trying to say that there is an outside reason for weighing morality, it is trying to tell you what morality is and how it operates. I see no reason why one could not have general principles that would take the form of ideals or the form of rules. I do not think at this time in the history of ethical theory we should go in for a kind of categorial imperialism. We should recognize that there are different constructions by which we talk about morality and that whatever phenomena lie at the base of morals, and whatever pressures, problems, difficulties, and contradictions arise in human life, we will find their expression in one place or another within any of these frameworks we may construct.

Third, I would propose that the understanding of the concept of morality is to be in terms of a set of functions: I mean the jobs that morality is doing in different periods in different phases of human life and so on, leaving open the question as to whether these jobs are really one or universal or involve sequences or stages. This question becomes a sociological one. But this is not to suggest that sociology is giving you moral standards, because you can even evaluate the functions. Just as you can ask whether the apparatus of law is able to handle certain types of questions and decide whether it is too gross or too rough, so you can very well decide that certain types of human problems cannot be handled by morality. You might just decide that morality is too refined for dealing with them.

Fourth, I should like to make a drastic suggestion to Kohlberg. I suggest that instead of referring to his stages as moral development he refer to them as stages of justice, or juridical development. Then he would not have to take on his own shoulders the burden of the whole philosophical profession to decide what is an absolute morality. It might turn out that the only developmental picture appears in this aspect of morality. There is no *a priori* rule that everything has to have a development. If Kohlberg finds that there is a development only with respect to justice this is a very important and interesting discovery. It is possible that other features of morality might show a developmental pattern. You might find a development in the types of love, for example, from a kind of initial dependency love to a self-assertive love to mature care and concern for others. Of course the fact that something has a development does not necessarily make it more or less important. Finding that there is a development in terms of justice is not the same thing as justifying the emphasis on justice.

KOHLBERG

Suppose one did restrict this Kantian domain, the development of which I have been considering, to justice. The thing that bothers me is that if that is what I am doing in my system, how do I then get to action? The moral man or the stage-6 man does not shock the victim in the Milgram experiment, for example, but the just man, given that justice is part of something bigger called morality, may or may not. As a psychologist I have to define the moral domain and not just a justice domain if I really want to get the ideas that I am dealing with back to the person. I wonder if you have a solution to that problem.

EDEL

I think it is less of a problem than you are suggesting, because the domain of justice is not something apart from morality; it is a great part of morality. Therefore I do not see where this would raise any problem with regard to your experiment. You can refer to morality if you understand morality as the critical evaluation of the principles, rules, and so on for our actions. A great part of this criticism is carried on in terms of justice. Now a problem might arise only at the points at which someone else would try to develop a counter indication for action on the basis of something outside justice. But this you have anyhow. For instance, if you get into an argument about justice and mercy, you may decide you want to make a distinction in justice between the kind of justice that includes mercy and the kind that does not.

KOHLBERG

As an alternative solution to the issue I could say that the whole system including stage 6 is defined in terms of justice because, for people who have articulated principles of justice, considerations of justice take priority over other moral principles in given contexts and situations.

NARVESON

I have not been able to see anything in your [Kohlberg's] characterization of the stages of your inquiry that would in any way require that the domain you are studying be less than the whole of morality – as marked out by Baier, for example. There is no reason why a man cannot have a supererogatory principle, such as the principle of benevolence, going well beyond what we think of as justice in the narrow sense, held on conscientious grounds and formulated on a notion of universalizability. Thus I do not think that Edel is at all right in criticizing you on this ground or in suggesting that you should restrict in any explicit way the domain of your inquiry. It does not seem to me that this is at all necessary and I certainly do not think that it is desirable, because I think you want to study not only a narrow band of moral principles but also the development of things like benevolence. I do not think you want to leave them out and I do not think you should.

CRITTENDEN

This would involve, would it not, a pretty substantial enlargement of the domain of justice? Perhaps Kohlberg does not really want to go that far.

KOHLBERG

There are psychologists' cant phrases that relate to the points Edel raised, such as ego-development, something that is broader than justice. It is in the sphere of human values and is related to the development of justice. Edel suggested that in fact a student of mine could have gone out and got 6 stages of love and that these could be tied into the system. However, insofar as these things have any real meaning in the individual's personality, I would not put them under the heading of morality either.

BECK

I think this takes you back to your original criticism of the "bag of virtues" conception of morality. It seems to me that a number of moral philosophers in recent years have found a great deal of value in this conception. They see it as getting us away from the overunified conception of morality and bringing us to an idea of a loosely connected set of character traits, which have various links and common features. If we try to concentrate on any one of these, or if we try to bring all morality under one rule or one type of rule, we will them be placed in a dilemma: should we try to make this rule a little more specific and so enable ourselves to judge particular cases, or should we make it more general and so enable it to cover all cases. There seems to be this tension, and I feel that we really must develop some sort of "bag of virtues" view of the matter, even though we realize that the "bag of virtues" only takes us a little bit further towards the degree of specificity that we need for making decisions in particular cases.

KOHLBERG

Can I be a social relativist on this particular point? The "bag of virtues" was fine for the Greeks in the sense that modal ideals of character could be acceptable. There they existed in the context of an unjust social order, that is, an order of a hierarchical arrangement of people with different types of character, as in Plato's conception of the ideal state. When modal virtues are really taken seriously they always come down to ego-ideals, modal character patterns, particularly in terms of education. I think this is what we get. I will be relativistic and say that I do not think that a social system built on the universalistic principle of justice can really take ideals of personality or ego-ideals or virtues or something of this kind as a definition for moral development.

BECK

That is not the point. I think that even in Greek times the good man was defined in terms of a set of virtues. It was not that you had different types of men within the culture and that these together made up the "bag of virtues," but rather that within a particular good man you would have a collection of virtues.

MELDEN

In recognizing the role of virtues we should take account of the way in which obligations and rights, the domain in which I think justice operates, provide certain boundary conditions for rational conduct. It seems to me that when we think of something like prudence or courage we think of excellences of virtues that human beings have; but not independent of, or completely cut off from, the maintenance of due regard for conditions of equity in dealing with other people. I object very much to the kind of Pritchardian identification of prudence with simple self-interest. Prudence is a virtue, it is desirable that a person be prudent. A man who is prudent is not a fool, neither is he just simply cunning in getting what he wants. There are conceptual links between the notion of prudence and the notion of fairness and equity: the way in which one manages to take account of the requirements of justice in one's thought and action. So I do not think we ought to say that virtues constitute a kind of bag or heap. I do not think they constituted such for Aristotle or for the Greeks, because there were certain boundary conditions that operated, within which certain identifiable characteristics of people were regarded, or named, as the particular virtues that they are. At the same time, when you emphasize justice and say that this is the whole of morality, it seems to me that you lose the point of the observance of the boundary conditions of our rational way of life. There are therefore virtues involved in what we call morality, and, if this means an enlarging of the morality which historically derives from (I suppose) the commandments of the deity or whatever, this is fine. I am not at all averse to the broadening or transformation of some of our conceptions of the moral law from certain of these root sources.

EDEL

May I just make a comment here? I think that in one way we are being unfair to Kohlberg's argument at this point on the virtues, because I think that it is a pyschological argument. The definition of a virtue usually involves a character trait, and a character trait is something on the basis of which you can predict people's reactions to some degree. Now it seems to me that what Kohlberg is questioning in this case is not our ordinary language but whether there is a viable concept of character trait on psychological grounds. To what extent can it really be used in the way that is claimed? Even in Kant we find that virtue seems to be a kind of continual effort of will rather than a host of specific virtues. It is interesting to look at the recent history of the theory of virtues. It was debunked by the social psychologists in the 20s because they were generally behaviouristic and because the Hartshorne and May experiment showed that you could not get enough predictability. It was revived in the 30s and the 40s on the basis of psychoanalytic material and the theory of personality. Philosophers have neglected the theory of virtues for a long time and are only now coming back to it. It seems to me that they will have to go into the psychological material in order to decide whether the concept of character trait is a viable one. Basically, it seems to be a psychological problem of the preconditions of a useful concept of morality.

NARVESON

I will try to add something to what Edel was just saying by picking up a point that both Crittenden and Beck have been making. I do not think that just because a man's morality includes more than justice, it must therefore go so far as to include everything of an evaluative sort. That is, there is no reason why it cannot have boundaries that include more than just considerations of justice in a general sense, and yet stop short of things about ways of life and styles of life and so on. Much as you may be fond of talking about these things, and important as they are to talk about, I still think that there is an extremely important reason for distinguishing between these and the domain of morality as a whole. Nevertheless, I do not think that just because you have a relatively unitary conception of what morality is – even as unitary as, say, the approaches of Kant or Mill – it in the least follows, as Beck seems to think, that you are therefore going to have an over-rigid principle that will keep you from accounting for something just because it is a unitary principle. Kant's work is a really splendid case in point. His large book, *The Metaphysics of Morals,* is divided into two parts. One is concerned with justice – what most people think Kant was exclusively concerned with. The other part is a good bit longer and is concerned entirely with the notion of virtue and leads to a general theory, which gives a place to the things that are ordinarily called virtues. Kant might not have done a terribly good job of elaborating it, but this is what he tried to do, and it is not at all clear that it was nonsense to try to do it. It may well be that given a single unitary principle, the facts of life nevertheless call for a division into a narrow area of justice and a much larger one of supererogatory virtues.

BECK

I think that you have misinterpreted both Crittenden and myself on this point. By referring to styles of life and the "bag of virtucs" wc do not mean to suggest that all virtues are moral virtues, but just that within virtues you have a subclass of moral virtues. I would want to insist upon the distinction between moral values and other types of value – and similarly with styles of life. Some parts of your life can involve aesthetic, or health, or economic value, and others moral.

With respect to the Kantian position, I would tend to say that there is simply an inconsistency in Kant here. There is, on the one hand, the statement of a pretty unified approach and, on the other, an attempt to bring this into line with the facts of moral life as we have it. Now there *may* not be this inconsistency. You may say that the possibility of a collection of virtues is allowed for in his main principles, but in that case it should have been brought out. My point is that you have to allow for some diversity and whether or not Kant did this is a matter of interpretation.

Incidentally, in answer to Melden's point, by using the expression "bag of virtues" I did not mean to suggest that there is a set of discretely divided virtues. I think that there can be, as I said earlier, a great many connections between virtues.

CRITTENDEN

In order to clarify my position if I can, let me say that I do not want to claim that the sum total of values to which one is committed equals the moral realm. It would be possible to consider morality, not so much as another distinctly marked-out area of value, but as a dimension which runs through all such areas. If one took that kind of analogy, then while morality would still be a relevant issue everywhere it would certainly not be equal to the sum total of values. Why I feel it is important to stress the total style of life to which we are committed at any given time is this: rationality or reasonableness, while I do not think it is strictly a moral principle, is crucial to depicting and to discussing clearly what is involved in morality and in being moral. The determination of what will in fact count as a sound moral reason or distinction or action or motive and so on is closely tied up with the kind of stand we take about the general set of values that determine our style of life. There is an interaction between reasonableness and the system of values that characterizes our style of life. The connection is circular but not necessarily vicious. On the one hand, we tend to specify what counts as reasonable in the light of the values that we are committed to, and, on the other, the sum total of values that we are committed to at any time are what we think is reasonable. If someone does not value being reasonable, nothing much is gained by demonstrating what it is reasonable for him to do. What I am trying to say is, I believe, closely related to the section of Gauthier's paper in which he talks about practical wisdom as being directed not to means but to ends.

CHAPTER II

Method and substance in moral education

ARE ATTITUDES AND PRECEPTS TO BE INCULCATED?

BAIER

Gauthier says in the last section of his paper that moral education is not really moral at all in one sense. It is not an inculcation of moral precepts or a teaching of moral attitudes; rather it simply involves showing people what they do. It is aimed not at those who lack practical wisdom and moral virtue but at those who, possessing these characteristics, nevertheless fail to do as they ought because they do not know what they are doing. Undoubtedly this is one thing that moral education might profitably include – although if you are thinking of separating moral education from other areas of education, it is not clear to me why you would want to include it under this heading rather than as part of training in how society works and so on. But waiving this for the moment, why does it in any way follow, or what is the reason for making the further claim, that education does not include the inculcation of moral precepts or the teaching of moral attitudes? Why are you excluding these other things which, I take it, have been traditionally regarded as the core of moral education?

GAUTHIER

The first stage in what I would want to call moral training involves training the child in certain dispositions to act, ways of responding to various situations. This is essentially a pre-reflective business which, if we are going to make a distinction between training and education, I should think is better placed under training. Then, if I am right, the next stage – the child becoming more reflectively aware of these dispositions in adopting some sort of over-all policy with respect to what he is doing – is something which no process of education is likely to achieve, something the child learns in a great many ways in the process of maturation. It is not just the process of socialization, because much is involved in acquiring a conceptual framework which I would not want to equate with socialization. In these processes there is nothing that I would see as an education in precepts, in the learning of certain precepts in a reflective way; in so far as the child quickly picks up precepts he tends to do so, I think, more or less pre-reflectively.

Real education, which has important moral implications, comes in teaching the child the consequences of what he does, enabling him to understand his actions in this further way. This process is essential if the child is to reflect on the precepts that he has picked up more or less pre-reflectively, to continue to hold some, to reject others. But the process is not directed so much at the precepts themselves as at giving the child some sort of information which he requires in order to reflect for himself on those precepts that he has picked up. That is why I tried to divide things up in the way I did and suggest that the most important educational part is not really moral education at all; and I agree that it is better carried on under some other headings.

BAIER

Suppose the child picks up these precepts unreflectively, then is given information about the consequences of, shall we say, low-level precepts – low-level in terms of the degree of generality. The information he gets might bring to light certain inconsistencies between these low-level precepts. That is, he may find that if he works out the consequences of acting on one of these low-level precepts he comes into conflict with other low-level precepts. At that stage, since the precepts have been picked up unreflectively, the question then arises, which of these has to give way? In the light of what higher principles are we to adjudicate between such conflicting lower-level precepts? And some reflective thinking about this, as opposed to merely drawing out what is usually called factual or causal knowledge about the consequences of acting in accordance with such principles, would be helpful. It is that which, I suppose, moral philosophy has usually taken to be its contribution to higher-level moral education; and I would have thought that if any objective matters can be extracted from the thinking of moral philosophers, this would form a legitimate part of properly moral education. To leave this entirely to the child or the growing adolescent, without theoretical assistance by spelling out what can be said clearly and soundly is to renounce one way, to renounce an important, and it seems to me perhaps a most legitimate, way of improving the moral standards of people in our community. I do not see why one should forego that.

SCRIVEN

Perhaps I can bring this general point home by an analogy from another area. When we teach children the laws of motion in their first or second physics course these consist of a number of platitudes, or two platitudes and something which is not entirely platitudinous at first sight but turns out to be platitudinous upon investigation. One of the platitudes is that for every force there is an equal and opposite force. Now the child looks at an ash tray crashing to the ground and somebody says there is a force of gravity acting on it. It seems pretty obvious that there is not an equal and opposite force or it would not crash to the floor. He does not know what to do with that. Is this a case of counter-example to that general principle? No, it cannot be because somebody would have noticed it before. So in some mysterious way this is still consistent with the laws of motion. And so on.

This procedure of trying to get the child from the point of having mastered the precepts to being able to apply them where and when they should be applied, even without the inconsistencies which Baier has referred to, is an immensely complicated process – so complicated that if you now ask a first-rate theoretical physicist which of the laws of motion is non-definitional, you cannot get a straight answer. It is far from a simple procedure to get children to absorb not the verbal form of the precept but its practical impact, and it seems to me that an *enormous* slice of moral education is involved in the process of trying to relate the precept to particular cases.

GAUTHIER

I am inclined to think that precepts are originally taught to the child in connection with particular cases. The child comes to learn the precepts and apply them, together. The first stage in application is handled in the very process by which the child comes to acquire the precepts.

I am also inclined to think that moral philosophers have tended to overstate the importance of higher-level precepts or general principles of action in people's actual moral behaviour. I would agree that there is something more than mere low-level precepts and an awareness of facts or what I call minor premises in the Aristotelian syllogism. But I am inclined to think that by and large this "something more" is to be found in certain general attitudes that the child picks up. Perhaps in our society on the whole these are utilitarian attitudes which the child comes to reflect upon in developing what I would call a moral policy. I see these not as a set of more general precepts but, if you like, a general way of proceeding or reasoning about moral questions; a general view of what sort of facts are relevant for deciding what you should do. It is not really possible to reduce this sort of procedure, these procedural principles, to what has been traditionally thought of as high-level moral generalizations or moral principles. So my argument is that the role of the alleged high-level moral principles has been considerably overstated by moral philosophers; that the process of moral development and the character of moral reasoning do not in fact reflect these higher-level precepts in the way in which they should if moral philosophers were right.

BAIER

I think what you have said could be taken either as a statement of what in fact is the practice of the common man or as a statement about what we should aim at getting the common man to do. If it is a statement of the first kind, then, although I do not know the facts very well, I am inclined to agree with it. If it is a statement of the second kind, I do not agree with it. I think there could be, as there are in other areas of education, progress; that is, we could get the common man to think harder and improve his performance. I do not think that we are doing it. This is an important general point.

From reading the papers that have been presented here one would think people were looking at a moral phenomenon which is simply to be characterized and explained and described in minute detail, whereas it seems to me that morality is a practice that we are engaging in and a very imperfect practice at that, although it has developed over many centuries and improved a little bit. We could get a lot clearer about it and we should not be satisfied with simply accepting what we find. That is, if this is not just like finding out how the solar system moves, it is something that we could improve in the direction of the good. I would rather say we could teach the man to do better than he is doing now by the ideal of morality that is already implicit in the way in which we morally talk.

GAUTHIER

I certainly agree with Baier that we are concerned with improvement, not simply with stating how people very imperfectly get along with moral reasoning. What we are disagreeing about, I think, is the way in which improvement is likely to take place. My argument, being rather schematic, would be that one reason we fail to make moral progress is that we have been seduced by the wrong model of moral reasoning. We have paid far too much attention to a model in terms of which general principles, our general moral principles, should be developed and taught to people. My argument is that there is nothing really wrong with the ordinary scheme within which moral reasoning takes place. Where we have gone astray, where we have failed to make sufficient progress, is in plugging in the minor premises and making people sufficiently aware of these. If we are going to improve people's moral practice it is in this area that we should concentrate our attention, not in the area of trying to articulate more clearly an ideal of morality and certain very high-order moral principles.

MELDEN

I wonder if I could raise a question apropos of what Baier has mentioned. He suggested a kind of two-tier reflection, is this not correct? You have specific principles and then presumably you have in some way to adjudicate between them in cases where apparently you have got to do one thing or the other and there are two incompatible kinds of precepts which seem to have application. What I am a bit worried about is moving too quickly from moral precepts to something else that is grandiose. Gauthier has also suggested some rather general considerations which can then be invoked – such as a utilitarian outlook. But I think we ought to look more closely at the kind of thing Scriven has just pointed out about the character of particular precepts that are involved and what indeed they do require us as reasonable beings to do. How should we regard and employ our moral precept and how, indeed, in the process of moral education, do we instruct children to become sensitive to their applicability, and to the respects in which they are to guide us in our choices and our conduct? I think we ought not to go too quickly to a higher level.

EDEL

Is it really necessary to take only one avenue? Gauthier called attention to the examination of the consequences in the use of precepts. Perhaps he puts this in too limited a fashion by saying that it is not itself moral. We have had at least two different suggestions as to what the consequences may do. Scriven seems to be pointing out that the consequences could clarify the meaning of the precepts themselves and what is involved in them; and Baier seems to be suggesting that they might also decide how to relate different principles and, even more, that they might overthrow some of the principles. So we have different roles for consequences.

It is possible that the notion of a consequence has been construed too narrowly. Take, for example, a question like patriotism. Presumably one of the lower-level principles is involved in the attitude of patriotism. There has been the problem in Canada, for example, as to what local patriotism and cultural patriotism should be. This problem would involve an application of the principle and value of patriotism to the particular case. But you can also explore the consequences of patriotism on a world-wide scale and then you might want to raise the question as to whether this whole precept itself might not be put aside or put down lower in the scale or hierarchy of principles. Is it not the case that the criticisms being made of Gauthier's kind of moral training here are not that going to consequences does not play a very important role in the educative part of it, but that it plays a variety of roles and the roles may be more far-reaching in restructuring the actual precepts themselves?

CRITTENDEN

I would like to make a comment on the third stage Gauthier talks of: the attempt to develop moral sensitivity by having people look at the consequences of their actions. I presume that what they have acquired up to this point are, first, a certain number of dispositions for acting with facility, and second, formal principles for resolving moral problems and thinking through to the correct decision. They have not been deliberately taught any substantive moral principles or ideals. (I noticed that in your paper you explicitly reject various ideals.) Then they come to look at the consequences. They are presented, let us say, with the example of the situation in Vietnam or the people in an impoverished area in the city. Obviously, from the language you use, your effort is to convince them that the defoliation of food-producing areas in Vietnam is undesirable, or that this is indeed sub-standard living accomodation for people and so is undesirable. I do not see that there is any reason why somebody who has come through the first two stages in a perfectly successful way could not simply reject these conclusions and do so with perfect moral sophistication in terms of the application of merely formal criteria and principles.

GAUTHIER

I think this is entirely possible. Indeed, I suggest at one stage that someone might have a general self-interested policy – something that I would consider not a moral policy at all – and certain dispositions to act which perhaps conform to this policy. And I would agree that such a person might be entirely unmoved by having the consequences of what he is doing or what society is doing pointed out to him. But

I do not think that the remedy for that is simply to try to teach him new principles or new precepts. To some extent at this stage, I should imagine, his dispositions to action have hardened to a certain degree; he has a policy, he has certain attitudes which he brings to bear on practical questions, and the question you might ask – how could these attitudes be changed at this rather late stage? – is certainly one to which I do not have any answer. However, I am inclined to think that this problem is perhaps rather less common than the problem to which I address myself in that last section of my paper: trying to make people aware of the consequences of what they do. I assume that by and large the attitudes people have, the dispositions that they have come to adopt, will lead them, if they reflect on considerations of the kind involved in the examples, to act in the sort of way that I imply is desirable here; even though it may mean altering certain precepts that they have.

Perhaps I could refer to a fairly well-known literary passage in *Huckleberry Finn* where Huck does not turn Jim in for being a runaway Negro slave. It is clear that in this situation Huck undergoes a very considerable moral development. The dispositions to act, which he has acquired in the past, the sort of policies that he has been brought up with, would have led him to turn Jim in in this situation. But what I want to suggest is that if he becomes aware, as he was never aware before, of what a Negro human being is like, he becomes aware in a quite new way of what the effect of his actions would be if he were to turn Jim in, what they would be if he were to let Jim go, and so on; that he sees his action in an entirely new light not because he has acquired new precepts, not because he has acquired higher-level principles on the basis of which he can adjudicate his lower-level principles and reject certain ones, but simply because of a new awareness of what he would be doing by turning Jim in. It is the development of this sort of awareness that I tried to focus some attention on. Now here, of course, it develops in an entirely informal way, just out of the situation in which Huck finds himself. What I did want to suggest was that education (or moral education) to a large extent consisted in putting people in these situations – if not in actual fact, then in getting them to think themselves into these situations – so that they gain this sort of awareness.

MELDEN

May I just ask apropos of that example: when Huck sees his action in a new light does this really mean that he sees certain effects of what he is doing?

GAUTHIER

Yes, I think it does.

MELDEN

Just that? That is all it really amounts to? This is what you were saying. Now you are forced either to stick with that or move off to Crittenden's complaint and accommodate yourself to it. Surely it cannot be the case that he merely sees that certain things are going to come to pass. He can regard these with total indifference. Why should they move him?

BECK

But surely the point is that if he does regard the situation with total indifference then he has not got these basic dispositions, and there is probably nothing we can do about it.

MELDEN

What dispositions to do what? Dispositions to engage in certain kinds of performance which have certain effects. That is all we have. So this would be my complaint: Gauthier has emptied out of the situation in which dispositions have been developed the kind of thing we would call the understanding of each other.

OLIVER

Let us suppose that Huck had chosen to turn Jim in. Let us suppose he had gone through the same agonies. Let us suppose he had envisioned the same consequences. Let us suppose that he had come to see Jim as a human being, and so on, but at the final moment his decision goes the other way. Then, is Huck more or less moral for having done all this agonizing?

GAUTHIER

Well, I simply want to say that, in effect, whatever decision Huck actually would make in the situation he does undergo a certain moral development.

OLIVER

Then he would undergo moral development whichever way his decision went?

GAUTHIER

Yes, given the account that Twain provides of what I want to call his new awareness here. Yes, he undergoes a development whatever he actually does. We may want to say different things about it depending on what he does, but that some sort of development takes place is independent of Huck's final decision in the situation.

SCRIVEN

That some development takes place or that the same quality of development takes place? Would you not want to say that perhaps he had improved even more if he can see that he should not turn in somebody just because he is a Negro.

GAUTHIER

Yes, I would. But I would also want to hold that some development in a greater moral awareness has taken place in any case.

ARONFREED

I do not understand your assent to Scriven's distinction. Why are you willing to grant that there is a difference of quality when Huck finally decides not to turn Jim in? Surely you would grant the possibility that Huck could, on very good moral grounds, decide to turn Jim in, not because he is a Negro, but for some other reason.

GAUTHIER

You mention other moral grounds. This would require something more than we are given in the story. I was trying to stick as closely as possible to Twain's actual development of the situation.

CRITTENDEN

Could I suggest here that this sort of difficulty over the example arises precisely because of the separation of those three stages that you have outlined in your paper. I know you have done this partly schematically, but it also suggests an almost chronological order. Now I think this is quite mistaken. The acquisition of whatever principles guide a person's behaviour should surely come along with the total feeling and experience involved in employing the principles in given situations. I think finally we get around to Melden's kind of argument. It seems to me that a more satisfactory account of the way in which a principle frequently works is to say that it helps a person see a situation in a different way, to redescribe the situation. It is not that much different, in a sense, from an aesthetic argument. Unless Huck's principles for treating other people have been acquired together with attitudes of respect, compassion, and so on, his seeing Jim as a person is hardly going to affect his moral perception of the situation.

BAIER

Could I cut in here? I am not happy about the suggestion that what matters in deciding whether an advance in the level of morality has occurred is how much the man has agonized over the decision. There is the suggestion that it matters very much which way he has decided. If you take the latter view you must admit the relevance and the validity of some reasons over others. Let me give you an example to show that there is, I think, much to be said for this side. Suppose the man who handed over Bonnie and Clyde had agonized about the question of whether to hand them over or not, considered the amount of money he would be losing if he did not hand them over, the kind of people Bonnie and Clyde were, the relationship which they had developed to his son, and all sorts of human touches about them. Might one not have said that nevertheless the decision to get the money was the wrong decision; that it did not show any great moral development on the part of this man, although he had agonized in coming to that decision. What matters about the question is whether he has got the hang of moral reasoning – just what reasons he uses, and how he evaluates them.

THE PHILOSOPHICAL CHARACTER OF MORAL EDUCATION: DOES IT AVOID THE PROBLEMS OF ETHICAL PLURALISM?

NARVESON

It seems to me that moral education in our society cannot but be philosophical. By this I mean in particular that it is not possible to "teach" morality by inculcating first principles (however "methodological" they may be) and drawing conclusions. Instead, what the instructor must do is to define concepts and problems and then try (hope) to show that solutions will be forthcoming by the inherent requirements of the discussion. That is to say, if the sort of conviction that (as Baier says) moral education as distinct from "training" aims at is to be reached, each student must think the question through to the bottom with nothing held back as being beyond question.

The peculiar and unique job of moral education is not only to get people to think in a certain way but also, because they are thinking about what they ought to do, to get them to act in the light of what they think. In this sense we cannot divorce the so-called cognitive and emotive aspects of morality. So it seems to me that the job of moral education is to get people by reflection to control their behaviour in certain general ways, and then one hopes that the way they act will be roughly the way that Baier commends. That is, I think that Baier is right, generally speaking, about the substance of morality.

CRITTENDEN

I think it is correct also to say that Baier is rejecting the view that moral education can be adequately carried on purely in terms of the formal criteria which specify the moral arguments or moral reasons or moral principles.

BAIER

May I comment briefly on this point. I would be very unhappy and would feel much less confident about anything that I have ever said if it were supposed that I am simply advocating a widely popular moral code, or, at least, one that is widely popular among academics. I feel that I am doing something more objective than that, something that I can justify in ways that the mere advocacy of the moral code is not able to do. Let me just sketch very briefly the kind of steps that I envisage for doing this. I suppose it would be generally granted that almost any social order is better than none, and that any social order, analytically and tautologically, implies the existence of compulsory rules. That is, it implies rules with which one has to confrom, and by this "has to" I mean that one can be forced to conform. Now, even if almost any social order is better than none, it does not follow of course that all these social orders that are better than none are equally good. From the point of view of the participants, the members of the social order, there is a great difference between alternative orders, that is, between alternative settlements of the necessary conflicts of interests that arise in the social context. Although they have other functions, compulsory social rules are especially designed to regulate conflicts of interests, and they regulate them in a variety of ways. Some sections of the community usually – I would say always – have a much better deal than other sections. The criteria of acceptability, as I call them, of social rules are those which we have in mind when we use moral talk, such as when we say something is right or wrong. When we say that something is wrong we imply that it violates a social rule which is not just a social rule but one which purports to satisfy the criteria of acceptability. One can immediately see what these are. They are those that when understood – and this is a core point for moral education – explain to each individual the necessity and beneficiality of having compulsory orders.

BECK

In giving an account of morality, it seems to me, one must take a moral stand. In fact, people in the discussion here have been exhibiting moral stands; for example, taking rationality and the common good as criteria of maximal value. To emphasize my point, may I say that I disagree with both of these as criteria. Rationality could never be the criterion of value (as Baier suggests it is in his book), because then you could not distinguish one area of value from another. Rationality has to operate on something; there have to be substantive questions about which one is rational. At this point people often try to salvage the situation by bringing in considerations of the common good to provide the substantive principle. But it seems to me that this will not do because then how does one solve those problems where the individual has certain peculiar rights arising out of his particular needs, desires, wants, satisfactions, and so on.

BAIER

I think that rationality is not a criterion of the moral order except in this indirect way: that it must provide a conduct regulator for rational creatures. That is all that I would mean. Also let me say that "rational" is an extremely weak criterion. It has been interpreted much more strongly than it ought to be. Anyone who is not irrational is rational. Although irrationality is an extremely strong negative epithet, I think that rationality is much weaker than reasonableness. That is, many people who are perfectly rational are not reasonable. We have been working here with the weaker criterion.

KOHLBERG

It would help me if Baier would specify the kind of argument he was really trying to construct in his paper: was it a legal-constitutional argument or a political argument or a philosophical argument? In the United States, if not in Canada, the problem of ethical pluralism involves the problem of a major constitutional veto. The set of rules for solving the problem on a legal-constitutional level is somewhat different from those of the philosopher in working out what is rationality or what is morality.

BAIER

I was trying to answer the question that I was set to discuss: the question of whether one could engage in moral education and avoid the problems of ethical pluralism by a purely formal teaching of ethics.

The conclusion that I arrived at after worrying about it for a while was, "no, one could not." One could not do justice to a proper conception of morality by a purely formal conception of rules, but one could – and I think that this is what I was suggesting in the last section of my paper – engage in moral teaching by doing the kind of thing that might be called methodology of ethics.

In the field of morality we are roughly at the stage of the alchemists or the phlogiston theory. We have all sorts of substantive views about what is wrong and a fantastic muddle in our minds about how we have arrived at these substantive views. A lot of disillusionment with morality is due, I think, to the fact that people simply do not understand why they should obey these precepts, and very often they do not understand rightly because they have a confused methodology. Clearly, one of the ways in which one can help here is by talking in a simple way about the technique for validating moral claims. This, surely, cannot be illegal, since one is not directly teaching moral precepts. The latter could not be arrived at except by applying these general principles to concrete situations which involve the knowledge of facts and consequences of actions. Now, that kind of education should take place in other disciplines. Psychologists and sociologists, for example, could tell you what happens if you engage in premarital sexual intercourse and masturbation and whatever else, and if you allow the population to grow at its present rate what happens to the food supplies and so on. All these, together with the principles and techniques for validating moral arguments, would enable the student to get an idea of which of these moral principles are defensible and which are not.

SCRIVEN

Although you have replied to Kohlberg's question by saying that in your paper you concluded that we could not avoid the substantive element, I think you are really saying in nonphilosophical terminology that we can. Surely the point of what you are saying is that as a matter of fact we can do everything that we really are most interested in doing without recommending a single substantial type of behaviour – and that is a terribly important point.

ARONFREED

I rather like this notion that you can, or that you might be able to, teach children about morality rather than teach them morality as such or moral decision-making. The thing that bothers me is that I really find it very difficult to envisage this abstract separation that we can make among ourselves when one is working in an actual teaching situation. Scriven is confident that if you put people together, their rational decision-making processes will bring them closer to agreement, reduce their rival alternatives, and so on. I have the feeling that his expectation would be confirmed, provided that the interaction occurs under the right circumstances. But the main problem, it seems to me, is one of how you can teach rational moral decision-making without teaching the assumptions from which the reasoning is to proceed; and if you could, what point would there be in doing it?

You can teach a child how to reason in mathematics; you can teach a child how to reason in moral philosophy. However, if you intend to have any impact upon the child's behaviour, the point is that you are not only going to have to teach him how to reason, you must also teach him whatever he should proceed from as he goes through this reasoning. Even if it were possible to imagine the curriculum in which you have restricted yourself entirely to talking about moral reasoning as opposed to substantive precepts or principles or values, I find it very difficult to imagine that you would have any impact upon the child's behaviour unless he had some starting points that he could use as referents for experiences in the past – that is, for his behaviour as such. The whole effectiveness of such a regime would depend on having some agreement beforehand on the assumptions with which you begin. As a teacher, you must use assumptions from which the moral reasoning proceeds. And these assumptions must have reference to things that the child cares enough about, that is, to instances where he has been engaged by his own past behaviour. Without that, I really find it amazing that anyone could even think that you would be able, on the basis of reasoning and without substance, to get the child to do anything. Why should he care?

BAIER

I entirely agree with that and I suppose that the game-playing that people like Piaget go in for does just what you are getting at. They do build up in the child certain attachments and commitments and then the peculiarly moral type of reasoning hooks on to these. My line begins with rationality in the area of self-interest, in which the child is taught to control certain inclinations because if he does not it will bring him long-range harm and so on. Then there are the very old-fashioned and very simple-minded devices, which undoubtedly could be improved on, like "well, how would you like that if it were done to you" (which encourages the child to identify with another), or "what if everybody did the same," and things of that kind. Now, that type of reasoning of course does not operate unless the child is already affectively concerned with what happens to the other fellow. But all that is necessary is that there be something to which the affect is attached. From the moment that is so, you can extend this affectivity to self-interested reasoning, and once you have that, if my approach is correct, you can extend it to moral reasoning. The kind of leverage point that you are looking for is given simply by the child's having something that he cares about.

CRITTENDEN

I do not think that you can resolve or avoid the problem of pluralism in the school context simply by focusing on methodological matters. Even if people follow a correct method there is no guarantee that they will come to the same conclusions. If the moral conclusions students reach are treated seriously, some at least will require action to be taken in the classroom or school or community. Surely at some point, then, students and teachers are going to be faced with alternative substantive decisions about what they should do here and now. I wonder how they decide in these cases on a course of action. Even if they agree, it is quite possible that they will be at variance with some moral belief held by a section of society and one on which the public school is supposed to maintain neutrality. So I think this is another aspect of ethical pluralism in which the concentration on methodology does not get us around the problem.

NARVESON

I am not entirely sure that we are in agreement on the meaning of the term "substantive," but let me see if I can give a more or less concrete example which might help. I would call the principle that we should regard everbody's interest and not just our own satisfaction a more or less substantive one (although Baier would think of it as more or less methodological). Now, supposing that a number of us agree on this point, we might still disagree as to whether choice A or choice B did in fact satisfy the interest of most, or something like that. That would be a substantive disagreement, but of a rather different sort from an initial disagreement on whether other people's wants should even be respected. It is obvious that if we have initially got an agreement on what I would call a high-level substantive principle (and which, as I say, Baier might regard as a methodological principle), namely, that everbody's interests alike are to count, this is going to rule out a wide range of obviously inequitable solutions from the start. But it is not going to resolve all disagreements because sometimes there will be both factual disagreements such as whether this or that program is in fact going to maximize the realization of interests. But surely if we can get as far as this point, we can adopt strategies of agreeing to disagree or to take turns. Substantive disagreements remain, but of another sort which are manageable and which do not, I think, produce a kind of crisis in the whole general idea of moral education.

SCRIVEN

It seems to me that when Crittenden says we have not handled pluralism he is suggesting that our goal should be to eliminate it in some way that is never achieved even in science. There is complete disagreement among many people over quantum mechanics and its relation to field theory. We cannot expect to eliminate all possible disagreements. The handling of pluralism is surely more of a practical problem. Can we, for example, recommend a procedure for moral education which will be legal if at all possible and make good educational sense and good moral sense. I agree with Narveson that it is extremely important that you get agreement about what to do when disagreements arise that cannot be resolved directly. A serious mistake in moral education is to fail to see that ethical relativism is not the same as agreeing to have procedures for refereeing differences and reaching compromises.

ARONFREED

I want to reflect on how unsatisfactory I find it to be told that "everyone's interests should be taken into account" is a substantive principle. This seems to be so vague and abstract that it would be much like resolving the scientific controversy that Scriven referred to by telling graduate students that the thing to do is to look at nature. Even if you were teaching an adolescent who understood what you meant when you said that we have to take everyone's interest into account, the question becomes: What are his interests? What are legitimate interests to take into account? Suppose the issue is the legitimacy of killing. When, if ever, is it legitimate to kill? What about war? We might start by telling the child that we have to take everyone's interests into account. But we soon have to ask about the substantive principles that one should use in determining whether it is ever legitimate to kill another man; and it seems to me that unless you somehow engage those principles, you are going to have no impact on the child's behaviour.

BAIER

In his paper, Loubser follows Parsons in distinguishing two aspects of the school's function: to develop in the individual both the capacity to perform roles that will be required of him and the commitment to perform these roles. I think that in our discussions here we have not always adequately distinguished these two sorts of things – the promotion of the capacity and the promotion of the commitment to do this. That is, when we consider the aims of moral education as producing mature moral beings or beings with the capacity for being moral, there are two different things involved: the inculcation of the capacity to perform the necessary moral reasoning and the commitment to perform moral reasoning when that is necessary and to act accordingly. And in reference to the second sense of being moral there was some question here about whether it is indeed the aim of moral education to produce it, or whether it was merely to produce the capacity for moral reasoning. I think that some people are very anxious not to do anything about the second element for fear of undue or immoral interference with the independence of the young mind. But it seems to me that the value that seems to be attached to the capacity for moral reasoning, quite independent of the commitment to acting in accordance with it, is rather empty. That is, if one does not attach to it the commitment to follow it, it is an idle exercise. I mean that it is an idle intellectual capacity that has been acquired for no great good. It seems to me that the important thing is that people should act in accordance with it because in the end, for the core of morality, we do need uniformity. We cannot let individuals decide without social disaster whether or not they will conform to the moral reasoning for which they have acquired the capacity.

CRITTENDEN

I certainly agree with this last comment. We have tended to focus attention almost exclusively on teaching people how to become very adept in the skills of moral reasoning. Provided that we can make the criteria of sound moral reasoning sufficiently specific, we are obviously talking about part of becoming morally educated. But from an educator's point of view I do not think it is an adequate account of what moral education is about. I think a moral educator is primarily concerned with helping to bring people to the position where they are committed to acting morally. This assumes of course that we avoid making too radical a distinction between thought and action.

I would also like to raise a question about the strong emphasis in some of the papers and comments on separating out the formal characteristics of moral argument from the content. Is it the case that it does not really matter what you finally choose to do or what you do in the light of your choice, as long as the way you make the choice fits certain formal standards of procedure believed to be appropriate?

NARVESON

I think we have to be careful not to confuse the form/content distinction with the thought/action distinction. One reason they are different is simply that a method or form by itself is not the sort of thing you can act in accordance with or not. Take Kant's categorical imperative of acting on a universalizable maxim. Well you just cannot act on that. The question is what do you think is universalizable and what is not. Until you have answered that question there is no way of telling whether a person's way of acting corresponds or fails to correspond with his beliefs. On the other hand, there are people who have very specific beliefs about what they ought or ought not to do but they fail to act, or apparently fail to act, in accordance with them. These are simply different distinctions which it would be quite a mistake to confuse.

KOHLBERG

Could I get some clarification on this talk about content and form?

CRITTENDEN

Take the example you use of students giving an electric shock to a subject in an experiment.* I gather that 80 per cent of the students at your stage-6 level decided not to go ahead and shock the subject and that 20 per cent of the students also at stage-6 level decided to administer the shock. Suppose I am a teacher and am presented with this as an example. I am interested in learning what I should do as a moral educator. I think it would be reasonable for me to ask this sort of question: Have I fulfilled my job as a teacher when I have helped students to get to the point of being able to resolve the problem in this manner? Although I may be convinced that the students who gave the shock acted immorally, should I try to persuade them about the content of their decision? Should I tell them that it was a bad decision even though their moral reasons for making it were excellent in *form*? Should I stop at that point and simply be content with getting them to such a level of methodological sophistication?

KOHLBERG

There are two issues here. One way we try to encourage mature or rational morality is to construct a value system in the school which is

* See above, pp. 78–9.

comparable with it. Let us say we decide to have universal humanism as distinctive of the school atmosphere. But, then, by our theory, what we get are stage-3 students copying the content of universal humanism in what they say, although still being conformists in spirit. The other thing is that it is theoretically possible to think of stage-6 reasons for wanting to fight in Vietnam but nobody does it. As it was pointed out, this is because of the factual assumptions involved.

OLIVER

The point is that the factual assumptions are quite questionable, and whether they are true or not is important. Uninformed people arguing at stage-6 level are sophisticated.

KOHLBERG

But that is part of the whole moral reasoning problem we have been talking about throughout this conference.

OLIVER

No, we have been talking about what rationality is and what stage-6 moral reasoning is, and how you get to it. We have not been talking about the reality dimension at all.

SULLIVAN

I want to come back to Crittenden's question about the 20 per cent of students who gave stage-6 reasons for shocking. I think that it is the kind of question an educator would be asking, assuming that his objective was to have everyone in the experiment come to see that they should refuse to co-operate. It also brings in the question of Kohlberg's stage 6 in the sense that we need to introduce some more individual variation. There could be other types of individual differences within that stage that we should look for to find out why the 20 per cent stayed in the experiment. The educator, I am sure, would be interested in these negative cases.

BAIER

I would like to comment on the same point. If we cannot give conclusive reasons as an answer to a moral question, we are not entitled to press beyond that. This is a failure of the theory. Without being able to demonstrate to the student that he has arrived at the wrong conclusions, one cannot say, "you have the best reasons there are but I do not want you to act on them." One's reasons have to be better, or else. Let me add this. I do not think that for all cases, particularly the tricky ones we have been discussing, we are able to give conclusive reasons as yet, and perhaps we never shall.

EDEL

The question of structure and content is a fundamental one, certainly for Kohlberg's scheme. As I see it, the structure of a building (for instance) is made of the same material as the rest of the building, or at least of something that is in principle the same: the structure is steel and the rest of the building is cement or wood and the difference is just in the kind of material. Bosanquet points out that it is the skeleton that sets the shape or framework of the body, but we must also remember that the skeleton is built up in the process of the development of the body, so that it is, as it were, a part of the body selected because of the properties it has for a particular job in relation to the rest.

On this basis, then, structure, if regarded as pure, cannot determine value. As Melden pointed out in a comment, universalizability, if formal, is just a feature of any predicate. You cannot get dignity out of that. For that matter, Peters in his *Ethics and Education* notes that justice is compatible with contempt and he appeals to our experience with bureaucrats who can be very, very just but who have no interest in us and push us around in other respects. If Kohlberg's stages are understood or interpreted in terms of different kinds of reasoning in moral arguments, they are only relatively formal – in the sense that a glass is relatively formal to wine or milk or water, but is material for the glass blower. Here again, as often, Aristotle is wiser than Kant (I am being dogmatic for provocative purposes, and you will recognize that this is part of the educative procedure). Kohlberg's sixth stage reflects the problem. It involves an appeal to conscience and morality within, but it leaves open the type of appeal. It has the bare "within" elements or the self-determination reference, but what this really means concretely depends upon the kind of self. I am reminded again of Aristotle's treatment of the question of selfishness in a comparable vein. Whether you should love yourself or not, Aristotle says, depends upon what kind of self you have. If you have a good self, it is worth loving and if you have a bad self, it is not worth loving. It seems to me that that remark is more profound than the whole subsequent history of egoism in ethical theories. It also fits beautifully with all psychological work on types of self and so on. It seems to me, then, that at this point Kohlberg's sixth stage is going to turn into frightfully different things depending on the picture of the self and self-regulation that underlies it. I do not see how he will be able to apply this stage without going into the content of at least the self. I do not mean that he cannot do this. But when he does, the sixth stage may yield a number of important substages and there probably will be cultural variations.

KOHLBERG

I wonder if it is fair to ask a group of moral philosophers this question: do you think that moral philosophy as it is taught at the college level is relevant to the stimulation of moral reasoning among high-school students?

NARVESON

It will be obvious from what I said earlier that I think moral education has to be philosophical. We want to avoid teaching children a set of ready-made answers to moral problems. The only way that we can prevent this is by doing moral philosophy, that is, by having teachers work with students in analysing their moral concepts so that they see answers emerge not from the teacher or from some authority outside but from their own minds. This is moral philosophy and until we have this kind of thing I do not believe we are going to have thoroughly morally educated human beings. It seems to me that when a teacher gets a number of students together to discuss questions with the hope that they will learn something moral out of it, one assumption is that a solution to the problem will emerge out of the intrinsic characteristics of the subject. It will not be artificially imposed by the flaunting of someone's will. In discussing the problem we will see that there is a solution or perhaps a narrow range of solutions the plausibility of which rests on the intrinsic merits of the grounds available for their support and does not rest on something arbitrary. The thought that morality is arbitrary is, I think, the chief danger in any genuine moral education. This is why I am so worried about the kind of teaching of morality that is done in parochial schools. What we want is a conception of morality and a set of moral principles that are the recommendation of impersonal reasons.

OLIVER

Yes, but I wonder what the teacher does. This is what bothers me. I have seen ethics taught at the college level and I do not get the impression that the teacher is standing there and waiting for moral philosophy to emerge.

NARVESON

That could be a function of the way a person teaches or more likely a function of the particular personality of the teacher involved. This is a very serious problem. I think that a good deal of work on the methodology of the college teacher of ethics would probably be very beneficial to the profession as well.

CRITTENDEN

Incidentally, which version of moral philosophy would you teach in a public school?

NARVESON

Putting the question that way is a misunderstanding of what is being done, or at any rate, what seems to me ought to be done – what most of us in the profession conceive ourselves to be doing. We are not teaching a moral philosophy. When we say we are teaching moral philosophy what we mean is just that we are considering certain concepts, considering the different things that various people have said about them: perhaps, as in my case, saying at various points that it seems to me that a particular position is stronger. But certainly I am not teaching a moral philosophy. I am trying to teach students as many alternatives as make any sense at all, that have been historically in any way viable, in any way influential. For example, I do my best to make it very clear exactly what a theistic position in ethics does and does not involve. I do come down very hard on theistic views in the end, but certainly I would deny very strenuously the suggestion that I am inculcating a position in the students.

CRITTENDEN

But this is what anybody who has ever indoctrinated could say.

NARVESON

Well, this may be. I think that a few of the students in the course would say something like this, but I would also say that they would have a very hard time presenting any evidence to support their case. Some of the smart students do come out disagreeing with me on this point but they do not understand what I have said on it. Certainly, I do not brainwash them.

EDEL

I think we ought to note that the situation in college is quite different from that of the high school. For one thing you have students who can read philosophical works and so forth. This is not in the least comparable to the high-school situation. Also the teacher in the high school cannot ignore the business of relating the elements of theory to practice and so on.

SULLIVAN

In reference to Crittenden's question about which version of moral theory should be taught, it seems to me that Narveson does make some assumptions about what constitutes morality.

CRITTENDEN

Yes, I do think that we need to get a bit more clear on what exactly teaching moral philosophy in the high school would involve. One could take the view that you are just going to expound in a descriptive fashion, as accurately as you can, the arguments for and against all the main ethical theories. Now I think that this can be done in a reasonably dispassionate and objective fashion. It is one way in which you could teach moral philosophy – teach about moral philosophy. But I gather that is not really quite what Narveson wants to do. It would not be a very satisfactory substitute for educating people to moral maturity.

If you are convinced that some ethical theory is better than another you will try to persuade students that it is the position they should accept and that the differences it makes for moral action should be reflected in the way they act. This gets us back to the pluralistic problem. I am concerned with it because we are vitally and directly involved with public-school education and cannot ignore certain real factors in our society which bear on what is done in moral education. Suppose you set about your task of demonstrating to a group of high-school students that the arguments in favour of any theistically centred morality are weak, refutable, and that any person who wants to be morally mature must simply abandon any attachment to a theistic framework for morality. If you are in the university setting it might be possible to conduct a theoretical discussion divorced from practice. But if you are engaged in the moral education of children you cannot ignore the question of consistency between what they learn in theory and their subsequent actions. If a theistic moral theory makes a difference in practice, then the rejection of it in a public school – with immature children who are compelled to be there by law – would seem to impinge on one of the areas of freedom which our pluralistic system guarantees.

I have used the theistic theory only as an example. Some of the participants of this conference have treated Kohlberg's stage 4 as a moral regression. For people who see the theistic principle as being central to and defining the nature of ethics, stage 4 would be put at the very top of his list. This of course is only one dispute. It would be interesting to consider the less dramatic but real differences for moral education between a naturalistic and prescriptivist ethical theory.

NARVESON

It seems to me that the teacher can try to bring out something which is objectively there in a very compelling but impersonal way. The demonstration that a certain position contains contradictions is an example of this: that is, showing the students that in order to maintain a certain position he must also entertain another proposition which is incompatible with it. Then you really have him. Nobody can believe, not even a thirteen-year-old given that he understands the concepts of logic at all, that it will work in fact. If you have got an argument which makes it plausible that his position does contain contradictions, the next move is up to the student. You say, "Now I do not see how we can get around this, but can you?" I am quite willing to bring in people to present the argument for a religious ethics. Perhaps eventually somebody will find a clear sense in which you can have a religious ethics that is buyable logically. I have not seen it and I do not see it coming. But I am always willing to give it a try. In this case I point out to the student, "Look, as far as I can see, these are contradictions. Are they contradictions?" And the student usually recognizes that they are.

SULLIVAN

Is it really that clear at the top? Can you really see the differences?

NARVESON

It is just not true that in order to know what an error is you have to know what the truth is. You can know that something is wrong without being able to show what is right. You can eliminate the position and you may not know quite where to go from there. Maybe there is not any ultimate foundation. I do not believe this, but it is a logical possibility that we have to face up to and I always try to do so. I include among other things a consideration of the kinds of positions called sceptical or existential (with a small e). All of these things have to be examined and presented to the class for their consideration. Maybe you can do something about it and maybe you cannot. I claim that in general we are able to do something.

SCRIVEN

It seems to me that Crittenden has raised a point that in its most general form gets back to the question of distinguishing indoctrination from education. Perhaps we should have discussed this distinction at some stage. Anyway I would like to mention some things that bear on it. A number of those doubts that have been raised in reference to pluralism are really tied indirectly with political considerations. That is, if I do a geography course in which I run through a whole lot of facts and theories and say which I think are the best and so on, nobody is going to haul me over the coals at the PTA. But if I do this in a course on religion or in a course on ethics, then I get into trouble even though I may be academically just as respectable in accepting defensible views. This is one reason why I run the line that ethics is a science. My general approach is simply that it is a social science and like any other science it can and probably can best be taught inductively; that is, with little emphasis on the substantive content, more on its method of inquiry and on student-discovery. It is normative but no more normative than engineering or lexicography or medicine. But of course its forms are ethical rather than practical, grammatical, or medical. It is just one of the studies of how we should behave to bring about some of our multifarious complex of ends. The study brings in anthropology, theory of games, economics, sociology, and psychology, in the same kind of way that engineering an instrument panel for an automobile does. The only difference is that ethics is the most general normative science just as physics is the most general descriptive science. Even that dichotomy is misleading, since ethics is descriptive of the value realm and physics is normative of the physicist's professional beliefs. We may just have to get a little hard nosed and say, "Look, there are a whole lot of things like the fact that you cannot found ethics on religion which are now, even politically speaking, so well supported by theologians as well as philosophers in general, that ethics is a perfectly respectable part of the curriculum and you cannot really complain that this is infringing on the Church-State thing."

Let me mention three very important types of nonindoctrinative moral education. A survey of comparative ethics, although it would have many drawbacks, is not without its merits as moral education. It enlarges your range of possibilities. This is extremely valuable in breaking down assumptions, for example, that man cannot live without property-conserving rules. So the comparative study is one thing. It is not propaganda, although it has an important educational effect. The second thing is that we study methods. On any question we look for the generalization that is relevant. This is what is always done in moral casuistry in whatever tradition. We learn how relevance is identified. No content is being pumped in, but something very important in moral education is going on. The third thing that we could do is employ inductive teaching procedures in which results could be reached by working from the students themselves. Here are three approaches which I think could be well defended against the claims of being propaganda.

On ethics courses: why is it that every person who goes to a university and takes an ethics course (which is a negligible minority of the total) works through the ritual of finding out what Aristotle meant by what his three translators translate in three different ways, and spends his time talking about metaethics? There is a long tradition beginning with Aristotle and Socrates of normative ethics and yet we do not, as a matter of fact, normally teach this at all.

KOHLBERG

I think that when moral philosophers start to reflect on their undergraduate courses in ethics in terms of what their educational goals really are, that is, what changes they want to produce in the people who come to those courses, they are immediately in the same business as the psychologists and the educators and the rest of us here who have been concerned about this. I do not think that the issue of age level is so important: whether the student is taking a college-level course in ethics or is taking a junior high-school course in ethics does not matter. What the educator needs from the moral philosopher is something about what can be done and what ought to be done in the light of his experience in teaching undergraduate ethics. But there are some questions I wanted to ask. To what extent should people who teach ethics at the undergraduate level be philosophers? I mean, is the assumption that ethics is part of philosophy rather than, say, part of social science correct? To what extent is there one professional tradition in ethics?

BECK

It seems to me that one of the major questions that moral philosophers are considering at present is whether they are competent to judge on substantive issues. To say that at the same time as they are considering these questions very seriously they ought to be teaching substantive moral issues is to make an unreasonable demand on them. I am all for setting up departments of ethical science in universities, but this is quite a different thing from saying that ethical philosophers should be teaching ethical science.

GAUTHIER

Well, I will come back to my position that one does not teach ethics. In effect this is what I was stating at the very outset. One teaches other things which are relevant to ethics but one does not teach the subject itself. I do not think it is a teachable subject. Unlike my friends here who teach ethics to undergraduates, I teach metaethics; and I teach metaethics, I suppose, because it was the only thing that I found clarifying in terms of my own moral thinking. In order to sort out how to think about moral problems it seems to me that what philosophers can say something about – and what I wanted – is a certain amount of metaethics and reflection on ethical reasoning. I think that the rest of what one wants should not be taught by teachers of ethics nor should it be taught by philosophers. But the rest of what one wants (as I said earlier) is an enormously expanded awareness of how society works, of what the consequences of individual actions within a society are, of what the consequences of the effects of social institutions are, and so on and on. One needs this without its being presented as ethics or put in terms of normative principles. The information has to be presented as objectively as possible and therefore by people whose job it is to understand society and who are not afraid of talking about all its aspects. What our students really need is a greater understanding of the world in which they are operating so that they can affect it. And they certainly want to do this. We do not need to motivate them in this sense, but we need to give them this understanding, which will make their actions more effective. And this, I think, should not be done by teachers of ethics but should be done more in the tradition of social studies and perhaps taught from a rather different point of view.

CHAPTER 12

*The theory of developmental stages in moral judgment**

SCRIVEN

I would like to christen a doctrine which runs through Kohlberg's approach and which is described as follows:

> I shall now present a third conception of moral education. In this conception the goal of moral education is the stimulation of the 'natural' development of the individual child's own moral judgment and of the capacities allowing him to use it to control his behaviour.†

I call this "the doctrine of original virtue." It is nice that a social psychologist should have replaced the doctrine of original sin.

KOHLBERG

It is not a matter of original virtues, but of natural virtues.

SCRIVEN

You have a theory of original, but needing to be uncovered, virtues. It does not begin with virtue. It works up to it in the natural sequence involved; it works up to the doctrine of justice in stage 6. That's the virtuous stage, right? So, we might say it is the doctrine of original *or* eventual virtue.

BAIER

Is that quite fair? Is it not the doctrine of the natural capacity for virtue?

SCRIVEN

No, that is too strong. Kohlberg does not argue that everybody will reach stage 6.

* For an outline of the stages see above, pp. 86–8.

† See above, p. 71; the passage is quoted from Kohlberg's original paper.

BAIER

Yes, it is too strong, but the other account is too positive.

KOHLBERG

The main point is that it is not possible to reach stage 6 without education – that is, if you use education in a very broad sense. For this reason I am not proposing a doctrine of original virtue.

SCRIVEN

Yes, except that education in the sense that includes being alive in a social environment is hard to avoid. Anyway, I do not think Kohlberg is committing the naturalistic fallacy in any of the forms he discusses. There is some sense in which he might be committing what could be called the "sympathetic naturalistic fallacy," which is to imagine that it is somehow better that we become virtuous naturally. It is certainly better with respect to society, but whether it is better with respect to ethics I am not sure.

KOHLBERG

Scriven has just referred to a major issue raised throughout my paper: the problem of the naturalistic fallacy. The question is, what bearing do certain "developmental facts" have on a philosophical conception of normative ethics? Everybody recognizes the relevance of the facts about development to talking about the means of moral education. But in reference to ends, to what extent is a natural end to be taken as a normative one? That is why I have tried to deal with all those forms of the naturalistic fallacy. Really the general question is this: if one assumes that my description is adequate (that is, a sequence of stages in which the highest stage is always the same), what are its implications for what morality ought to be or for what moral education ought to be?

EDEL

On these problems of the naturalistic fallacy I would like to briefly draw your attention to three different kinds of questions that are here involved and their relationship. One of them, of course, concerns the stages (S1 to S6) in Kohlberg's thesis. I am not going to refer to the evidence for these stages because that is an empirical matter. But if you take the descriptions of the types involved and lift them out of the context of Kohlberg's stages, it seems to me that you will still have a set of moral patterns. Long before we were fortunate enough to have Kohlberg discover the developmental stages which are here involved, we did have all of these as moral patterns: the pattern of the utilitarian, the pattern of the egoist, the pattern of justice, and so on. Thus we can speak of these apart from any kind of order simply as a diversity of moral patterns (M1 to M6). These moral patterns, by the way, might be arranged in the order of which is more moral or more desirable or better or more justified, and so on. Now in addition to developmental stages and the moral patterns, the whole theory of justification is a quite different issue. There are various patterns of justification also (J1 to Jn). Notice I say "n" here because there may be more or less than 6. We have to look at the kind of justification that is given when one of the Ms is said to be better than another. Given developmental stages, moral patterns, and types of justification, I wonder whether Kohlberg's analysis or system presupposes that you first make some judgments about the moral superiority of Mn to M1? If it is an independent question, to what extent will you then discover that the ordering of M1 to Mn is related to the empirically established order, S1 to Sn? Does the latter make a difference to the judgment of moral preference or moral betterness or anything of that sort, or is it an independent matter? It seems to me that if we made these distinctions we could at least be clear about some of the issues involved in what is or is not a naturalistic fallacy, as well as the separation of the various domains.

SCRIVEN

We should perhaps focus on a special difficulty which I think a number of you will have felt in Kohlberg's stages. This is the difficulty of distinguishing between stages 5 and 6. Kohlberg comes out with a remark that stealing to save a life is all right because it is just. As a matter of fact he puts it into one long sentence, which I think can be quite instructive. He says: "We know it's all right to be dishonest and steal to save a life because it is just, because a man's right to life comes before another man's right to property. We know it is sometimes right to kill because it is sometimes just."* That first sentence would read better to me if one said simply: We know that it is all right to be dishonest and steal to save a life because a man's right to live comes before another man's right to property. That is, it seems to me that one should not suggest that the appeal to justice here is necessarily an appeal to the other man's right to life or that it is translatable in such a fashion. Justice is concerned with rights in a complicated way but not in this particular way. What we have here looks like surplus moral metaphysics and poor moral philosophy – in fact, poor moral phenomenology too because I am not sure that this is the way people nor-

* Scriven is quoting from Kohlberg's original paper. The latter has been revised in the light of this comment. See above, p. 58.

mally report their moral experiences. The only way to get a stage 6 beyond stage 5 is not in terms of the summary I have quoted. Nor do you get it by down-grading a mere appeal to equal rights in comparison with the appeal to justice. There are places where Kohlberg argues that the appeal to rights is a sign of stage 5, whereas the appeal to justice is a sign of stage 6, but here he is also translating justice.

If you refer to Appendix 1* where he outlines the stages, you will notice that there is no reference in stage 6 to justice. This is hard to reconcile in some respects with various things he says in other places. There is a distinction in the descriptions given in the main table which I find much more defensible. It is what I have called elsewhere the distinction between active and passive morality: that is, between the passive regard for the rights of others and the active love for others which generates that respect. I suspect that Kohlberg may have introduced the identification of stage 6 with the appeals to justice more recently that when he composed that table and that it may be superfluous or, at any rate, misleading.

NARVESON

I think you have quite properly taken Kohlberg to task for not presenting stages 5 and 6 as distinctly different. I would want to go a bit further than this and say that I have considerable doubts about the discrimination of most of the stages from most others. Most philosophers would regard a stage-6 orientation as a *sine qua non* of the moral point of view. Nevertheless, even supposing that a conscience (and in some general sense, a principles) orientation is a *sine qua non* of moral orientation, it would be possible to argue, and it has in fact been done, that the only conscionable thing to do is to be at stage 4 in certain specific senses. For example, some theological ethicists would maintain that human obligation ought to be to a personal God – endowed, to my mind, with some rather arbitrary characteristics. I think that these people are wrong, but it is a question in moral philosophy, and it would take a good deal of argument to see whether their position would do at all.

Let me go a little bit further. I want to argue that there is something to be said for certain aspects of every one of the stages Kohlberg describes. Clearly the obedience-punishment orientation is not something which we want to abandon. One could correctly claim that the later stages qualify it in one sense or another, but one would surely not want to say that having an obedience and punishment orientation is itself a sign of moral inferiority. And look at the phrase "trouble-

* See above, pp. 86–8.

avoiding" in Kohlberg's description of stage 1. Depending on how you construe trouble or what kind of trouble, you might very well argue that the entire structure of justice is orientated to trouble-avoiding. This relates to the general question of the logical relation among different ethical theories, which is a philosophical question by no means settled at present. Disagreements are very widespread among philosophers on these points and I do not think that any study which relies on their having been settled and sets up a clear order of precedence, as Kohlberg seems to do, is at all satisfactory.

Now let me make a connected point about the logic of the discrimination of these stages. It might be the case that in the theoretical situation you can more or less discriminate the series of stages. The first stage is in a sense the natural set of somebody who has not learned much at all yet. I think that stage 1 in Kohlberg's scheme is probably like this, although I am not entirely sure. One might then conjecture about a series of stages such that the later ones are those which you would arrive at by applying logic and science to what you had begun with. You would have to show that the hypothetical list of stages did in fact have an intrinsic logical order such that the later ones are the ones which follow logically as you push the analysis more thoroughly and as you find more facts than you had in the earlier ones. If the stages are discriminated according to this kind of principle, it would then be very plausible to suppose that there would be a developmental process of the kind Kohlberg maintains because one main thing that is supposed to characterize human development from infancy to middle years is increasing knowledge and intelligence (I mean intelligence in the sense of increasing ability to deal with arguments, etc.). I think Kohlberg is claiming that the later stages in his scheme are morally better than the earlier ones. After all, the judgment that X is more mature than Y does have a moral ring to it. It may be that he would want to claim that this principle has been involved in settling the stages, and, if so, well and good. But I would want to see it argued more carefully, and I would want to see the stages more precisely distinguished.

There is one more note I would like to add. I do not understand very clearly the kind of claim that is being made when Kohlberg says that the stages are such that you cannot skip any of them. It is being maintained, I believe, that empirical evidence shows that these stages are never skipped over. If it is only a kind of statistical generalization, then I would not quarrel with it. But my observations of a very small number of children, notably my own, would indicate that the hypothesis of unskippable stages is simply false.

CRITTENDEN

A sentence in Kohlberg's paper is, I believe, specifically connected with what Narveson has just been talking about. He says "the step-by-step sequence of stages is invariant because it represents an inner logical order of moral concepts, not because it represents an order wired into the nervous system or into the educational practices of the culture."* Now it seems to me that the philosopher who is trying to co-operate in this kind of inquiry is of most use in pointing out what statements do count as moral reasons and the conditions which are relevant to their being accepted as moral reasons. I do not see that the moral philosopher can really do any more than offer his informed opinion as to whether the reasons given in particular circumstances are moral or not moral. Certainly I think that it is impossible for him to derive from the inner logic of moral concepts a rank order of responses into five or six stages such that stage 1 includes the least moral reasons you can give and each succeeding stage morally better reasons, in a rigid logically ascending order up to a stage 6. To claim that there is an inner logical order in the quality of moral reasons is quite different from claiming that in order to perform certain cognitive functions you need to have a certain level of intellectual development.

KOHLBERG

The table on pages 89–91 setting out stages in the conception of the worth of human life is meant to illustrate that, as the same people progress step by step, the same concepts about the value of life are at a different level of differentiation and integration for each stage. You can state what this progression is in terms of many dimensions – its being more universal, for example – but in each case there is a differentiation of the moral value of human life from all kinds of extraneous considerations such as whether the husband loves his wife and so on. These are spelled out for each stage. This is only one example of the kind of detailed logical analysis we have tried to go through to show the sense in which each of the stages involves a distinction or differentiation not made at a previous stage – and yet is also more integrated.

In this sense I think you can show that the stages do meet the criteria that Narveson mentioned, that there is some kind of a logical order to the sequence. As a psychologist you ask why there should be this kind of step-wise movement when you look longitudinally at the same people over time. Then you immediately have to make the kind of logical analysis that I mentioned. But then the question is how that kind of logical analysis is related to moral justification, why one

* See above, p. 48. The passage is quoted from Kohlberg's original paper.

stage is better than another. We have an internal logic, and when we talk about ethical justification of a moral system we sometimes do it in metaethical terms and sometimes from within a realm of ethical discourse. If you want to say that stage-6 morality insures the survival of the individual who holds to that morality, that would be adopting a non-moral or second frame of reference, it is not a justification by reference to moral terms. What I am trying to deal with is this: if you put a stage-2 and a stage-3 person together, the one at stage 3 is going to influence the one at stage 2 and not vice-versa when they argue. This is an empirical fact. What is it about each of these stages that this should be the case? It seems to me that the problem is close to moral philosophy.

MELDEN

I still feel rather confused about the relation between the stages, and I think that I share Narveson's uncertainty. He suggested that by a kind of logical deduction (if he did not suggest this, it is at least a possibility) one could proceed from stage 1 to stage 2, that we do have notions like obedience and punishment and responsibility operating at stage 1 but that a person at this level is not aware of all of the entailments. Let me present it in this way: I do not have a very high opinion of cats and dogs in respect to their ability to engage in thinking of any sort, but I am sensible of the fact that when I punish them I am doing something quite different from what I did when I had occasion to punish my children. All of these notions like punishment, obedience, responsibility are, it seems to me, enormously complicated. It may be that the notion of punishment is being used in the description of stage 1 in some radically truncated form. If this is the case and there is a conceptual connection between the stages, the conceptual seeds are present in stage 1. However, it is not that you proceed by a kind of deduction from 1 to 2 but rather that as you are going from 1 to 2 to 3 and so on there is a great deal more information, conceptual enrichment, etc.

KOHLBERG

With regard to punishment, for example, I would say that it is an aspect that is present at every stage, but that the conceptions of punishment are different at each stage. By this I mean what one would give as an example of fair punishment, for instance.

MELDEN

Let me break in at this point. To say that the conceptions are different is not really to face the issue. It suggests that we have different senses and this is a philosopher's kind of gambit which I think we ought to be very careful about employing. What we have really are not different senses of the term but, if you wish, different features of a concept which are present here but omitted there. In other words, we are dealing with conceptually related notions. So let us not speak of different senses of different conceptions but rather of different articulations of the same thing, with features missing at earlier points but becoming very rich and complicated at the end.

KOHLBERG

As a mature subject discussing that story about stealing the drug, I may worry about going to jail. But we treat that as a "non-moral" reason, whereas at stage 1 or 2 it is the reason for not stealing. In this sense even concern about avoiding the punishment does not drop out of the system completely but it drops out of what can be called the moral system. The mature individual is making a psychological statement about himself in saying that he fears punishment but he does not view this as a morally legitimate reason for deciding not to steal the drug. Orientation to punishment has dropped out, but other conceptions of punishment will have come in at the higher level. I recognize that the issue of punishment is a bothersome one because it gets back to the question of rational praise and blame.

BECK

If the process of going through the stages is dependent upon increasing cognitive development and gaining access to certain information, could not the stages be altered by giving the children different knowledge at a particular stage? It seems to me that there are two factors at work here. One is the logical question, the other is the sociological one: that children in their development come into contact with various sources of experience, which determine the cognitive material that they receive.

KOHLBERG

When you look at the graphs in which you get the same age trend in different cultures and when you see that progression from stage 3 to stage 4 occurs at age 10 for one person and at age 20 for another, although they are both of average IQ, it becomes hard to make the definition of the stages as specific as you suggest with regard to teaching content.

BECK

In your findings the stages are still kept intact even if they come at a later age. Can you envisage a situation where the stages might vary because the cognitive development of the child varies due to accidental features of his environment?

KOHLBERG

These stages presuppose, among other things, Piaget's stages of logic. This means, for instance, that you cannot reach the principle level of moral thinking until you have what Piaget calls formal operations – the capacity for formulating principles of a hypothetical-deductive sort and for theory formation or whatever you want to call it. A theory of society is involved in stages 5 and 6, and it is not until adolescence that you find people using formal theories in this way or being concerned about logical consistency for its own sake and so on.

PASKAL

I wonder why someone should stop at any one level or what accounts for the difference between one person who makes the transition from stage 3 to stage 4 at age 10 and the other who makes it at age 20.

KOHLBERG

Well, this is a complicated question. The regularity of the progression is suggested by the fact that the correlation between moral maturity, say at age 13 and age 25 is 90, but the ones who are advanced at age 13 tend to have retained their advantage – and this is without much variation in IQ. The difference in social experience and so on is an answer to the question about delay. Why people get stuck at particular stages is partly contingent upon the stage. The policy of "you scratch my back and I'll scratch yours" or "everyone for himself" is stage 2, but it does correspond to the way the world is to a certain extent. It is adaptive to the environment. So there is not too much going on in a person's moral experience that would shake up such an interpretation of the moral order.

SULLIVAN

In the other cultures you have studied there are very few people at stages 5 and 6. Is there something about the American culture at this present point in history which is stressing justice over other considerations such as charity? The point I want to make is that your stages seem to be very culture-bound: other cultures could not reach those higher stages you have defined simply because they do not have those types of preoccupations.

KOHLBERG

Let me say that the longitudinal evidence is not really so satisfactory, because we do not have that many stage-6 people in our samples to say that they always went through stage 5. But if there is a natural development so that the conception of moral principles developed only after universal constitutional law, that is, if there is a kind of movement from a constitutional legal outlook or mode of thought to what philosophers have been concerned about, and if moral philosophy as a stage-6 game depends on having gone through the constitutional legal frame of reference, I should think that this would be interesting in terms of an analysis of what moral philosophy is all about. It really has not been very clearly documented. We use stage 6 as a watershed. Of course, certain things that you or I might think are high-level morals at stage 6 in fact may be displayed by people who have never reached stage 5. But these do not get included in the system. Specifically, let us take the word "principle." This word is a *cliché* in our culture and so an individual may say, for instance, that you should steal the drug to save your wife because the highest principle is loyalty to one's family. Now although the word "principle" is used, the response is not to be scored at stage 6 because it is just a different way of saying that you should be nice to your family, and using the word "principle" adds nothing to it.

ARONFREED

I think it might be worth pointing out that many of the questions now being raised about the logical order of the stages and the possibility that change in cognitive power accounts for these apparent developmental changes in moral thought have also been raised by psychologists in much more general form. They have been concerned with the cognitive nature of the developmental changes that take place in children's verbalization of moral thought. It is possible that the cognitive changes one sees in moral development rest on transformations of operators in the child's cognitive capacity, which he becomes able to apply in sequence to the material that he gets, so to speak, from his transactions with the social environment. If that were the case, one would expect to find some similarity, or perhaps identity, between operators at work in moral development and the kinds of transformation of operators that the child uses in his conceptions of the physical world – time, space, conservation of quantity, and so on. Of course, once one entertains such a notion it leaves open the possibility that there is nothing intrinsically moral in the changes themselves which make up the sequence of moral development. The moral content involves particular kinds of representations. So the changes that occur have to do with changes of operators that are found in the child's cognition of the social and physical world in general. They have no intrinsic moral status whatsoever – any more than the changes in the child's conception of number have moral status.

GAUTHIER

I am still concerned with some of the logical issues relating to the connection between these stages of moral development. I think Kohlberg was suggesting that we would on the whole agree that the stages represent some sort of development, that the later ones are in some way higher than the others. If one looks at what Jim says* at age six about the worth of human life and what he says at age sixteen, my own reaction to his comments is that between ages thirteen and sixteen he has absorbed all that religious nonsense which has led to a regression in his thinking. His original position – in which he says it is all right for the doctor to "mercy kill" a fatally ill woman who requests it because it is really up to her – is one to which we are gradually moving with respect to suicide after going through a period in which our laws, on religious grounds, made suicide a crime. Euthanasia is an even clearer example.

This leads me to the point that stage 4 is one about which recent moral philosophers have not, I think, said very much. Their silence tends to suggest that stage 4 does not have very much to do with morality and that in a way it is more in the nature of a cul-de-sac into which people get themselves, perhaps because of mistaken views held on other grounds. Indeed, recent moral philosophers (good ones, I mean) have not seen either stage 3 or stage 4 as of importance in a rational development of morality. If one looks, for example, at the sort of argument that Baier, after Hobbes, has been developing, one sees something like a direct relationship between stage 2 and what is roughly stage 5. One can see how stage 5 could come rationally out of stage 2 by this sort of argument. However, the relationship between something like stages 3 and 2 would require a quite different sort of explanation, I should think. It might be the case that a child who wanted the approval of his fellows gradually became aware that the "good boy" orientation was needed to secure it and so passed from naïve egoism to the "good boy" orientation by a process of increasing awareness of what was necessary to get the satisfaction he wanted and which he could not get while he remained at stage 2. This could perhaps represent a change in the child. He has come to have certain wants or

* See above, p. 90.

needs that he did not have before. I am not familiar with the processes of development here and so I cannot say whether the child acquires new wants or needs for social approval that would lead him into stage 3. But what is clear, I think, is that the relationship between stages 2 and 3 cannot have the same sort of conceptual character that the relationship between stages 2 and 5 could have in something like the Hobbes-Baier argument. So I am inclined to think that if there is, as it were, a logic to this development, it is going to involve the addition of a good many empirical premises particularly with respect to stages 3 and 4: what people want in terms of the approval of others, what they are exposed to in terms of statements about the alleged super-authorities like God, and so on. Whether a person gets to stage 4 or not might very well depend on the sort of information to which he is exposed. But these particular stages really have little to do with the logic of moral development.

NARVESON

I think that Gauthier is entirely right in what he has just said. That is, certainly the development could not be purely logical, but at the very least it would have to take into account increasing perceptions of various kinds of facts as well. It might be that what you would get would not be a linear development but one with all kinds of detours and variations in it.

On another point, something I said earlier may have been misleading. I more or less suggested that if we had intrinsically ordered stages, then we would expect *a priori* that these would also be the stages of a person's actual development. But I think it is clearly not true that this is what we may *a priori* expect. There is a quite straightforward counter-example. It is very well known that in mathematics, stages of thought that clearly presuppose some of the others are learned first. It is much easier to teach arithmetic before quantification theory even though logically, at least as we now understand mathematics, the theory of arithmetic would presuppose quantification theory. In general, the fact that something is logically presupposed by something else proves nothing about which of the two is going to be known first in the actual development of any individual. People often have flashes of intuition which go way ahead of their command of the intervening theory in a fully elaborated system.

LOUBSER

I have a few points to raise in this discussion of the stages. The first is about the sequence of stages 3 and 4. On the basis of general considerations of socialization in the family, reaction to parents and so forth, I thought that there might be good reason to expect that those two stages would be reversed. If one looks at the child going through these various stages in terms of the types of content and environment involved in each, there are at least three factors on which they vary. One is the authority dimension, that is, authority as a source of moral value; another is the egoist-orientation in terms of the satisfaction of needs of the individual himself; and a third is the individual's relation to other social objects not necessarily arranged on the authority dimension, perhaps his peers as reflected in the "good boy" pattern of orientation. On the authority dimension, for example, it seems to me that stages 1 and 4 are consecutive stages, that stage 4 would logically and psychosociologically follow from stage 1. Similarly stage 2 seems to be clearly prior to stage 5 on both logical and psychosociological grounds.

The logical problem is of course a difficult one. One would think that the considerations of logical order would be the same for relating, say, stage 1a and stage 1b as for relating stages 1 and 4 or stages 2 and 5. But the logical considerations in relating stage 4 and stage 5 would involve a jump from one social dimension to another, from a morality based on an authority dimension to a morality based on the expectations and the influence of others who might be peers. There seem to be both logical and psychosociological reasons for a more differentiated way of relating these stages to one another than Kohlberg's sequence of stages or levels would imply.

CRITTENDEN

I still think that philosophers should be primarily concerned with what counts as a sound moral argument or what are good moral reasons – just as they are with other kinds of arguments. Any stage that a child or adult human being might be at, with respect to skills in making valid arguments, is irrelevant to the question of validity and invalidity itself. If we know that people typically go through a number of stages distinguished by the kinds of reasons given for making decisions on what ought to be done and if we agree on what constitutes moral reasons, we might then say that it is logically inconsistent for someone both to be at stage 2 and seriously to give sound moral reasons. Or we might say, as Gauthier has just said, that in fact anyone giving stage-4 reasons is not giving moral reasons. But I do not think that philosophers as such are concerned with the genesis of moral reasons. And I do not think they can support the claim that the order of Kohlberg's stages is logically demanded by the nature of moral concepts.

BAIER

If your point is about the meaning of the term "moral," I think it is well-taken. It is only when we get to the higher stage that we describe it as a higher type of moral reasoning. But if we are generous about this type of thing, let us forget about whether the word "moral" properly applies to various stages and just say that these involve types of practical reasoning and that there is a hierarchy among them in the sense that the higher you get on the scale the clearer you are about the advantages of employing this higher type of reasoning in certain contexts.

CRITTENDEN

But then is it necessarily a logical hierarchy apart from being the kind of development that psychologists in fact have found?

OLIVER

I think that there is one very important point that has not been pursued. It is the fact that the higher stages as Kohlberg has discovered them are more persuasive even for someone who is one or two stages below. Such a person feels that somehow the reasons of the highest stage are better than the ones that he can give. This is not a logical matter; it is psychological.

NARVESON

I do not see how you can say that persuasiveness is purely a psychological matter because, after all, when a person is persuaded of something, what he is persuaded of is that the argument in question is better. He has to have a notion of reasoning in order to be able to be pursuaded about anything by any kind of argument whatever. To say that it is just a kind of incidental psychological fact that X is more persuasive than Y strikes me as being most implausible.

ARONFREED

You are claiming that someone may not be persuaded unless there is essentially an appeal to reason. But I might persuade a child merely by virtue of the fact that, in talking about the moral dilemma in one particular way, I am using words which the child picks up as a signal. That is, I might use "big" words: obviously words which he does not quite understand but which he feels are the ones to use when answering in that situation. It depends on what you mean by persuasion.

NARVESON

But notice that the context in which this point was raised was that of argumentation; that is, Oliver was talking about arguments between people at different stages. The analysis of persuasion as a straightforward S-R simply cannot apply.

OLIVER

Let me show what I wanted to say by an example. Suppose you say to a person, "Was the violence at Lexington and Concord a good thing?" And the person says, "Yes." Then you say, "Why?" And he says, "Because they were fighting for liberty." Then you ask, "Were the riots in Newark a good thing?" He replies, "No, they were just terrible." And you say, "Well, weren't they fighting for liberty?" At this point some people would say, "That's different" and they will go on and draw a distinction to qualify; others will say that it is different, but they will be very upset because they somehow know that the analogy is useful and persuasive, that it shows the need for more moral argumentation but they cannot handle it.

SCRIVEN

I am bothered about the objections that the philosophers are raising. I do not know why we are getting so tied up about the fact that people do respond in this sequence to these types of argument. As I understand some of the criticism, it is essentially of the form that it is impossible that they should, but they do. The objective fact is that you can get high interjudge reliability in assessing the level at which your particular response should be judged. Therefore, the stages are objective. They are not intrinsically confused; they are intrinsically complex. The sequence of development is, as Oliver has just brought out, logical in one very important sense. It is also logical in the sense that it does represent in many respects an increasing differentiation of complex matters – not that this springs *a priori* from the brow, but because in the course of interacting with their social environment people are forced into making further distinctions. Now the claim that this represents a hierarchy that philosophers should regard as an improvement in the moral level of these children seems to me one that philosophers perhaps have the most right to object to. But I do not think that it is one that has so far been extremely well-sustained. Gauthier's point was a very good one. However, it is much less important that philosophers agree that stages 4 and 2 should be in that order with respect to some abstract notion of superiority, morally speaking, than that this be a sequence of persuasiveness, a sequence in which the end point is admitted to be much higher than the first point, and that by and large it represents a person's discriminations and hence has some inherent plausibility. Anyway, Kohlberg would have to stick with the same sequence for all the other reasons, and it would still be a very useful sequence since it tells us something about the way things do go for all children with respect to persuasion and, therefore, moral education, which is what this is all about.

KOHLBERG

But are you really saying that the philosophical objection is altogether irrelevant? Suppose the philosopher were to argue with me that in some moral sense stage 3 is better than stage 4. Do you mean that he is not raising anything that would need to be of concern to a moral educator?

SCRIVEN

No, it would depend entirely on other facts such as whether half the children in the United States are getting stabilized in stage 4, whereas if their education was a little different they would stabilize at stage 3. Then the philosopher's argument will become very important, but only then. I mean it is not important provided people peak out at stage 5 or 6.

KOHLBERG

Yes, but in fact most people in the society peak out at stages 3 and 4.

SCRIVEN

Then it depends entirely on the question of how irreversible that situation is. Let us argue about the question of whether moral education at the moment gets people to as high a stage as it could. That is an important question. If you say it only gets them to stage 3, but that it would be better if only it got them to stage 4, then a philospher who proves that 3 is better than 4 has made a very good point about your conclusions. But that is a special point and it is not relevant to the general question of the validity of the thesis.

LOUBSER

May I just ask whether the empirical evidence is unequivocal about the relative position of stages 3 and 4.

KOHLBERG

Yes. I would have to say that being a good liberal humanitarian with some remaining "good boyishness" in me, I liked stage-3 children better than stage-4 when I first met them. In fact I put stages 4 and 1 together as Piaget did, in what he called the heteronomous or authoritarian orientation. But although things are a little trickier with stages 5 and 6, I do think that the kind of sequence we have here, the change from stage 3 to 4, is pretty typical. Stage 3 is a very difficult one to maintain. It is not too plausible to have a morality based just on the notion of being nice to people – you get into terrible binds in deciding who to be nice to.

GAUTHIER

Well, it seems to me that one of the problems that is to be faced in moral education is the arrest of people at your stage 4, which, as I have argued earlier, philosophers quite rightly leave out of their account of morality. Perhaps some of the problems that are emerging in our society have to do with the rejection of stage 4. It is just possible that the natural order of development is not the most desirable here and one should, in one's moral education, try to get people around stage 4. In other words, one should try to upset the natural order and in educating children get them directly from the earliest stages to stage 5 so that they by-pass stage 4.

KOHLBERG

If you could persuade a child of 12 at stage 2 to take a stage 5 or 6 point of view I suppose there would be much to be said for it.

SCRIVEN

Gauthier was just saying that it would be important to try it. But you have tried giving children arguments two stages too high and they cannot take them. It does not affect them. If arguments one stage higher will move them and arguments two stages higher will not that is a pretty thorough experiment.

MELDEN

Do you mean that if you give stage-5 reasons to children at stage-2 they understand the argument but are not persuaded or do they not quite get the hang of the argument?

PASKAL

There is a problem in this for me also. If the findings of studies by Turiel, Rcst, and others are accepted as supporting the notion that children's level of morality can be best modified by presenting them with the next expected stage in their moral development, why should this happen? Why should showing a child how to think about something cause him to think that way? If a stage-3 child is exposed to arguments representing each of stage-4 and stage-5 judgments it is predicted by Kohlberg, Turiel, et al. that the child will incorporate the stage-4 level reasoning into his own judgmental behaviour. Why? To say that this happens because stage 4 rather than stage 5 is the next highest level of functioning is begging the question. How does the child know that – unless there is programmed within him some apparatus for recognizing what the next highest level looks like?

It seems to me that it is almost impossible to account for a child's accommodation to the next stage without some notion of readiness for a specific experience; some idea of an inborn course of development. That is, given that the child has had the opportunity to organize his experience at some level, he becomes ready, *at some point,* to perceive or conceive the next higher level of cognitive organization. The order of specific readiness defines the seemingly inevitable course of development. The specific readiness for the next level is constituted by some kind of recognitory apparatus. The problem for reaserch is to discover the principles which define what makes a cue distinctive at each developmental level. That is, what is the rule for choosing examples which produce "optimum disequilibrium"?

To induce development we need to know when the child is ready to *attend* to cues which will lead to the next level of structural development. Whether an individual is ready to change or not – that is, to attend to the cues which can potentially induce structural change – depends on whether his structural organization is at the point at which the recognitory apparatus for the next level of functioning has been activated. And the point at which "the gate is sprung open" is undoubtedly a matter of individual differences. For example, there are undoubtedly individual differences among children in the number of experiences they need to have with conservation of mass before this becomes a stable structure and the child is then ready for the next step. And the characteristics of the stability of structural organization may well be significantly different among children, given different levels of intellectual functioning. I would suggest that it is the set of variables that influences this development that investigators have only just begun to explore (e.g., Brim, Kohlberg, and White 1967). They have to do with individual differences in psychological processes through which the child structures events in this world. These include both affective/motivational features and memory/attention features. It is differences among subjects, with respect to these variables and how they affect the organization of cognitive structures, that would be expected to account for whether subjects change when exposed to higher levels of cognitive functioning.

CHAPTER 13

The cognitive and the affective in moral action

COGNITION AND THE CHANGING OF BEHAVIOUR: THE RECOGNITION OF PUNISHMENT IN MORAL CONTEXT

ARONFREED

What impresses me is that the overwhelming evidence from common observation, as well as a certain amount of formal work that psychologists have done over the years, indicates that children's behaviour is very insensitive to what we have been talking about as moral education in this conference. I wonder, for example, whether the kind of moral education that has been suggested here would result in any modification of their behaviour, or whether it would simply result in their being able to hold conversations in moral philosophy. Of course you may have no interest in modifying their behaviour. But if you do, I would entertain the most serious reservations about teaching in the sense that it has been talked about here. To take just one example: Hartshorne and May showed years ago, in a rather trivial way, that Sunday-school education and many other contacts with the institutional teaching of norms had no effect upon children's behaviour in honesty situations.

Recently, I returned from a conference in which someone reported the following study. It was a study of five hundred children in which the idea was to find out what would influence the children to give something valuable that they had won, which now belonged to them, to somebody else. What the experimenters essentially did was to pit exhortations using moral principles against merely providing the opportunity for the child to see someone else give first. They arranged the design in such a way as to cross all of the possible variations of having this so-called modelling effect together with and without exhortation. It turned out that all of the exhortations in all of the variations had no effect whatsoever upon the behaviour of these third- and fourth-grade children. But merely seeing someone else give did facilitate their own behaviour of giving. It did not matter, in this case, what the source of exhortation said. Even if he told the children to be greedy and keep everything for themselves, the children did nevertheless give if he himself set an example of giving. I do not know what to make of these rather obvious findings in any detailed way, but I think that they should be taken into account.

SCRIVEN

What you are saying shows that you cannot teach physics with singing commercials; and morality is intellectually, as I conceive it, probably the most difficult subject in the curriculum. All the studies that have been done consist in discovering the remarkable fact that you cannot teach morality in a trivial way. The Hartshorne and May study shows you that the boy-scout program for teaching morality is wasted and that Sunday school is wasted. Certainly, on the intellectual level that we have been talking about here it is obvious that they would be; they are completely non-intellectual, completely non-rational, they are simply exhortatory and you need not expect them to have much effect. You could say that they *might* have such an effect and it is interesting to discover that they did not. But you cannot *expect* anything to have much effect that does not undertake a very serious, long-term examination of the immensely difficult connection between the precepts and the practice, which is the first step that we have been talking about.

Let me defend what the philosophers are up to in these terms: there is not any hope at all that any program of moral education, given that it is a pretty complicated business, is going to be worth much unless you can get some sort of rationale for the structure of morality clear in the minds of the people who are doing the moral educating. There is not some magic way in which you can divorce the understanding of what morality is from teaching about it. You cannot get teachers who have no conception of the principles of physics, although they have been through a school of education where they got a science teaching credential, to teach the PSSC program. There is no reason to expect that morality is somehow going to be much easier. On the contrary, it is going to be much harder. You are up against the emotional prejudices, the tendency to rationalize, the conflicting pluralistic background of the child in the home, all of which work against you; whereas in physics you get a *tabula rasa* to work with. So it is going to be one of the toughest of all the educational undertakings, and it is never going to work unless you can get some idea about how the structure of morality operates or what it is like intellectually. Without getting into the academic fallacy of thinking you must have a sort of abstract theory of morality all tidied up before you can get anybody to teach the first steps of it, I do think we should set our sights very high in the intellectual dimension before we can expect any pay-off from the practical side.

ARONFREED

The problem is whether anyone with a morality that is very well developed can teach moral education without taking into account these behavioural components that we have been talking about. We have talked essentially of making the teaching device more sophisticated, in much the same way that somebody would say that the teaching of mathematics has been poor and we can work out better programs such as the SRA program, and so on. This has turned out to have a certain grain of truth in it. But while I agree that it is very difficult to teach moral education without some very clear concept in the mind of the teacher, the problem is whether you can teach it to the child even if the concept is very clear. For example, you have said that we have to overcome the emotional prejudices in early experiences which are given to the child in the home. I would argue, quite to the contrary, that you will never be able to teach moral education unless you build on these emotions – that strong affective dispositions are precisely what you need to engage in the teaching of moral education. Without them you will never get anywhere.

HUNT

In reference to experiments cited in Aronfreed's paper, if we think of these three features – the behaviour, the person, the environment – we can consider the degree to which the paradigms represent something that might take place in the real-life situation. Frequently, behaviour in experiments of this sort involves choice situations where the youngster is presented with few possibilities. It seems to me worth noting here that these constraints on the child rule out many possibilities which exist in the real-life situation. That is, in the real-life situation we can integrate the responses, we can make other responses, we can look at them in new ways, we can reorganize them, we can construct other alternatives.

If we consider the environment, we can ask how representative it is or, to use Egon Brunswik's phrase, what "ecological validity" it has. What is the child's concern with the strange adult who is putting his hand in front of a toy saying it is for the older children? What does this have to do with situations of socialization when he is dealing with his parents? I think we need to raise issues of this sort in terms of how a child views the circumstances. I would argue, for example, that one of the key issues here is the importance of making the observations under non-surveillance conditions, that is, with the experimenter leaving the room. It is very difficult to assume that we have an environmental condition which is private in any sense of the word as long as the child is in the school building. I would suggest that it is extremely difficult in terms of the environmental impingement on him to assume that we are dealing with anything like a private internalized circumstance when the child is still confronted by these kinds of constraints. I want to say also that I think there has been a good deal more care in this set of experiments than many psychological experimenters have exercised in this regard. It is very difficult to deal with the issue; it may be that it is impossible to study experimentally what people do in private.

The third aspect of the situation, the qualities of the person, seems to me to be important. Aronfreed takes the position in his paper that we can view development, if you will, in terms of going from an external to an internal orientation. Well, if this is the case, it should follow, I suspect, that the children who are seen in the experimental circumstances will vary in terms of their position on this particular dimension and their responses might be seen in this light. We need to think about the effect of certain experimental conditions in relation to the youngster we are working with. We know, for example, when there are sensory limitations – if we are dealing with the blind child or deaf child – that he is differentially receptive. I think the same thing applies to different kinds of children. These then are some of the issues that seem to me to be important in the generalization of a paradigm, when we go from the laboratory to the real-life world in the three dimensions.

The issue of awareness is an important one for the argument here. Again it is very difficult, I think, to get an accurate estimation of awareness from a youngster, in terms of the situation. Is he comfortable in telling the experimenter about it? Are there other ways of getting at awareness where we do not have to use verbalization? Can we use indices of awareness, which will indicate how the child would behave in other circumstances? I felt that the issue of the non-cognitive, the non-aware mediation, perhaps needed to be considered a little more critically here.

Aronfreed comments about the lack of correlation between children's moral values, their verbalizations, and their behaviour. It seems to me that one of the reasons that we have these low correlations, which are sufficiently voluminous now that we can accept them, is that they do not take account of the conditions under which the behaviour occurred. If we take account of the conditions under which the child is behaving in process terms, I think that we can get a better idea of some of these relationships. Is he behaving under a surveillance condition? Is he behaving under conditions where there is a normative influence? Is he behaving with his peers? Is he behaving where there is no one around?

CRITTENDEN

Could I raise a question about the experiments you [Aronfreed] refer to in the early part of your paper? I did not have a chance to read the detailed report to which you refer. As I understand it, however, children were discouraged in some cases from choosing a more attractive doll in preference to a less attractive one by the use of punishment expressions or the withholding of candy or other rewards of this kind, if they went ahead and did choose the more attractive toy. Now one problem I have here is this: if the language that was used by the experimenter really expressed or even contextually expressed moral disapproval, the experimenter would be misleading the children, because clearly this is not a situation of moral choice, and if he did not use language that even contextually could be taken by the children as being moral punishment, then I do not see how you can with much reliability extrapolate from that sort of situation to one which does involve moral choice-making.

ARONFREED

The best answer that I can give is to suggest that you read the report. The fact of the matter is that in the paradigms, the basic procedures are such that the experimental agent of socialization does not indicate any sort of cognitive structure for the child – either about why the child is being punished or about what the contingencies of punishment are. So not only is there not moral disapproval, but there is no evaluation of the child's behaviour in the ordinary sense; there is merely punishment. In other paradigms, there is evaluation of the child's behaviour with respect to certain dimensions of value which do not appear to me to be moral in character. I do not suggest anywhere in the paper that these are moral choices the child is making; moral choices are choices which are informed by moral judgment. One of the problems of this conference, I take it, is the question of what moral judgment is. But the experiments are addressed to the problem of how you can get internalized control over behaviour to begin with, as a base line from which to begin talking about what sorts of cognitive structures can then be engaged in this control. And I think it is true that moral cognitive structures can be engaged for the control of behaviour. The closest thing to it, I would say, in any of the experimental paradigms that I described here is a particular set where we evaluate a child's behaviour in terms of his intentions. This would make it clear that we are punishing him for his intentions. That is the only one where a component that some people have thought is relevant to moral judgment is engaged in the experiments.

CRITTENDEN

However, do you not think the child brings to an experimental situation a whole range of associations in the use of particular words, to the facial expression of the experimenter when he is issuing punishment statements, and so on.

ARONFREED

I am sure he does. That is why we do experiments. That is to say, that is why we distribute children randomly across conditions and create artificial paradigms which treat them all as equal subjects.

CRITTENDEN

I am aware that this is done, but it does not meet the difficulty I have.

MELDEN

Perhaps the question being raised by Crittenden is related to this: is the child hurt or is he punished? A deprivation is not punishment; it could be imposed sadistically or irrationally. It seems to me that if the child recognizes it as punishment, there is a kind of moral gloss which is being used here.

ARONFREED

I am not really sure what question you are asking. You might be asking about the nature of punishment, the concept of punishment.

MELDEN

I think punishment is bound up with the notion of guilt and this suggests the question raised by Crittenden. The account of the experimental situation might go wrong.

SULLIVAN

Although you [Aronfreed] do not inject evaluation into the situations, does not the subject do this? If I walked over and hit you now without saying anything, you could do a lot of inferring, for example, about how I value your person or what you are saying. You can expect even children to be doing this, too. Sometimes they ask why they are being punished.

ARONFREED

We do inject evaluation into some paradigms. In other paradigms – the initial ones – the experimenter does not evaluate the child's behaviour overtly. Does the child possibly use evaluative dispositions that he already has to interpret what is being done to him? Of course he does. The experiments are not based on the notion that children are non-cognitive creatures merely because they are not being given a verbal explanation about their behaviour in certain paradigms.

KOHLBERG

I do not know whether Melden's question is raised in a psychological sense. If so, it is very important from the point of view of the psychologists. If one child is beaten up by another in a fight this is not "punishment." That is, there is no context in which he has been doing something bad, and the beating has a quite different effect on him than if it had been given by his father or somebody like that. If little Johnny minds his baby sister and is spanked by his mother when she returns, he thinks he has been bad. If he ill-treats his baby sister, and receives a kiss and some candy when his mother returns, he thinks he has been a good boy. There is a gradual differentiation with age between the goodness of the act and the actual receipt of punishment or reward. In many cases there must be some evaluative context of the child's being good or bad if he gets a punishment.

ARONFREED

He may well bring in evaluative thought. However, it is a problem if one wants to demonstrate that the evaluative apparatus which he brings with him has anything to do with the experimental effects which I described. That is, the effects have to do with the differences among the conditions, and the differences among conditions have to do with the timing of punishment, and the timing of punishment has to do with certain presuppositions about Pavlovian conditioning mechanisms. In that limited sense, certain of the paradigms do confirm predictions which need not take evaluative capacities into account.

The child's cognitive structures may also engage affective control of behaviour. It does not have to be merely a question of conditioned behavioural control without the mediation of cognitive structures. The child's representation of what is happening, including the most sophisticated kind of evaluative representation, may also control his behaviour. But the interesting and inescapable fact is that some of these timing effects for internalized control of behaviour may be obtained with dogs. That is a sobering thought from the point of view of the large theoretical perspective that needs to be dealt with in accounting for how a child, given a certain amount of social experience, controls his behaviour in the absence of surveillance. It is also true, as I point out in the paper, that once you begin to give the child a cognitive structure, and to vary the timing of punishment in relation to that cognitive structure, independent of the timing with respect to the act itself, you can get effective control over behaviour, which actually is more powerful than that which you can get on the basis of pure conditioning (to use the term here for communicative purposes).

KOHLBERG

The question is what, if anything, your experiments have to do with moral behaviour in older children or adults, regardless of what they have to do with dogs. Is the actual control of children's behaviour in complex moral situations really a function of the kind of mechanism you talk about? It is not clear whether you are saying that they are or they are not. The fact that you can, in certain circumstances, condition a response does not in any way indicate that this is the way control is exerted in real life or in development. There are a lot of reasons to think that it is not. That is, moral conduct in real life does not involve repetitive situations and punishment where the same behaviour is repeatedly punished. If you look at what adults and even children do in the way of moral control, there is very little of this regular repetition of punishment in their history that you can trace as causing that kind of control.

ARONFREED

Is that a statement of hope or a statement of fact?

KOHLBERG

I think it is in one sense a statement of ignorance. I just cannot find many analogies, in the first place, of repetitive punishment as really producing differential responses in a moral situation. For instance, take cheating on tests at school or elsewhere. In addition to the moral judgment factors which are really rather powerful predictors of whether children will cheat or not (that is, if there is maturity in moral judgment and so on), there are these ego-control factors which are also rather powerful predictors of whether children will cheat or not. These ego-control factors (represented by things like attention) differentiate children independently of moral level or moral judgment and are differentially predictive of behaviour; in other words, good old-fashioned will in a certain sense. There is some evidence for a kind of will factor which leads people to differentially follow the moral judgments that they themselves make in the situation. Now it seems implausible to trace differences in that relatively general control factor to any kind of conditioned history. While your studies show rather powerful control of behaviour by punishment, the naturalistic studies of moral behaviour – relating to child-rearing practices and so on – show very little relationship between punishment histories and children's behaviour. So the long range, or more global, effects in natural situations are not necessarily something that you can extrapolate from your experimental view.

BECK

It seems to me that the only objections that were raised to Aronfreed's experiments were assuming the theory with which Aronfreed disagrees, namely, that the cognitive structure which children impose upon the task and the experiment is a significant factor. I think the theory lying behind the experiments is that it is not nearly as significant a factor as has been thought. What we need to investigate is just what types of behaviour can be stamped in or stamped out using techniques of this kind. And while I agree that there must be some categorization of these acts, because certainly there is not repetitive punishment of exactly the same act but of the type of act, need it be a moral categorization?

EDEL

It does not necessarily have to be a moral categorization in terms of the picture given by Aronfreed's paper. But let me ask this question specifically: in the kind of problems that come before a nursery-school teacher, are there any that would fit under this paradigm of implanting and so on, any kinds of problems that could really be treated in this way? Or are you dealing here with elementary mechanisms of an isolated sort that have no lesson for this?

ARONFREED

What do you mean by the term "isolated"? From what are they isolated?

EDEL

Let me put it in terms of the question I raised. Take the case of the nursery-school teacher and the kind of problems she meets – whether it is children fighting over paints or something of that sort or whether it is one child hitting another just in a random way or not sitting still and so on. What would be the application of this claim assuming that one wants to question it: that internalized control of conduct does not presuppose operations of conscience, cognitive elements, and so on? Would you have any recommendations along these lines as to how to implant certain kinds of attitudes?

ARONFREED

No, I would not have any recommendations, in the sense that I do not particularly care to make recommendations to people about how to rear their children. That is not the aim of the research. But if you are asking me whether there is anything that goes on between a nursery-school teacher and her children to which these paradigms apply, I think the answer is, in a sense, obvious. I would say that her interaction with the children is in many respects essentially these paradigms, regardless of whether she is confronted with problems or not.

Let me add that questions about whether this is really punishment, for example, come down to the question of what you mean by punishment. Now, strictly speaking, many of the effects of these paradigms can be produced if we simply think of the child's behaviour as being sensitive to what we might call aversive outcomes of any sort. Now there are some aversive outcomes that you might want to call punishment. This is a question of definition. I myself prefer to use the term punishment for an aversive outcome where the child perceives that the outcome is intended to suppress or modify his behaviour in some way. It is punishment if he perceives it to be contingent on, and intentionally directed towards the modification of, his own behaviour. I think it would be interesting to make that distinction and to use the term punishment in that way. It is not to say that you must have punishment in that sense in order to produce the effects which are produced in some of these paradigms. In some cases, you do not need anything that even corresponds to what we would ordinarily call punishment in order to produce behavioural effects like those described here. For example, you can have a withdrawal of expected rewards and produce similar effects.

KOHLBERG

People in different ways bring up the issue of what the relevance of this kind of experiment is to moral education. I think I would like to put it from this point of view. We all know that the situational management of behaviour by teachers in the classroom depends on reinforcement processes to a considerable extent, rewards primarily. Now this is classroom management in some sense rather than moral education. It is not intended to have long-range effects on the child's moral character every time the teacher says, "That's good" or something of this kind to the child. The teacher mostly is not concerned about what the children do behind her back. She is concerned about controlling their behaviour in the classroom and she is not really very worried about whether a child would or would not do whatever it was the teacher wanted him to do at the moment, were he all alone or in some other situation. In your paradigms you are very much concerned with what the child will do when the adult's back is turned or when he is alone. In part that concern seems to come from the fact that all our notions of morality and conscience are based on this internalization notion, what the person does without external rewards and constraints. But it is not clear to me really how your findings, or the kind of experiments you do, bear on moral education in any different way than the standard Skinnerian type of study in which you show that if the teacher says, "That's good," it will increase the rate of verbal response of the child or something like that.

ARONFREED

These paradigms are not Skinnerian. The experiments are not based on the supposition that the internalized control of behaviour is entirely a function of conditioning. The acquisition of values is not, in my opinion, a problem of conditioning. It is an entirely different level of phenomenon. The question of how cognitive structures are acquired by the child, how evaluative operations are acquired by the child, are not problems of conditioning.

KOHLBERG

I am really asking whether you want to make a distinction, from the point of view of the kind of acquisition techniques that are involved, between classroom-management procedures as these terms are applied to an educational context, and moral internalization or moral education.

ARONFREED

Well, I would not suppose that punishing a child at different temporal intervals in relation to an act would give him any moral values, if that is what you are asking me about. If you are asking me about how this applies to moral education, it is difficult for me to answer because I do not know yet what you mean by moral education. If you are talking about something that would affect the behaviour of the child, then I would suggest that these paradigms are relevant to moral education. I do not know whether they have immediately translatable practical consequences, but I think that they are the outline, as it were, of the theory of how to control the child's behaviour with internal monitors.

SCRIVEN

It seems to me that the two of you are to some extent trading blows that do not quite land. Aronfreed says that since the teacher negatively reinforces the children and his is a theory of negative reinforcement of certain sub-areas of behaviour, it is obviously relevant. Kohlberg replies that the point is not that something as general as that is relevant to moral education but rather that it has to be something much more like what goes on in circumstances that we normally take to be moral education. I do not think this objection is met by saying that there are some features of these circumstances that are matched in Aronfreed's case. Moreover I do not think that Aronfreed thinks so either, and there are two points which, I believe, show this. First of all there is his statement that punishment is not just negative reinforcement as the Skinnerian understands it. It surely has to be something more complicated, in particular, something perceived by the recipient as designed to extinguish the behaviour. That clearly makes it different from punishment of rats and so on in the traditional way in which the word punishment has been used. But that is still only a necessary condition; punishment in the morally relevant sense requires more than that. It requires also that the recipient be able to distinguish between the case in which it is clear that the authority figure is trying to extinguish this behaviour and the case in which the authority figure has some very special kind of reason for wanting to extinguish it. The reason may not be at all clear, but at least it is not that the authority figures do not like this behaviour as such. The process of development is partly the process of the child's learning to distinguish between the intentional extinguishing procedures in general, and the moral case, of getting to the point where he is able to say, "Sure, Mommy punished this kid but maybe he wasn't in the wrong. Maybe she shouldn't have punished him." The second point is that Aronfreed is obviously interested to some extent in behaviour which will continue to manifest itself in the absence of the authority figure. In these respects I think he is moving nearer to the case of moral education.

In spite of his perfectly legitimate willingness or desire not to insist that he is doing research on how to manage classrooms or how to bring up children, it seems to me he could perhaps meet some of the questions that have been raised by a more serious attempt to think of cases in ordinary childhood development which really matched this. Now Kohlberg tends to prove his point that Aronfreed's work is irrelevant by saying, "Look, in the case of cheating how often do you repetitively punish children? You don't." But that is not the only sort of case, and he cannot prove his general negative statement by giving one example. Let us look at a few other cases. In the household situation it seems to me the child is repetitively punished for transgressions that he continues to make in a number of ways, for example, food mismanagement and interaction with other siblings. I would like to hear Aronfreed's view on whether there are not such cases, which match rather closely his own, and whether in those cases he wants to recommend particular kinds of procedures as opposed to others.

ARONFREED

I think I subscribe to most of what you said, particularly about the perception of punishment. It is clear that without having any moral notions, the child may perceive that he is being punished contingent upon his behaviour, with the external intention of suppression of the behaviour. The moral notions come from adding something beyond the perception of intention in the aversive outcome. There has to be some sort of evaluative structure that we are willing to treat as moral and that the child perceives as having moral considerations in it. I would continue to insist, however, that the control of these structures over behaviour is always fundamentally grounded on affective mechanisms. There are obviously great discrepancies between what children know and how they behave, and this of course raises the problem of what the relationship is between cognition and behaviour. I have been at some pains to stress the affective nature of the relationship. There must be affective binding of some kind.

In response to your other point: clearly aggression, dependency on parents, distribution and possession of material goods are issues of socialization in the home about which various kinds of evaluative structures, including moral structures, are built up. There are each day, contrary to what Kohlberg has suggested, a massive number of opportunities for the child to experience aversive outcomes of all kinds. Some are very subtle; they do not necessarily involve punishment in the ordinary sense. They may be a frown, a warning signal, a withdrawal of affection, a withdrawal of some other anticipated reward. These things go on every day, and of course the point is that they are powerful in terms of behaviour even though they are not necessarily moral.

SULLIVAN

In relation to the distinction that Baier makes in his paper between social training and morality, I wonder if he would comment on how he sees this type of research. Is it veering more towards social training?

BAIER

One thing I alluded to that bears on this is that even with the cognitive element in punishment that Aronfreed admits, it is not yet the concept of punishment relevant to morality. That is, one has to recognize the social pressure, not merely as pressure designed to control behaviour (to extinguish certain forms of behaviour, encourage others), but as imposed for other reasons. I think one can now play around with the degree of sophistication that one wants to build into the concept of punishment. If one takes the minimal requirement, I think as Scriven puts it, it must at least be recognized as being more than just someone wanting to push us around so as to achieve different forms of behaviour by us. Or we can take it all the way up to recognizing the legitimacy of the requirement on us, of the form of conduct for whose neglect the punishment, this kind of undesired result, is imposed upon us. That is then a matter of definition, and I think that if one gives a full account of morality that treats punishment as an element in morality, it would involve recognition of the legitimacy or justifiability of the imposition of that form of social pressure. This would make one of the differences between socialization and acquiring a morality, or being taught a morality.

AFFECTIVE MECHANISMS AND THE CONTROL OF BEHAVIOUR

NARVESON

I have two related questions. In replying to one of the comments, you [Aronfreed] said that the observations you made showed that controlled behaviour is fundamentally grounded in affective mechanisms. One of the questions I wanted to ask is what exactly that is supposed to mean. I can think of various meanings it might have in which it would seem to me to be false or a non-statement or a tautology.

The second question refers to what you say in your paper, following up the point that punishment without cognitive structure can produce internalized control of behaviour: "These commonplace observations remind us that human beings are animals, that animals are highly conditionable, and that morality has very little force in vast repertoires of internalized control over social conduct."* This might mean that morality is the kind of thing that does not have much force by, as it were, its inherent nature, that it is inferior in force to lots of other behavioural controls, or it might mean simply that, in general, human beings – at least small ones – do not very often control their behaviour by reference to moral mechanisms in particular. In the first interpretation it will be an extremely important statement I think for our purpose, but in the second it simply means that people, and especially small children, do not very often react specifically in response to moral structures. It would perhaps say something about what kind of goals a program of moral education might have, namely, to see to it that people more often respond to moral controls.

ARONFREED

Let me respond to the second question first. I am not sure what the conflict between the statements is. I did mean essentially that moral decision-making is not engaged in vast repertoires of internalized control. I did not mean it to apply to little children particularly, but in fact to bigger children as well – even adults. On the other question, I have learned to be very cautious about responding to the "what does that exactly mean" type of questions. I am using the term "affective" as I think most psychologists would tend to use it. You said that you could think of many meanings that it might possibly have. Perhaps you could list some of these and I could tell you which one applies.

NARVESON

Yes. The word "affect" might be understood to have what I suppose philosophers would call a mentalistic sense in which it referred to a sort of internal experience. For example, I sometimes feel pretty awful about something I've done and I suppose you might represent that as a sort of "affect." But it is very rare that I rule my behaviour by reference to specific waves of feeling either in anticipation or otherwise. On the other hand, "affect" could mean just what you are experiencing when you control your behaviour.

SULLIVAN

Let me suggest what I think Aronfreed has in mind. In this situation I think he is asking about what brings people to take a moral point of view, to apply their moral judgments in action.

* See above, p. 186.

ARONFREED

That is the reason for wanting to talk about affective mechanisms. In response to Narveson's question about what exactly do we mean, let me be quick to admit that it is rather difficult to specify what the properties of affective states are, primarily because psychologists do not know anything about emotion or affectivity. They use it mainly as a construct handy for accounting for certain kinds of experimental effects, such as the ones I have reported in this paper. But I am referring, as Narveson has apparently suspected, to positive or aversive experience. As for the distinction Narveson tries to make between the two meanings of affect, in both cases he is talking about experience.

NARVESON

Yes, but there is the difficulty that if something like the second interpretation is true it may well turn out to be the case that the statement is a tautology. A reason why some people would say that behavioural control is fundamentally grounded in affective mechanisms would be to deny that it is grounded in some other kind of mechanisms, for example, rational or cognitive ones. But the point I want to make here is this: if the statement that the behaviour is fundamentally controlled by affective mechanisms is meant as just a kind of tautology, then the question remains as to why the person feels that way under those circumstances. The answer may be that it is because he has figured out that it is wrong. I may feel awful after I've done something which I perceive to be wrong, because I have concluded on the basis of various observations and premises and general theories that this was the wrong thing to do. My feeling may well be what you called "affective." But this would prove nothing whatever, I would think, about the fundamental mechanisms of behaviour in another sense. It may very well be that the fundamental mechanisms of behaviour, that is, whatever it is that forces a fully mature being to feel in certain ways, are his cognitive structures. This would be entirely consistent with that statement you made about affective mechanisms. So I was not entirely sure what you meant when you said it or how it was supposed to have related to our general program here, which is to talk about moral education. As I see it, moral education would be concerned primarily with what, I suppose, you would call cognitive structures. Of course this is said with the understanding that the cognitive structures in question are for the purpose of conditioning behaviour, which very well might mean that they are not successful unless they produce some affect as well.

BECK

It seems to me that the model Aronfreed is trying to break away from has been very well put by Narveson: the model that when we come to a moral decision or a moral action we shift into a different realm, the rational or some other, in which there are different forces at work and different mechanisms. I think the model that Aronfreed is trying to suggest is one in which there are basic affective mechanisms that are not peculiarly moral, although there may be a distinctive selection of them in connection with moral behaviour. His broad definition of conscience suggests that if we try to concentrate on some particularly moral mechanisms of behaviour, such as Narveson's suggestion of rational mechanisms, we will not get anywhere because in fact even moral behaviour is based on pretty ordinary sorts of mechanisms without which we just will not get a behavioural change.

LOUBSER

I was wondering whether what Aronfreed has in mind depends somewhat on a distinction between the types of activity that are involved in conditioning. In other words, on the one hand, there is the unpleasantness of being sanctioned by one's father or being punished, as you put it, in terms of the child's interpretation, and on the other, the type of activity which it seems to me you have in mind when you talk about affective mechanisms that are involved in the acquisition of values as a part of the acquisition of conscience. Once you have an acquired internalized control mechanism that operates as what you call conscience, it seems to me more difficult to cope with the types of question that Narveson has posed here. In this case moral reasoning becomes very much a part of figuring out the affective consequences of certain actions, whereas when you do not have internalization, the affectivity is more a matter of the kind of conditioning practised.

SULLIVAN

There may be other mechanisms besides punishment and some of the paradigms that psychologists talk about. To operate on the categorical imperative, let us say, in any substantive way takes a quite lively imagination. It may involve a lot of cognitive skills in putting yourself in the situation of the other. While you are making your judgment, if it has any kind of real substantive value for you, it must mean something to you to know what this other person or group might be feeling. I think Gauthier and Oliver in their papers talk about using the imagination in moral problems. This might be another mechanism. Perhaps it is not so easy for psychologists to work with it.

NARVESON

I wonder if I could ask what a mechanism is in this context. Why do we call these things mechanisms?

SULLIVAN

An example of a mechanism would be conditions that make a person, let us say, move from simply judging how he ought to behave to behaving that way.

EDEL

It seems that one of the reasons why the distinction between the cognitive and the affective becomes such a serious question among the philosophers is that the emotive theory has made such a sharp separation between the two. In a way, Aronfreed has disarmed us by saying he does not know what the affective side is, that he has no clear psychological theory of it. Yet the philosophers do want to know from psychologists whether the affective side has to be taken as operating separately on rules of its own and merely tied by some sort of associative device or experience to cognitive elements or whether, as the Deweyans and the Sartrians and so on have maintained, there is a motivational structure in the very emotional reactions, and thus cognitive elements. The initial separation of the cognitive and the affective is itself the very question at issue. Thus we have this very strange situation in which it is the theory of emotions that helps to determine the kind of picture of morality that is given, yet when we look to you for the theory of emotions your answer sends us back to the issue that Narveson was raising.

GAUTHIER

A lot of this discussion has arisen from the example that you [Aronfreed] gave of the child who verbalizes about moral matters but does not act on his verbalization. Now, are you intending to suggest by this sort of example that moral verbalization has an essentially epiphenomenal character in respect to behaviour or simply that it is quite possible to verbalize in this way without being affected or without acting on one's verbalization, although it is equally quite possible that one would act on it?

ARONFREED

I doubt whether my memory storage mechansims can hold all of the questions that have been raised. Let me start with Narveson's comments.

I suppose that you are aware of the fact that I am not eager to subject the concept of "affective" to epistemological analysis at this point. The concept is used by many psychologists essentially as a construct in order to deal with what the relationship is between what you are doing, let us say, to the child and what he is giving you by way of output in behaviour. It is not entirely without properties. For example, when I speak of an aversive affective state, I mean that the experience is aversive to the child and he will do things in order to reduce it – that it is sometimes possible to arrange contingencies in such a way as to show that particular stimulus events have aversive values for him and that he will do things to get rid of them. So we want to give it certain properties even though it is very difficult to formulate them in any elegant way.

Let me go on and try to respond to your comment about the implication of all of this for moral education. You have asked whether, in my argument that affective mechanisms are fundamental, I am saying that behaviour is not rationally controlled in this domain. The answer to that question is, "yes." I am saying that behaviour is not rationally controlled. It is possible to have a reason, and to have the reason obtain some control over behaviour, but I suspect that in most instances the control is not based on reasoning *per se*. If a person reasons or has moral cognition, the control that can be exercised over behaviour, I would continue to insist, in the last analysis has to be affective. I do not pit affective against cognitive in the way that ethical theorists often have. What I suggest is that cognitive structures control behaviour by the affect that has become attached, coupled if you like, to the consequences of that reasoning, to the representations or operators which are arrived at as a conclusion of the reasoning.

On whether cognition enters at all into affect, whether affect has its own set of rules, the only thing I can say is that I have been using the term affective here in a very primitive way. In fact, the only distinction that I would make now would be between positive and aversive affective states. That is, I have talked about a generalized dimension of affectivity. If you want to get into the psychology of emotion and ask, for example, about the nature of the properties of a specific affect, such as a moral affect or jealousy or rage, I think that most psychologists tend to do experiments that appear to be predicated upon this assumption: that affective states, specific qualities of affective experience, are not defined merely by my use of the term "affective" as being positive or aversive. Affects are in cognitive housings, or have cognitive properties, which define the quality of an affective state. So, when I am speaking of "affective" here, I do not necessarily mean all of the specific qualities of affective state which do demand, in fact, some kind of cognitive housing in order to give affective experience its qualitative properties; that is, the experience which makes one emotion seem different from another.

KOHLBERG

Let me cite a research study which bears directly on Edel's question about the cognition-affect relationship. We have been circling around two questions. One is the question of the relation between moral cognition and the moral affect itself. And the second is the question of the interrelation of moral cognition and moral affect in moral choice. Psychologists for a long time worked from the psychoanalytic model in which moral choice was essentially the conflict between the lust of the flesh and feelings of guilt, and moral choice or moral decision was some kind of quantitative and miserable outcome of these conflicting affective forces. Guilt was always the central, say, moral emotion. In order to study guilt we took delinquent boys; we knew what naughty things they had done, and we could talk to them about them. We got a variety of ratings of how intensely they felt guilt, on a kind of common-sense level, about the things that they had done. This turned out to be highly correlated with their level of moral judgment which we usually think of as a cognitive phenomenon. In fact, the various ratings of guilt done from different points of view, different systems, did not relate any better to each other than they did to the moral principles that the person was using – his conception of justice or whatever you want to call it. So, empirically the cognitive structuring of his situation was in fact also the structuring of his affective reponses.

From my theory of cognition and affect I would say that if an adolescent, for example, thinks about doing a naughty act and he has vague anxiety in the pit of his stomach, and then says, "That's the voice of my conscience telling me how guilty I will feel if I do it," he has made a cognitive interpretation of that feeling in the pit of his stomach. Another kid says, "I feel butterflies in my stomach but I'm not going to be afraid of the cops. To heck with it." The feeling in the pit of his stomach is the same. It is the cognitive structuring of whatever was the conditioning anxiety that determines both how it is experienced and the way in which it enters into action. Affect cannot be qualitatively distinguished without reference to cognitive structures. Schachter and other experimental social psychologists have physiologically aroused different people in different social situations and have shown that the same arousal was experienced as anger in one situation and as something else in another by the people involved.

I think the question of the relation of cognition and affect in morality, in moral development at least, has to be kept separate from the other issue of whether rationality determines behaviour or moral choice or something like that. What is the difference between people acting in accordance with principles of physics which they know and their acting in accordance with moral principles? I would say that while people do not always act in terms of their knowledge of physical principles, on the whole they do. I would say the same thing is true of their action with regard to the moral principles that they accept, their moral cognitions. However, the difference between physical and moral principles is that the latter embody certain affective components in themselves. You cannot have a conception of justice without some sort of affective reaction being involved, whereas you can have such a conception of a physical principle.

BAIER

I have two questions in relation to one of your [Aronfreed's] responses. You said that cognitive structures, or whatever the exact phrase was, can affect an action but in fact do not. Now when you say that they can do that but they do not, what would the "do not" refer to: to the subjects you have studied, or would you say that this was generalized over the whole area of human conduct? And the second question: would you regard it as desirable to move from the state in which cognitive structures do not influence action to the state in which they do?

ARONFREED

Although I do not remember exactly what I said, it was not that cognitive structures may control behaviour yet do not, but rather that they *need* not. What I am trying to suggest, in fact, is that cognitive operations are part of the processes which may enter into the control of an act, but that their control is exercised through affective mechanisms no matter how complex the cognitive operations may turn out to be. You ask whether I meant the conclusion to apply in general to human conduct or only to my own subjects. The answer to that is clear: one does not do experiments merely to show that fourth- and fifth-grade students in certain schools have particular propensities. On the other question about the desirability of changing this situation, I can only say that what I am trying to do is to spell out nature. It is natural philosophy for me, not moral philosophy.

BAIER

I understand that. It seems to me that earlier you suggested by implication that there was something blocking the introduction of cognitivity into the moral field; that one could not introduce it or that it would not be effective, that one had to morally educate in some other way. Now I gather that you say that it can be done that way, though as a matter of fact very often it is not the case that these cognitive structures work effectively. If this point is correct, and if you do not object to the introduction of these cognitive structures, why do you object to the account of moral education that was presented earlier as being somehow starry-eyed and Utopian?

ARONFREED

Because it was not an account of moral education. We have yet to arrive at an account of how that occurs. Given that we can agree (an open question) on what values should be placed neatly in the child's head, the problem remains, of course, that one needs to have a theory of the acquisition of values, so that we know what the curriculum should look like mechanically. I have only been at pains to suggest that I doubt that the kinds of strategy I've heard – with the exception of what Gauthier suggested, because I think there may be something to that – are likely to produce modification of behaviour. I think that most of the strategies that I have heard here are likely to produce children who can hold more intelligent conversations with moral philosophers about the nature of moral action and so on. But as to whether that will have any influence on their behaviour, I am really quite uncertain. I think, perhaps, that if one wants to teach children moral values, or moral reasoning, or the application of precepts to particular situations, it might be good to put them in a situation of direct confrontation: interaction types of situations where people are behaving and somebody (the teacher) is talking a language of moral value in connection with observable kinds of behaviour in much the same way as it happens in the home. What happens in the acquisition of the child's values in the home is that much is said and much is done simultaneously, without anybody making conscious decisions about how to do it.

BAIER

Well, then, I suppose there is no disagreement here; I entirely agree with what you have been saying just now. I thought you had a stronger objection, an objection in principle based on some psychological theory of the impossibility of influencing behaviour by cognitive means.

PASKAL

There appears to be agreement that intention or cognitive structure must constitute part of the definition of what defines morality in human behaviour. That is, we need to know what are the individual's intentions, what are the arguments influencing his behaviour. Hunt's paper suggests that in order to educate or change an individual we should know what are his current cognitive and affective structures, and should engage in manipulation attempts within the context of the individual's particular mode of functioning. To put this program into effect we need to tie down several points, namely: (1) what is the goal of the attempted manipulation, that is, what constitutes moral behaviour? (2) what is a reliable measure of the individual's mode of functioning? and (3) what is the most effective method of achieving the desired changes?

The first question has been under discussion in the course of this conference. The question of the development of a reliable instrument to measure cognitive and affective structures has been tackled by several investigators. Kohlberg's and Hunt's scales are the two examples we might consider from Hunt's paper. Kohlberg's method of scaling involves scoring verbal behaviour in terms of the logical and value structures which he uses to describe that behaviour. Similarly, Hunt's approach is to obtain samples of the individual's verbal behaviour and to impose a structure on these. Hunt appears to derive from what an individual says about one particular thing how he constructs his world in general. Both of these measures have been shown to have some degree of reliability.

The third and principal issue to which Hunt addressed his presentation is the description of effective methods of changing behaviour. The suggested operating principle is to "match models," that is, give the child what fits him best. Kohlberg and Turiel and their colleagues have found that children are most apt to show development in their level of moral judgments if they are exposed to judgments which are one above their current level. Hunt has shown that behaviour of young children can be modified if they are exposed to a particular environment, and the extent of the modification depends on an interaction between the individual and the environment. I would like to point out that although both of these are used as examples of the application of the matching-models notion, they may be different. Kohlberg measures the subject's cognitive structure, exposes the child to a different cognitive structure, and then looks for changes in the subject's cognitive structure. Hunt measures the subject's cognitive structure, exposes him to an environment with changed contingencies, and then looks for changes in the subject's behaviour within this changed environment. (I have not been able to find data that indicate that the subjects' possibly changed cognitive structures have been evaluated after experience with the changed environment.)

In a sense, then, Hunt's approach is not unlike that of operant investigators, except that he uses a test to find out what changed contingencies should be introduced for any particular child. The central difference between Kohlberg's conceptualization and that of operant people is that Kohlberg makes the assumption that what someone *thinks about* his behaviour affects his behaviour. And so we should learn what variables determine his cognitions. To change his behaviour, then, we should change his cognitions. The operant position is that behaviour can be accounted for more effectively by knowing what the observables are, without paying attention to how these interact with central (i.e., internal) structures.

Attempts to use the matching technique to stimulate development of moral judgment within Kohlberg's framework must show that it is largely experience with the next highest level of moral judgment that is effective. Thus, the burden of support for such a technique rests heavily on Turiel's data. The problem is, does it work? If you give a child a particular experience, the next level of moral reasoning relative to his, does it change his moral judgment? There is some indication that it is not as successful as people might want it to be. Anyway, the problem is to find out whether the method works.

SENSITIVITY IN MORAL DECISION AND ACTION

OLIVER

I want to say something about what we might call moral sensitivity, that is, sensitivity to what is happening around one. It seems to me that questions about the preconditions of moral sensitivity to experience that would feed into some kind of structure have an important common interest for psychologists and philosophers. Because Kohlberg is simply concerned with the nature and development of the structure, the whole conversation focuses on that – without any concern for what are the prerequisites or relevant experiences to be fed into the structure in the first place. If you will look at some of our leaders (for example, in our pacification program in Vietnam), I do not doubt that they have very adequate structures and are very moral people in the sense that we are talking about moral people, but they are inadequate in other ways. You see John Kennedy's funeral procession and it really hits you, then Martin Luther King's and finally Robert Kennedy's. By that time you are inured to this sort of thing happening. It seems to me that this is partly why young people who care are so upset and impatient with us. I mean, we are worried about the structure of reasons but we are not concerned generally, as psychologists or as philosophers, in the sense of reflecting very much about obvious atrocities in real experience.

KOHLBERG

Let me just say a couple of words about Oliver's dissatisfaction with both his own approach and my approach. It is not clear whether the dissatisfaction should be expressed in the title "Is Morality Enough?" or "Is Reason Enough?" or "Is Reasoning Enough?" There is more to reason than verbal reasoning, as I think Oliver points out, and there is more to morality than either reason or verbal reasoning, and there is more to the good life than morality. In one way or another Oliver raises all of these issues in his paper. I will simply point out the distinctions among these issues. The distinction between reasoning and reason: does reasoning always suggest something purely cognitive, whereas morality involves the rational passions? Some passions are both more moral and more rational than others, and that tends to be missing in the usual notion of verbal reasoning. That is, a sense of justice, respect for human dignity and the other things that are implied in my stage 6, are not just words, they are affectively loaded orientations – in the way that the impassioned sense of justice of Martin Luther King is a rational passion in contrast to, say, the stage-4 moral indignation of the John Bircher or the stage-2 Black Power sense of vengeance ("Burn, baby, burn"). Those involve different emotions as well as different concepts of justice. We usually think of a rational or mature emotion as good because it helps direct conduct, that is, it helps us to act morally. But I think that Oliver's treatment points out that it has many other human functions as well, many of which can be said to be aesthetic: for instance, to experience tragedy in literature – at least Greek tragedy – one must have the moral base for reacting to the hero's end as fated, inevitable, and earned, and yet see this hero as a basically good man. That is, it depends on a certain level of moral development, sophistication; it is capacity to experience tragedy, as Oliver points out. Even to have a tragic sense of life is part of maturity and experience, regardless of what it does for moral conduct.

When we raise the aesthetic issue, then, we are in part answering the question of why morally educate the child, what good is morality. Part of the good of morality is not moral, it is aesthetic. So the aesthetic and the affective are both part of a broader conception of moral education. I think that Oliver's paper eventually deals with the whole broad field of human and social development. I have not dared to do this, but I think it has to be done when we get into education. That is, we have to ask, "What is this doing to the child?" and sometimes we cannot answer that in terms of a formal conception of morality.

I just want to end by saying that we are in agreement in viewing moral development, moral maturity, as both the cause and the consequence of full participation in a community. That is, according to me, sense of participation in the social order, role-taking opportunities and so on within existing institutions, are the social experiences that are important in moving the child upward, but it is also the case that the capacity to participate in the community is dependent upon moral maturity.

MELDEN

I would like to come back to what Oliver was saying about moral sensitivity. I think it contrasts very sharply with this affect-cognition kind of distinction that was presented in an earlier phase of our discussion. I think the notion of feeling as a kind of internal sensation, the sort of thing that comes and pushes and gets limbs moving and so on, and the notion of an experience as if it were in some way neutral with respect to our convictions, are quite wrong. Also, I think it is dangerous to think of the whole moral enterprise as if it were a matter of calculating virtue and effecting ends that we simply want. What really distresses these young people very much is just this: they are led to believe that the rest of us view these dreadful occurrences without sharing the frightening, traumatic experience of them. In moral education it is very important not just to link the things that befall human beings with the cost and consequence in some casual way, but also with human feeling, which seems to be part and parcel of, or very closely connected with, the proper understanding of those events. To see human beings as human beings is not just to be able to discriminate between people and posts. It is the way of relating to another person that marks the distinction between a psychopath and an understanding human being. I think Oliver is absolutely right in that, without attention to this facet of experience, we cannot really make any progress in getting what we want in the way of moral education. The neglect of it renders rather anaemic and academic so much of philosophers' talk about human action and human beings.

EDEL

I think it is historically wrong to say that moral sensitivity has not been dealt with by the great moral philosophers. You can start all the way back with Aristotle's discussion of the man of practical wisdom in which the close relationship of desire and feeling on the one hand and cognition on the other is taken to be the mark of a fully mature man. In the phenomenological writers (Hartmann, for instance) you have a tremendous emphasis on moral sensitivity. You have it in the whole history of the eighteenth-century sentimental philosophers.

But I do not want to leave it simply as it is dealt with at a theoretical level. Let me take the case that you (Oliver) have mentioned. There is a serious danger, I think, in the position that you advance, if it results in the cutting off of theory from what I will call for want of a better word, "feeling." The typical problem that is suggested by you is the behaviour of students, for example, in the moral criticism of the older generation by the younger generation or the protests at Columbia and Berkeley and so on. Shortly after Robert Kennedy's assassination, I happened to be at a Commencement speech given by Arthur Schlesinger, Jr. He attacked the whole idea and approach of the New Left (Marcuse and so on) as if it were a new kind of Sorelianism – a myth of violence that was deliberately anti-rational. Now, if you are going to set off these aspects of theory and feeling one against the other, I think you are likely to deserve that interpretation and do an injustice to what the students themselves are doing. I think that many of them do not have an anti-theoretical outlook. Their action is based on what they believe are the necessities of the situation and the idea of the role that confrontation plays in the opening of feelings and the breaking down of barriers. This could simply be an assertion of feeling, or it could be a criticism of the stages of theory that have been reached at the particular time. I believe that students are acting on a theory; whether it is a Kropotkin type of anarchism or anything else, it is a theory. I am not raising the question here of whether the theory is right or wrong. But, you see, I do not think that you can help the understanding of it if you try to interpret it as an anti-theoretical attitude. The very central question is how the two are brought together. The history of ethics is rich in the attempt to deal with this, and if it does nothing else, it can set up an ideal of the morally sensitive man in which being a good theoretician is an integral element.

MELDEN

I think that you are quite right about Aristotle. He has paid attention to feeling and so on. However, I think that there has been a neglect by philosophers of some of the complexity, and hence there has been a failure to notice that some of the ways in which we do in point of fact think about moral matters are perhaps not adequate to the task. At the same time, nothing of what I said about experience or feeling in any way justifies any repudiation of rationality. I want to insist most emphatically that being reasonable, understanding, intelligent, perceptive, and so on involve many different sorts of things. We must not think that rationality and the ideal of rationality are committing us to just one technique. There are lots of ways in which we reason about human events and I simply want to leave the door open and suggest that perhaps the concept of experience is a good deal richer than some of us think because of the rather impoverished, I would say conceptually impoverished, models with which we approach it.

OLIVER

I have a colleague who made what I think was a wise and profound statement. It was to the effect that in more recent times academics and adults generally have moved towards a much more tentative, pragmatic view of the world and life; a much more analytical and flexible view, not based on natural law or natural principles. Students see this, but they see it as a process of cold analysis which the academic community encourages as appropriate for the classroom. Now his point was that behind this analytical, cold tone, there is great uncertainty and moral agony on the part of faculty, but they do not choose to communicate it. The student is thrust into a world that is in many ways absurd and meaningless, and he feels it. Because the teacher analyzes it without communicating the feeling and agony that he in fact feels, the student strikes out at him even though he shares the common concern. This is a dimension of what I am calling moral sensitivity in moral education that I think is extremely important even at a pragmatic, pedagogical level.

CRITTENDEN

As I understand it, our task in relation to moral education is to try to state the ideal a little more clearly and fully than it has been in the past. This involves seeing the kinds of connection between what we have labelled as cognitive and affective, thought and action, and trying to get a clearer picture of how these would be related in an ideal moral education program. Then of course we have to vary the ideal picture according to the actual condition of the people who are being educated in a given place and time. For some of us, perhaps most of us, our recent experience of people being educated has been in North American universities. However, that does not speak (by any means) for the whole population even at that age, and in some countries it speaks for a relatively much smaller proportion. On the question of stressing affectivity, what is actually done to translate the ideal of moral education would depend on the situation. In some cases I think that there would be need to inject, or put emphasis on, the cognitive aspects because the emotive had been so overplayed. In the training programs of Nazi Germany, for example, affectivity ran riot and produced a fantastic effect in action.

OLIVER

Take modern France. You do not have to go to Nazi Germany. Do you carry on the kind of discourse that we have been talking about with the students who are throwing cobblestones at you? How do you interact with them?

CRITTENDEN

To emphasize the point I was just making, I would certainly distinguish in my method of approach between university students, particularly if they are throwing cobblestones, and people of the same age who are, for example, working in a factory and who perhaps have not yet taken to throwing cobblestones.

LOUBSER

May I just point out that I think Oliver's point is well taken when we shift our attention to moral education as distinguished from certain problems which moral philosophers, psychologists, and sociologists feel that they have to solve before they can engage meaningfully in moral education. After all, moral education is a composite phenomenon in which we have to communicate a certain content – certain concepts, precepts, and what have you – to individuals whose stage of moral development we have to take into account. It seems to me that the point Oliver is driving at is that the content cannot be at a level of abstraction or in a realm of ideas that is divorced from the type of environment in which people's moral sensitivities are either blunted or activated every day. From that point of view the requirement of the current situation in which people have to act as moral agents is an extremely important perspective, I would say, for moral educators to take into account. I would go so far as to say that it is important even for moral philosophers to take it into account if they care to communicate with students about the current state of affairs and the problems it poses to modern man. More generally, it is important because, as symbol-using animals that create structures around themselves for various purposes, we very often get entangled in our own institutions. This is why it is necessary that the analysis of the structure of institutions, particularly those originally set up to achieve purposes derived from knowledge of the developmental processes of individuals or the way in which moral reasoning is most adequately done, must be a part of the process of moral education.

[During the course of this long discussion of the cognitive and affective aspects of moral education, the participants came to be divided into two fairly distinct groups. At least, it seemed this way to a member of the audience whose comment suitably closes this section. The speaker is Michael Kubara, a graduate student in the Department of Philosophy, University of Waterloo.]

Listening to both sides of the table, one gets the feeling that there is not so much a substantial disagreement as there is a disagreement in emphasis. On the left we have an emphasis on the emotional aspects of moral education, and on the right we have an emphasis on the rational and conceptual aspects. But with regard to the emphasis, I should like to say a few words on behalf of the right. This business about concepts and feeling is not a new chestnut. Hume, for example, pointed out that unless there was a feeling aspect in evaluation and moral concern, morality would not get off the ground. Hume also pointed out that if people let morality be simply a matter of feeling, they were letting in a lot of inequities. And this was pointed out by one of the participants who wants to emphasize the feeling aspect (Oliver). You pointed out yourself that we witnessed J.F.K.'s assassination, and we witnessed King's assassination, and then Robert Kennedy's assassination, and our feelings became muted. We became callous, and this is simply a psychological fact. That is what Hume noticed a long time ago; that our moral feelings are notoriously a function of space and time. We do not feel as intensely about atrocities that happened, say, a thousand years ago, and we do not feel as intensely about atrocities that are happening in Indo-China. The point is that our feelings are notoriously ephemeral. Although they are a necessary condition for moral concern, they are certainly not sufficient, and, in order to balance the facts of feeling, you need principles. You need a clear, rational perspective in order to accommodate for the inequities that are built into feeling. But of course this is not to minimize the fact that without the feeling aspect morality would be irrelevant. One constructive point which could come out of this is simply that you have to know what kind of feelings to channel and in order to do this you need the rational, clear statements of the aims of moral education. Nobody wants to deny that one of the objectives of a moral educator is to achieve this kind of sensitivity or feeling. But as I said previously you have to have the right kinds of feeling and the right kinds of thought.

This book
was designed by
ELLEN HUTCHISON
under the direction of
ALLAN FLEMING
University of
Toronto
Press